THE IRISH TIMES: A HISTORY

For Emma, Kieran and Conor O'Brien
&
Dara and Mark O'Connor

THE IRISH TIMES

A History

MARK O'BRIEN

FOUR COURTS PRESS

Typeset in 10 pt on 13.5 pt Sabon by
Carrigboy Typesetting Services for
FOUR COURTS PRESS LTD
7 Malpas Street, Dublin 8, Ireland
e-mail: info@fourcourtspress.ie
and in North America for
FOUR COURTS PRESS
c/o ISBS, 920 NE 58th Avenue, Suite 300, Portland, OR 97213.

A catalogue record for this title is available
from the British Library.

ISBN 978–1–84682–123–3

Printed in England
by MPG Books, Bodmin, Cornwall.

Contents

Illustrations

appear between pages 160 and 161.

Abbreviations

ACA	Army Comrades Association
AoA	Articles of Association
BBC	British Broadcasting Association
B&F	*Business and Finance*
CB	*Catholic Bulletin*
CC	Controller's Correspondence
CRO	Companies Registration Office
DDA	Dublin Diocesan Archives
DE	Dáil Éireann Debates
D/J	Department of Justice
DPGU	Dublin Print Group of Unions
D/T	Department of the Taoiseach
DUP	Democratic Unionist Party
EM	*Evening Mail*
FCO	Foreign and Colonial Office, London
ICTU	Irish Congress of Trade Unions
II	Irish Independent
IPR	*Irish Political Review*
IRA	Irish Republican Army
IRB	Irish Republican Brotherhood
IT	*Irish Times*
LSF	Local Security Force
MA	Military Archives
MEP	Member of European Parliament
MP	Member of Parliament (Britain)
NA	National Archives (Ireland)
NL	National Library (Ireland)
NUJ	National Union of Journalists
OCC	Office of Controller of Censorship
PRO	Public Record Office, London
PCMR	Press Censorship Monthly Reports
QUB	Queen's University Belfast
RAF	Royal Air Force
RPC	Review of Press Censorship

RTÉ	Radio Telefís Éireann
RUC	Royal Ulster Constabulary
SDLP	Social Democratic Labour Party
SE	Senate / Seanad Éireann Debates
SI	*Sunday Independent*
SIPTU	Services, Industrial and Professional Trade Union
SPB	*Sunday Business Post*
SR	*Sunday Review*
TD	Teachta Dála
TCD	Trinity College Dublin
UCC	University College Cork
UCD	University College Dublin
UCDA	University College Archives
UUP	Ulster Unionist Party
WIT	*Weekly Irish Times*

Acknowledgments

THIS BOOK IS THE result of a two-year Government of Ireland post-doctoral research fellowship provided by the Irish Research Council for the Humanities and Social Sciences to which I extend my thanks. The School of Communications, Dublin City University facilitated the research, which was conducted under the guidance of Professor John Horgan. My thanks also to former head of school, Brian Trench. For legal advice, I extend my thanks to Mark O'Connell, BL. For help with illustrations thanks to Declan Tuite, David O'Callaghan and Sarah Maher of DCU, Clodagh Kingston of Dublin City Library and Archive, and Lady Anne Arnott.

Those who agreed to be interviewed and those who responded to correspondence enriched the research. My thanks to Conor Brady, James Downey, Brian Fallon, Ronan Fanning, Paul Gillespie, Renagh Holohan, Richard Keatinge, Dennis Kennedy, Geraldine Kennedy, Mary Maher, Frank McDonald, Gerry Mulvey, Louis O'Neill, Cathal O'Shannon, Andy Pollak, Don Reid, Lorna Siggins and Andrew Whittaker. To those who felt they could not grant interviews I extend my thanks for having considered my request.

My thanks also to those who supplied material they came across in the course of their own research or who passed on knowledge of the existence of relevant material. Thanks to John Horgan and Gary Murphy for passing on material they came across in the US National Archives, to Eunan O'Halpin for the information on his late uncle's papers in UCD Archives and to Jack Lane and John Martin and the *Irish Political Review* for copies of the letters discovered in the Public Record Office in London. My thanks also to Gerry Mulvey for a copy of the first *Irish Times* stylebook, to Lorna Siggins for a copy of a talk delivered by the late Ken Gray on the history of the *Irish Times* and to Michael Viney for an advance copy of a chapter on his time at the paper. My thanks also to Sarah MacDonald and Br Paul Hurley of *The Word* for sourcing and sending me a copy of an interview with Douglas Gageby. Thanks also to Seamus Dooley of the National Union of Journalists.

The research was facilitated at various institutions: my thanks to Paul Sheehan, Librarian of DCU Library, Noelle Dowling of the Dublin Diocesan Archives, Victor Laing of Military Archives, Pat Sweeney of the National Library and Seamus Helferty of UCD Archives. Thanks also to the staffs of the National Library, National Archives, Kerry County Library, Business Information Centre Dublin City Council Library, the Companies Registration Office, the Registry of Friendly Societies, and the Births, Deaths and Marriage Office. For permission to reproduce illustrations thanks to Martyn Turner, Frank Kelly, Eoin McVey, and the *Irish Times*.

Thanks also to Paul Connors and Helen Shaw. Thanks also to Keith McCarthy, house hunter extraordinaire. Finally, my thanks to Michael Adams, Martin Fanning and all at Four Courts Press for their enthusiastic reception of the idea and their professionalism in bringing it to fruition.

Preface

THE *Irish Times* is Ireland's oldest national daily newspaper. Established in 1859 as the voice of southern unionism and staunchly opposed to home rule it was ultimately forced to make its peace with an independent state in 1921. From then on it kept a wary eye on developments. It abhorred the new state's emphasis on all things Gaelic and equally abhorred de Valera's tampering with the Anglo-Irish treaty. It was the bane of the censor throughout the Second World War during which the state and the paper were, as the minister for defence, Frank Aiken, put it, 'at daggers drawn'. During the 1950s it became the voice of liberalism before transforming itself into the 'paper of record' during the 1960s. It became a trust in 1974 and is, today, the country's authoritative newspaper of choice. It has always generated, and sometimes been the centre of, controversial news stories, from the Mother and Child controversy in 1951 to the heavy gang exposé in 1977 and from the Bishop Casey scandal in 1992 to 'Bertiegate' in 2006. This book is a history of the *Irish Times*, and, given that newspapers are different things to different people, so too will this book. Some may be interested in the earlier history of the paper, others in the contemporary period. Some may be mainly interested in the paper's journalism, others in the commercial development of the company. Some may be interested in how the paper evolved, others in how it broke major stories that shook up Irish society. All things considered, this book brings together the most important elements of all these aspects and will hopefully spur a wider interest in the history of Irish newspapers and in Irish journalism generally.

CHAPTER I

'A First Class Daily Paper'

> In its fifty years of existence the *Irish Times* has had one change in ownership and no change in policy ... We have supported every national movement, and all legislation, that seemed likely to promote Ireland's prestige and welfare as an integral part of the United Kingdom and the British Empire. Honestly, and to the best of our ability, we have resisted every action and every measure that seemed to us calculated to injure or retard that great aim.[1]
>
> The Irish Times *on its first fifty years*

A s Lawrence E. Knox put the finishing touches to the first edition of the *Irish Times and Daily Advertiser* he could hardly have imagined that his tentative publication would go on to become one of the most respected journals of news and opinion in Ireland and the world. What he did know was that he had identified a gap in the market for a conservative journal to champion the political and economic union of Great Britain and Ireland – a union that had been increasingly challenged from the 1840s onwards. The famine of 1845–51, during which one million people died and another one million emigrated, had shattered many people's faith in the union. Relations between landlords and tenants had plummeted to their lowest level and would culminate in the land war of the 1870s. Religion was another bone of contention; although roughly 80 per cent of the population professed the Catholic faith, the official state religion was Protestantism in the guise of the Church of Ireland. Political dissent was never far below the surface, and the year before Knox's publishing initiative Irish separatists had established an organisation that would play a central role in breaking the union that the *Irish Times* was established to support. The Irish Republican Brotherhood, and its belief in physical force to achieve political change, would take centre stage several times over the following sixty years – each time roundly condemned by the paper.

But all this lay in the future, and in the 1859 general election Ireland returned 57 (out of 105 Irish seats) conservative members of parliament. It was towards this constituency, the mercantile and administrative class that was predominantly Protestant and unionist and which believed passionately in

15

maintaining the status quo vis-à-vis politics and religion, that Knox aimed his new paper. Knox himself came from a conservative, wealthy and Protestant background, being the eldest son of Arthur Knox, from Co. Mayo, and Lady Jane Parsons, daughter of the earl of Rosse. Born in 1836, he obtained a commission as a lieutenant in the British army and served throughout the Crimean War of 1854–6 during which he was promoted to the rank of captain. In 1859 he devoted his energy to establishing the *Irish Times* and (as his obituary noted) 'for energy and devotion to business he had few superiors'. In 1868 he was elected as an MP for the borough of Sligo, representing 'the Conservative interest'.[2]

The arrival of Knox's paper was well timed. The 1850s was a decade of significant change in the Irish newspaper industry. In 1855 Ireland had approximately one hundred newspapers but by 1859 another thirty had been established.[3] Up to this point newspapers had been taxed in three different ways – a tax on advertisements, a tax on newsprint and a stamp duty on each newspaper copy which entitled the paper to be delivered by post without extra charge. The advertisements tax had been imposed in 1712, entailed a duty of one shilling on every advert and was abolished in 1853. The tax on newsprint, imposed in 1757, entailed a duty of $1^{1}/_{2}d$. per pound of paper and endured up to 1861. The stamp duty was the most crippling of the three taxes: as well as increasing the cover price, it involved the stamping of each newspaper. Introduced in 1712 at a rate of $^{1}/_{2}d$. a sheet, it had risen to $1d$. in 1836. It was abolished in 1855 and prompted a spur of growth in the newspaper industry.[4]

Knox's *Irish Times and Daily Advertiser* first appeared on Tuesday 29 March 1859 as a newspaper published on Tuesdays, Thursdays and Saturdays. In its early days, the paper published two editions – the mid-day edition at 2 p.m. and the evening edition at 5 p.m. – and it joined an already crowded Dublin newspaper market, which included the *Freeman's Journal, Saunder's Newsletter*, and the *Daily Express*. Indeed, the *Irish Times* title itself had existed previously between October 1823 and July 1825. This first incarnation had nothing to do with Knox's paper and folded in 1825 when it acquired the *Dublin Journal*, relaunched itself as the *Morning Courier and Dublin Journal* and then collapsed within a few months due to labour problems with its printers. With his offices located at 4 Lower Abbey Street, Knox also published the *Weekly Advertiser* every Saturday – a free sheet that supposedly had a 'guaranteed circulation' of 10,000 copies per issue.[5]

Describing itself as a 'New Conservative Daily Paper', Knox's *Irish Times* consisted of four pages, each with six single columns of type. The first page was devoted exclusively to adverts while the news on the other three pages was broken up under such headings as 'Fashion Intelligence' which listed the doings, comings and goings of members of the royal family, the aristocracy and high ranking officers of the armed forces; 'Assize Intelligence' which consisted of court reports; and 'Foreign Intelligence' which carried news from around the world. News from around Ireland invariably came under the heading 'From Our Correspondent'. Announcements of births, deaths and marriages were initially treated as news, and the paper only began to treat such announcements as chargeable adverts in 1860.[6] It also carried a lengthy report on the proceedings in the house of commons and a stock and share list for the Dublin exchange. Sports news was assembled under 'Sporting Intelligence' and listed the results of various cricket matches, coursing events and horse-race meetings, while race tips for future meetings were given under the heading 'Sporting Prophecies'. Knox was determined to give his paper a distinctive identity and in its first leading article, or editorial, he outlined its philosophy. While conceding that it was 'true that every religious and political party is already fully represented in the Press', he also observed that 'every Irish journal which has any circulation to boast of is the special advocate and mouthpiece of a sect or party'. This situation was 'the natural result of the intense divisions that have hitherto characterised our social state'. Times were changing, however, and Knox believed that a new political order was emerging:

> Every year sees a larger and larger proportion of our population indifferent to the manoeuvres of faction, disgusted at the arts of the demagogue and sincerely desirous of laying aside their mutual prejudices and labouring together for the good of their common country. Men of this stamp dislike to be classed and ticketed off even under such mild denominations as Liberal or Conservative. They are anxious for good government, but care little in whose hands the government may be placed. They desire to see measures discussed with reference to their essential merits rather than to their party bearings. Warmly interested in whatever concerns the real progress of Ireland, whether moral or material, in the elevation of the standard of life among the labouring classes, in the general diffusion of education, in the security of property and of the fruits of the poor man's industry, they view with more than indifference all attempts to favour any one class or creed at the expense of the just rights of the others.[7]

It was to this critical and discerning constituency that the paper would address itself. There was, however, a contradiction inherent in its objectives. It would support critical viewpoints vis-à-vis what was best for Ireland only if such viewpoints were firmly grounded in the belief that Ireland functioned best as part of the British empire:

> As Irishmen we shall think and speak; but it shall be as Irishmen loyal to the British connection, and proud to share in the destinies of the only first-rate Power in Europe that has known how to combine social order with individual freedom. We shall not be given to the manufacture of national grievances, or to complaints that the interests of Ireland are neglected in the Imperial Parliament; but shall rather inculcate the doctrine that the share of consideration which Ireland receives in the Legislature depends and will always depend on the class of representatives she sends there.[8]

Regarding the pressing political matters of the day, the paper believed that the position of the established church should be 'left undisturbed' and that it was 'safe and right to extend the franchise to the more intelligent and well-conditioned portion of the working classes'. It was opposed to the secret ballot, believing that the 'democratic tendency of the measure, except so far as Ireland is concerned, has been overrated by its promoters'. It surmised that few issues could compete in importance with that of land reform, and noted that 'the fact that so many distinguished members on different sides of the House have brought forward Bills on the subject is a sufficient proof that some further security than now exists is needed to induce the tenant to invest his capital in the improvement of his farm'. Taking all this into consideration, Knox declared his ambition to 'make the *Irish Times* a first rate Irish newspaper complete in its details, sagacious and consistent in its policy and faithfully reflecting the opinions of the most independent, intelligent and truly progressive portion of Irish Society'.[9] In the 1860 edition of the *Newspaper Gazetteer,* Knox described the *Irish Times* as 'the Protestant and Conservative daily newspaper'.[10]

EARLY DAYS

As founder and proprietor Knox took a keen interest in the paper's editorial content but very little is known of the paper's early editors. Its first editor was Dr George Frederick Shaw who, having presided over the paper's production for its first couple of weeks, resigned because he found 'the onerous work of an editor incompatible with the accomplishment of his important [Trinity] College duties'. His successor was his nephew, the Revd George Bomford Wheeler. A Trinity graduate, Wheeler served as a curate in Dublin's North Strand area before becoming chaplain to the Smithfield Convict Depot in 1859. During this time he wrote articles for a variety of publications such as the *Daily Express* and *All the Year Round*, a periodical established by Charles Dickens.[11] Wheeler became editor in July 1859 and continued in that post after he was transferred as rector to Ballysax, Co. Kildare, where he was killed when his coach overturned one evening in October 1877. His obituary noted that 'As a writer he was possessed of a singularity acute intellect, a rarely cool and impartial judgment, great facility of comprehension and a particularly neat and graceful style.'[12] Wheeler oversaw the paper's initial success; just fourteen weeks after its launch it became a daily paper, its edition of 7 June 1859 announcing that 'In consequence of the great success that has already attended the *Irish Times*, the Proprietor has been induced to establish it as a Daily Paper, to enable the Conservative members of the community to enjoy a first class Daily Paper, at a far cheaper rate than was ever yet published in Ireland.'[13]

Nonetheless, there were some minor teething problems. Shortly after it commenced daily publication one of its reporters, a Revd Mr Frew, applied to the Great Southern and Western Railway for a free pass over the company's system. This was a privilege granted to newspaper reporters, and when the superintendent of the railway refused to issue a pass, Knox complained to the company only to be informed that 'free passes can only be given to legitimate reporters'. He also had difficulty in obtaining an affordable rate from the same railway company for the carriage of the paper. In October 1859 he complained about its charges and in reply was offered the same terms as applied to other newspapers – £10 per month. In April 1860 he suggested to the company's directors that they consider the *Irish Times* when placing adverts, but again met with a frosty response; he was informed that the directors did not propose to make any changes in their advertising arrangements.[14]

The paper's production process also posed problems in that the printing machines of the time inhibited expansion. Production of the infant *Irish Times* was a laborious affair, with the entire paper being set by hand in cold metal type. Every individual letter was picked from a case by hand and arranged to form words that were sorted into lines of type, which in turn were assembled into columns of type. These columns were then compiled into flat pages or 'formes', which in turn were locked in iron frames or 'chases'. These 'chases' were then secured on the bed of the printing machine. Sheets of paper, fed into the machine by hand, travelled around a revolving cylinder that impressed them on the 'formes' of type that were inked by rollers as they reciprocated to and fro on the bed of the machine. The number of individual paper-feeding positions provided on the machine governed output. The company's first printing machine was a four-feeder that could produce between 4,000 and 5,000 printed sheets an hour; but these were printed on one side only and were completed on a second machine. The completed copies of the paper then had to be folded by hand, and the tops of the pages, known as the 'bolts', were uncut. The task of cutting the 'bolts' so that the paper could be read was the task of the reader, or more likely, since most of the early readers of the paper had domestic servants, the task of the butler or batman.

Disassembling, or 'dissing', the pages of type after the paper was printed, was a slightly quicker process. Every individual character had to be put back into its case; the upper-case for capital letters and the lower-case for small ones – printing terms that are still in common use today.[15] But this laborious process and the limited capacity of the printing press hampered the early growth of the paper. As the paper's jubilee edition observed, it had 'been the fate of many newspapers to find their infancy beset by commercial and financial difficulties. The early difficulties of the *Irish Times* were mechanical not monetary. The needs of an expanding newspaper were held in check by the limitations of the printing press.' All the paper could do in terms of enlargement was to increase its page size – 'and this it continued to do until it became positively unwieldy and unsightly' – or resort to printing an independent supplement. Initially, each page consisted of six columns of twenty-three inches of type, but by April 1861 each page had eight columns of twenty-seven inches of type, and by 1867 this had increased to nine columns per page. This unwieldy page size continued until the end of 1869 when the installation of new printing machines allowed the paper to double its size to eight pages of six columns of twenty-three inches of type. By 1873 it was up to twelve pages per issue.[16]

As regards circulation, the paper published its own figure every day between February 1860 and June 1862. On 8 February 1860 it announced that its circulation for the previous week had been 8,720 copies per day. By December 1860 daily sales stood at 11,372 and the paper claimed 'the largest circulation ever before attained by any newspaper in Ireland and with four exceptions in the United Kingdom'. Twelve months later, daily sales stood at 16,085, and in June 1862 it claimed a daily sales figure of 16,988.[17] In October 1862 Knox commissioned a British company, W.H. Smith & Son, to distribute the unstamped issues of the paper to the Dublin trade after having experienced difficulties with a previous distributor. The company's Irish manager, Charles Eason, reported that 'The *Irish Times* have recently closed with one who took 400 copies, Davis of Blackrock, and put the man in prison for the debt due to them, and they have an advertisement daily in their paper inviting the public to transfer their orders to our boys.' Later that year W.H. Smith took over the stamped distribution of the paper to its regular subscribers. The calibre of its readership prompted Eason to observe that 'the list of the *Irish Times* will certainly promote new business. Some of the names are really very good.'[18] In its new-year edition of 1 January 1867, the paper claimed a circulation figure of 20,000 copies per day.[19] By 1871, of all the Dublin dailies, the paper had the largest annual account with W.H. Smith: £4,603 compared to £2,918 for the *Freeman's Journal* and £2,069 for the *Daily Express*.[20]

A NEW OWNER

Despite Knox's hope for a settled political scene, the 1860s was a decade of division as the Irish Republican Brotherhood organised around the country in preparation for an uprising to establish an independent Ireland. When that rising occurred in March 1867 it was quickly crushed, and the paper declared that it was for the best that the movement had made its move, 'for now the absolutely idiotic character of the movement is incontestably proved'.[21] The sporadic nature of the engagements between the IRB and crown forces prompted one letter writer to observe that their tactic was 'to weary out the troops by causing them to be sent here and there on a wild goose chase'; he demanded that 'every Fenian found guilty of treason suffer the extreme penalty, otherwise there is nothing to prevent this business going on for months, to the disgust and annoyance of everyone, and to the destruction of the prosperity of the country and the ruin of many'.[22] For its part, the paper believed that poor economic conditions, insecure employment and lack of imperial investment in Ireland played its part in propelling certain classes of people towards rebellion. While those who were in 'constant occupation had a stake in the quietude and order of the country', those who were not 'had not the influence of work or intelligence to preoccupy his mind; he was open to the insidious arguments of designing men, and therefore it was that the Fenian hordes counted almost solely of ragged youths, labourers out of work, and dissipated outcasts of the cities'. It called on the government to establish 'dockyards and naval arsenals in Ireland, to be at once centres of employment and examples of progress and of industry' and believed that the expenditure on such endeavours would 'be less in amount than the cost of periodically crushing attempts at insurrection'.[23] According to the memoir of one prominent Fenian, John Devoy, the paper had at least one Fenian on its staff – William O'Donovan – though not until after the rising. A proficient French speaker, O'Donovan had been dispatched to Paris in 1865 to act as a courier between John Mitchel in France and IRB leader James Stephens in Ireland. According to Devoy, 'William got to know Paris very well during his trips, and, after the failure of the Rising, the *Irish Times*, although a Tory paper, made him its correspondent there. He remained in Paris many years and was there during the Siege and the Commune, and his letters were very interesting when he could get them out.' The paper later sent O'Donovan to Spain during one of the Carlist insurrections and after this he returned to Dublin to become one of its leader writers.[24]

The paper's edition of 25 January 1873 contained deep black lines between its columns announcing the death of its founder, at 36-years-of-age, the previous day. According to the leading article, Knox had been suffering from an attack of scarlatina and 'was unexpectedly taken away in the midst of a career of usefulness, and when he was most hopeful for the future of his country'.[25] His funeral was a large one; 150 carriages, including Dublin's lord mayor in his state coach, formed the funeral cortege. Knox's funeral carriage was drawn by four black horses and the 'literary staff and representatives from the printing department of the *Irish Times* walked two abreast, as mourners, on the right of the hearse, while the commercial staff occupied a corresponding position on the left'. Immediately after the hearse came the 'Band of the Irish Times', members of parliament, judges, mayors 'from several important boroughs, including Belfast' as well as 'vast numbers of clergymen, noblemen, and gentry of the country, and leading members of the mercantile community of Dublin and its neighbourhood'.[26]

Following Knox's death, his widow put the paper on the market and sold it to the highest bidder, Sir John Arnott, in May 1873 for £35,000.[27] Born in Aughermuchty, near Glasgow, Scotland in 1814, Arnott had come to Ireland in 1834 to find his fortune. Described as 'a courageous and largely successful Victorian entrepreneur', success followed Arnott, and his later business interests included Arnott & Co., Belfast; Arnott & Co., Dublin; Cash and Co., Cork; Baldoyle and Cork Park Race Meetings; the City of Cork Steam-Packet Company; Arnott's Brewery, Cork; the Passage Docks Shipbuilding Company, Cork; and the Bristol Steam Navigation Company.[28] He served as lord mayor of Cork from 1859 to 1861, was knighted by the lord lieutenant in November 1859 and also represented the borough of Kinsale as an independent MP between 1859 and 1863. A committed philanthropist, he presided over an investigation into the conditions of children in the Cork Workhouse and during this time the Irish Poor Law Relief Bill, dealing with the welfare of children, was introduced, to which Arnott lent his support by joining the select committee on the issue.[29]

On 27 May 1873 the paper's leading article explained the change in ownership and reported that, on the day he concluded the purchase, Arnott had visited the paper to inspect its various departments and to address the staff. Having examined the building and concluded that 'important sanitary improvements' were required, Arnott also inspected the printing machinery, and orders were placed for 'more powerful engines and boilers, and for steam presses that will throw off double the present number of copies per hour'. The new machines arrived quickly, as in November 1873 the paper advertised its old machinery for sale. The machinery in question consisted of two 'Middleton Four-Feeders' one of which could print 5,250 copies per hour and the other 4,750 copies per hour, one 'Wharfedale Two-Feeder' which could print 3,000 copies per hour and three 'Livesey's Folding Machines'.[30] Additions were also to be made to the editorial staff, and it was announced that special care was 'to be taken with commercial and industrial topics, hitherto, in Sir John's opinion, somewhat neglected'. In his address to the staff Arnott declared his intention to provide 'every compositor and pressman in his employment with improved house accommodation'. Arnott owned what the paper described as 'a large extent of building ground at the north side of the city within convenient distance of Lower Abbey street' and on one such site he 'undertook to build neat and comfortable houses for the *employées* of the *Irish Times*, and to fix the rent at a figure lower than that which they now pay for their crowded and unwholesome town lodgings'. This announcement was met with applause, as was his pledge to his workers that he would 'not desert them either in sickness or old age'. Arnott, the article concluded, wished to develop the paper as 'an instrument for the material regeneration of Ireland, and as a fearless, able, and well-informed exponent and leader of Irish opinion'.[31] Below this leader was a letter from Arnott addressed to the paper's readers in which he pledged that 'its columns shall continue to be devoted to the interests of the country, to the promotion of harmony and good feeling amongst all classes; in fine, to whatever is truly useful, loyal and patriotic'. The paper being, as Arnott put it, 'independent of all party considerations', he pledged that it would not fail 'to criticise both the great parties of the country, whether sectarian or political', and he assured its readers that it would 'neither spare the errors nor hide the merits of either'.[32]

After its takeover by Arnott, the paper flourished. On 3 April 1874 it changed its name from the *Irish Times and Daily Advertiser* to the simpler *Irish Times*. In July 1875 the *Weekly Irish Times* was launched as a compendium of the week's news, and it continued publication in various guises until March 1958. In its initial incarnation the paper had a circulation of between 16,000 and 21,000 copies per week. In October 1880 the *Evening Irish Times* was launched as the publication time of the *Irish Times* had been brought back from mid-day to early morning. The evening edition entailed one page change to include the latest market reports and news. Circulation stood at around 1,000 copies per day and the paper survived until June 1915.[33] All this expansion resulted in a need for larger premises, and in March 1882 the paper relocated from Lower Abbey Street to 31 Westmoreland Street. On 20 March 1882 it published its first edition from there and noted that 'the rapid advance of the paper' had prompted the move. It also informed readers that it now had its own reporting staff in the house of commons which enabled it 'to give the fairest representation of every side of opinion, and in particular of Irish opinion on Irish affairs'. The paper estimated that, at this time, it was printing from 'sixteen to seventeen or more columns of debates, comprising nearly forty thousand telegraphed words per night'.[34] This investment was to pay dividends in terms of circulation; in 1873 daily sales had stood at 15,500 but as the issue of home rule came to dominate the political agenda daily sales gradually rose to 25,000 in 1885.[35]

In November 1873 the paper devoted substantial space to reporting the home rule conference held in Dublin under the auspices of Isaac Butt's Home Rule Association. For its issue of 22 November 1873 it printed a twelve-page edition to cover the closing proceedings of the conference and noted that it constituted the 'largest daily paper ever published in Ireland'. Surprisingly perhaps, given its deep attachment to the union, its leading article gave a glowing account of how the conference had been conducted and the argument advanced. It remarked that few who believed that the 'intimate connection with England has been a great gain to Ireland were prepared for a convention so honourable to the members composing it, characterised by such a constant spirit of constitutionalism, decorum and sincerity, conducted with so much order and ability'. The proceedings had been marked by a 'display of dialectic talent, of self-control, of mutual concession, and of patriotism, which would have done credit to many a National Assembly more strictly representative in character'. Neither did it have a problem with the concept of home rule; the conference delegates had outlined 'a programme which, if it be sincerely carried out, does not seem to threaten the stability of the Empire; and that by the terms of their resolutions they have anticipated all demands that could be made for a substantial guarantee of the loyalty of their intentions'. It also criticised the coverage given to the conference by the London press: 'Garbled extracts of speeches, which, if fully given, would bear quite another interpretation, have been submitted to the English public as condemnatory of the utterances of the speakers; and these passages seem to have been deliberately chosen with the view of throwing ridicule on an expression of opinion, which, we repeat, was the earnest outcome of deliberations in which a highly respectable and loyal section of the Irish nation were engaged.' All things considered, it called for the issue to be 'fairly argued between the leaders of Irish public feeling of all parties' before a final position was 'forwarded to our fellow-subjects on the other side of the Channel'.[36]

Such positive coverage continued the following year when the Home Rule Party put forward an unsuccessful motion for home rule in the house of commons. The paper noted that, although 'the Home Rulers knew that an overwhelming majority would vote against them, they spoke gallantly as if there existed a chance of victory'.[37] But as the party subsequently began to obstruct parliament by proposing endless amendments to legislation, reading long passages of text into the record and demanding votes on every issue, the paper expressed its scorn for such tactics. At the height of the party's obstructionist phase it commented that 'the Irish members – the Irish irreconcilables – have held the House at their mercy, have successfully hindered the whole course of business, and have completely crippled the Commons'. As the 1877 parliamentary session came to a close, it adjourned 'amid the derisive astonishment and contemptuous laughter of all who have been so long assured that Great Britain alone possesses the model of a constitutional Parliament'.[38]

The paper was more sympathetic to the issue of land reform. When Charles Stewart Parnell became president of the Land League in October 1879, it observed that since Catholic emancipation in 1829 'the dissatisfaction of the Irish farming classes has laid at the root of all popular movements'. While the IRB had 'held out the ownership of the soil as their chief bait to those whom they sought to convert to their views', so too had O'Connell's Repeal Association, and the Home Rule Association believed 'that a native Parliament would give effect to their hopes in a somewhat kindred way'. Thus it supported land reform and declared that the 'object of the Land League, as affirmed by resolution, are – firstly, to bring about the end of rack rents, and, secondly, to facilitate occupiers in obtaining the ownership of the soil. Both objects, considered *per se*, are fair and desirable'. There was nothing 'announced by the promoters of the Land League at which the public, or any section of the public, need be shocked or frightened'.[39] Such sentiments notwithstanding, reporting on the activities of the Land League was sometimes precarious. Prominent Land Leaguers often referred to the paper as the 'Liarish Times' and resented the presence of its reporters at League meetings.[40] At one meeting, William O'Brien, having finished his speech, turned to the paper's reporter, Andrew Dunlop, and asked him to retire from the meeting. When asked why he should leave, O'Brien replied, 'Because you are not here as an ordinary newspaper reporter, but as a spy.' After rejecting this claim, Dunlop left the meeting, but having mounted his horse drawn carriage found it surrounded by angry Land Leaguers who untied the horse and upended the carriage, forcing him onto the ground. When O'Brien repeated his claim Dunlop retorted, 'It's a lie and you know it.' O'Brien then had to be restrained by several clergymen from assaulting Dunlop who left the meeting under police protection. Forced to walk to the next town, Dunlop encountered a mob waiting for him and was assaulted several times before reaching the post office where he took refuge until the local police sergeant arrived to escort him to the railway station. Shortly afterwards, David Arnott, the joint manager of the paper, asked Dunlop if he would cover O'Brien's tour of the United States and Canada. Dunlop refused, believing that the assignment 'would probably be a somewhat dangerous one' and a somewhat futile one if, as he suspected, O'Brien would not allow him to attend any meetings or functions. The assignment was subsequently abandoned.[41]

With crop failures leading to evictions in the late 1870s, agrarian conflict gripped the countryside as the Land League organised mass protests. Eager to resolve the situation, prime minister William Gladstone passed the 1881 Land Act that established a land court to resolve issues between landlords and tenants. The paper welcomed this initiative as 'a confession on the part of Government that in the agrarian condition of the people of Ireland there exists grave and real grievances'.[42] But Parnell refused to support the legislation because it did nothing for tenants with leases or who were in arrears of their rent. When he was arrested and accused of preventing the land act from working, the paper observed that Parnell had declared 'moral war' against the government and called on the public to 'keep excitement within bounds, so that in no hour of intense feeling any person or persons shall involve themselves in any further collision with the law'.[43] After the Land League declared a rent strike and agrarian disturbances escalated around the country, Gladstone entered into secret negotiations with Parnell that ultimately led to the Kilmainham treaty of May 1882. This entailed Gladstone extending the terms of the Land Act to include those formally excluded from its remit, and Parnell expressing his support for the legislation and calling on the Land League to end its protests. Aghast at these developments, the paper accused Gladstone of 'subserviency to the Irish Party' and declared that the deal was 'an assured domination of the Parnell section of Members over the rest, and over the Castle and country'.[44] A few days after Parnell's release the paper printed a special Sunday edition published 'under circumstances of the most unexampled and startling character'.[45] The news of the events of the previous day made page one – the events in question being the brutal stabbing to death of the chief secretary, Lord Frederick Cavendish, and the under-secretary, Thomas Burke, by members of an unknown secret society called the Invincibles. Condemnation of the murders was swift from both the Home Rule Party and the Land League, and the paper accepted that whatever one thought of Parnell and his policy of popular agitation 'no Irish party entertains the slightest idea of regarding less lightly than its hideousness requires, an atrocity for the dark depths of which the records would be searched in vain'.[46]

'ENGLAND CASTS US OFF'

In the 1882 edition of the *Newspaper Gazetteer*, the *Irish Times* described itself as 'Moderate-Conservative' with 'a circulation far exceeding that of any other newspaper in the country'.[47] Between 1882 and 1892 its daily sales gradually rose from 23,500 to 28,500.[48] But it did not have the largest circulation. This distinction fell to the paper associated with Parnell and the Home Rule Party, the *Freeman's Journal*, which had a circulation of approximately 43,000 in 1887.[49] Although these figures come from the newspapers themselves, the 1885 accounts of distributors, W.H. Smith, indicate that while the *Freeman's Journal's* account stood at £12,437, that of the *Irish Times* stood at £8,644. The paper's readership was, for the most part, confined to the greater Dublin area with the *Freeman's Journal* having a much wider circulation:

In 1887 Eason's Belfast house held 14 standing orders for the *Irish Times* and a like number
of the *Freeman's Journal*; through agents it supplied 17 copies of the *Irish Times* as against
150 copies of the *Freeman's Journal* ... A newsagent in Newcastle West, Co. Limerick,
regularly handled 50 *Freeman's Journals* (and a sole copy of the *Irish Times*) ... Limerick
bookstall handled 116 copies (but only six copies of the *Irish Times*).[50]

Sales of the paper within the greater Leinster area were buoyant, however. In
August 1878 a bookstall in Bray sold 174 copies of the *Irish Times* every day
compared to 156 copies of the *Freeman's Journal*. Thus there existed the
'dominance by a unionist paper in Dublin, and by a nationalist paper outside
the capital'. With no other successful conservative paper, the *Irish Times* was
'the undisputed voice of Dublin unionism'.[51]

By the mid-1880s the paper was anti-home rule in a much stronger vein
than it had been in 1874. By this time it was edited by James A. Scott, 'who
steered it successfully through the difficulties and dangers of the Home Rule
crisis in 1886'.[52] Born in Edinburgh in 1829 Scott was, at one time, joint editor
of the *Evening Mail*. He was editor of the *Irish Times* between 1878 and 1899
and was a founding member of both the National Association of Journalists
and its successor, the Institute of Journalists.[53] After the 1885 general election,
Parnell's Home Rule Party held the balance of power and, when it became clear
that William Gladstone would consider home rule in return for Parnell's
support, the paper accused him of casting aside 'the principle of equal legislation for all the parts of the Kingdom'. As the paper saw it, Gladstone would
'retain only nominal influence for the Crown in Ireland under a shackled
prerogative, and would subject more than one-third of the native Irish people,
spoken of in an exclusive sense as the "loyal minority", to the rule of a majority
curbed only by such guarantees as Mr Parnell would offer, who already has
refused any'.[54] In a subsequent leading article it warned loyalists 'that their
interests are already betrayed as far as Mr Gladstone can betray them, and that
there is not a day to lose in declaring their obstinate resistance to the betrayal'.[55]
When the details of Gladstone's proposal were confirmed, the paper attacked
the terms upon which home rule was proposed and what it saw as Gladstone's
abandoning of loyalists:

England casts us off, gets rid of us – that is the great temptation offered to her by Mr
Gladstone – and in getting rid of us keeps us under a control not to promote our own trade
and manufactures, while bearing all our own burdens and losing all the advantages of any
real Imperial rights. From a national point of view, is this an honest plan? Is this not
another selfish English plan? ... The shape in which Mr Gladstone presents the whole
design, and the manifest object of it, would do the utmost that ingenuity could to reconcile
the Irish loyalists to cast adrift from a perfidious companionship, and prefer even the hard
lot of a battling minority to the almost harder lot of a betrayed minority, leaning upon
England only to be deserted and insulted by her.[56]

Home rule was an issue that the paper's proprietor, Sir John Arnott, felt passionately about, and as the debates on the issue came to a close he wrote a series of letters to the London *Times* in which he proposed his alternative policy for Ireland. In one such letter he suggested that the executive based at Dublin Castle should be put in the hands of Irishmen. Observing that the 'principal functions are in the hands of strangers', he asked whether there were 'no Irishmen fit to fill those places?' Could not the chief secretary, he asked, be 'an Irishman of energy, popularity, and shrewdness – say Mr Parnell himself, with a seat in the Cabinet, and "carte blanche" to develop Irish national industrial resources by the best means that local knowledge can devise'. He also suggested the formation of 'a Grand Parliamentary Committee of Irish Members, selected from the Counties and Cities, to meet in Dublin once a year ... to investigate bills for local requirements'.[57] Arnott's proposals fell on deaf ears, as did Gladstone's own arguments for home rule. When, in June 1886, the home rule bill was defeated after one-third of Gladstone's own MPs voted against it, the paper observed that the bill 'was lost altogether through the action of the Liberal Party itself, in repudiating the Liberal Premier, and rejecting and reprobating his policy'. It called for equanimity on the part of its readers; it would 'be as idle for the loyalists to indulge in jubilant and extravagant shouts of victory as it would be for the nationalists to deny the right of a majority to determine the Imperial policy'.[58]

'A MEAN AND MISERABLE STORY'

No such equanimity attached itself to the fall of Charles Stewart Parnell four years later. In November 1890, Parnell's former colleague, William O'Shea, sued his wife Kitty for divorce and named Parnell as the other man. Victorian public opinion was scandalised, and the Home Rule Party split in two. The paper reported the divorce case extensively, although it conceded that the formulaic proceedings 'did not at all justify the absorbing interest which the general public has all along seemed to take in the case'. It was 'one of the most unsensational suits ever brought before the courts, outside, of course, the personality of the distinguished co-respondent of the suit'.[59] But while the case itself might not have been sensational, its outcome certainly was. When the court essentially branded Parnell an adulterer, the paper described the saga as 'a mean and miserable story, which from beginning to end is a narrative of paltry deceit'. It had 'no wish to turn the scandal to political account', but, it declared, the verdict made it 'impossible to regard him as occupying that position of dignity which hitherto he has held'. Parnell was 'himself responsible for the depreciation of his character, and if condemned by the public for a lapse of honour and of honesty that have irretrievably wrecked the reputations of smaller men, he has only himself to blame'. The revelations struck 'a heavy blow at his reputation' and the behaviour laid bare to the public was 'wretched in its duplicity and disgrace, and, while they condemn it, they cannot but regret that it has dragged down a great name'.[60]

When the Catholic hierarchy issued its denunciation of Parnell, the paper printed what it called the 'supremely important document' and opined that the conclusion it pronounced would be 'received universally with the respect which is due to the position and authority of those eminent prelates'. That conclusion – that Parnell was guilty of 'one of the gravest offences known to religion and society' – would, it believed, 'exercise the largest effect'.[61] When the Home Rule Party split, it declared that the consequence would be 'further commotion in our country' and observed that those 'who support the Unionist principle have no call to rejoice in it'.[62] Nonetheless, it was generous in its tribute to Parnell when he died ten months later. While it was 'enough to add that his errors were very great, and the injustice which he did to his own social class flagrant', it also acknowledged his contribution to improving the living conditions of the tenant farmers and his political skills even if, as it believed, they were wasted on trying to secure home rule. 'His moral lapse', it concluded, 'will not forbid gratitude among those who profited by his struggles on their behalf, and it will not affect the judgment of those who lamented the waste of his energies in a labour that has proved a momentous failure.'[63]

Momentous failure or not, the issue of home rule continued to dominate the political agenda. In 1892 Gladstone introduced a second home rule bill, and the paper reflected the hardening unionist attitude as the bill wound its way through parliament. Ulster was portrayed as the powerhouse of opposition and, when unionist protests climaxed in the large scale signing of the Belfast Convention, it observed that 'Ulster is a word of larger meaning and weight than ever'. It was 'an impertinence without example to ask the Ulster million to hand over power, to jeopardise the interests of such a community, to a political leader who has not so much as vouchsafed mention of the character of his design'. Ulster, it concluded, was a power to be reckoned with:

> Ulstermen have the demand to make that they shall be masters of their own future, and they will not suffer English Radicals or Irish Factionists, or both conspiring, to take from them, whether by force or fraud, their birthright of British equality, or their treasure of personal freedom ... Ulster from to-day becomes such a power in the Kingdom as United Ulster never before has been, and the disunited and distracted Southern Provinces compare with it most sadly.[64]

When the bill was passed in the house of commons, the paper predicted that the house of lords would do 'a duty to the Empire' and kill the bill.[65] When the lords did exactly that, it triumphantly observed that 'It was flung out of the House of Lords this morning by a vote which is signal and impressive ... The majority of 378 is unexampled. It is record breaking.' The campaigns for and against home rule had, it contended, 'arrested business, occupied men's minds to the damage of enterprise, caused bitterness and poisoned society'. 'It would be best for Ireland', it concluded, 'that we never heard more of the Home Rule Bill.' But while home rule slipped down the political agenda, it would resurface in 1912. By that time the political ethos of the paper would be redefined twice more: in the 1887 edition of the *Newspaper Gazetteer* it described itself as 'Independent (i.e. Liberal-Conservative)' and in 1895 as 'Unionist'.[66] But whatever about being bad for the country the home rule saga was good for circulation. Daily sales of the paper rose from 29,187 on the day of Gladstone's introduction of the bill to 43,381 the following day. It had a smaller increase on the day following the bill's defeat in the house of lords; sales jumped from 30,353 to 33,377.[67]

IRISH TIMES LIMITED

The masthead of the paper's edition of 29 March 1898 was surrounded with thick black lines, as was the page that carried its leading articles, the first of which announced the death the previous day of Sir John Arnott. The passing of 'one so conspicuous in Irish enterprise, in public spirit, in unselfishness and good works' would, his obituary observed, 'be mourned by all classes of our countrymen'.[68] Subsequent to this, the trustees of his last will and testament, his widow and his son Sir John Alexander Arnott, held the paper in trust for two years. In November 1900 a new entity, the Irish Times Limited, was created to acquire and take over as a going concern the *Irish Times* and its sister publications, the *Weekly Irish Times* and the *Evening Irish Times*. The prospectus for the company indicated that it was a profitable one. For the year ending December 1895 it made a profit of £27,829; the corresponding figures for the following two years were £31,196 and £33,771. For the year ending March 1899 it recorded a profit of £35,367 and to March 1900 it made a profit of £29,227.[69] The company's first chairman and managing director was Sir John Alexander Arnott and by virtue of article 103 of the company's articles of association he was entitled to hold these positions until his death or retirement. The first board of directors boasted four members of the Arnott family – Sir John Alexander Arnott, David Taylor Arnott, Loftus Percival Arnott, and Cecil

John Maxwell Arnott – as well as the general manager James Carlyle, each of whom was required to purchase at least £1,000 worth of shares.

The original share capital of the company was £450,000 divided into 55,000 preference shares of £5 each, and 35,000 ordinary shares of £5 each. The vast bulk of the ordinary shares were acquired jointly by the new Sir John Arnott and his wife. The ordinary shares were significant in that only ordinary shareholders were entitled to receive notice of, attend and vote at AGMs. Preference shareholders could only attend meetings convened to alter the company's articles of association, to consider the sale or winding up of the company or if dividends went unpaid for more than six months. In all such meetings ordinary shareholders were entitled to one vote per share held, while preference shareholders were entitled to one vote per five shares held. Thus, those who held the ordinary shares controlled the company. Significantly, no ordinary share could be sold or transferred to a non-member of the company without the consent of the board so long as an existing member was willing to buy the share at a fair value. This provision did not apply to ordinary shares held by Sir John Arnott and his wife who reserved the right to transfer their ordinary shares to any person.[70]

Both the share structure and the voting rights of shareholders were amended over the years. In June 1904 the 35,000 ordinary shares of £5 each were divided into 175,000 shares of £1 each. These 175,000 shares were in turn divided into 105,000 preference shares of £1 each and 70,000 ordinary shares of £1 each. Again Sir John Arnott and his wife retained the bulk of the ordinary shares. The share register of 1921 lists them as jointly holding 66,386 ordinary shares with Sir John Arnott holding another 404 ordinary shares in his own name. The voting structure was also amended so that ordinary shareholders were entitled to one vote per every five shares held and preference shareholders to one vote per twenty-five preference shares held. In January 1920 it was agreed that, upon the death or retirement of Sir John, all shareholders would have the right to receive notice, attend and vote (according to shares held) at the company's AGM.[71] Nonetheless, Sir John remained as chairman and managing director of the company until his death in 1940.

'TYRANNY OF THE CLAP-TRAP PATRIOTS'

At the beginning of 1900 the paper expressed its belief that 'the real difficulties of Ireland are economic and agrarian, rather then political'. For nearly twenty years 'much of the energy which could have been profitably applied to the development of the country's material interests has been expended in a vain and unpractical pursuit of the *ignis fatuus* of Home Rule'.[72] With the arrival of the new century it believed that it was time for Ireland to settle down within the United Kingdom and for its politicians to devote themselves to improving social and economic conditions. But even though home rule had been thwarted, the political power of the Protestant and unionist community was not as strong as it had once been. Land reform – such as the Ashbourne Land Purchase Act of 1885 – had resulted in the transfer of land ownership from the old ascendancy class to Catholic farmers. In addition, electoral reform had resulted in the introduction of the secret ballot in 1872 and near universal male franchise in 1884. In addition, the late 1800s witnessed the rise of a number of organisations, which, while not necessarily advocating home rule, stressed the differences rather than the commonalities between Ireland and Britain. These organisations, such as the Gaelic League and the Gaelic Athletic Association, which set about reviving the Gaelic language and Gaelic sports respectively, helped stress a distinct culture and national identity from those of Britain. The period was also characterised by a growth in militant nationalism.

One issue on which the paper and militant nationalism differed was the Boer War in South Africa. While the Irish Transvaal Committee held anti-recruitment meetings, the paper was determined to do its bit for the Irish regiments and organised the Irish Regiments' Widows' and Orphans' Fund. It also issued an appeal to its readers to send in donations of clothing to be forwarded to the troops. A letter written by the paper's London correspondent to the London *Times* outlined the success of this appeal by declaring that a consignment of forty tons had been dispatched to the troops – '9,237 pairs of socks, 13,000 pairs of laces, 701 dozen handkerchiefs, 160 pairs woollen undervests and drawers, 1,000 shirts, 110 suits of pyjamas, 450 caps and tam o'shanters, 350 cardigan jackets, and jerseys, 300 scarves, 40 cholera belts, and other comforts'. As the correspondent put it, the contributions had come 'from the humble peasant to the highest in the land throughout Ireland'.[73] The war resulted in increased circulation; daily sales rose from 31,000 in 1898 to 40,000 in 1900.[74] Such was the demand for news that the paper published on Christmas Day 1899 when the war was at its most critical phase. The previous week had become known as 'Black Week' due to a series of setbacks for British forces, so a decision to publish was taken to keep readers up to date with developments. However, a Christmas truce had been agreed upon, and so there were no major developments to report. In addition, all transport had been cancelled for the holiday and overall the decision to publish on Christmas Day was 'in the nature of a fiasco'.[75]

After the death of James A. Scott in 1899, the paper's London editor, William Algernon Locker was appointed editor. Born in London in 1863,

Locker had edited *The Globe* between 1891 and 1895 and was editor of the *Morning Post* between 1895 and 1897. He edited the *Irish Times* until 1907 and from then until 1924 was the paper's London correspondent. He was also assistant editor of *Punch* magazine between 1915 and 1929.[76] Locker's editorship saw a rise in circulation, helped no doubt by numerous royal visits. On 5 April 1900 sales hit 73,789 on the occasion of the visit of Queen Victoria. On 22 July 1903 sales hit 52,811 when King Edward VII visited Dublin. Everyday circulation remained buoyant throughout the early 1900s and stood at 36,000 copies per day in 1904. Given that the *Irish Times* was aimed at a very specific readership, the launch of the *Irish Independent* in 1905 should not have had any major impact; but the new competitor was cheaper, and by 1910 circulation had fallen to 33,000 copies per day. Nonetheless, advertising revenue remained steady and the *Irish Times* made a profit of £29,466 in 1905.[77]

By this time, the paper had employed a female staff reporter, Annie Bethune Maguire, who covered social functions; she was 'a well-known and popular figure at the Viceregal Lodge and the Castle under several vice-royalties'.[78] By this time, too, coverage of sports had expanded, with the emphasis very much on rugby, cricket, coursing and horseracing. Much coverage was devoted to Ireland's first triple crown victory in 1894, though the coverage of the first modern Olympic Games held two years later was more sparse. While the paper reported the success of Dublin's John Pius Boland in reaching the finals of the single and double tennis competition, his success in winning two gold medals went unreported.[79] Horse racing was the sport that received most coverage: the Arnott family had interests in the Cork and Baldoyle racecourses, and Maxwell Arnott was a horse breeder and trainer. In 1902 the Phoenix Park Race Company, of which Sir John Arnott was chairman, opened the Phoenix Park racecourse and the following year the Irish Times Ltd purchased the premier horseracing journal, the *Irish Field*.

It was also around this time too that James Joyce, whilst living in Paris, made his writing debut in the paper. In a letter to his mother he had mentioned: 'It would be quite easy for me to send any kind of news to that intelligent organ – motor news, dead men's news, any news – for I have all the Paris papers at my disposal.'[80] Joyce's father forwarded the suggestion to a friend of his, Matthew O'Hara, who was a reporter with the paper, but the delay in getting any answer prompted Joyce to remark: 'I am seriously thinking of entering the church if I find editors and managers and "practical" people so very stubborn as they appear to be'.[81] Shortly afterwards, Joyce's mother wrote to inform him of O'Hara's instructions: 'O'H says you may send him any *fresh* news you can pick up in Paris under cover to *himself Matthew O'Hara* and he will work it up for you, so try him with the first thing you can find.'[82] In April 1903 Joyce submitted a tortuous interview with Henri Fournier, a French motor-racing driver who was due to race in Ireland the following July. Part of the interview consisted of a convoluted exchange that involved both men trying to convert kilometres into miles by first trying to figure out how many yards there were in a mile. When they agreed the conversions and it emerged that the speed of Fournier's car would be roughly sixty-eight miles an hour, Joyce's response was, 'It is an appalling pace! It is enough to burn our roads ...'[83]

Another writer making headlines in the early 1900s, though for very different reasons, was John Millington Synge, whose play, *The Playboy of the Western World,* met with riotous opposition and vociferous protests from nationalists when it was staged at Dublin's Abbey Theatre. Set on the western seaboard, the plot centred on the welcome given to an outsider who had supposedly killed his father but whose popularity drops when it emerges that he had not. The play, as the paper put it, gave 'offence to a very large number of the Dublin community, who maintain that it is utterly untrue to life and a travesty on Irish character'. As a consequence, protesters interrupted the proceedings on a nightly basis:

> A considerable section of the audience strongly resented the notion that such a state of affairs could be taken as a correct reflex on western peasant life, and showed a determined resolve to interrupt the representation ... and kept up a sustained outburst of hissing, booing and groaning ... At intervals the groaning and hissing were varied by the singing of 'A Nation Once Again' and 'The West's Awake'. Vigorous stamping of feet and slashing with sticks of the woodwork created an indescribable din, as the result of which the voices of the actors were completely drowned.[84]

As the play's run continued things got worse:

> Groans, hisses and cheers were given with lusty vigour, and the din was increased by the valiant efforts of a performer on a penny trumpet, but the "music" he produced was almost completely drowned by the angry interchanges which passed between the stalls and the back portion of the pit ... Cheers, groans and stamping of feet were continued in a most persistent manner ... A further remark in reference to a certain inside female garment led to renewed scenes of disorder, and the cross-fire between the audience was intensely funny. One man yelled out, 'That's worthy of the slums of London'. 'Shut up your mug', cried another; a third man chimed in with 'Go to h——'. 'That's your country', was the retort, but the rejoinder was absolutely crushing, 'Go home and kill your father'.[85]

For its part, the paper saw the dispute as one between artistic expression and the sanctimonious view of Irishness fostered by some political parties. While it conceded that the happenings of the play 'would be uncommon in any civilised country', it noted that 'the "Irish-Ireland" critics of Mr Synge's play have decided that it would be absolutely impossible in Ireland'. The objectors had 'founded their objections on a theory of Celtic impeccability which is absurd in principle, and intolerable when it is sought to be rigidly imposed on artistic considerations'. No impartial observer could 'defend for a single moment the *Sinn Féin* party's crude and violent methods of dramatic criticism'. All in all, it commended the Abbey Theatre for its persistence in keeping the play running in spite of the protests. It was high time 'for thoughtful Irishmen of all parties to make a stand for freedom of thought and speech against bodies which seek to introduce into the world of the mind the methods which the Western branches of the United Irish League have introduced into politics'. It was for this reason that the paper expressed its support for 'the plucky stand which the National Theatre Company is making against the organised tyranny of the clap-trap patriots'.[86] But as the 1900s progressed, the paper would do more and more battle with those who openly advocated Ireland's complete separation from the British empire.

CHAPTER 2

Tumultuous Times

The twenty-seven years of his editorship were stormy years for Ireland, calling for almost infinite tact and strength on the part of an editor. Mr Healy's whole nature was conservative, and he was in charge of a conservative newspaper; but within a few years after his long term of office began, the old foundations of Irish life were shaken to the roots.[1]

John Healy's obituary in the Irish Times

IN 1907 JOHN EDWARD HEALY succeeded William Locker as editor when Locker returned to London. Born in Drogheda in 1872, Healy studied classics at Trinity College where he edited the college magazine and in his final year wrote leading articles for the *Evening Mail*. From there he graduated to the *Daily Express*, of which he became editor before he left to pursue a career in law. While studying to become a barrister, Healy kept up his contacts in journalism and was, at various times, the Dublin correspondent for the London *Times*, the editor of the *Church of Ireland Gazette*, and an occasional leader writer for the *Irish Times*. Called to the Bar in 1906, he practised law for a few months before taking up the offer of editing the *Irish Times*.[2] When he became editor, the paper was a twelve-pager and cost one penny a copy. Its austere appearance and layout had not altered dramatically over the years; each page was still printed in eight single columns of dense type. Pages one to three consisted of classified adverts and three-column-width display adverts for Dublin's main department stores. Page four carried the sports news – horse racing, greyhound racing, cricket, golf, athletics, soccer, bowling, tennis, polo, but no coverage of the GAA. The editorial page carried theatre listings, leading articles, a column called 'Court Circular', which, under the emblem of the royal coat of arms, kept readers informed of the latest happenings at Buckingham Palace, and a 'London Letter' about proceedings at Westminster. Another column, 'From the Times of Today', consisted of a London *Times* article expounding on current events. The 'Fashionable Intelligence' column listed the doings and comings and goings of various nobility, while another, 'Naval and Military Intelligence', listed the arrivals, departures, appointments and promotions of senior military personnel. Alongside foreign and domestic news, financial news and law reports, the paper also printed 'Church of Ireland Notes', an indicator of the paper's target readership.

The first fourteen years of Healy's twenty-seven-year editorship were a time of profound upheaval. The granting of home rule, the great lock-out, the First World War, the 1916 rising, Sinn Féin's election victory in 1918, the war of independence, the establishment of the Irish Free State and the civil war all occurred under his watch. Healy was a staunch unionist who believed that Ireland would disintegrate politically and economically if the link with Britain was broken. The paper's unionist ethos was at its strongest under Healy, and this left the paper with a legacy that it found difficult to shake off. But once the Free State became a reality, it was forced to come to terms with the new order, which it did with grace and tact, although many republicans never forgave it for its editorial stance during the 1916 rising. With John Redmond's Irish Parliamentary Party holding the balance of power in Westminster and the veto of the house of lords abolished by the Parliament Act of 1911, home rule seemed inevitable. All the government had to do was pass the bill three times and, even if it was rejected by the lords each time, it would become law on its third passing by the house of commons.

'AT THE POINT OF A BAYONET'

Despite this inevitability, the visit by George V to Dublin in July 1911 gave succour to Irish unionists and the paper; it noted that the visit 'vindicated Dublin's ancient claim to be ranked as the second city in the Empire',[3] and it took comfort in the fact that northern unionists were against any opt-out clause for Ulster that would leave southern unionists to reconcile themselves to a parliament in the predominantly nationalist south. It noted that in speech after speech 'our northern friends have declared that to secure their own safety at the expense of those less able to protect themselves would be a treachery comparable only to a surrender to Home Rule itself'. The cause against home rule was 'not the cause of a province, of a class, or of a creed, but the cause of the whole country'.[4] A unionist demonstration in Dublin in October 1911 saw the paper report Ulster Unionist Party leader Edward Carson as having said that Ulster 'would not dessert the Southern Provinces' and that 'Ulster wanted no separate Parliament'. The protest had 'linked up the whole of Unionist Ireland in stern and steadfast opposition to the Government's policy of Home Rule'. There was 'going to be no "split" between Ulster and the Unionists of the south' because Ulster would 'never make a mockery of her Unionism by an inglorious and base attempt to shelter herself within a separate Parliament'.[5]

When, in April 1912, the Liberal government introduced its home rule bill, the paper declared that the country was on 'the eve of a prolonged and probably bitter conflict'. Compromise, in any form, was not on the agenda: 'It is to the fact of Home Rule, and not to the conditions of any Home Rule Bill that Unionist Ulster is still so firmly hostile as it was in 1886 and 1893.'[6] In September 1912 opposition stepped up a gear when over 200,000 unionists signed the Ulster Covenant that declared their right to use 'all means which may be found necessary to defeat the conspiracy to set up a Home Rule Parliament in Ireland'. This ambivalence towards violence was mirrored within the paper. Despite the fact that the covenant represented a refusal to recognise the legitimacy of parliamentary democracy, the paper simply observed that the Ulster unionists had 'convinced every open mind in the United Kingdom that the men who sign the Covenant to-day will keep their word. This is the only fact that counts. They may be right or wrong, loyal or disloyal, patriots or rebels; but they have taken a course, and nothing will turn them from it.' Home rule could 'only be imposed on Ulster at the cost of civil war'.[7] The only part of the proceedings that gave it cause for concern was the way in which religion had crept into the ceremony. It reiterated its 'dislike for the introduction of religion into politics' and declared that no church was 'entitled to bind all its supporters to a political creed – much less to a political collect'. It expressed concern that, at a meeting at the Ulster Hall, a clergyman had claimed for the church 'a right to lay the Divine measuring line on every attempted form of legislation bearing on the character, the freedom and the well-bring of the people'; that was 'a very dangerous claim for Churches which denounce the doctrine of infallibility'.[8]

In its new year's day editorial of 1913 the paper declared that 'political feeling, particularly in Ireland, has been embittered to an extravagant degree'.[9] Not only had relations between nationalists and unionists become strained; so too had relations between northern and southern unionists. In the house of commons, Edward Carson, despite his previous utterances, proposed an amendment to exclude Ulster from the scope of home rule. Although the amendment was rejected, it caused much anxiety to southern unionists who did not relish the 'proposed abandonment of Southern Unionists to the mercies of a Nationalist Parliament'. The paper dismissed Carson's assertion that exclusion would not be a betrayal of southern unionists because Ulster Unionist MPs at Westminster would protect their interests: it retorted that 'a dozen Ulster Unionists at Westminster (counterbalanced as they would be, by a dozen Ulster Nationalists) could not lift a finger to help the Irish minority under a Home Rule Parliament'. Home rule itself represented a better prospect: 'an Irish Parliament containing a substantial and vigorous minority from North-East

Ulster would have, at least, a few redeeming qualities'. Ulster it declared, 'must stand or fall with the whole of Unionist Ireland'.[10] When the house of lords rejected the bill, the paper opined that without the agreement of Ulster Unionists, 'no scheme, large or small, for the betterment of Irish government can be feasible, or even conceivable'.[11] As the bill wound its way through the commons a second time, the paper declared that home rule would 'never become law in the province of Ulster except at the point of a bayonet'.[12] When the lords rejected the bill for a second time, it claimed that Ulster would be 'absolutely justified in resisting it by every means in her power'; by doing so, Ulster would be 'the champion of British liberties against an unexampled tyranny' and civil war would 'become not merely a necessity but a virtue'; home rule could only be enforced 'at the cost of revolution'.[13]

'NO LARKIN'

In Dublin a revolution of a very different kind was brewing. For several years Jim Larkin had been building up the Irish Transport and General Workers Union and, through the tactic of sympathetic pickets, had forced many Dublin employers to recognise and negotiate with the union. Larkin met his nemesis in William Martin Murphy, the owner of Independent Newspapers and the Dublin United Tramway Company, who, as head of the Dublin Employers' Federation, organised nearly 400 employers to face down Larkin's union. In August 1913 Murphy dismissed all his employees who refused to sign a declaration revoking their union membership. As a conservative newspaper the *Irish Times* supported the employers and had no time for the union that had tried 'to make itself the arbiter between masters and men in all the varied commerce and industry of our capital'. Aggrieved employees had nothing to gain 'by entrusting their case to an agency whose interest is agitation rather than settlement, and to which the public opinion of Dublin is definitely hostile'.[14] The union retaliated during Horse Show Week when 200 tram drivers and conductors walked off the job. The paper described their action as 'a crime against the civil welfare and the public peace', and added that it regarded 'as public enemies, the men who deliberately organised the strike and used the unfortunate strikers for their wicked purposes'.[15] Its view of Larkin's union and its methods was succinctly summarised in one paragraph:

> The essential fact is this – that a single organisation is now exercising an abominable tyranny over the working classes of the city. Its object is to control the relations between masters and men in every branch of local industry. When recognition is refused to it a strike follows. The whole trade of Dublin is dislocated in order that a single firm may be brought to its knees. The organisation has no mercy on the sufferings of the poor; it never spares a

thought for the welfare or reputation of Dublin. The present tramway strike is a characteristic example of its policy and methods. With the object of forcing itself upon men who hate it, this body did not hesitate to try to 'hold up' the business and pleasure of Dublin in the most vital week of the whole year. The thing is not merely a nuisance; it has become a danger and a degradation.[16]

It praised the 'fine stand' taken by William Martin Murphy, which had 'put heart into the whole city'. On 3 September the Employers' Federation locked out all its employees and by the end of that month, with 25,000 workers locked out, the scene was set for a winter of hardship and discontent. Despite its pro-employer stance, the paper admitted that it could not say that 'labour has no real grievance in Dublin, or that many employers would not be wise to reconsider their attitude to its fair demands'; when normality was restored, 'certain reforms which have long been desirable in the industrial conditions of Dublin will become practicable'. But such reforms would have to wait until it had 'ceased to be possible for self-styled champions of labour to support anarchy in the workshop with riot in the street'.[17] One major grievance was the appalling living conditions that Dublin workers and their families endured. These were brought into stark relief when, in early September 1913, two tenement houses collapsed in Church Street, killing seven people. To call the tenements overcrowded would be an understatement; as the paper noted, 'One of the houses sheltered five families of twenty-six persons, the other six families of about twenty persons'. Such conditions were, it acknowledged, 'responsible not only for disease and crime, but for much of our industrial unrest':

> In such places there can be no happiness or content; there is not even, as we have just seen, any real security for life and limb. The workers, whose only escape from these wretched homes lies in the public house, would not be human beings if they did not turn a ready ear to anybody who promises to improve their lot. They have not sufficient education to distinguish the false appeal from the true. The members of the Irish Transport Workers' Union live, for the most part, in slums like Church Street. Their domestic conditions make them an easy prey to plausible agitators. We believe that, if every unskilled labourer in Dublin were the tenant of a decent cottage of three, or even two, rooms, the city would not be divided to-day into two hostile camps.[18]

But any solution would have 'to wait upon a return to normal conditions of industrial life'; Dublin employers were 'fighting for the very life of the city, for the right not merely to do their business in their own way, but to do it at all'.[19] Nonetheless the paper set up a 'Church Street Accident Fund' to receive public subscriptions for the forty people, many young children, left homeless by the collapse. Readers were invited to send in subscriptions and among the first to contribute were the Dublin Metropolitan Police (£54), Sir John Arnott (£10) and an anonymous contributor who went by the name 'No Larkin' (£1).[20]

The question of who should pay for Dublin's proposed new art gallery was also a topic of debate at this time. The Cork-born art collector Sir Hugh Lane had offered a collection of paintings to the city of Dublin on the condition that Dublin Corporation build a permanent site for their exhibition. The offer was eventually rejected on the grounds of cost, though not before many Dublin luminaries had voiced their opinion on the matter in the columns of the *Irish Times*. In one such letter, William Martin Murphy stated that it was 'revolting to think that the week of the Church Street holocaust' was the time for the Corporation to again debate Lane's offer, which involved, as he put it, 'spending public money in building a picture palace over the River Liffey'. The appalling condition of the tenements was, Murphy concluded, 'the question of questions for Dublin'.[21] In the same issue, the paper published a new poem by W.B. Yeats, *On Reading Much of the Correspondence against the Art Gallery*, that accused Ireland of fumbling in 'a greasy till' and declared the death of romantic Ireland.[22] In its editorial introducing the poem, the paper explained that 'Mr Yeats sees behind the opposition to the Art Gallery project a tendency of mind which he fears may grow on us in Ireland ... He feels that there is a danger of our people becoming hardened to the worship of materialism and commercialism.' The paper itself was in favour of the art gallery and declared that if the Corporation rejected Lane's offer, then 'the city will deserve the reproach which Mr Yeats makes against those who have grudged the money and the granting of Sir Hugh Lane's conditions'.[23]

As more and more employers locked out their workers and the lock-out looked as if it might go on indefinitely, the tone of the paper's editorials became more apocalyptic. It continued to call on employers to join the lock-out and was under no illusions about the sufferings that a prolonged lock-out would involve or how that would focus the minds of workers and their families:

> There is no possibility of negotiation with James Larkin's Union. It must either crush or be crushed. The great Anarch has been crushed in other cities where he has been tackled boldly and strongly. He will be crushed in Dublin also. However protracted this battle may be, it can have only one end. The whole industry and intelligence of the city are behind the employers. We deplore the suffering which this struggle is going to inflict on the workers and on their innocent families, but that suffering will bear fruit in the disenchantment of experience. With one or two conspicuous exceptions, the employers are now resolute and united. This fight will see the end of syndicalism in Dublin.[24]

At the end of September, a Board of Trade inquiry into the lock-out was established which ultimately found against Larkin's tactic of sympathetic strikes but also against the employers' demand that workers renounce trade union membership. The employers' rejection of the report prompted George Russell

(Æ) to write an open letter, 'To The Masters of Dublin', to the paper; it was an eloquently damning indictment of the behaviour of the Dublin Employers' Federation:

> Those who have economic power have civic power also, yet you have not used the power that was yours to right what was wrong in the evil administration of this city. You have allowed the poor to be herded together so that one thinks of certain places in Dublin as of a pestilence. There are twenty thousand rooms, in each of which live entire families, and sometimes more, where no function of the body can be concealed, and delicacy and modesty are creatures that are stifled ere they are born ... The men whose manhood you have broken will loathe you, and will always be brooding and scheming to strike a fresh blow. The children will be taught to curse you. The infant being moulded in the womb will have breathed into its starved body the vitality of hate. It is not they – it is you who are the blind Samsons pulling down the pillars of the social order.[25]

By February 1914 the majority of workers had been starved back to work. As the paper noted, the settlement was 'the very worst kind of settlement – virtually "settlement by starvation"'. Indeed, it struck a human note in reminding its readers that the 'brooding discontents which exploded in the mad attempt to "hold up" Dublin gathered force and volume in the pestilential atmosphere of the Dublin slums'. Echoing Russell's letter, it noted that it was 'a cynical commentary on our social sense that we needed the stimulus of the strike to realise the squalor and misery which, in the last analysis, produced it'. If 'the citizens of Dublin are now inspired to sweep that squalor and misery away, the strike will have had at least one good result.'[26] With its disruption to Dublin business life, the lock-out had an impact on the paper. Its annual report for the year ending September 1914 noted a decline in advertising revenue in the later months of 1913. The early part of 1914 was marked by an outbreak of foot and mouth disease that caused the cancellation of the Spring Show, while the outbreak of the First World War caused the cancellation of the Horse Show: two shows that 'annually brought to Dublin enormous wealth and business activities'. The war also led to 'a serious falling off in advertising revenue' and involved 'very heavy expenses in procuring for our readers news of the campaigns from all quarters of the world'. However, circulation increased to 34,000 copies per day and the company managed to return a profit of £30,995.[27]

'THAT JAUNDICED ORGAN OF WEST-BRITONISM'

During the lock-out the plight of the workers' children came to the fore and the issue of proselytism, or religious conversion, raised its ugly head. Both Protestant and Catholic lay organisations ran food centres in places of worship, and this fuelled suspicions of charities using free food to convert the poor. Where charity ended and conversion began was a sensitive issue at the best of times, but during the lock-out it became a hugely emotive topic. Hungry children were viewed as being especially vulnerable to conversion, and although it condemned the practice of proselytism, for the *Irish Times* there was a certain pragmatism attached to the process. It declared that it 'would much prefer a little child to be a well tended Roman Catholic with food in its stomach than a neglected and starving Protestant in the slums – and *vice versa*'. A Catholic clergyman, the Revd John Gwynn, denounced the above viewpoint as 'rank paganism', forcing the paper to outline its objection to the motive rather than the outcome of proselytism:

> For some years, perhaps, an infant has lived in the slums, utterly neglected, starving, surrounded by every kind of vice and wickedness. Then through some accident – often the imprisonment or death of a drunken and worthless parent – somebody is induced to take an interest in the infant's soul. Persons who, for years, had ignored its cry for bread become desperately concerned about its religion. Other persons of a different Church fling themselves into the fray. In the end the child finds food, decency, and education in some institution, Protestant or Roman Catholic. If no o *sum theologieum* had been aroused about its soul, it might have lived or perished in the slums. Nobody, Protestant or Roman Catholic, might have lifted a finger to save its body ... The proselytisers, Protestant and Roman Catholic, fight over the souls of children whom they would leave to the misery of the slums if those children's bodies only were concerned.[28]

It was on this very issue that the paper became the subject of fierce criticism from the *Catholic Bulletin*. The criticism centred on its coverage of the sacking of a Protestant clerk, G.H. Walton, from the publishing company M.H. Gill & Son. In October 1913 the firm dismissed Walton on the grounds that he had admitted to being a Protestant proselytiser. The issue came to light when charity colleagues of Walton wrote to the paper to highlight his dismissal after thirty-nine years of service with the firm. Since this had happened at a time when the air was 'full of promises of religious equality and toleration for the Protestants', they called on all those who believed in 'the principles of religious and civil liberty to intervene and correct a manifest injustice'.[29] This prompted a letter from the company's secretary, Patrick Keohane, in which he stated that Walton had admitted to being 'actively engaged in certain objectionable practices' with certain Protestant institutions that meant to 'all Catholic minds, one and only one, aspect, namely proselytism – and that in one of its most insidious forms'. The company's directors had concluded that it was inconsistent 'with their obligations as recognised Catholic publishers that a gentleman engaged in such practices should continue in their service', and so Walton was given one month's pay in lieu of notice upon his forced resignation. Keohane pointed out that the company had many Protestants in its employment and that while its directors had 'no quarrel whatever with Protestantism' they could not employ any person 'endeavouring to wean little children from the faith of their fathers'.[30]

In an editorial, the paper declared that there was 'a disparity of evidence'; if Walton had spent his spare time 'feeding the poor without any ulterior motive', then Gills had treated him 'not merely harshly, but brutally'; if, however, by 'means of tea and bread and butter' he had 'tempted little children to swallow his theological opinions', then he had behaved 'foolishly and with a lamentable want of what we may call Christian delicacy'. It again expressed its dislike of proselytism by dismissing 'religious "conversions" which are not the outcome of spiritual and intellectual conviction' and declared that free breakfasts to the poor should not 'be compromised by any sort of religious service'. Proselytism had done an 'immense amount of harm in Dublin by preventing the hearty co-operation of Protestants and Roman Catholics in works of social reform'. Notwithstanding all this, it concluded that Walton had been treated 'very badly'. In his free time Walton, 'exercising the civil and religious liberties of his citizenship, did certain things of which his conscience approved'. Gills' action had set a precedent, which 'if many employers were to assert it, would justify the hardest things that Mr Larkin has said against employers as a class'. It expressed confidence that the incident would 'surprise and alarm all Irish Protestants and many fair-minded Catholics' and called on nationalist politicians to outline what they thought of Walton's dismissal. If such politicians stayed silent, then both Protestants and Catholics could only take 'utterly divergent views of the meaning of the words "civil and religious liberty"'.[31]

Not surprisingly, the issue prompted a flurry of letters to the paper, though none from Walton himself. When his charity colleagues declared that Walton had 'never opened his mouth on the subject of religion on any occasion at the Breakfasts',[32] Keohane replied that the board 'did not think it necessary to point out that Mr Walton was a waiter not a preacher at the Sunday morning breakfasts'. Intriguingly, the paper did not publish this riposte from Keohane.[33] Other contributors had more success in getting their views printed. A Catholic correspondent pointedly asked, 'Do we not try to convert others to our own faith?'[34], while a Protestant employer, Robert Gibson, wrote to say that if he found a Catholic employee trying to convert Protestant children he would sack him. Gibson fundamentally opposed proselytising and declared that 'the Roman Catholic, or the Protestant, who tries to pervert little children is neither a good Catholic nor a good Protestant, and utterly unworthy of the name of Christian'.[35] Another correspondent denounced the sacking as hypocritical because he had bought a copy of a Catholic periodical in Gills' shop, the back page of which was 'an appeal on behalf of the Society of the Holy Childhood for funds wherewith to "buy" the infants of parents of the Pagan communions, in order to rear them as Roman Catholics'.[36] Other correspondence debated the innocent or ulterior motives of free food[37] and whether Walton's treatment was symptomatic of what Protestants could expect under home rule.[38]

The *Catholic Bulletin,* which was published by Gill & Son, entered the fray the following month with a stinging rebuke of the *Irish Times* coverage of the issue. Its editorial was denounced as being 'strung together by the shabby misrepresentations, the cunning innuendoes and the bare-faced half-truths which one mostly expects from that jaundiced organ of West-Britonism'. Its policy on letters also came in for criticism: it had 'suppressed two authenticated letters written in self-defence' by Keohane but had published 'a full score of communications, many of them anonymous, most of them seething with bigotry, and all more or less prejudiced'. And it had shown its own 'sense of political and religious tolerance' by changing Gills' address from O'Connell Street to Sackville Street, thus 'eliminating in its arbitrary little way the name of one of the greatest friends of human freedom of any age, in favour of that of one of the most obscure of the many obscure adventurers that ever came to prey on this country'.[39] The *Catholic Bulletin* also took the unusual step of inserting a supplement entitled 'A Challenge to the *Irish Times*' which noted that two letters sent by Keohane 'in reply to all these disgraceful imputations, calculated to bring public odium on their house, were suppressed by the *Irish Times*'. The paper's conduct was denounced as 'cowardly and contemptible' and nothing short of 'journalistic blackguardism'. Catholics should not, it concluded, 'be intimidated by the stale slanders of the Ascendancy and their hoary bogey of Catholic intolerance'.[40]

HOME RULE AGAIN

In 1914 the issue of home rule and the possible exclusion of Ulster again dominated the political agenda. The paper took exception when *The Spectator* observed that the only options facing the government were an acceptance of exclusion or civil war. Exclusion would, the *Irish Times* opined, condemn the country to 'an eternity of national weakness, industrial impotence, and sectarian strife' and leave southern unionists as 'a helpless minority in a community embittered by the loss of Ulster'. There were 'some worse things than civil war, and one of them is the betrayal of loyal friends'.[41] In March 1914 the Liberal government moved a considerable amount of army units up north, prompting the paper to remark that 'His Majesty's troops have always been popular in Ulster, and will continue to be popular there until they are ordered to attack the rights and liberties of the community'.[42] However, the cavalry brigade based at

the Curragh refused to move north and fifty-eight officers resigned. This put the
paper in a difficult situation; while it shared the officers' belief that force should
not be used to quell Ulster's resistance, it could not be seen to be encouraging a
mutiny. True, anything 'which stood between Ireland and the passing of the
Home Rule Bill, with its logical consequence of civil war, might be regarded
with satisfaction by Irish Unionists', but it could not 'rejoice at the incalculable
development in the situation'. That the government contemplated the use of
force in Ulster was 'tragic and terrible'; that the army refused to obey was 'even
more important and more sinister'.[43] The paper ultimately blamed the
government, which had tried to 'provoke Ulster into disorders which would
give the Government an excuse for pouring an overwhelming Army into the
Northern Province, and nipping civil war in the bud'.[44]

The prospect of civil war moved ever closer when the Ulster Volunteers
landed a large consignment of guns at Larne in what the paper called 'one of the
most daring, most skilful, and most perfectly organised achievements in modern
history'. Despite reporting that 35,000 Mauser rifles and 3,500,000 rounds of
ammunition had been smuggled into Ulster, it described the event as 'apart from
any question of legality or wisdom, a truly remarkable achievement' and opined
that 'there is no man in Ireland to-day – not even the most extreme Nationalist
politician – who is not proud that this thing was done by Irishmen and in
Ireland'. It was equally ambivalent about the legality of the occurrence: 'The
Volunteers will argue – quite soundly, as we believe – that they have broken no
law in importing these 35,000 rifles. It seems to be certain that they did not
break the King's peace. The suasion which was applied at a few critical
moments to a few policemen and Customs officers appears to have been strictly
moral, though of course, its objects were well aware that it had a physical
sanction.'[45] Whatever the faults of this line of reasoning, the paper was at least
consistent when, three months later, the Irish Volunteers, formed in Dublin to
ensure that home rule was delivered, landed its own consignment of weapons.
It admitted that it could not 'criticise the conduct of the Nationalist Volunteers
in landing a cargo of rifles at Howth yesterday. We cannot fairly blame their
almost exact imitation of deeds which we have not condemned in Ulster.' It did,
however, express concern at the way in which events were unfolding; the state
of the country was 'desperately critical'; the administration was 'helpless and
discredited'; and the nation was 'divided into two rival armies' with passions
running 'stern and high'.[46] It declared that there was 'no effective government
in Ireland' but also noted that the 'present cloud will be found to have a silver
lining if confronted by a common danger'.[47]

That common danger arrived courtesy of the First World War, which saw
home rule suspended and the Ulster and Irish Volunteers pledging to fight a

common enemy. In what the paper called 'this competition of patriotism', both sets of Volunteers were 'acting in unison and inspired by a common love of country'.[48] It welcomed John Redmond's call for members of the Irish Volunteers to join the army and noted that if both unionists and nationalists were 'going to fight shoulder to shoulder in this war, to share the same baptism of blood, the same suffering and glory in the same holy cause, the end of the war will find a new situation in Ireland'.[49] But it hardly did Redmond any favours when, commenting on a recruitment rally in Dublin at which Redmond and prime minister Herbert Asquith spoke, it observed that it was 'a new thing in Irish history that a great meeting of Nationalists should have concluded with the singing of God Save the King'.[50] Redmond's call split the Irish Volunteers, some of the executive of which believed that the movement should only serve an Irish government. When those who disagreed with Redmond publicly chastised him, the paper accused them of siding with Germany and warned of the consequences of a German victory:

> Anything that weakens the Empire's arm at this terrible crisis must be a help to the Germans; therefore, anybody who seeks to keep Irishmen from joining the Army must want the Germans to win ... A German conquest of this country would be worse than any calamity that has ever overtaken it in all its mournful history ... If our Volunteers were to offer the slightest resistance, our towns would be laid low, our cathedrals and public buildings ruined. Irish priests would be shot and tortured; and the honour of no Irish girl, the life of no old man or child, would be safe. After the conquest Ireland would be reduced to the condition of Prussian Poland. We would be crushed by German taxation. Every Irish sentiment, tradition, and instinct would be trampled into the earth. All this must happen if Germany defeats the British Empire.[51]

The Ulster Volunteers had no qualms in joining up and were cheered on by the paper: 'Every soldier from Unionist Ulster who falls in this war, every act of Ulster Unionist heroism shown against Germany, will make still more impossible the thing which Mr Asquith already regards as unthinkable.' The paper was highly enthused by the war; at last, it declared, 'the dream of generations of Irish patriots has come true: the whole of Ireland, Unionist and Nationalist, Protestant and Roman Catholic, is united in a great and holy cause'.[52] Indeed, as his obituary noted, John Healy was 'a member of almost the first party of journalists to visit the Western Front'.[53] The paper also published lists – under the heading 'TCD and the War' – of Trinity College graduates who had enlisted, and declared that the Book of Kells would 'be dethroned by a copy of this War List – in future the Library's dearest treasure'.[54] Throughout the war it also published lists of Irishmen who were killed in the conflict under the heading 'Roll of Honour'.

'THE SURGEON'S KNIFE'

As Easter 1916 approached, the paper warned of rising tension within the capital and of the activities of the Irish Volunteers – their 'open sedition in the streets of Dublin', their 'sinister traffic in firearms and ammunition', their 'grossly disloyal speeches', their 'rabid sheets' – and concluded that some 'dangerous motive may, or may not, underlie the whole business'.[55] On Easter Monday that motive became apparent, and the next day's paper observed that it had 'never been published in stranger circumstances than those which obtain to-day'; an attempt had been made 'to overthrow the constitutional government of Ireland [and] to set up an independent Irish Republic in Dublin'.[56] Production of the paper had continued as normal that Monday night, but after it was printed Healy received a request from the government to delay its issue to the public and 'the *Irish Times* actually issued to the public on that date was in greatly reduced form'. In the weeks following the rising, the company offered for sale a limited number of copies of the Tuesday edition as originally printed, believing that it would 'form an interesting souvenir of the Irish Insurrection of 1916'.[57] Given the location of its city centre offices, the paper found itself caught between two positions – O'Connell Street held by the rebels and Trinity College held by British forces – which gave its reporters a unique insight into the fighting. Indeed, the staff found themselves trapped in the building for the best part of a week. To ease the cabin fever, the general manager, John J. Simington, secured a barrel of porter that was rationed out at intervals until it was gone.[58] The company's storage depot on Lower Abbey Street was destroyed during the shelling of the city centre. Despite these setbacks, the *Irish Times* published more editions during the rising than any other Dublin paper; the insurgents occupied the offices of Independent Newspapers in Middle Abbey Street and the *Daily Express* opposite City Hall, while the offices of the *Freeman's Journal* in Princes Street suffered damage by shelling. In his later dispatches as Irish correspondent of the London *Times,* John Healy gave an insight into the production of the paper during that week:

> On Monday night I went to my own newspaper, and until Friday night I was virtually a prisoner in its office. We were the only newspaper in Dublin which tried to 'carry on', and we succeeded until Thursday. On that day we were reduced to a 'folio of four pages'. Dublin was utterly cut off from the outside world. Of what was happening in Dublin we knew only what could be gleaned by the brief excursions of brave men who faced death every time they left the office door. We learned afterwards that the General Officer then commanding had sent at least one brief communiqué to the English Press, but this was denied to the only newspaper in Dublin.[59]

Despite being able to publish most days, the paper's reportage was limited by a multitude of factors; the government's declaration of martial law under General John Maxwell, the imposition of press censorship, the inability to communicate with its London office, the difficulty and danger that getting near the fighting entailed for reporters and the fact that the police instructed Healy to turn off all lighting within the building.[60] On the fourth day of the rising it declared that there was 'little or no news (we admit frankly) in the only newspaper; that, however, is not the newspaper's fault, and it may claim, perhaps, as a merit that it comes out at all'. Strangely, it was forced to recommend activities other than reading a newspaper to its readers: a father could 'cultivate a habit of easy conversation with his family ... put his little garden into a state of decency' or do some 'useful mending and painting about the house'. Reading the works of Shakespeare also came highly recommended.[61]

The company later made up for this lack of coverage by publishing a triple issue of the *Weekly Irish Times* on 13 May 1916 that contained full details of the rising: lists of the casualties, reports of the damage and the proclamation of independence itself. This is, perhaps, the most famous of all *Irish Times* front pages; its front-page banner headline mistakenly labelled the rising the 'Sinn Féin Rebellion in Ireland'. In its round-up of the more curious sights of the rising it declared that 'In some instances respectably-dressed persons took part in the looting. One man fitted on a stolen suit of clothes in the street.' 'Ladies with bare feet were seen wearing sealskin coats and jewellery in Sackville street during the looting'; and 'Even costly pianos were looted and rolled along the roadway in Henry street.'[62] Referring to the damage caused on O'Connell Street it noted that 'While the insurgents had possession of the Post Office one of their number spent some time shooting at Nelson's nose, which was swept clean away. The figure of Nelson is now minus an arm and a nose.'[63] A year later the company published the 286-page *Sinn Féin Rebellion Handbook*, which reproduced all the contemporary reportage of the rising and detailed maps of the battle sites. It also included accounts of the courts martial, the activities and trial of Roger Casement, the two commissions of inquiry into the rising and full lists of those killed or taken prisoner.[64]

After the insurgents surrendered, the paper published an edition dated 28 & 29 April & 1 May 1916 and explained that, although its staff had attended for work, the fighting around its offices made publication impossible towards the end of the week. Indeed, such was the demand for news that circulation of the paper jumped from a daily average of 37,000 copies to 46,500 copies in May 1916.[65] In an editorial it observed that the 'Sinn Féin Insurrection' would 'pass into history with the equally unsuccessful insurrections of the past', the only distinction being that 'it was more daringly and systematically planned, and more recklessly invoked, than any of its predecessors'. It attributed 'a certain desperate courage to many of the wretched men who to-day are in their graves or awaiting the sentence of their country's laws', but declared that the real heroes were 'the gallant soldiers who were poured into Dublin, including at least two battalions of famous Irish regiments'. 'Our veteran troops in France', it solemnly declared, 'seldom had to face a more fiery ordeal, and could hardly have done better than these lads fresh from the training camps.' It also demanded that the government take stern action against the rebels:

> We now know, beyond yea or nay, the extent, the power, the motives, and the methods of the seditious movement in Ireland. All the elements of disaffection have shown their hand. The State has struck, but its work is not yet finished. The surgeon's knife has been put to the corruption in the body of Ireland, and its course must not be stayed until the whole malignant growth has been removed. In the verdict of history weakness to-day would be even more criminal than the indifference of the last few months. Sedition must be rooted out of Ireland once and for all. The rapine and bloodshed of the past week must be finished with a severity which will make any repetition of them impossible for generations to come.[66]

Two days later it claimed that 'The country has no desire that punishment should be pushed to the point of mere revenge, but in the interests of national peace and safety, it demands that stern justice shall be inflicted on the authors of one of the most deliberate and far reaching crimes in Irish history.'[67] Another two days later it observed, 'By all means, let justice be tempered with mercy. But the leaders of the insurrection must be made incapable of further mischief; the conditions which made it possible must never be permitted to recur.'[68] When the *Freeman's Journal* returned to production, it accused the *Irish Times* of 'blood-thirsty incitement to the Government'. The paper rejected this charge as 'wicked nonsense'; while it had 'called for the severest punishment of the leaders and responsible agents of the insurrection', it had also 'insisted that there shall be no campaign of mere vengeance'.[69]

The paper's letter page was inundated with opinions on the rising and the British response. W.A. O'Brien, an Irish soldier in France, noted that 'The news of the disgraceful line of action adopted by a section of Irishmen was received by the real Irishmen out here with profound regret and shame ... this rebellion is nothing short of an insult to the memory of those brave fellows of Irish regiments who fought so well, and gave up their lives, at Gallipoli and on the Western Front.'[70] In contrast, W.G. Fogarty of Galway declared that the rising was the result of 'bad government and bad example set by the North of Ireland and by the Curragh officers'. In reference to the unionist gun-running at Larne, Fogarty declared that 'nobody in these islands should forget who it was who showed how gun-running should be carried out; who first interfered with the freedom of the King's highway; who first cut telegraph wires; who first seized post offices and police barracks, and threatened officers of the Crown with deadly weapons'. Those who committed such offences 'were not answered with executions, or proclamations, or martial law' and the government 'should shoulder its own share of blame for what has happened'.[71]

The paper disagreed with John Redmond's call for a halt to the executions that followed the rising. As it saw, it the leaders of the rising were 'able and educated men [who] appreciated thoroughly the nature of their enterprise and the consequences of defeat'. The suggestion that 'the sterner punishment has become indefensible, not because it may not be deserved, but because an unhappily large number of persons has deserved it' lacked 'logic [n]or common-sense'.[72] The unionist community was 'grieved and bewildered by the Nationalist Party's half-hearted denunciation of rebellion, by the orgy of newspaper misrepresentation which denounces Sir John Maxwell as a von Bissing, by the torrent of slander that has been poured on troops who have performed a painful task with equal courage and forbearance'. The paper did not deny that mistakes were made; it supported calls for a public inquiry into the killing of Francis Sheehy Skeffington who was shot by a British officer as he tried to prevent looting, but it concluded that 'mistakes were hardly to be avoided in the terrible pressure of events'.[73]

As the executions continued, public opinion shifted towards the rebels. As one republican recalled, 'The army and the *Irish Times* demanded blood, and blood they got. But when Sir John Maxwell shot to pieces the Government of the Irish Republic he put an end to the English domination of Ireland.'[74] As details of the executions emerged, moderate nationalist opinion was horrified. A little over a year later, the *Irish Times* was reporting this shift in public opinion. As the rebels reorganised themselves as Sinn Féin the paper declared that 'a party of confessed extremists is "out" to strike another blow at the heart of England, and to make British government in Ireland impossible by every means in its power'. It noted that 'the seeds of another rebellion are being sown in Ireland before the dismal *debris* of the late rebellion has been cleared from the streets of Dublin, and while women are still in mourning for the husbands and sons who were murdered in that dreadful week'.[75] When, in July 1917, Eamon de Valera was elected as MP for East Clare, it noted ominously that 'An important election has been won on a policy of revolution'.[76] A national general strike in protest at the prospect of conscription being imposed earned the party much support and ensured the non-publication of the paper on 23 April 1918. The following day it observed that 'No newspapers were printed in Dublin yesterday. Some of them were in sympathy with the anti-conscription movement; but in all cases – and the *Irish Times* shared the common fate – the general withdrawal of labour made publication quite impossible.'[77] Eight months later Sinn Féin won 73 of the 105 Irish seats in the Westminster elections on the basis that it would set up an Irish parliament in Dublin. The stage was set for the ultimate showdown.

THE ARRIVAL OF SMYLLIE

It was in this immediate post-war period that John Healy recruited an employee who would have a profound effect on the paper and who would ultimately succeed him as editor. Robert Maire Smyllie was born in Shettleston, near Glasgow, Scotland, in 1893, the eldest child of Robert Smyllie, a Scottish printer, and Elizabeth Follis, a Corkwoman. When he was still a child, the family moved to Sligo town. One account of the family's move held that Smyllie senior inherited some money and took over the conservative *Sligo Times*. The appointment of a manager, who, over a period of time, pocketed much of the cash paid to the newspaper for classified advertisements and subscriptions ensured the paper's collapse. The family then moved to Belfast, where Smyllie senior took up a post as assistant editor of the *Belfast Newsletter*.[78] By this time, however, Smyllie junior had made his way to Trinity College. During the summer break of 1914 he travelled throughout Europe working as a tutor to the son of a wealthy American and had the misfortune to be in Germany when the war broke out. Picked up as an alien citizen, he was interred in a civilian imprisonment camp located in a disused racecourse at Ruhleben, just outside Berlin, for the duration of the war. It was here, among inmates of all shades of political beliefs, that Smyllie's education was completed. Ruhleben camp was, as his obituary observed, 'packed with distinguished men, and men of political distinction, whose company and conversation smoothed down many of his social and intellectual corners'.[79] Left to their own devices, the inmates organised debating competitions and language and politics classes to help pass the time. Smyllie was centrally involved in the camp's Society of Irish Players that organised plays for the camp's inmates. Indeed, Smyllie and one of his fellow inmates, William Jackson, wrote a play, *The Night of the Wake*, which was so well received that 'it had to be repeated twice'. The society also performed *Cathleen Ni Houlihan*, *The Playboy of the Western World* and *John Bull's Other Island*; the performance of *John Bull* was 'the result of a hint from the authorities that the society's next play should be one in which the scene was not a public house or a sheebeen'.[80] Smyllie was also involved in producing the *Ruhleben Camp Magazine*. It was here too that he deepened his interest in European affairs and acquired fluency in German.

After the war Smyllie returned to Sligo to find his father's paper had collapsed. On his way home through Dublin, however, he had stopped off at the offices of the *Irish Times* to enquire about work there. It is possible that he had established some previous contact with the paper. In its edition of 31 December 1918 it had reproduced the text of a document that had been handed to prisoners leaving Ruhleben by members of the Soldiers' Council, the body that had orchestrated the November revolution in Germany. The document was an innocuous text praising the virtues of the revolution, and the paper recorded that it had been sent the document 'by an Irishman recently released'.[81] It is possible that this document came from Smyllie. Either way, Smyllie's grasp of European affairs and his ability to converse in German greatly impressed John Healy. No sooner had Smyllie arrived back in Sligo than an offer of work came through from Dublin. Would he, Healy enquired, be interested in covering the peace conference at Versailles for the paper. Shortly afterwards Smyllie was in Paris, where he spent the best part of a year reporting on developments at the peace conference. He scored a scoop in the form of an interview with British prime minister David Lloyd George that was quoted in most of the world's press.[82]

But the topic of most interest to the paper was the arrival of a Sinn Féin delegation that unsuccessfully demanded a hearing at the conference on the grounds that the war had been fought for the rights of small nations and that, therefore, it had a right to put the case of Ireland to the conference. With Sinn Féin having kept its pledge to set up an independent assembly in Dublin, the arrival of the delegation caused a stir among the international press. According to Smyllie, the general consensus among reporters was that while the delegation would not be granted a hearing, all agreed that 'a definite settlement of the Irish Question was an absolute essential to the world's peace'. But, according to Smyllie, 'most foreigners refuse to take the Irish Question very seriously, and the proceedings which have just taken place in Dublin seem to have evoked more mirth than sympathy among the nations of the Continent'.[83] For its part, the paper dismissed Dáil Éireann as 'a solemn act of defiance of the British Empire by a body of young men who have not the slightest notion of that Empire's power and resources and not a particle of experience in the conduct of world affairs'. As far as Healy was concerned, Sinn Féin was a front for extreme socialists; while one half of the party consisted of 'a body of idealists who nurture themselves quite honestly on visions of an independent, but peaceful and pious, Ireland', the other advocated a policy that had 'submerged unhappy Russia in shame and ruin'. The party proposed, Healy believed, to 'apply the principles of Lenin and Trotsky to Irish affairs' and was 'working for the disintegration of society and the confiscation of all property, public and private'.[84]

WAR AND TREATY

As the war of independence gained momentum and the Ulster Unionist Party came to accept partition as inevitable, it prepared for the creation of a six-county state that would ensure the long-term survival of a unionist majority. Not only was Ireland to be partitioned; so too was Ulster, with counties that had large nationalist populations being ditched. When, in March 1920, the Ulster Unionist Council took that very decision, the paper was scathing, and prophetic, in its criticism:

> It has resolved to slam, bar and bolt the door of six counties against the other twenty-six, and it has given the Government fair and full notice of its purpose ... The Unionists of Cavan, Monaghan, and Donegal are thrown into outer darkness, unwilling victims to the perpetual segregation of the six-county area ... They have accepted a term of self-government which will give them complete control of their own fortunes. They have re-established the Tudor Pale – save that on this occasion some half-million of the King's loyal subjects are outside it ... Their case is that they have saved their own peaceful and prosperous corner from the ruin which the Government is preparing for the remainder of Ireland ... The six counties voted yesterday for absolutely permanent partition and for nothing else ... In the first place, the Unionists of Cavan, Monaghan, and Donegal were sacrificed on the alter of permanent partition ... If these counties were included in the Northern Area, the Nationalist vote might be large enough at some future time to enforce overtures to the Southern Executive, and that danger the Ulster Unionist Council has resolved to remove at any cost ... In passing this Bill it will pass a measure for the permanent division of Ireland, for the maintenance of sectarian strife, for the perpetuation of all the grotesque machinery of tri-sected railways and double judiciaries. It will doom the Irish people to secular unsettlement, and will convert thousands of law-abiding men to the cause of revolution.[85]

By now the war of independence was raging in earnest and the country was consumed by what the paper called 'an orgy of general lawlessness'.[86] Sinn Féin, it noted, was determined to 'to tear an Irish Republic out of the very heart of the British Empire'.[87] But the tactics of both sides came in for sharp criticism. It noted that 'police and soldiers, maddened by the cold-blooded slaughter of their comrades, have taken vengeance in hot blood'. Such reprisals were 'wholly wrong' and no government could 'tolerate the "wild justice" of individual revenge'.[88] It had strong words too for republicans. The events of Bloody Sunday in which Michael Collins' squad killed fourteen British agents was described as 'Dublin's most dreadful day since Easter week of 1916'; a country whose capital city could 'be the scene of fourteen callous and cowardly murders, on one Sunday morning [had] reached the nadir of moral and political degradation'.[89] Overall, 1920 was a year in which the pursuit of 'a hopeless ideal, supported by a reign of terror, reddened every month in the year's calendar with blood'.[90]

The paper was also aware of its own vulnerability. In May 1921 the Dáil agreed upon a boycott of English goods and, having made representations to various newspapers, the acting minister for labour informed the Dáil that he 'had got an undertaking from the *Freeman's Journal*, the *Irish Times,* and the *Independent* papers that they would not publish any advertisements for Belfast goods or for English goods on the Prohibited List'.[91] As one reporter remembered: 'The atmosphere got such that the *Times* editor John Healy once found himself against a wall before drunken Auxiliaries who half-seriously invited him to say his prayers, and the then leader-writer, Robert Smyllie, wondering what might hit him from one side or the other in the conflict.'[92]

According to Smyllie, John Healy and himself were arrested on Bloody Sunday by a party of drunken auxiliaries (British soldiers) who insisted that they 'were Sinn Féiners and, consequently, must be shot'. Taken to a house and put facing a wall, they were spared further harm when the householder recognised who they were and rang Dublin Castle. Shortly afterwards, Smyllie and Healy were rescued by a group of British officers sent from the Castle.[93]

One reporter, Chris O'Sullivan, secured an interview with Eamon de Valera. An Australian, O'Sullivan was looking for a quick way out of Dublin, which had become 'too sticky' to work in. He figured that an interview with de Valera would be syndicated all over the world and be his ticket out of town. He thus asked a London-based Australian news syndicate headed by Keith Murdoch (the father of media mogul Rupert Murdoch) to give him credentials for the interview. Realising that such an interview would be syndicated with risks of biased use, he asked Murdoch to guarantee in the credential that nothing in the interview would be altered except by the deletion of a complete question and related answer. This safeguard, according to O'Sullivan, helped establish his good faith with republicans. After initial contacts with republican messengers, O'Sullivan was summoned to meet Erskine Childers, the republican director of information, who probed him for several weeks on his motives. O'Sullivan convinced him that, as well as being his ticket out of Dublin, it was a priceless opportunity for the republican leadership to put its case before the world. Childers eventually agreed and O'Sullivan promised to report back after the interview and supply a copy of what he sent to London.

Several weeks later O'Sullivan was picked up from his home by a car of armed men and driven to a Georgian mansion on the south side of the city. A twenty-minute interview with de Valera followed, during which O'Sullivan asked him what position Britain would be in to defend itself, if, after agreeing to a republic, a war situation developed in which it found itself being attacked from Ireland. According to O'Sullivan, de Valera answered that 'in that event Britain would have the right to throw her troops across Ireland' to repel the attack. O'Sullivan posted his report of the interview to London as soon as it was typed and went back to Childers with a copy that same evening. Childers read the report 'with considerable upset' and demanded that its publication be cancelled, arguing that no republic could agree in advance to another power throwing troops across its territory. O'Sullivan thought his international scoop was in tatters but then remembered the undertaking not to make any changes except for the deletion of a question and answer. He immediately drafted a telegraph to Murdoch in which Childers requested that the contentious question and answer be dropped. Curiously, Murdoch later replied that he had already decided to exclude that question and answer. The copy of the interview released to the world's press in June 1921 was minus the question and answer about Britain's position in time of war, and O'Sullivan left Dublin bound for Russia.[94]

The following December the paper welcomed the Anglo-Irish treaty: it meant 'an end of age-long strife, gives to an Irish Free State a place of profit and honour in the community of the Empire, and promises to close the ancient breach between North and South'.[95] Southern unionists were 'surrendering most of all'; they had lost 'the host of laws, institutions, traditions, and ideals that bound them to Great Britain' and were 'entrusting themselves to the good-will of a majority from which politically, they have suffered much, and with which in the past they have had little in common save the love of Ireland'.[96] As the split within Sinn Féin became apparent, the paper observed that the Dáil was 'not being asked to decide between an independent Irish Republic and an Imperial Free State'. The idea of a republic had been 'abandoned by the leaders of *Sinn Féin* on the day when they accepted Mr Lloyd George's invitation to Downing Street [and] was dead long before the plenipotentiaries signed the Articles of Agreement'. In a swipe at the hardliners it noted that they would not be happy 'until they have build an Irish Republic on the ruins of the Irish Free State'. It warned that the country wanted peace and that the Dáil's 'ratification of the Agreement by even a trifling majority would justify an immediate start with the legislation for the establishment of the Free State'.[97]

When the new year came and went with no sign of a decision being taken, the paper turned its sights on Eamon de Valera and declared that no man had the right to 'condemn his country to ruin for the sake of his personal convictions'. In a prophetic statement, it noted that the man who insisted 'on having his own way at this vast expense is like the ancient chiefs whose funerals entailed the death of half their households'.[98] When, in January 1922, the Dáil voted to accept the treaty, the paper warmly welcomed the decision. Addressing southern unionists, it declared that they would have to 'adjust their minds to an entirely new set of ideals and ideas … Ireland is their country and her future must be their future.' It expressed confidence that there would be no

'Babylonian exodus'; it attached little importance 'to the wild abuse of Southern loyalists which came from one or two excited speakers in the *Dáil*' and much importance 'to Mr Griffith's promise that, so far as he can have his way, all minorities will get fair play and full consideration in the Irish State'. All southern unionists, it concluded, would 'do their best to make the new settlement a success'.[99] The same could not be said for all Irish nationalists; shortly afterwards, the country was plunged into a bloody civil war.

CHAPTER 3

A New Order

More money is spent on dress among all classes of the community and the penultimate fashions of Paris are flaunted in Kerry and Connemara. Dancing has become a craze in every part of the country. In itself dancing is no sin, but it becomes a grave danger to the morals of boys and girls when it invades the small hours and is lubricated with the poisons of the illicit still.[1]

The Irish Times *on life in the Free State*

IN THE AFTERMATH OF the treaty what might be called the paper's natural constituency declined dramatically. In 1911 the Church of Ireland had 249,535 members in the twenty-six counties but by 1926 this had dropped to 164,215 and to 145,030 in 1936. Emigration to Northern Ireland and Britain, the withdrawal of the British army and their families, and the burning out of landlords all contributed to the decline.[2] That said, circulation remained relatively steady: in 1920 daily sales stood at 32,500; by 1922 daily sales reached 34,500 and by 1926 stood at 36,500.[3] This rise reflected the political turmoil in the country, and as the civil war worsened the paper set its sights on Eamon de Valera. What right, it asked, had he 'or any other man to ordain that all the guarantees of peace, freedom and fruitful toil that the Treaty enfolds shall pass away in one high funeral gleam, like the grandeur of the Four Courts?'[4] In contrast, William Cosgrave was 'a rock of common sense' and the ideal choice to lead the new state because he had 'no violently extremist past to live down'.[5]

But despite its support for the government in its fight against the anti-treaty forces, the paper questioned the censorship it imposed. In July 1922 the government ordered that all newspaper proofs be submitted to its censorship office prior to publication.[6] Among the matter censored were details of troop movements, 'comments likely to cause disaffection in the Army, or in any way affect their morale or discipline or the quality of their combatant force', and 'matters calling for the overthrow by other than constitutional methods of the Parliament and Government or bringing them into contempt or leading to general lawlessness or disorder'.[7] The government was also sensitive about how newspapers treated its publicity. At a meeting in July 1922 it was mentioned that 'the attitude of the Dublin newspapers was very unsatisfactory, and it was decided that representatives of the Dublin newspapers should be summoned for interview at regular intervals, with a view to putting the situation clearly before them'.[8] These interviews had the desired effect; a later memo recorded that 'the interview with the Editors of the "Freeman's Journal" and the "Irish Times" had produced a good effect, and that current numbers of these papers had shown a considerable improvement on previous issues'.[9]

The anti-treaty faction was just as sensitive. In September 1922 various newspapers were threatened with reprisals over their coverage of the conflict. This prompted the paper's general manager John J. Simington to communicate with a republican contact of his. According to the surviving correspondence, Simington argued that the paper had 'criticised impartially Free State and Republican questions'. The internal IRA correspondence also mentioned the security situation at the paper: 'There has not been any guard on the I. Times. The owner (Arnott) wanted one put on but Simington (the manager) is against it. If Simington does not apply for a guard and anything happens he will be personally responsible ... Simington is a decent man and he wants guidance.'[10] Whether such guidance was forthcoming or not, the paper escaped any attack. Not so its editor, John Healy. During the civil war, shots were fired through the windows of his house as a warning.[11]

Given the newness of the state machinery, there were moments of confusion. In September 1922 the paper noted that it had been told that 'the military censorship had been abolished' only for it to be replaced by 'a sort of censorship, which we know not whether to describe as military or civil'. It had been prevented from publishing two reports, one concerning the alleged mistreatment of anti-treaty prisoners and the other concerning the evidence and verdict at an inquest. This 'undefined, spasmodic' censorship was, it noted, 'a grave nuisance' and the suppression of news, 'except on the most clearly defined principles', would only 'generate suspicion and distrust'.[12] Replying to a Dáil question, the minister for defence, Richard Mulcahy, denied that censorship had been ended but conceded that it had 'been relaxed practically to vanishing point'. While newspapers were not required to submit proofs prior to publication they had been warned that occasionally 'material will come their way, the publication of which is not compatible with general public safety'. Such material still had to be submitted to the censor and, if the government became aware of material 'being circulated for publication that it is in the public interest to prohibit', a general order banning publication would be issued to all newspapers.[13]

In November 1922 the government expressed considerable angst at the fact that the paper referred to the anti-treaty forces as 'Republicans' rather than as 'Irregulars' as desired by the government. It took particular offence to headlines such as 'Republican Offensive' and 'Leading Republicans Arrested' and concluded that 'It cannot be said that this paper definitely supports the Irregulars; but by such methods as the above it presents their case in a way that is misleading to the average mind. This was the first paper to yield to Derrig's threat. It has consistently called the Irregulars "Republicans" ever since.'[14] The issue of how to refer to anti-treaty forces continued after the civil war ended, as the ban on using military rank when referring to anti-treaty personnel was reaffirmed in a letter from the government's director of publicity, Sean Lester, to various newspapers in May 1924. Shortly afterwards, the advertising manager of the *Irish Independent*, T.A. Grehan, wrote to Lester to tell him how, when he told a customer wishing to insert a memoriam notice that the paper was prohibited from using military ranks, 'the advertiser tore up the advertisement and told us it was merely a matter of prejudice with us and said he would go round to the *Irish Times* and get it in without difficulty'. The notice subsequently appeared, with the military rank, in the following day's *Irish Times*. When Grehan rang Simington at the *Irish Times*, the latter expressed the view that 'so long as Newspapers were allowed to refer to the ranks of deceased Republicans in their Editorial Columns, he did not see why they should not be allowed to do so in the Advertisement Columns'. Seeking a ruling on the issue, Grehan suggested the ban be dropped as it caused 'a good deal of friction and unpleasantness, in dealing with the parties concerned'.[15] Lester sought guidance from the ministry of home affairs and noted that it was clear that 'the "Irish Times" challenges the authority of the order which was conveyed to them at the same time as to the "Irish Independent" on the 15th May last'. In Lester's opinion, either something had to be done 'to deal with the *Irish Times* if this publication is an offence, or to admit the justice of *Irish Times'* refusal to comply, and to inform the other newspapers that no restriction will be placed on such notices'. Lester believed that there was 'a good deal to support Mr Grehan's opinion that the time has arrived when this restriction should be withdrawn although it would be rather unfortunate to do so as a consequence of the defiance by the *Irish Times*'. The ministry replied that it could not find the original order relating to the ban and the use of military rank in anti-treaty obituaries continued.[16]

'THE TYRANNY OF IDEALS'

After the civil war the paper maintained its strong support for William Cosgrave and Cumann na nGaedheal. The alternative was unthinkable, for, as it observed during the 1923 general election, no man had 'more responsibility than Mr de Valera for the country's losses and miseries during the last eighteen months'. He had 'preached war against the State' and his followers had 'sought to over-ride the will of the Irish people by a tyranny of violence'.[17] Despite its support for Cosgrave, the paper criticised his administration whenever it detected efforts to 'Gaelicise' the new state or the influence of Catholic doctrine on legislation. In particular it objected to the introduction of compulsory Irish in primary schools and a ban on divorce, both of which it saw as impinging on the minority's civil liberties. While it acknowledged that Irish was 'an ancient and rich language', it strongly opposed it being 'forced down people's throats or made a test of loyalty to the Free State'.[18] There was a danger that 'in the hands of perfectly honest enthusiasts, the Irish language may be turned into an instrument of oppression' and, while it welcomed educational reform, it expressed its fear of 'that most plausible of tyrannies – the tyranny of ideals'. While the minority had 'no grudge against the Gaelic culture' they would resist 'any attempt to force it upon their schools against their will or to make it a condition of their rights as citizens of the Free State'.[19]

In 1924 the government made Irish compulsory in secondary schools and linked its teaching to exchequer funding. While the paper recognised that the language had 'historical, sentimental and literary claims upon the people's goodwill', it believed that sentiment was 'being pushed to the extremity of injustice'. After 1928 no student would be able to obtain the intermediate certificate without passing an examination in Irish, and schools that did not teach Irish would lose exchequer funding. Under this new regime those hardest hit would be 'the schools, largely Protestant, which educate boys for professions and services that either are over-stocked to-day, or do not exist at all, in the Free State'. The education of pupils would be 'strangled' by compulsory Irish as it would demand so much of the pupil's time that 'in his later school years he will be handicapped hopelessly in his pursuit of Greek and Latin, French and German'. The government was, it declared, 'guilty of a flagrant injustice and of a grave blunder'; the southern Protestant population was 'the most stable ... the most law-abiding, most industrious and more progressive element in the State' and this legislation adversely affected it by 'interfering with their liberty of thought and action and wounding them through their children'.[20]

In November 1926 it speculated that the minority was not vocal enough against compulsory Irish for fear that such protests 'might be misconstrued as hatred of the language itself, as contempt for national ideals or a form of sectarian prejudice'. It also criticised what it perceived as the lack of leadership from other Protestant institutions – 'Dublin University is dumb; the bishops, save for a few polite remonstrations at diocesan synods, are dumb' – and called on such institutions to be more vocal.[21] The call had the desired effect. In a letter to the paper a few days later, Dr A.A. Luce, a prominent Fellow of Trinity College, declared that, while optional Irish was a 'hardy plant in its native soil', compulsory Irish was 'eye wash, political window-dressing, dope for Republicans, anything but a genuine educational subject'. In a remarkable insight that has stood the test of time, Luce observed that 'The orator pretends he is going to speak in Irish, but after a few broken sentences he drops into English. The tax collector begins his letter in Irish, but demands the money in English.' Compulsory Irish was 'a wrong to Protestant parents' because it drove 'a wedge between them and their children', it reflected the 'one-nation theory' of Irish nationalism, and there was 'little or no Protestant literature in the language'. It was, he concluded, 'an instrument of political and religious tyranny'.[22]

These editorials and Luce's letter led some commentators to suggest that the paper was engaged in a sectarian campaign against the language. The minister for education, J.M. O'Sullivan, accused the paper of an attempt to 'stir up sectarian strife' and of 'hostility to the native language'. The paper reiterated that it was against compulsion, not the language itself – a fact ignored by the minister who was determined to charge it with 'the crime, or disease, of invincible sectarianism'. The Protestant community hated 'the accusation of sectarianism' which, it declared, 'would be exposed in its full falseness if the tens of thousands of Roman Catholics who are equally hostile to compulsion would come into the open'.[23] The minister's speech gave encouragement to the Catholic Bulletin, which observed that 'the various outposts and forts of the English garrison have, in regular succession, and with remarkable unison, opened fire'. Their contribution was, it declared, 'directed against all the essentials of Irish culture' and the stance against compulsory Irish was 'against the very idea of the Irish Nation as it really is'.[24] Such criticism went over the head of John Healy. The paper continued to carry Irish words in italics and even went so far as to substitute the name Kingstown for Dun Laoghaire in its reports of parliamentary debates. This practice prompted one Fianna Fáil TD, Sean Brady, to complain that he had been misreported by the paper and to 'protest very strongly against the action of the "Irish Times" in persistently going to the trouble of changing the official name of Dun Laoghaire to Kingstown'. The practice was, he contended, a 'grave disrespect towards the laws of the Free State, because the Free State Government actually went to the trouble of officially bringing in a Bill which included a change to this name Dun Laoghaire'.[25]

The Catholic teaching on divorce was also enforced. Before independence a person seeking a divorce had to present a private bill at Westminster. On the assumption that the Free State would adopt the same procedure, three private bills were lodged with the private bill office of the Oireachtas. But since no standing orders existed for the introduction of divorce bills, the three bills lay in legislative limbo for several months. In February 1925 President Cosgrave proposed a motion that banned any such bills from being introduced on the basis that anything that weakened marriage was bad for society.[26] The paper urged caution in the matter; if the motion were passed, the Free State would 'deny to its citizens a right which is inherent in citizenship of every part of the Commonwealth of British Nations'. It proposed the establishment of special courts to hear matrimonial cases as had happened in another dominion, New Zealand, and concluded that a ban on divorce would do nothing for Irish unity, as the people north of the border would never give allegiance to a state 'that would diminish by as much as one particle the rights of their imperial citizenship'.[27] When Cosgrave's motion was passed, it accused the government of 'raising a new and truly formidable barrier between the two parts of Ireland' and of imposing 'on some citizens, present and future, disabilities which exist in no other Dominion of the Commonwealth'. The best feature of the debate was, it remarked, 'its exhibition of a zeal for the nation's morals which some day, will perhaps, exert itself to banish drunkenness and vice from the streets of Dublin'.[28] For its trouble, the paper again incurred the wrath of the *Catholic Bulletin*, which declared that the paper's editorials were 'pleasant reading, no doubt, for those "Catholics on the make", who derive their ideas from the Ascendancy journal'. It also took issue with the fact that numerous Catholic charities, schools and religious orders advertised in the *Irish Times* during the summer months and claimed that the paper was 'careful not to have its Divorce Symphonies coincide in tune, or even indelicately adjoin, such lucrative Catholic contributions to its pages'.[29]

THE SOLDIERS OF DESTINY

By the mid-1920s Eamon de Valera began to reconsider his policy of parliamentary abstentionism but, as the paper observed, the country did not care greatly whether 'Mr de Valera chooses to call himself President of an Irish Republic or Grand Purple Emperor of the Ineffable Order of Rosicrucians'.[30] In June 1927 Fianna Fáil fought its first election and, unimpressed with de Valera's new incarnation, the paper declared its belief that Cumann na nGaedheal 'with all of its defects of policy and outlook, is the only bulwark of the country against chaos';[31] Fianna Fáil could offer nothing 'save disaster – a substitution of unsettlement for settlement and of destruction for construction'.[32] As polling day drew near it again took de Valera to task:

> When the Anglo-Irish Treaty was signed in December 1921, Mr de Valera and his friends declared themselves to be against it. Dáil Éireann was convened to decide the issue, and the

> Republicans did everything in their power to defeat the Treaty. They failed. If Dáil Éireann
> had rejected the Treaty, they would have accepted its decision in the name of democracy;
> but, because the majority went against them, they declared that democracy was wrong.
> Then there was a general election. Once more a decisive vote was registered in favour of the
> Treaty, but still the Republicans refused to accept the popular mandate.[33]

The assassination of the minister for justice, Kevin O'Higgins, finally put an
end to de Valera's abstentionism. The Electoral Amendment Act obliged Dáil
candidates to declare their readiness to take the oath of allegiance and to take
their seats within two months of election or accept their forfeiture. The paper
observed that the legislation was 'designed, rigorously and patently, to "queer"
Mr de Valera's "pitch"'; if he still refused to take the oath he would become 'a
permanent and constitutionally impotent tenant of the political wilderness'.[34]
The legislation had the desired affect, and on 11 August 1927 the paper
reported that Fianna Fáil had decided to enter the Dáil and take the oath of
allegiance after having decided that it was an 'empty political formula' that had
'no binding significance in conscience or in law'.[35] As the paper reported it, the
party whips, Frank Aiken, Gerry Boland and Sean Lemass were the first to take
the oath. Over the course of two-and-a-half hours the forty-four Fianna Fáil
deputies arrived in groups of two or three to take the oath. De Valera himself
was among the last to go through the procedure.[36] For the paper it was too little
too late; it pointedly asked why, if de Valera really believed the oath was
meaningless, 'he waited five years to enter the *Dáil*; and why, in the name of
common sense, has he squandered so many words in the interval in
denunciation of this empty formula?'[37]

Fianna Fáil's entry into the Dáil dramatically altered the political landscape
and almost immediately the leader of the Labour Party, Thomas Johnson,
proposed a motion of no confidence in the government. The envisaged result
was a minority government composed of the Labour Party and the National
League supported but not joined by Fianna Fáil. The paper derided this
proposition as Fianna Fáil government by proxy. Some days before the motion
was to be voted on, it had a scoop. Robert Smyllie happened to meet Johnson
and two of his colleagues at a bus stop outside a hotel in Enniskerry, Co.
Wicklow. When Johnson and his company got on the bus to Dublin, Smyllie
entered the hotel and on learning that the men had spent three hours in its
garden-house he went there and searched the waste-paper basket wherein he
found a pile of torn-up paper with writing on it. He spent two hours
reassembling the torn paper on which was written Johnson's list of names for
the new cabinet should the motion of no confidence succeed and the Labour-led
minority government come into office.[38] The paper published the list the day
before the vote.[39] The success of the motion depended on how the National

League voted: its members supported the motion, but the Dáil divided evenly and the ceann comhairle cast his vote in favour of the government causing the motion to fall.

The paper was jubilant, and declared that 'Mr de Valera may control some future Government but not as the result of a mere parliamentary manoeuvre, and not without direct responsibility to the nation'.[40] However, it soon found itself at the centre of rumours to the effect that it had helped engineer the survival of the government. One National League deputy, John Jinks, was present for most of the debate but did not vote, and his absence immediately became the subject of speculation. In an interview, his party leader, Captain William Redmond, stated that Jinks had declared his support for the motion at a party meeting that morning, and claimed that 'he must have been "spirited" away as a result of methods of a century back'.[41] Rumours abounded about how Jinks had missed the crucial division. One rumour had it that Jinks was given a stern talking to by independent unionist TD, Major Bryan Cooper, and Robert Smyllie, who convinced him to miss the vote on the basis that his Sligo-Leitrim constituents had not mandated him to put Fianna Fáil into power. Another rumour had it that the two men treated Jinks to a liquid lunch before putting him, less than sober, on a train back to Sligo. In an interview with the paper Jinks himself gave a more mundane account of his absence. He denied that he had been talked into missing the vote, stated that he had always opposed the motion, and explained that he did not stay for the division because he did not want to cause a split in his party. He described the rumours regarding his absence as 'sheer invention'.[42] Whatever the cause of his absence, the rumours outlived Jinks' political career. Despite having survived the vote of no confidence, William Cosgrave called an election and Cumann na nGaedheal again formed a government. Although John Jinks lost his seat, his name lived on. When the national stud farm bought a new racehorse, it was given the name 'Mr Jinks'; the horse went on to win the 1929 English Two Thousand Guineas, at odds of five to two.

'AN IRISHMAN'S DIARY'

Despite being as different as chalk and cheese, the editorial team of John Healy and Robert Smyllie saw the paper through the 1920s with gusto, helped in no small manner by Smyllie's acquaintance with W.B. Yeats. According to one contemporary account, Smyllie and Yeats were on friendly terms; both had strong Sligo connections, and Smyllie even claimed that he had attended a séance with Yeats.[43] When the news that Yeats had won the 1923 Nobel Prize for literature came through on the wire, John Healy, knowing that Smyllie was on familiar terms with the poet, asked him to telephone Yeats for a comment. According to one account, when Smyllie gave Yeats the good news, the latter responded by saying, 'How much, Smyllie, how much is it?'[44] Needless to say, the paper did not repeat the esteemed poet's words, preferring to report the exchange thus: 'A telephone message from the *Irish Times* Office was the first intimation which Mr Yeats received of the high tribute which had been paid to his work. He had known nothing whatever about it, and was not even aware of the value of the prize.'[45] Apparently, Smyllie, for years afterwards, took great delight in repeating Yeats' less than artistic reaction in the Palace Bar. Yeats also handed Smyllie a scoop in February 1926. Knowing that republicans were intent on causing disturbances during a performance of Sean O'Casey's *The Plough and the Stars*, he visited Smyllie to deliver the text of the short speech he intended to deliver in the event of such disturbances. When the disturbances did occur, the paper was in the unique position to report what nobody – amid the hissing, shouting, fighting and stinkbombs – in the theatre could hear. The next morning it exclusively reported that Yeats had accused Dublin of having 'rocked the cradle of genius'.[46] Referring to protests about the appearance of a prostitute in the play, it caustically noted that the people of Dublin 'need not pay anything to see counterfeit prostitution on the stage of the Abbey Theatre. They can rub shoulders with the real thing on every night of the week in the central streets.'[47]

Nonetheless, Healy was, as one reporter put it, 'a man of remarkable inflexibility of mind' and the paper 'still clung to its old attitudes'.[48] He 'clung jealously to the few links that still bound the two nations, and watched with sadness their gradual loosening by Mr Cosgrave's Government and their virtual destruction under the presidency of Mr de Valera'.[49] Two such links were the Horse Show hosted by the Royal Dublin Society and Remembrance Day held throughout the empire to commemorate the war dead – two annual occasions at which the British army had always appeared in full regalia under the previous regime. During the 1920s the paper devoted extensive pictorial coverage to both occasions. Every August and November it carried pages of photographs of the various titled dignitaries visiting the Horse Show and of the remembrance ceremonies at the Cenotaph and the Wellington monument in Dublin's Phoenix Park. Very often it took delight in recording the fact that 'God Save the King' was sung with gusto by the assembled crowds. Such hankering for the past did not go unnoticed by republicans. As Todd Andrews saw it, while Healy was 'a west British pedant ... who could not accept the fact that the establishment of the Free State represented a major change in Irish relations with Britain', the paper was 'a stodgy and poor imitation of the London *Times* and was read, almost exclusively, by Church of Ireland clerics, Trinity dons and the remaining occupants of the "big house" and their minions'.[50] Indeed, this was the popular view of the paper during the 1920s, and a *Dublin Opinion* cartoon from that decade succinctly captured it: purporting to show the inner workings of the paper, almost everyone is wearing either a top hat or a scholar's mortarboard. In the background a printer stands between a 'Semi-Colon Scatterer' and an 'Italics Inserter' and the only reference works on the shelves are *Burke's Peerage* and numerous copies of *Who's Who*. In the wings the social editor is alarmed to hear that there were no peers on that day's mail boat from England, the occupants of the 'urgent news' department reminisce about the first Castle ball, and the 'Irishman's Diary' cubby-hole is occupied by a peasant and a pig. In the foreground a gentleman enquiring about the whereabouts of the editor is told that he is most likely gone to either Sackville Street or Kingstown.

Throughout the 1920s the paper averaged eight to ten pages and cost two pence a copy. It was still printed in eight single columns of type, although the occasional use of photographs from the early 1920s onwards broke up the dense text. By 1923 the paper had a page devoted to photographs provided for the most part by its first staff photographer, George Leitch, a former aerial reconnaissance officer with the Royal Flying Corps. The 'Court Circular', 'Fashionable Intelligence' and 'Military Intelligence' columns were merged into one column – 'Court and Personal' – which still carried the emblem of the royal court of arms. While debates at the Oireachtas were obviously reported, another column, 'Imperial Parliament', kept readers up to speed with developments at Westminster. Women's journalism also began to appear in the 1920s although it was confined to columns such as 'Woman and Her Home' and 'Recipes for the Cook'. By the mid-1920s GAA games were reported on, though in very sparse detail. That said, the paper reported on the annual traditional Irish music festival – the Feis Ceoil – very prominently. It also began a 'Books of the Week' column. December 1927 saw another novel editorial innovation: as assistant editor, Robert Smyllie introduced a new column, 'An Irishman's Diary', on 14 December 1927. In its original format the column was a day-to-day miscellany of individual paragraphs contributed by various reporters and edited into a running order by Smyllie under the pen-name of 'Quidnunc'; the Latin for 'What next?' On Saturdays, Smyllie himself wrote the column under the pen-name 'Nichevo', a column he continued to write until his death in 1954.

Also initiating change was the general manager, John J. Simington. Having joined the paper at the age of sixteen in 1878, Simington became general manager in 1907, retained that position until 1941 and remained a board member until his death in 1949.[51] It was Simington who oversaw the paper's revolutionary transition from hand-set type to mechanised production by

Linotype machines at the turn of the century. Linotypes produced lines of type from molten lead; this allowed the rapid setting of text in solid lines of brand-new type every day. This hot metal technology was the basis of newspaper production up to the 1980s. Printing innovations, such as the rotary press, soon followed. The rotary press was based on the principle of converting the printing surface from a flat forme of type to a rotating cylinder. It printed from a cylindrical surface onto a reel or 'web' of paper, producing complete copies of the paper in one operation and delivering them cut and folded.[52]

Simington also overhauled the paper's distribution system. In 1931, together with Independent Newspapers, the *Irish Times* entered into a contract with the Great Southern Railway Company for the provision of a dedicated newspaper train. While this innovation had much to do with ostracising the soon to be published *Irish Press,* the change ensured that the paper arrived around the country much earlier. Previous to this, the paper had travelled on the overnight mail train, arriving in Cork at 10.55 a.m. Under the new system the newspaper train left Dublin at 4 a.m. and – with various connections along the way to serve the west and south-east – arrived in Cork at the much earlier time of 8.15 a.m. The paper also remained profitable. The annual return for the year ending September 1921 recorded a profit of £29,196; and the three subsequent years yielded profits of £30,354, £39,386 and £49,151.[53] However, sales began to slip in the late 1920s – from 36,500 in 1926 to 31,500 in 1928 and 30,000 in 1930.[54] It also had the distinction of being the first newspaper to cross the Atlantic ocean by air. In April 1928 a German aristocrat, Baron Gunther von Hunefeld, Captain Hermann Koehl and the commanding officer of the Irish air corps Major James Fitzmaurice, succeeded in making the first east-to-west transatlantic crossing. The *Bremen* set off from Baldonell Aerodrome for Long Island, New York but crash-landed thirty-six hours later on a frozen water reservoir at Greenly Island in Canada. According to one account, several *Irish Times* journalists were present at Baldonnel to see the plane off, and one of them gave Fitzmaurice a copy of the paper to carry on the plane.[55]

'A GRAVE MENACE'

In August 1928 the paper published the government's censorship of publications bill in full.[56] The legislation was designed to establish a censorship board that could ban indefinitely any periodical or book if it were judged to be 'indecent or obscene' or if, in its general tendency, it were judged to be 'detrimental to or subversive of public morality'. Although the paper had welcomed film censorship – 'since many of the films which come from the neurotic studios of

Los Angeles and Berlin are quite unfit for presentation in public' – it was more circumspect when it came to literary censorship.[57] It conceded that some mechanism of censorship was needed in the case of 'indecent newspapers and of certain obviously "quack" advertisements', but it believed that the bill went 'beyond this legitimate purpose'. It viewed with suspicion 'the looseness of its terminology and the wide powers with which it arms the Minister for Justice', and expressed concern that the bill might lead to censorship of literature and political and economic writings that appeared to be contrary to the views of the Catholic majority. Would, it inquired, the term 'public morality' include 'religious questions, and may honest speculation in this sphere be reported to the censors because, perhaps, a majority of the citizens dissent from it?'[58] The bill was 'a grave menace to moral and intellectual freedom' and, since the term 'indecent' was defined as anything 'calculated to excite sexual passion', the minister for justice could 'suppress substantial portions of the Bible, much of the world's finest love poetry, and – since the bill embraces art – many of the world's loveliest pictures'. Likewise, since the term 'public morality' was not defined, the minister was 'free to decide that most of the ancient classics, some of the greatest novels, and scientific works like "The Origin of the Species" were subversive' and to ban them.

Noting that the bill provided for severe penalties for advertisements and articles that encouraged or advocated birth control, it pointedly asked by what right did the government 'seek to enforce the teachings of one Church upon those members of other Churches who claim the right of public judgment in the matter of birth control?'[59] The impact the bill might have on the minority community was a core feature of its objection to the bill, which it described as a 'truly formidable instrument of oppression' with which future governments could 'assail political views and religious convictions'. The minority recognised that the 'country's outlook and the main texture of its thought are, and will continue to be, Roman Catholic'; it respected the 'traditions and sincerities of the Roman Catholic majority'; and it was 'anxious to live on the best of terms with them'. All it asked in return was that 'their constitutional rights as good subjects of the State shall be sacred under any and every Government; and those rights include the fullest liberty of soul and mind'. While the minority would 'gladly concede a Gaelic-Catholic culture to all who desire it', the paper objected to it being 'forced upon citizens who have no desire for it'.[60] When the first list of banned books – three novels and ten books on various aspects of contraception – was published, the paper opined that the whole censorship regime would, in the long term, be wholly counter-productive:

> The legend 'Banned in the Irish Free State' in a publisher's notice will make the fortunes of
> novels which, without this aid, might fall still-born from the press ... It is probable that not
> twenty per cent of the reading public was aware yesterday of the existence of the three
> novels; and it is almost certain that not one Irish woman in fifty thousand had known
> anything of the ten works of obstetric sociology. Now all these books will be subject of tea-
> table talk and will line the pockets of passengers from Holyhead to Kingstown ... The truth
> is that any form of intellectual censorship is a moral anachronism ... Furthermore, in these
> days of railroad, steamship, aeroplane and wireless 'broadcasting', the physical restrictions
> of a literary censorship cannot be enforced. It is wholly possible that in the near future one
> of Mr Fitzgerald-Kenny's [the minister for justice's] lucky thirteen may be the subject of a
> wireless discussion from London or Daventry, to which every Irish possessor of a valve set
> will have free access.[61]

In a Dáil debate shortly after the act became law, deputy Patrick Little of
Fianna Fáil declared that the paper went 'out of its way to publish lists of books
which are censored' and called on the minister for justice to 'use all the powers
he has to prevent an abuse of that kind'.[62] From then on, the paper, under a
succession of editors, would never cease to campaign against the censorship
regime, or, in its own words, it would never shirk from the 'defence of the
ordinary commonsense and decency of this country against the Government
paternalism that would treat every adult citizen as if he wore short trousers'. It
would forever be puzzled by the proponents of censorship who, 'while
professing the belief that Irishmen, exceed all other races in virtue, spoil the
whole argument by a paradoxical insistence that every possible occasion of sin
shall be removed as far as possible from them'. It seemed that supporters of
censorship could never 'make up their minds whether the people of Ireland are
genuinely the honest, high-minded, demi-angels of tradition, or debased
troglodytes who must be driven willy-nilly into decency by boards'.[63]

'A FIERCE AND FUTILE IDEALISM'

When, in January 1932, William Cosgrave called a general election, the paper
did not hesitate in taking sides: Fianna Fáil's manifesto, with its promise to
abolish the oath of allegiance, incurred the wrath of the paper's editorials. There
could 'be no compromise between the two policies which are set before the
electors':

> One is a policy of upsetting, the other of building; one spells war, the other peace; one
> repudiates the Free State's place in the British Commonwealth of Nations, and the other
> seeks to strengthen it. The two policies can be outlined in as many sentences. Mr de Valera's
> party proposes to refuse payment of the land annuities, to remove the oath of allegiance
> from the Constitution, to abolish the office of Governor-General, and to establish state

socialism on the Russian model, behind unscaleable tariff walls. The policy of President Cosgrave's party is based on a growing friendship with Great Britain, on the highest development of trade with that country, and on a more careful management of the national finances.[64]

The choice made by the electorate would 'put an enduring mark on the future fortunes of the state'. Fianna Fáil was a party of 'unrepentant activists' characterised by 'a fierce and futile idealism'. Its ascension to power 'would be a fatal guarantee of international trouble, of internal disorder and of economic folly'; all its policies offered were 'an isolated Free State, torn by domestic tumults'. In contrast, the outgoing Cosgrave administration offered 'strong government at home and a steady and wise extension of the State's economic borders'. Its policy of 'good terms with our best customer' constituted 'sound business, sound policies and sound patriotism'. It was, of 'first importance that Mr Cosgrave's policy shall receive a clear mandate from the electors'.[65] However, unlike previous elections in which Fianna Fáil had effectively been voiceless against such criticism, by 1932 the *Irish Press* was up and running and played a central role in spreading the party's message and countering such criticism. As polling day approached, the *Irish Times* summed up its perception of what a victory for either party would mean for the country and its inhabitants:

> If Mr Cosgrave wins, the good government of the last ten years will be consolidated; the failing efforts of lawlessness will be crushed; a basis will be laid for reconciliation with Northern Ireland; the farmers' future will be secure under the economic aegis of the British Commonwealth, and, as a member of the Commonwealth, the Free State will hold a high place in the world. If Mr de Valera wins, lawlessness will lift its head again, and the citizens' present sense of security will vanish; the Anglo-Irish settlement will be denounced; the North will be repelled forever; the Free State will be isolated from civilisation; and her farmers will find in British tariffs their deadliest enemy instead of their most bounteous friend.[66]

Noting that less than 70 per cent of electors had voted in the September 1927 election, the paper calculated that an increase of 10 per cent in voter turn-out would ensure the return of Cosgrave's government with a comfortable majority. Throwing caution to the wind, it made this prediction with 'the utmost confidence'. It was convinced that among those who had not turned out to vote in previous elections were many unionists who, 'while they have accepted the benefits of Mr Cosgrave's Government, have failed to overcome their dislike of its origins'. Determined to rally these voters to the government's side, the paper called on them to 'put duty before tradition or prejudice'. This duty was twofold. Firstly, there was the duty of 'self-preservation': if Fianna Fáil took office, 'the wealth and security of every citizen, including the ex-Unionists will be impaired and perhaps gravely imperilled'. Secondly, there was the duty 'of loyalty to Ireland and to the Empire': if Fianna Fáil took office, the Free State would 'become an Ishmael from that Empire which the ex-Unionists, their sons and their ancestors, have helped to mould'. Election day, then, was a 'paramount day for the exercise of the old Unionism's finest virtues – loyalty and patriotism' – to be reflected in a vote for Cumann na nGaedheal.[67] On polling day it declared that while every ex-unionist in the Free State deemed 'himself a patriot and an imperialist', he would be neither, if, through abstention, the country relapsed 'into chaos and is divorced from the British Commonwealth'. The duty for every ex-unionist was 'clear and urgent'.[68]

In spite of those efforts, Fianna Fáil became the largest party in the Dáil and took power with the supporting votes of the Labour Party, a fact that helped soften the blow for the paper. The arrangement was 'a poor barrier against all the accidents and arts of politics', but 'a bargain for power means mutual concessions' which meant that de Valera's 'larger and more daring plans must be postponed'. Revolutions, it pointed out, were 'not made on the slender basis of a majority of six or eight votes'. The paper hoped that 'the new Government's education will be swift and intensive and that within its ranks and in the country disillusionment will follow hard upon the heels of knowledge'. In a sideswipe at de Valera, it declared that while 'the price of this adventure may be high ... the results will justify it. In Hans Andersen's story, a costly pageant was needed for the discovery that the Emperor had no clothes.'[69] Almost immediately de Valera introduced a bill to remove the oath of allegiance, and the paper accused him of provoking 'a direct quarrel' with Britain. Reflecting its imperial mindset, it declared that 'unchallenged repudiation must have momentous reactions on the whole Empire; already the Indian nationalists are making perilous capital out of Mr de Valera's policy'.[70]

De Valera's decision to cease re-payment of the land annuities also came in for criticism. The land annuities were payments due to the British exchequer in re-payment of loans advanced to Irish tenant farmers at the turn of the century to enable them to buy land. De Valera's decision to keep the money for the Irish exchequer prompted the British government to increase duties on Irish imports and sparked a damaging economic war that lasted until 1938. The paper described the British government's response as 'a necessary measure to balance the British budget [and] the inevitable result of Mr de Valera's decision to violate an international agreement.'[71]

June 1932 provided a respite from de Valera's assault on the treaty. For most of that month Dublin was awash with papal flags and bunting as the city hosted a eucharistic congress. Thousands of pilgrims descended on the city for the week-long international religious festival during which, as the paper put it,

'Roman Catholic Ireland testified to her faith with a unanimous and whole-hearted fervour, to which Protestant Irishmen must render the highest tribute'.[72] The paper gave extensive coverage to the week's events, in writing and in pictures. It reported the comings and goings of various church dignitaries, the stoning of trains carrying pilgrims from the north, the 'beautiful voice of John McCormack' and the noisy interruption to the pope's broadcast on radio from Rome by aeroplanes 'used by English Press representatives for the purpose of getting photographs'.[73] It also carried a report on the papal high mass, 'Million Minds with a Single Thought', which captured, unwittingly perhaps, the paper's unease at the one size-fits-all ethos at the heart of Catholicism: 'It was at that moment of the elevation of the Host, the supreme point in Catholic ritual, that one fully realised the common mind that had swallowed up all individuality in the immense throng. Flung together in their hundreds of thousands, like the sands on the seashore, these people were merely parts of a great organism which was performing a tremendous act of faith, with no more ego in them than the sands themselves.'[74]

THE GOVERNOR GENERAL

One ego that had not lost the run of itself during the eucharistic congress was that of the governor general, James McNeill. The Fianna Fáil government had adopted a policy of deliberately snubbing McNeill at official events. On one occasion this had resulted in the immediate exit of two government ministers – Frank Aiken and Sean T. O'Kelly – from a reception at the French embassy upon the arrival of McNeill. On another occasion, when McNeill had accepted an invitation to a function hosted by Dublin's lord mayor, the army band had been withdrawn from the event. This policy came to a head during the eucharistic congress. McNeill, who, as the king's representative, would have taken precedence over the head of government, was not invited to any of the functions associated with the event. Having corresponded with de Valera several times without getting any satisfaction, McNeill released the correspondence to the national newspapers – a move that saw the government invoke the Official Secrets Act. A news story in the *Irish Times* outlined the exact sequence of events. On the afternoon of Sunday 10 July the paper received various letters from the governor general with a request for their immediate publication. The documents were prepared for publication but at 1.15 a.m. the paper received a phone call from the minister for justice with instructions that they were not to be published. This was quickly followed by a visit from a high-ranking member of the Garda Síochána with an order to the editor declaring that the documents were confidential state papers and prohibiting their publication under the Official Secrets Act.[75] However, McNeill had also sent the documents to newspapers in Northern Ireland and Britain and, in an attempt to prevent their distribution, Gardai seized various incoming newspapers at the mail boat at Dun Laoghaire and at customs checkpoints along the border.

At this stage, however, the government knew that it had been beaten and allowed the Irish newspapers to publish the documents, or, as the paper put it, the government 'abandoned its foolish attempt to muzzle the Governor-General'. McNeill's charges were, it noted, 'of a sort that is rare, indeed, in the history of the British Commonwealth'. In the letters, McNeill complained that government ministers had 'treated him, not once only, but on several occasions during recent months, with deliberate discourtesy'. Noting that McNeill was 'a cultured, quiet and courteous gentleman', the paper assumed that 'if he were a private citizen, no Free State Government or Minister would have sought to affront him – especially in the exalted season of the Eucharistic Congress'. The logical conclusion, therefore, was that the government was snubbing MacNeill 'because he is the King's direct representative in that Dominion of the British Commonwealth of Nations which was created by the Anglo-Irish settlement'.[76] When, later that year, de Valera succeeded in having MacNeill replaced by Domhnall Ua Buachalla, the paper accused him of having 'degraded the Viceregal Office'.[77] To all intents and purposes this was the end of the office of governor general; Ua Buachalla, a shopkeeper from Maynooth and a 1916 veteran, refused to take up residence in the Vice-Regal Lodge, did not appear at any official functions and merely signed whatever de Valera put in front of him.

THE 'UNABASHED DICTATOR'

Another individual run out of office by de Valera was the commissioner of the Garda Síochána, General Eoin O'Duffy, who was closely identified with Cumann na nGaedheal. De Valera felt that O'Duffy 'was likely to be biased in his attitude because of past political associations' and so dismissed him in February 1933. The paper opined that if this was how de Valera was going to treat public servants, then he should 'abandon his pretence of democracy'.[78] When William Cosgrave proposed a motion condemning the action, de Valera retorted that he had seen 'an article in the Irish Times suggesting that Deputy Cosgrave should bring in a motion of this sort' and wondered aloud whether 'Deputy Cosgrave brought this motion in at the instigation of and to please the Irish Times.'[79] The following July, O'Duffy assumed command of the Army Comrades Association. Also known as the National Guard and formed in the midst of the 1932 general election, the organisation had ostensibly been established to look after the welfare of ex-servicemen but ended up providing protection for Cumann na nGaedheal candidates against attack by the IRA. The latter part of 1932 and the general election campaign of 1933 had been marred by violent clashes as political rallies turned into pitched battles between treatyites and anti-treatyites. This was at a time when, as one reporter put it, 'election meetings were a form of open-air theatre with audience participation in the form of chants such as "Murderer", "Perjurer", "Spanish Bastard", "Seventy-Seven", "Who fed the birds at Ballyseedy?", often accompanied by sticks, stones, rotten eggs and fresh cow dung, as well as periodic chargings of the police and the platform'.[80]

The ACA's uniform consised of a blue shirt and beret – hence the nickname 'The Blueshirts' – and it also adopted the Roman or fascist-style salute. For its part, the *Irish Times* was in two minds about the merits of O'Duffy and his organisation. It urged unified and robust opposition to de Valera's government but despaired at the opposition parties: Cumann na nGaedheal was 'at the ebb of its fortune', the Centre Party had 'made no useful contribution to the national stability or welfare', and the arrival of the ACA added another 'formidable element of disunion'. It believed O'Duffy 'brought into public affairs a spirit of energy and discipline' but it had mixed feelings about the political orientation of his organisation: 'Its organisation is distinctly Fascist, but its professions are democratic. It is constitutional but it desires large and, as yet, vague changes in the present system of parliamentary government.' The net result was 'three Oppositions, which to-day have few points of contact and no common policy'.[81] When de Valera eventually banned the ACA, the paper acknowledged that he was entitled to do so. It contrasted, however, his promptness in banning the ACA with his tolerance of the IRA. Noting that there was no doubt that the ACA constituted a 'semi-military body' and that the government was 'entitled to suppress, and ought to suppress, all military or semi-military bodies except its own authorised forces', it accused de Valera of being 'cynically inconsistent'. While the ACA was 'not an armed force and cherished no unlawful designs against the Constitution', the IRA was 'not merely semi-military, but military and in open conflict with the Constitution' and was 'known to have a large influence in the Government's counsels'. Either the government was 'afraid to give equal treatment to the National Guard and the Irish Republican Army' or it was engaging in 'an act of political revenge'.

Nonetheless, it advocated a calm response to the ban. Praising 'the new hopefulness, vigour and discipline' that the ACA had brought into public life, it called for these qualities to be translated 'solely to the tasks of political organisation and unity'.[82] It called for the unification of all constitutional parties opposed to Fianna Fáil, and seemed to be prepared to give O'Duffy the benefit of the doubt, on the understanding that his excesses would be curtailed in any new party. He had 'outlined an ambitious scheme of political reform, which seems to be inspired by Signor Mussolini's great work for Italy' and the paper seemed to approve of his proposal, 'by means of a chastened franchise and by various methods of vocational representation, to break the stupid rigours of the present parliamentary machine'. Notwithstanding all this, it declared that de Valera's government would 'not be dethroned by shirts of any tinge; the real instrument of its downfall must be the plain black-and-white of the ballot paper'; so, the most pressing issue was the 'coming together of all the Constitutional forces in a single party and a single purpose'. Such was the need for removing de Valera from power – albeit by constitutional means – that the paper proposed that 'Agreement, for the time being, might be limited to means for the present Government's defeat; all questions of portfolios and of domestic policy could be postponed until that essential aim had been achieved.' As a 'semi-military *dux* and the head of a banned organisation', O'Duffy could 'create nothing but trouble'; but as 'an organiser of much ability, with a large political following in the country', he could 'make himself really formidable to the Government'.[83]

When, in September 1933, various parties amalgamated as the United Ireland Party – or Fine Gael – with O'Duffy as president and William Cosgrave as vice-president, the *Irish Times* was ecstatic: while only a short time previously the country was 'looking cheerlessly down the unbroken vista of a road to ruin', the merger ensured that the 'hearts of all good citizens are inspired with new hope and courage'. It declared that 'Men of all creeds, classes, and callings must support the United Ireland Party' and proclaimed its belief that if the new party made 'good use of its time and of its fresh resources', its call for electoral support would 'find a prompt and generous answer'.[84] The ACA, however, had not gone away. When the government proscribed the National Guard, it circumvented the ban by renaming itself as the Young Ireland Association, and after the merger of opposition parties it supposedly became the youth wing of the new party. The government did not believe this, however, and in December 1933 it banned the Young Ireland Association. In response, the paper accused de Valera's government of acting 'as ruthlessly as the Nazi Government in Germany when it thinks it is being threatened by a powerful opponent'. While it held 'no brief for the "Blue Shirts"', as it did not believe that 'organisations which are based on continental models are suited to the genius of the Irish people', it failed to see in what respect the Young Ireland Association had 'broken the law'.[85]

In an effort to rid Irish politics of the Blueshirts, the Dáil passed legislation that prohibited the wearing of uniforms and badges and the use of military titles in support of a political party. When the Senate rejected the bill, de Valera promptly introduced a bill to abolish the Senate, a move that was greeted with apoplexy by the paper. At last, it announced, de Valera had 'discarded the last pretence of respect for constitutional Government'. The 'unabashed dictator' who had 'no use for a Constitution that is not his slave' had finally been revealed. His reaction to the Senate's decision was 'a threat to citizens, of every party and creed, who claim the fundamental liberties of citizenship in a democratic state', and his 'persistence in his design to abolish the Senate or to suppress the political organisation of the rival party' could only result in 'constitutional chaos'.[86] In a editorial entitled 'Towards Dictatorship', the paper questioned de Valera's commitment to constitutional politics and likened the abolition of the Senate to the creation of a dictatorship along the lines of Hitler and Mussolini:

> If he secures the disappearance of the Senate, he actually will have as much personal power as Signor Mussolini or Herr Hitler; for he will control the Dail, the majority of whose members tremble at his nod, and he will be freed from the inconvenience of a critical Second Chamber. Yet nobody pays more lip-service to the ideals of democracy than the President of the Executive Council, although it must be confessed that his conversion has been comparatively recent. The majority of the people at one time had no right to do wrong. It had no right to approve of the Treaty, for example, or to keep Mr Cosgrave's Government in power for ten years; but now it can do no wrong. The possession of a single vote majority in Dáil Éireann entitles President de Valera to tear the Constitution into shreds, to treat everybody who does not agree with him as an enemy of the State, and to wave aside as frivolous irrelevancies all suggestions that do not emanate from his own brain … The only remaining safeguard of popular rights is a general election; one of these days the President may decide that it, too, is superfluous.[87]

The legislation to abolish the Senate was, of course, rejected by that house, which suspended the legislation for the statutory eighteen months. The final sitting of the Senate took place in May 1936, and the paper marked its demise by noting that henceforth the Dáil would 'render implicit obedience to President de Valera', who would 'wield a power that even Herr Hitler or Signor Mussolini might envy'.[88]

As regards the political opposition that de Valera could not get rid of, Fine Gael, despite the paper's high hopes, was going nowhere fast. The party failed to make an impact during the 1934 local elections, and O'Duffy's increasingly hysterical speeches embarrassed the moderate wing of the party. In September 1934, under pressure from the Fine Gael leadership, O'Duffy resigned as president of the party and was replaced by William Cosgrave. What the paper made of all of this is unclear. A printers' strike between July and October 1934 ensured that it was off the streets for the best part of ten weeks. When publication resumed at the beginning of October, it opined that nearly everyone must have been 'affected directly or indirectly by the stoppage – from the investor who must keep abreast of the stock markets to the housewife seeking to engage a new cook, or the humble citizen who wishes to know the winner of the 3.30 race'. The world, it noted, was a much different place than it had been when publication had ceased. The most notable occurrence was 'the death of Field Marshal von Hindenburg, which led to Herr Hitler's immediate assumption of supreme power in Germany, and the endorsement of his action by a remarkable plebiscite'. Closer to home, despite its previous high estimation of him, the paper did not mourn the exit of O'Duffy from Irish politics. His resignation from the presidency of Fine Gael had 'put an end to what from the outset was an uneasy fellowship'. O'Duffy had been 'an admirable Commissioner of Police; but he never was a politician and, sooner or later, a breach with his more widely experienced colleagues was bound to occur'.[89] The paper still regarded de Valera as a threat to democracy; in an editorial in October 1934, it again classed him with Hitler and Mussolini:

> To all intents and purposes President de Valera, although he relies on a democratic vote – possibly the most democratic in the world – is a dictator. Herr Hitler abolishes the entire Constitution of Weimar with a stroke of the pen; President de Valera tears up the Free State's Constitution piecemeal. The one is a dictator and boasts of the fact; the other preserves the *façade* of democracy, behind which he works his own unfettered will. When the Reichstag was in Herr Hitler's way he promptly got rid of it, just as Signor Mussolini got rid of the Italian Parliament. When the Free State Senate tried to thwart President de Valera's dictatorial plans, he did precisely the same thing in a different way.[90]

It demanded that Fine Gael pull itself together and challenge de Valera's government in a coherent manner by providing effective opposition. Acknowledging that the Blueshirt saga had 'played havoc with the whole organisation of the United Ireland Party', it expressed the hope that 'the episode of General O'Duffy will be forgotten now as quickly as possible, and that under Mr Cosgrave's guidance, the United Ireland Party will formulate a vigorous and far-reaching policy'. The lack of an effective opposition meant that the Free State was 'drifting towards a republic through lack of a positive lead in any other direction'. What the opposition needed was a policy that would 'challenge President de Valera's programme at every step'. Luckily, the paper had such a policy in mind. What Irish politics needed was 'a man who will be sufficiently bold to announce definitely that he is opposed to a republic, and that the *Saorstat's* future lies within the framework of the British Commonwealth'.

While it acknowledged that 'such a man might find himself in the wilderness for a time', it expressed its 'sufficient confidence in the innate good sense of the Irish people to believe that eventually he would win through'.[91] As the 1930s progressed, however, the country would move further and further away from the commonwealth.

CHAPTER 4

Smyllie's Reign

When, in these trying times, it's possible to work on the lower slopes of a national newspaper for several weeks without discovering which of the scurrying executives is the editor, I count myself fortunate to have served under one who wore a green sombrero, weighed twenty-two stone, sang parts of his leading articles in operative recitative, and grew the nail on his little finger into the shape of a pen nib, like Keats.[1]

Patrick Campbell on Robert Smyllie

In May 1934 John Healy died, having served as editor for twenty-seven years, and was succeeded by his deputy, Robert Smyllie. In personality and temperament the two men could not have been more different. As his obituary recorded, Healy was rather stern and aloof: 'In books, perhaps, he found a closer intimacy than in his fellow man ... his habits inclined to those of the recluse, rather than those of the man of affairs, and during the last ten years of his life he nourished few personal contacts with Irish politics or society.'[2] Smyllie was the complete opposite. A gregarious individual, he revelled in the company of others, particularly in the Palace Bar on Fleet Street where he held court on a nightly basis, receiving all manner of established and aspiring poets, artists, novelists, playwrights, and journalists into his company. In appearance, too, the difference between the two men was marked. While Healy had been a tall, slim, rather stiff individual, always impeccably dressed, with a trim, tidy moustache, Smyllie was the complete opposite:

A nose that might have been moulded by a child turned loose in the kitchen on baking-day – with features and figure to match. Physically, there's a dumpling quality about Smyllie, come to think of it. A sort of amateur pastry-cook effect, with a moustache made out of pluckings from the yard brush that just doesn't belong anywhere. The whole, as they say, nicely browned to a turn, with the further scattering of yard brush bristles for hair, and there – pictorially at least – is Mr R.M. Smyllie, the Editor-in-Chief of the *Irish Times*.[3]

But it was in terms of politics that the difference between the two men was most pronounced. Whereas Healy had been irrevocably opposed to the Free

State pulling away from Britain and 'had fought every step of the way, using all the weapons, from cold logic to ridicule, in his stylistic armoury', Smyllie was of a more pragmatic disposition.[4] While he was undoubtedly a monarchist and a supporter of commonwealth membership, he approached these issues from an Irish rather than an imperial angle: Healy criticised the country's move away from Britain because he believed it was bad for the commonwealth, whereas Smyllie criticised it because he believed that it was bad for Ireland. In an interview in 1941, Smyllie outlined the paper's editorial policy:

> Our policy is to advocate the maintenance of a strong Commonwealth connection, while insisting, no less strongly, on Irish political independence. In other words, we are in many ways the only real Sinn Féin paper in existence. Ireland must be a free country politically, but economically she must work in the closest co-operation with Johnny Bull. We preach the freedom of the individual as well as the freedom of the state.[5]

Compared to Healy, Smyllie had 'the contemporary outlook; he knew that "West-Britonism" as a policy or a point of view was dead'.[6] He knew he could either preside over a newspaper that remained aloof from the development of a new state that was the near contradiction of everything for which it had previously stood, or instead give it a new position in Irish journalism by making it relevant to Irish life. Wisely, Smyllie chose the latter option, and in an interview outlined what he saw as the major changes that the paper underwent during his tenure:

> When the British left Ireland in 1922, the bottom fell out of the world in which the *Irish Times* previously had existed. Quite frankly, we had been the organ of the British government. The bulk of our readers were British Civil Servants and Army people. We had now to write for a totally different public. In other words, we had to write for a public that simply wouldn't have had us on their tables before. We pictured them, largely, I think, as young men and women just left school, just down from the universities – the people who were going to be the voters and the leaders of the future. It's always been held against us that the people we write for have been old ladies and colonels – for 'dug-outs' in the Kildare-Street Club. That's certainly not true to-day.[7]

Not that that the paper performed a complete u-turn on any issue. As one reporter put it, while it 'made clear its acceptance of the new order in general, it did not pretend to welcome it all in detail'. On the contrary, it 'frankly attacked "Gaelicism" and mental narrowness'.[8] One part of 'Gaelicism' that caused a problem was the Irish language, the increased use of which in the affairs of state posed problems for reporters:

> It was humiliating to have to ask what on earth the Secretary to the venerable President, Douglas Hyde, meant when he rang the Irish Times to give the names of people who had

attended some ceremony at his residence, in Phoenix Park, Áras an Uachtaráin. He gave me a string of names, most of which were familiar because they were little different in pronunciation from the English version. But some were incomprehensible: Walsh became 'Breathnach'. Interspersed between them, too, from time to time, came the repetition of what sounded like 'Argusarborn'. To have to ask ... what it meant, was as embarrassing, as the discovery that all it meant was 'with his wife' – Proinsias MacAogain agus a Bhean turned out to be the Minister for Defence, Frank Aiken, and Mrs Aiken.[9]

Nonetheless, Smyllie presided over a remarkable transformation of the paper that ensured its survival. As one commentator noted at the time, he brought 'tolerance to the *Irish Times* and in the columns of the paper offered the only forum available at the time where free discussion of ethics and religion could take place'. Such a policy ensured that, in social issues such as divorce, censorship, and the Spanish civil war, its editorial viewpoint was 'definitely at variance with the Catholic standpoint'. As regards its low circulation, the commentator noted that what it lacked in circulation it made up for in the quality of its readership which was concentrated 'principally among the educated and influential classes, not only Protestant but also Catholic'.[10] Even those opposed to commonwealth membership were impressed with the changes wrought by Smyllie. As Todd Andrews later remarked:

> Under Smyllie's editorial direction its readership extended to businessmen and bank clerks, members of rugby football clubs, academics of the national university and even more significantly, civil servants and members of the government. Smyllie accepted that he was an Irishman owing unequivocal allegiance to Ireland ... He obviously had a free hand from the proprietors of the paper and his influence derived from the fact that he wrote from the standpoint of a free and independent Ireland rather than that of a province, regrettably and possibly temporarily, separated from the motherland ... Smyllie, in fact, integrated the *Irish Times* and what it stood for with the Irish nation and he was more than welcomed by the ruling group and by the civil servants in particular ... When anyone in the civil service offices told you that he had seen such and such an item 'in the paper', you knew that he was referring to the *Irish Times*. Favourable comment from the *Irish Times* made a minister's day. Favourable comment from the other two Dublin dailies was of no importance to them.[11]

Such praise from republicans would have been unthinkable in Healy's day, and illustrate how far Smyllie re-orientated the paper away from its old unionist philosophy. In the 1930s circulation generally hovered around the 25,500 mark.[12] Throughout the decade it averaged twelve to fourteen pages during the week, and, with addition of extended sports reporting and property advertising, fourteen to sixteen pages on Saturdays. Adverts still dominated the front page, despite the arrival of the *Irish Press* in 1931, which, from day one, had put news stories on its front page. One reason for the paper's persistence in devoting its front page to adverts was that it was a financially lucrative practice, and, given the paper's limited circulation, it needed this revenue. Even the death of King George V in January 1936 could not persuade the paper to drop the practice for a day, although it did announce the death in bold typeface beneath the masthead with the mournful headline 'Death of the King'.[13] Each page was printed in seven columns of single type, which, with the addition of double-column introductory paragraphs under a set of three to four headlines made the layout more attractive to the eye. Photographs also began to be placed within the text, although the photograph page continued to cover events such as the Spring Show, country shows, race meetings and political events. Letters to the editor were still dispersed throughout the paper, as was foreign and home news. In contrast, financial news was collated in the 'The Financial News and Notes' page. Women's journalism still consisted of the 'Of Interest to Women' column that contained sections such as 'Fashions from Paris', 'This Week's Recipe', and shopping tips under the heading 'I saw Last Week'. In the paper's two pages of sports reporting, the emphasis was very much on horse racing – a sport favoured by the Arnott family – although rugby football, association football, hockey, table-tennis, golf, rowing, cricket, greyhound racing, lawn tennis, billiards, coursing, yachting, angling, badminton, polo and boxing also received much coverage. Reportage of GAA games was minimalist, although coverage of the All-Ireland Finals usually merited more attention and the odd photograph. Business-wise, the paper continued to be profitable; the annual returns for the years ending September 1937 and 1938 recorded profits of £22,707 and £21,955 respectively.[14]

JOURNALISTIC LIFE

Along with change in the paper's politics came a change of atmosphere that allowed all manner of eccentricities to flourish; none more so than the nightly routine of sending the paper to press. Each evening around 5 p.m. Smyllie would rush through the front door of the building and race up the main staircase to his office, brushing past the various visitors and hangers-on who had gathered in the lobby hoping to have a word with him:

> In anticipation of his coming, the front office was frequently occupied by a straggle of supplicants – impoverished old acquaintances to whom he gave small sums of money, crackpots seeking publicity for their crazy schemes, a well-known briefless barrister needing money for a cocaine 'fix', an elderly lady from some respectable suburb, banging her umbrella on the counter and demanding an interview with the Editor. Like many heavy men, Smyllie was surprisingly nimble on his feet and could move swiftly through the beseeching throng and up the stairs to the next floor. Sometimes, if too sorely tired, he might turn on the landing with a sweeping gesture and quell the mob with a shout:

'Pismires and warlocks stand aside!' Then he would vanish into his den, leaving trailing clouds of pipe smoke in his wake.[15]

Having reached his office he would deal only with any business that could not be postponed before heading to the Palace Bar, which, located across the road from the paper, was the centre of artistic life in Dublin. Its clientele consisted of a veritable who's who of writers, poets and artists that included poets Fred Higgins, Seumas O'Sullivan, Ewart Milne, Louis MacNeice, Padraic Fallon, Patrick Kavanagh, Donagh MacDonagh and Austin Clarke, and painters Harry Kernoff, William Conor and Sean O'Sullivan. Other regulars, at one time or another, included the sculptor Jerome Connor, the writer Oliver St John Gogarty, political cartoonist and founder of *Dublin Opinion* Charles E. Kelly, novelist Leslie Montgomery (better known as Lynn C. Doyle), the actor Liam Redmond, Cathal O'Shannon (then secretary of the ITGWU), the playwright Brinsley MacNamara, literary editor of the *Irish Press* M.J. MacManus, Smyllie's assistant editor Alec Newman and the paper's advertising manager G.J.C. Tynan 'Pussy' O'Mahony. O'Mahony, father of comedian Dave Allen, was a legend in his own right. Nicknamed 'Pussy' because someone once caught him trying to teach the office cat how drink milk from a saucer, he had a reputation for pulling elaborate pranks, mostly at Smyllie's expense. On one occasion he rang the newsroom announcing that, as president of the Gaelic League, he would be delighted to attend that afternoon's rugby international if only he could get a ticket. Spotting the news value of such a person attending a 'foreign' sporting event, Smyllie gave up his own ticket and discovered the truth too late. On another occasion, Smyllie set out from the office to a Masonic banquet with the instruction that he should be called back if some news emergency should occur in his absence. While the nature of the news emergency was not recorded, the manner of his recall was: 'It was O'Mahony who eventually burst into the hall. "Gentlemen", he announced to that very Protestant gathering, "I bring you all a blessing, and a special message of greeting from His Holiness the Pope".'[16]

It was among this clientele of established and aspiring artists that Smyllie held court on a nightly basis, seated at a central table towards the rear of the bar. Cartoonist Alan Reeve neatly captured the typical Palace Bar scene in 1940. A gifted New Zealand cartoonist, Reeve contributed caricatures of well-know, Dublin artists, academics and public figures to the paper's books page in late 1939 and early 1940. In his cartoon 'Dublin Culture', Reeve captured the clientele of the bar for prosperity, with Smyllie located in the exact centre of the drawing, wearing his trademark broad rimmed hat, his arm outstretched for a cigarette. It was here that Smyllie hired many of the paper's most celebrated

writers, including Patrick Kavanagh and Brian O'Nolan, better know perhaps
as Myles na gCopaleen. Kavanagh was present on the occasion of the infamous
'Poet's War' that erupted in the bar one evening in winter 1939. According to
Kavanagh's account, the row, described by him as a 'wild hooey ... over Louis',
began when Austin Clarke insulted Louis MacNeice with the immortal words
'Let him go back and labour, for Faber and Faber.' Fred Higgins then entered
the fray, defending MacNeice with a reference to Clarke's nervous breakdown.
Padraic Fallon, in turn, defended Clarke, and a bout of less than poetic fisticuffs
then erupted. So moved was Kavanagh by the occasion that he wrote a ballad –
'The Battle of the Palace Bar' – about the night, although it survives only in
fragmentary form:

> They fought like barbarians, these highbrow grammarians,
> As I have recorded for the future to hear.
> And in no other land could a battle so grand
> Have been fought over poetry, but in Ireland my dear![17]

In his memoir Lionel Fleming recounted that he heard it was Kavanagh himself
who delivered the infamous line that ignited the fight. The only other detail to
reach Fleming was that 'Alec Newman, before hurling himself into it, had first
prudently handed over his false teeth and glasses to the barman for safe
keeping.'[18]

The nightly routine continued when Smyllie returned to his office to put the
paper to press. He would again run the gauntlet of hangers-on before holding a
conference with the assistant editor, Alec Newman, regarding the topics on
which they would base their leading articles. This done, and before proofs came
up for correction, the joviality would begin. Brandy would be passed round,
Smyllie would light his trademark black briar pipe, the gramophone would be
activated, dominoes would be played, and occasionally, Smyllie, who was an
impressive baritone, and Newman would sing operatic limericks with lyrics that
left nothing to the imagination. Newman, a classics graduate of Trinity College,
had joined the paper as a full-time leader writer in 1930 and became assistant
editor when Smyllie became editor. Born in Waterford and reared in Belfast, he
was recruited by John Healy on a freelance basis to contribute book reviews.[19]
He was, one colleague recalled, a talented linguist in every sense of the word;
'when he had had a few too many, he could fairly turn the air blue [use
expletives] – an attribute, which, in later years cost him dear'.[20] A newer recruit
was Alan Montgomery, the son of novelist Leslie Montgomery, who joined as a
trainee reporter in 1934.

Both Newman and Montgomery would edit the paper in succession to each
other, and it was this triumvirate – Smyllie, Newman and Montgomery – that

put together the first ever *Irish Times* stylebook.[21] 'Bureaucratic language', it
contended, 'is the source of dull English. When the plain meaning can be
discerned, there is no reason why we should not give it'. 'Every item', it stressed,
'should be intelligible to the man who has not seen a paper for twelve months,
or who has just landed from Siberia'. Among the more notable instructions
contained in the extensive stylebook was a rule stipulating that 'News appears
in a page, not "on" it' – a throw-back to the days when John Healy had argued
that the only thing that could appear 'on' a page was a stain or mark after it
had been printed. Another rule stipulated that reporters should 'Compare sizes
of towns and other places in foreign news with Irish towns and counties rather
than English' – a sign of Smyllie's recognition that the *Irish Times* was an Irish,
not an English, newspaper. It being an Irish newspaper, the weather had to
make an appearance: 'The weather has to figure many times in every issue of
the paper. Let us be as short as possible about it. If it rains hard, say so; but do
not begin with a rigmarole about the uncomfortable "conditions".'[22] Smyllie
was a stickler for grammar and had a particular aversion to split infinitives and
sentences that began with the words 'And' or 'But', as Patrick Campbell, of 'An
Irishman's Diary' fame, found out:

> Bertie crossed out the ands and the buts with roars of pain and outrage. 'Never, never begin
> a sentence with a shuddering preposition!' he cried. 'A preposition has never initiated a
> sentence and never will'. A split infinitive drove him to bang both fists on the desk. 'To
> actually justify!' he snarled. 'To actually justify. Listen to it. It turns the stomach. If you
> must – 'actually to justify' – but what's 'actually' doing there anyway. It's superfluous. It's
> even otiose. The graces of style, Mr Campbell. The graces of style'.[23]

The working conditions of the average reporter at this time were, to say the
least, tough. Twelve-hour days, a six-day working week, no minimum wage and
no pension scheme ensured that 'most reporters stayed at their work, unless
rescued by a legacy, until chronic illness or death removed them'.[24] Although
both the National Union of Journalists and the Institute of Journalists existed,
neither yet had the clout to force any improvements in working conditions. As
far back as 1927, the NUJ had sought negotiations on wages and conditions
with newspaper proprietors, who responded by insisting that they would only
meet the NUJ if it acted jointly with the Institute of Journalists – a union the
NUJ regarded as next to useless.[25] It was not until after an industrial dispute
involving printers in 1934 that proprietors finally recognised the NUJ as a
legitimate trade union.[26] The public perception of the profession also left a lot
to be desired. As one reporter recorded, there was 'a certain stigma on the
profession; an assumption by the public that reporters are all seedy and rather
unscrupulous men, with a taste for drink, an ignorance of grammar, and a

capacity for never getting their facts quite right'.[27] Another noted that reporters were viewed as 'seedy, scruffy creatures who would turn up at funerals and weddings, wanting lists of people who attended, scribbling down names on the backs of envelopes, and invariably, to judge from the next day's *Irish Times*, getting them wrong'.[28] Despite, or perhaps because of, these conditions, there existed a strong sense of camaraderie among all reporters who tended to look out for one another:

> The presupposition was that if anything newsworthy happened in and around the capital on a weekday before mid-day it would be reported in the evening papers – the *Herald* and the *Mail*, which newsboys, still barefoot, would bring onto the streets early in the afternoon. It would be time enough, then, to put a quick call or two – not to the scene of the event, but to one of the reporters who had covered it, to check whether there might be some particular *Irish Times* angle. There was rivalry for circulation between the newspaper owners, and up to a point between their editors and the higher-ranking staff writers, but very little between the reporters. If for any reason one of them arrived late for some briefing – by, say, a minister, in which the hand-out happened to be accompanied by some unforeseen but important off-the-cuff remarks – he could usually rely on obtaining a 'black'; a carbon copy of what one of the reporters would put in his own newspaper, or failing that a telephoned run-down of the other man's notes.[29]

Indeed, the 'allegedly cut-throat nature of journalism was ... largely a popular illusion'; reporters from all the national titles 'tended to stick together in a self-protective, almost Masonic fraternity; sharing all, or nearly all, of what they learnt'.[30]

'THE GLAMOUR OF HITLERISM'

In June 1936 de Valera's government declared the IRA an illegal organisation – a move welcomed by the paper, which noted that the state could no longer 'wink at a secret and more or less organised political army which refuses to recognise that the State or its laws have any authority in Ireland'.[31] The move followed a spate of IRA killings that included the shooting dead of retired Admiral Somerville at his home in West Cork in early 1936. The elderly ex-naval officer was killed for writing letters of recommendation for local men who wished to join the British navy. The admiral was a relative of one of the paper's reporters, Lionel Fleming, who was sent to cover the story. In his memoir he recorded that this was one of the worst moments in his career. He arrived at the scene to be greeted by his relatives who were unaware that he worked for the paper and who welcomed him with the words; 'Oh Lionel, how kind of you to visit us in our trouble. We've been so bothered by those dreadful reporters.'[32] In 1941, Larry de Lacy, a sub-editor, found himself caught up in an IRA internal feud. De Lacy was a brother-in-law of then IRA chief-of-staff Stephen Hayes, whom the northern section of the IRA believed to be an informer. Kidnapped and tortured, Hayes wrote a concocted confession that stated he was passing on sensitive information to two government ministers and to his brother-in-law at the *Irish Times*.[33] Around the same time de Lacy disappeared, and despite the best efforts of his colleagues at the paper he could not be found or contacted. Having implicated de Lacy in his false confession, Hayes escaped from his captors and sought sanctuary in a police station. Just as the paper was reporting this twist in the saga, de Lacy showed up for work. The belief in the paper was that de Lacy had been kidnapped on the basis of the false confession, interrogated and then released, although as one colleague recalled nothing was ever said about his absence from the paper: 'Larry resumed work at the office as if nothing had happened. Not a word was said by anyone concerning this mystery which had everyone guessing for weeks. Larry said nothing, The Editor said nothing. Colleagues said nothing … It was said that after his kidnapping he always carried a revolver'.[34] Indeed, another reporter recounted the story of how one day he found a loaded revolver on the floor of a lavatory in the *Irish Times* building. He walked out of the lavatory with the gun pinched between his nervous fingers, to have it reclaimed by its rightful owner – de Lacy – who calmly took the gun and put it in a concealed holster.[35]

As well as watching out for the improvements in democracy at home, the paper kept a keen eye on its deterioration abroad, inspired no doubt by Smyllie's avid interest in European affairs. His holidays were usually spent on the continent, and while there he would often write major feature pieces on the country he was visiting. After a holiday in Germany in 1929, Smyllie had written a series of articles entitled 'The New Germany' which was subsequently published in booklet form by the company.[36] Editorially, the paper was, in 1936, surprised that the German people had 'yielded to the glamour of Hitlerism, with its Swastika banners, its gaudy uniforms, its catch-words and its fantastic promises'.[37] It declared that 'everybody who knows and appreciates Germany's real *Kultur* must grieve at this great nation's abandonment to an unworthy hysteria' and expressed confidence 'that the people who gave birth to men of the stamp of Goethe, Beethoven, Hegel, Mozart, Schiller and Bach will not tolerate for long the arrogant pretensions of Hitler'.[38] The new regime's treatment of Jews also came in for criticism: it declared that 'Germany's efforts to "purge" herself of the least trace of Semitism have made her Government seem both tyrannical and absurd in the world's eyes'.[39] As Hitler turned a democracy into a dictatorship, the paper suggested rather caustically that he seemed to be inspired by de Valera's approach to politics:

In some respects Herr Hitler seems to have taken his cue from President de Valera. No sooner had he come into power than he decided to ignore the Treaty of Versailles, just as Mr de Valera decided to ignore the Anglo-Irish Treaty of 1921. The Weimar Constitution went the way of the Free State Constitution ... Herr Hitler – again like Mr de Valera – claims a popular (or is it a divine) mandate for everything that is done.[40]

In November 1936 Smyllie wrote – under his pen-name 'Nichevo' – a penetrating fourteen piece feature series entitled 'Germany under Adolf Hitler'.[41] One article from the series noted that the German Workers' Front resembled 'a gigantic trade union, lacking only the right to strike.'[42] He also cast a cold eye on the Nazi anti-Semitic campaign that was 'being waged throughout the country with unabated fury' and noted that Jews were leaving Germany in large numbers and by any means possible in spite of the fact that they had to abandon their considerable wealth as they fled. 'Even Jews at times', he concluded, 'will prefer freedom to opulence'.[43] As the regime's treatment of the Jewish people worsened, the paper observed that, although in the long run the German people would 'become revolted by the sheer cruelty of the Nazi campaign against the unhappy Jews', for the moment Germany's 'conscience seems to be in the keeping of the National Socialist Party, which, in turn, is controlled by a handful of Jew-baiters'.[44] In November 1937, after travelling extensively in Czechoslovakia, Smyllie wrote another feature series, 'Carpathian Contrasts', that was published in booklet form and which resulted in him being awarded the 'Order of the White Lion' by the president of the Czechoslovak Republic shortly before it was overrun by Hitler's army.[45] As this was a foreign decoration, the Czechoslovakian government asked the Irish government whether it would have any objection to Smyllie receiving the honour 'in recognition of the contribution he has made to a wider knowledge in Ireland of Czechoslovakia and her people'. The minister for external affairs, Eamon de Valera, recommended that no objection be raised because the services for which Smyllie was being awarded were 'of a cultural nature, similar to those for which other foreign decorations have been bestowed on Irish citizens'.[46]

'A FASCIST JUNTA'

This strong adherence to freedom of thought and expression cost the paper financially when it came to its coverage of the Spanish civil war. In the words of one historian, it published 'some of the most factual, balanced editorial analyses to be found in Europe'.[47] Whereas the pious, Catholic-orientated *Irish Independent* supported the fascist rebel leader General Francisco Franco, and the *Irish Press* did not takes sides, the *Irish Times* was unrepentant in its

support for the democratically elected socialist-republican government that
came to power with radical plans, and which alarmed the monied classes and
the clergy. In an editorial, it outlined what it saw as the background to the
conflict:

> At the last general election a Government was returned to power in a perfectly democratic
> way. It was a Republican Government, with certain leanings towards Socialism; but nobody
> could question its credentials ... The Government admittedly was anti-clerical, as most
> Left-wing administrations on the Continent are. It incurred the wrath of the priesthood as
> well as of the grandees ... and its attitude towards Church property very naturally gave
> grave offence in sacerdotal circles ... The big landowners and monied classes took sides
> with the Church, and the stage was set for a bitter struggle between the Popular Front and
> the allied forces of Conservatism.[48]

This, however, was not a universally shared view; the paper noted that the
conflict was being 'distorted grossly by Europe's yellow press'. Spain had 'a legally
elected government' the authority of which had 'been challenged by certain officers
of its own army, who would normally be regarded as common or garden traitors'.
However, by some 'curious metamorphosis', the government had 'been made to
appear as the usurping party while the rebels are hailed as patriotic heroes'. Not
surprisingly, the paper reacted with alarm to Franco's statement that, if successful,
he would 'establish a military dictatorship as a prelude to setting up a corporate
State on the model of Portugal, Italy and Germany'. 'In a word', the paper
proclaimed, 'he is a Fascist'.[49] Just how strongly the paper believed in
democracy can be gleamed from its statement that 'if the IRA should appeal to
the people, and as a result, should find itself with a constitutional majority, we
should regard it, and none other, as the legitimate Government'.[50] To get a first-
hand account of what was going on in Spain, Smyllie dispatched a reporter,
Lionel Fleming, 'to go down on the Republican side' with the instruction that
he did not care what conclusions were reached so long as they were honest. In
his memoir Fleming recounted his experiences:

> So I did go down and tried to be honest, chronicling the fact that the Republicans were
> burning down churches and that many of them were addicted not only to Communism but
> to the far more fascinating and attractive ideal of anarchy ... But I did also put on record
> the fact that this was a legitimate struggle, both against the evils of Nazism and Fascism
> (which were to become very obvious indeed in the succeeding years) and the claim of the
> Catholic Church, that it should be allowed to control almost every aspect of Spanish life.
> The parallel, I suppose, was fairly obvious, though I had not contrived it.[51]

As the conflict escalated, the paper observed that there was a 'deliberate
effort to represent the war as a resurgence of the "Catholic" against the "Red"
spirit', whereas the conflict was really between 'a Fascist junta which seeks to

impose a military despotism upon the country and a population which has tasted, for the first time, some of the sweets of democracy, and does not wish to forego them'.[52] It also rejected claims of rampant anti-clericalism on the part of the government and the militia set up to defend it, noting that the violence was 'being directed not against religion, but against the Spanish clergy, who always have identified themselves with the aristocracy and land-owning classes'.[53] Such a view conflicted sharply with that of the Catholic church, and, as Fleming observed, it did not take long for the church to react:

> The publication of my first articles was followed by the arrival, in our office, of a very polite priest. He told Smyllie that, by pure chance, he had been talking to several of our more prominent advertisers, who had hinted that, unless the *Irish Times* discontinued this series of articles, they would feel compelled to withdraw their custom. He spoke, said the priest, as a well-wisher of the paper; he would not like to see the *Irish Times* lose money. He was shown the door.[54]

The warning was not a hollow one. In August 1936, Hugh Allen of the Catholic Truth Society wrote to the president of Blackrock College and chairman of the Catholic Headmasters' Association, John Charles McQuaid, suggesting that, given 'The conduct of the Irish Times in reference to the Spanish crisis', the association 'might now agree to put that paper out of bounds for members of the Association, as far as advertisements of their schools are concerned'. Such schools advertised in the paper for the simple reason of attracting the business of well-heeled Catholics who read the paper. Stating the obvious, Allen noted that, 'If all agree not to advertise in this anti-Catholic organ, the necessity of advertising in it will disappear.' Would, he enquired, McQuaid bring this proposal forward for discussion at the association's next meeting?[55] When forwarding his agenda items to the association's secretary, McQuaid listed the 'Irish Times' as the second item to be discussed.[56] A second letter from Allen to McQuaid a couple of days later thanked him for doing the 'needful' against the paper, the editor of which, Allen proclaimed, was 'a Mason, and his actions are taken in sympathy with Masonic brethren in Barcelona'. He even went so far as to outline an argument that McQuaid might use in advocating an advertising ban at the meeting:

> The argument in favour of advertising in the Irish Times is that it is <u>necessary</u>, in order to reach a certain class of Catholic who reads the paper. The answer to that argument is that the type of Catholic who reads the Irish Times will hesitate to send his child to an Irish school in any circumstances. He exports his children. But there may be exceptions. If there are, they will send their children to Irish schools without the aid of Irish Times publicity. When the time comes for them to choose a school, they will go out to procure information. They will seek for it wherever they can get it, in the Independent or the Irish Times. When one considers the amount of Catholic money spend on school advertisements in the Irish

Times, one wonders is it justified commercially. After all, Catholic readers of the paper are comparatively few. Some of them are beyond Catholic influence, the rest are commercially hardly worth all the competition. I made up some time ago – two years back, I think – that one issue of the paper carried about £175 worth of Catholic school advertisements.[57]

The minutes of the Catholic Headmasters' Association meeting of 22 October 1936 indicate that Allen's letter was read to the meeting. Scribbled notes record the result of the subsequent discussion as 'Irish Times: Sympathy. Leave to Head of Schools'. Nonetheless, the motion had an effect on the paper. In the month of August 1936 it carried twenty-eight adverts for Catholic schools and in September carried a further eight adverts. During the same period the following year, the paper did not carry any adverts for Catholic schools.[58] But if ecclesiastics thought that removing advertising from the paper would influence its editorial policy, they were wrong. While such a boycott obviously hit the paper's finances, Smyllie was, according to one reporter, an editor determined to 'fight all forms of obscurantism, political or religious, whatever the cost in advertising revenue'.[59] If he felt that 'the employers were in the wrong in some labour dispute, no amount of wailing about lost advertisements or broken friendships would sway him to allow them to get away with it'. He could also be relied upon to back his reporters against unwarranted complaints: 'But against pressure from outside – especially if there's any attempt to browbeat a reporter – they can rely on him absolutely, in such matters. Smyllie is immovable. Many a time his attitude must have infuriated his employers; to give them credit, they have let him have his way.'[60]

AN 'ILLEGITIMATE REPUBLIC'

In December 1936, King Edward VIII confirmed the paper's worst fears when he decided to abdicate the throne to marry American divorcee Mrs Wallace Simpson. The affair had been an open secret for some time; while the 'gutter Press of the United States of America' had the king's name 'splashed across its lurid columns in a manner than has been most painful to loyal Britons throughout the world', Irish and British newspapers had withheld the facts from the public 'not, indeed, because any pressure has been brought to bear from high places, but simply because the newspapers of these islands try to maintain a tradition of decent reticence in regard to such matters'; now the storm had broken, and, as the paper saw it, the king had only one option: 'Edward the man must subordinate his human emotions to the royal duty of Edward the King.'[61] When the abdication was confirmed, it urged restrain on the part of Irish politicians meeting to discuss the crisis. Stating that the link to the crown was a 'precious possession of those Irish citizens who combine an abiding love for their own country with an almost mystical attachment to the British Throne', it appealed to 'Ministers and deputies alike to exercise the wise and dignified restraint that marked yesterday's proceedings in the House of Commons'.[62]

Restrain was not on the agenda, however, as de Valera introduced two bills under guillotine so as to ensure their quick passing in the Dáil. The Constitution Act removed all mention of the king and the governor general from the constitution, and the External Relations Act limited the functions of the crown to external affairs such as the appointment of diplomatic representatives and the signing of international agreements as advised by the government. The paper was outraged and accused de Valera of seizing the opportunity 'with almost embarrassing haste, to take advantage of the new position for his own purposes'. It was typical of his 'confused process of thought'; while internally the Free State would 'become a sort of illegitimate republic'; externally it would 'remain an integral part of the British Commonwealth'. Ultimately, it concluded, it was all 'an elaborate sham' because there was 'no question of secession from the Commonwealth'. No matter how de Valera dressed up 'the Saorstat in republican trappings', it remained 'just as much a part of the Commonwealth as Canada or New Zealand' and his 'attempts to convince his followers that he does not recognise the King [were] simply childish'.[63]

But it was not all head-to-head antagonism. Throughout the 1930s the paper supported Fianna Fáil's policy of increasing taxation on commodities rather than increasing income tax. In May 1936 William Norton of the Labour Party observed that it was 'obvious from recent issues of that paper, and recent comments in the editorials, that the *Irish Times* regards the present Minister [Sean MacEntee] as an absolutely ideal Minister for Finance, from the standpoint of the people it represents'. MacEntee had, Norton declared, 'in the viewpoint of those who are responsible for the production of that organ ... done much to repair the mischief caused by the provocative policy of the President of the Executive Council'.[64] In a later debate James Dillon of Fine Gael was more blunt: the paper had, he said, 'been taken into the bosom of the Minister for Finance' and had discovered 'a new financial gospel'. In a reference to the motto of the de Valera-dominated *Irish Press*, Dillon announced that he expected the *Irish Times* 'to emerge one of these days in very small print describing itself as the *Irish Times* or "Small Truth in the News"'.[65] Later still, when the paper again supported Fianna Fáil's policy of not increasing income tax, Dillon sourly pronounced that the party had so 'intoxicated Westmoreland Street' that every member of Fianna Fáil should frame the article so that when 'his confidence in the present Minister for Finance begins to flag he can reassure himself that Westmoreland Street is pleased, the *Irish Times* is satisfied, and what more could any loyal supporters of the Fianna Fáil Party ask than that their Minister for Finance should have measured up the most pleasurable anticipations of that pillar of national feeling in Ireland, the indomitable *Irish Times*?'[66] Such was Dillon's distaste for this economic meeting of minds that he eventually declared that Fianna Fáil was 'welcome to their new recruit'; the paper had 'been wrong in the public life of this country for the past 82 years and it would be a shame to spoil its record now'.[67]

The paper also supported Fianna Fáil's stance on the Spanish civil war. In February 1937, in pursuance of an international non-intervention agreement, de Valera introduced the Spanish Civil War (Non-Intervention) Act, which forbade Irish citizens to enlist for either side of the conflict. For once, de Valera and the paper had the same viewpoint on an issue, a viewpoint that the paper acknowledged was at variance with public opinion. It was unquestionably true 'that the greater part of the Irish people sympathises with General Franco's cause and is anxious to see him acknowledged as the rightful ruler of Spain' and that the country, 'if free to indulge its inclinations, would send far more volunteers to General Franco's forces than those of Senor Caballero's Government'. However, it congratulated 'Mr de Valera's Government on its clear vision and on its willingness to act in concert with the whole civilised world'.[68] In contrast, it castigated Fine Gael, which, 'for some reason best known to itself', had decided 'to make matters as difficult as possible for the Government' by forcing 'a long and fatuous debate', the tactics of which were 'pointlessly obstructive'. The party had protested against the bill 'on the totally irrelevant ground that the Free State Government ought first to recognise General Franco as the *de facto*, if not the *de jure*, ruler of Spain', and 'many of those who took part in the ensuing debate seemed to have the haziest ideas regarding the Spanish war'. It pointed out that while it could not 'be accused of any undue sympathy with President de Valera's general policy', in this instance he had 'acted with admirable correctness'. While opportunists had been 'yelling themselves horse in an effort to make the Spanish war an issue in this country, and to try to place the Government in a totally false position', de Valera had 'never [has] lost his head' and had 'refused to allow himself to be stampeded'. In contrast, Fine Gael's proposal that the government recognise Franco as the rightful ruler of Spain was 'patently absurd'.[69]

A 'LONG AND RATHER DREARY DOCUMENT'

The rapprochement did not last long, as some months later de Valera released the text of his new constitution. On 1 May 1937, the paper published, in full, the text of the document and observed that de Valera had 'drafted his new Constitution as if Great Britain were a million miles away', for nowhere within what it described as the 'long and rather dreary document' was there any mention of Great Britain or the commonwealth. Nonetheless, the document was 'couched in admirably simple language, eschewing the complexities of legal forms'. This, it opined mischievously, was due to the fact that it had to be 'translated scrupulously into Irish'. The paper made no mention of the 'special position' accorded to the Catholic church, probably because the right of religious liberty was granted, but it noted with concern the 'special clause in the new Constitution to prevent divorce'. It gave a cautious welcome to the guarantee to 'freedom of conscience and speech', but noted that there was 'a suspicious reference to the Press' that required 'careful scrutiny'. It was, however, the ambiguity about the country's relationship with the crown and commonwealth that really made it anxious. There was no mention of the commonwealth, but neither was there any mention of a republic; was Éire in or out of the commonwealth? To such a question, the paper declared, Bunracht na hÉireann gave no answer; it merely suggested that Éire was 'neither fish, flesh, nor even a good red herring'.[70]

The coronation of George VI a few days later interrupted the paper's discussion of the new constitution. It published an eight-page supplement on the coronation, and noted with some regret that alone of the nations that comprised the commonwealth, the Free State was not represented officially at the ceremony. Nonetheless, its editorial ended with the refrain 'God Save the King'.[71] The following day, it reported angrily that 'certain individuals, representing themselves as members of the Irish Republican Army, an illegal organisation, visited our branch office in Cork, and demanded the removal from our windows of the photographs of the King and Queen'. This was an unacceptable 'attempt to enforce an unofficial censorship on an Irish newspaper'.[72] But it was by no means an isolated incident; two years previously the paper had received a communication from the Federation of Old IRA Associations asking it not to publish photographs of the annual Armistice Day ceremonies. In response, the paper published both the letter and the photographs.[73] It was this exact issue – censorship – that resulted in some of the paper's strongest editorials against the new constitution and indeed de Valera himself. Referring to the provisions for free speech in the constitution, it noted that, while one section guaranteed 'the citizens' right of free thought and speech', another required that this right not 'be used to undermine public order or morality, or the authority of the State', and yet another made the 'publication or utterance of blasphemous, seditious or indecent matter a punishable offence'. Why, it asked, was the government 'not frank about this business'; why did it

not just 'admit outright that it proposes, under the Constitution to control the
Press?':

> Evidently it wishes to maintain the democratic principle of freedom of speech and thought
> as a pleasant fiction, and to deny the reality of such freedom. May we remind Mr de Valera
> that there are no more ardent exponents of free speech in the whole world than Signor
> Mussolini and Herr Hitler, who insist that the newspapers of Italy and Germany are free to
> print precisely what they please? The only limitation which they impose is that the
> newspapers shall act only in accordance with the good of the State – in other words, with
> the doctrines of the Government.

It expressed its 'deep dislike for this sub-section of the Constitution' and
pointed out that the provisions were 'so wide that it can be invoked to meet any
occasion in which the Government of the day may have reason to fear criticism;
indeed, it can be so interpreted as to impose a complete censorship upon the
Press at any time, and for any length of time'. As would happen during the
Second World War, the provisions opened 'the way for a condition of affairs in
which no view but the Government's will be available to the public at large'. De
Valera, it noted, might as well have had drafted the article thus: 'The State
guarantees liberties for the exercise of the rights of free thought and speech,
subject to the Government's approval.'[74] In another editorial it took him to task
for being 'the sole begetter of this unique instrument'. It was clear he himself
had 'conceived the original idea of a new constitution; he drafted the document,
apparently taking legal advice when he wanted it, and depending on the light of
nature when he did not want it; and finally he acted as its sponsor in the Dáil,
revealing himself in the process to be one of the supreme egoists of our times'.
That one person should do all this was 'utterly incredible'. But, as it pointed
out, de Valera was no ordinary person:

> President de Valera some years ago announced blandly that when he wished to know what
> the Irish people wanted, he merely looked into his own heart, where, it seems, he was able
> to discover the clue to every riddle. He considered himself to be the ultimate repository of
> the national psychology. He was the Irish Sir Oracle, and when he oped [sic] his lips let no
> dog bark. As a kind of corollary to this piece of unparalleled vain-glory, he delivered
> himself of the notorious dictum that the people have no right to do wrong. Coming from a
> Cyrano de Bergerac, such silly gasconade might be amusing; coming from a national leader,
> it is tragic.[75]

In the subsequent election and referendum, the paper called on the
electorate to vote for Fine Gael and to reject the new constitution. Facing up to
commercial reality, though, it carried election adverts for Fianna Fáil for the
first time – including one full front-page advert consisting of a cartoon of
William Cosgrave as a turkey with his ruffled feathers as broken election

promises.[76] On the eve of polling day, it was 'glad to admit that in many ways President de Valera's Government has confounded its former critics, including ourselves; that it has acted fairly and uprightly towards the political and religious minorities, and that its Ministers, on the whole, have done their jobs conscientiously and well'. Nonetheless, Cosgrave's party stood unambiguously for the 'Free State's continued membership of the British Commonwealth of Nations' and so the paper urged its readers 'to go to the polls tomorrow and to vote in all cases for the Cosgrave candidates'. It was equally forthright in advising readers on how to vote in the referendum. It proclaimed its belief that 'the new Constitution was entirely unnecessary; that it is an amateurish document designed to catch the votes of the masses; that it contains at least one definitely dangerous clause in respect of the Press, and that, by its omission of even the most oblique reference to the Commonwealth, it is based not upon reality but upon humbug'. Consequently, it advised readers 'to vote against it' and was confident that 'if all the voters do their duty and go to the poll to-morrow, Fianna Fáil can be defeated and the new Constitution consigned to oblivion'.[77] In the heel of the hunt, neither de Valera nor the constitution were so consigned, and when the latter came into effect in December 1937 the paper again criticised the ambiguity regarding the country's position vis-à-vis the commonwealth. Describing the new constitution as 'a kind of empty formula', it observed that:

> The outstanding feature of the whole business is the fact that citizens of the new Éire will continue to be treated as citizens of the British Commonwealth of Nations ... While he remains at home, apparently, the Irishman will have the green flag wrapped around him, but as soon as he sets foot on the mail boat he will enfold himself in the Union Jack ... They will be Republicans at home and Dominionists abroad. They will be in the Commonwealth, but not of it. They will ignore the King in Ireland; when they take a trip to the Continent or the United States of America, they will claim his protection. In some respects the new position may be humiliating; but when all is said and done it will be harmless make-believe.[78]

'SPINNING MACHIAVELLIAN PLOTS'

Despite the difference of opinion over the constitution, relations between the paper and de Valera began to thaw when the latter initiated negotiations with the British government with a view to ending the economic war that had erupted in 1932. The issue of partition was raised early on in the negotiations, with the paper offering a solution: a united Ireland within the commonwealth. It was, it declared, 'utterly absurd that a small country such as Ireland should be cut in two'. While 'the abolition of imperial symbols and the attempt to revive Irish as a spoken language' in the south had alienated northern unionists, the south was 'associated with the Commonwealth grudgingly, and only for purposes of purely selfish interest'. The basic cause of this 'sulky enmity' was partition. The remedy for this 'calamitous condition of affairs' lay only with 'the people of Northern Ireland, whose passionate loyalty to the Throne and the Empire never has been in doubt'. Would they, it asked, 'not meet their fellow-countrymen in some way, for the sake of the Empire, as well as for that of their own common motherland?' Showing that it had reconciled itself to the new regime in the south, the paper could 'assure them in all good faith that they have nothing to fear from the majority in the South'.[79] While the issue of partition was not resolved, a trade agreement with the UK was reached, and the paper was ecstatic at the reconciliation of the two governments:

> British Ministers of the most hardened Tory type have discovered that Mr de Valera and his colleagues are not like the Anthropophagi, or men whose heads do grow beneath their shoulders – in fact, that they are normal human beings ... The Irish also have made their discoveries. British Ministers do not sit up all night spinning Machiavellian plots in which to ensnare the guileless daughter of Houlihan ... We congratulate Mr de Valera on the fact that an agreement has been reached – a fact for which he deserves the nation's gratitude.[80]

In a rare display of praise it declared that de Valera 'showed real courage when he initiated the negotiations that led to the present settlement' and 'displayed gifts of true statesmanship when he went to London'. But it had mixed feelings about the return by the British admiralty of the treaty ports of Cobh, Berehaven and Lough Swilly. True, 'British occupation of these ports constituted a substantial limitation of Irish sovereignty' but 'Ireland's best interests would be served by a defence pact between this country and Great Britain'.[81] In the subsequent general election, the thawing-out continued. The election of June 1938 was the first time that the paper did not call on its readers to vote for Fine Gael. Neither did it call on its readers to vote for Fianna Fáil. While rallying 'those survivors of the old regime – called, for want of a better term, ex-Unionists' to exercise their franchise, it did not 'presume to guide these ex-Unionists, or anybody else, in the difficult choice' of whom to vote for. Instead, it hoped they would 'be inspired not by their memories of the past, but by their ambitions for the future.'[82] It did, however, have occasion to chastise Sean T. O'Kelly, who, in the course of an election speech, 'informed the good folk of Manor Street [Dublin] that he and his colleagues had "whipped" poor old John Bull, and that, with God's help, they would whip him again'. It noted that O'Kelly would not 'whip anything more sensitive than the white of an egg' and expressed its doubt that 'his fearsome threats against England will keep many Londoners awake at night'.[83] When Fianna Fáil was returned to power, the paper declared the result 'eminently satisfactory'. With the treaty ports back in Irish hands and a promise by de Valera to renovate these defence facilities, 'Éire's defence will be safe in his hands; and for that reason, if for none other, we confess that we are glad that he has been returned to power'.[84]

As Europe headed towards war, the paper was resolute that, when the hour came, the Free State would stand shoulder to shoulder with Britain against the totalitarian regimes of the continent. From the mid-1930s onwards, the paper dismissed the concept of Irish neutrality as unfeasible. In 1935 it asserted that 'When war comes we shall be in it; and, if we are not on Britain's side, so much the worst for us.'[85] The following year it dismissed neutrality as 'merely childish', declaring that 'without a working arrangement with Great Britain, our little State would be utterly helpless'.[86] In 1937 it asserted that 'neutrality would last precisely so long as Britain's enemies would wish it to last'.[87] When, in February 1939, in an interview with an American news agency, de Valera reiterated his government's policy of neutrality, the paper described the idea as 'admirable, if it were at all possible'. The reality, as it saw it, was that 'Irish neutrality in a war involving the British Empire would be as impracticable as Scottish neutrality'. In the event of war, 'there could be no hope for a neutral Ireland'; the only option the country had was to 'make common cause with Great Britain'.[88] But neither the government nor public opinion saw it that way, a fact that did not deter the paper from continuing to advocate the state's involvement in the looming conflict. It tried a variety of arguments to try to woo public opinion away from neutrality. One such argument centred on the country's geographical position. While the paper recognised 'that the desire of the Irish people is to keep out of war', it pointed out that, given the strategic position of the island, the reality was that 'any power that is at war with Great Britain will be at war with Ireland, whether we Irish like it or not'. When the war came, 'Ireland will stand or fall as Great Britain stands or falls'.[89]

It also highlighted the anti-Nazi sentiment that it detected in the Irish population. It did not detect 'any particularly fervent pro-British feeling in Éire', but it did divine 'a deep hatred of Germany's Nazi system, and of everything for which it stands'.[90] It suited Germany 'to perfection that the twenty-six counties should remain neutral during a war in which she and Great Britain were involved', and the state would only remain neutral 'as long as Herr Hitler's fighting forces are satisfied to respect her neutrality'.[91] Contrasting the influence of both counties on the state, it observed that while 'Great Britain's influence upon Ireland may be bad, from the point of view of our extreme Republicans … the influence of Germany, if they should overcome the Western democracies in a major war, is likely to be a great deal worse'.[92] Such reasoning was to no avail, and as the drift to war gathered momentum the paper became increasingly anxious about what the policy of neutrality entailed. In 1939 it insisted that it was 'high time that the people of Éire should know precisely where they stand in relation to the international crisis ... If the Government has a policy, Mr de Valera ought to explain it in open Parliament.' Given the 'radical difference between the British and the Irish interpretation of this country's constitutional status', Britain would not tolerate Irish neutrality:

> The British continue to regard Éire as a Dominion, and our citizens as British citizens. Mr de Valera regards Great Britain as a 'foreign' country, with which, for the sake of convenience, Éire has certain working arrangements. With the first shot of the war all this make believe will be blown sky-high ... If Éire is a 'neutral' country, it will not be in the same position vis-à-vis Great Britain as Holland, Switzerland or Belgium vis-à-vis Germany. In these days of unblushing Realpolitik Éire's neutrality would last just as long as it might suit British policy, and not a moment longer.

The paper was at pains to point out that it was not being unpatriotic or playing devil's advocate; it simply believed that 'when some of our Irish super-patriots are talking about neutrality it is well that they should know what they are talking about'. When war came, it would inevitably 'be a dirty business on all sides', and the state would 'be as helpless as a feather in a gale of wind'.[93] The government's lack of planning also came in for criticism. There was 'a rumour that somewhere in the background, a Government department has been accumulating gas-masks for the civilian population, and that some day, when it has accumulated nearly enough, it may risk distributing them to the people for whom they were originally intended'. This, it noted, was comforting, even though there was 'some doubt as to which may reach the citizen first, the gas or the mask'.[94] Despite the thaw in relations between the paper and de Valera's government, throughout the war years the relationship was again at daggers drawn as the paper locked horns firmly with the government's censorship apparatus.

CHAPTER 5

'Nippon go Brath'

We were, as we still are, pro-British, inasmuch as we believed, and continue to believe, that the system of democracy which exists throughout the British Commonwealth, represents, for all its faults, the highest achievement that yet has been made by man as a political being.[1]

Irish Times editorial, 12 May 1945

URING THE SECOND WORLD war Smyllie and the *Irish Times* begrudgingly supported the Free State's neutrality.[2] When war was declared, it noted that, 'while the sympathies of this newspaper need no advertisement, we recognise the wisdom of Mr de Valera's decision, and shall give it our loyal support'.[3] But along with neutrality came media censorship that allowed for the suppression of news and comment, which, in the government's opinion, threatened domestic stability, encouraged domestic partisans (namely the IRA), or gave any of the warring parties any reason for questioning the authenticity of Irish neutrality. Whatever about neutrality, the paper was opposed to censorship and spent the war years battling against the censor's blue pencil. The day after Germany invaded Poland, the Dáil passed the Emergency Powers Act that gave effect to Irish neutrality and media censorship. Two days later, the editors of all the daily newspapers were summoned to Government Buildings and addressed by the controller of censorship, Joseph Connolly. As no censorship service had yet been put in place, he asked the editors to avoid giving publicity to matters that might impair Irish neutrality. The various editors responded 'fairly well' to Connolly's request, but while the specifics of the press censorship were being prepared it became apparent that such voluntary censorship was not at all satisfactory from the government's point of view:

Many complaints were received of objectionable matter in some of our daily newspapers, the chief offender being the 'Irish Times' which published reports and letters of a definitely partisan nature. It seemed to the studied policy of this paper to undermine our neutrality. Running through all its editorials was a suggestion that our neutrality was unreal and of a temporary nature. Such phrases as 'the temporarily safe shelter of Éire's neutrality' frequently appeared.[4]

By mid-September 1939 the censorship service was up and running and the editors were again summoned to Government Buildings for a 'frank exchange of ideas' about censorship. Before the meeting took place, Joseph Connolly wrote to de Valera outlining his take on censorship and stating that he expected most resistance to emanate from the *Irish Times*:

> Our lines have all been aimed at preventing publication of anything that would in the slightest degree impair our neutrality but it is already evident that it is going to be difficult to keep out of 'opinions', leaders and sub-leaders the suggestions (a) that we are not really neutral, (b) that we cannot continue to be neutral, (c) that we are wrong in being neutral, (d) that the big majority of the people are opposed to the enemies of Britain ... it seems likely that we will have definite difficulty in the case of certain papers such as the 'Irish Times' in restraining them from tincturing all or most of their material with a definitely pro-British tinge and, particularly in their leading articles, getting them to follow a strictly neutral line of argument.

The government could, he believed, adopt a strict censorship 'preventing any and every comment which could in any way be interpreted as favouring the British' or it could allow 'reasonable latitude or liberty in arguing for the support of the anti-German forces'. The first option could bring the government to 'the point of an open breach with papers like the "Times" where they may either refuse to obey our rulings or force us to take action up to the stage of fine or suppression or both'. Since government supporters and nationalists generally were watching carefully 'to see what latitude will be permitted to what are looked upon as pro-British elements and papers and will be quick to criticise anything that may seem to favour the British or pro-British tendencies', he advocated 'strict censorship if it became obvious that we are not going to get that full co-operation from the "Times" and such papers that we deemed necessary'.[5] Connolly was correct in anticipating that the strongest objections to censorship would come from the *Irish Times*. At the meeting Smyllie objected to the restrictions placed on the expression of opinion on the merits or shortcomings of the belligerent countries or their competing ideologies. Connolly responded by pointing out that Smyllie 'should remember that the volume of opinion represented by his journal was but a fraction of opinion in this country and might be fuel to certain disturbing elements in this country'. The official record of the meeting is illustrative of the different positions taken:

> Mr Smyllie said that at times even a journalist must act at the risk of spending a period in Mountjoy. He would have no hesitation in condemning, for instance, a bombing attack on Belfast. He pointed out that Holland, Belgium etc are neutral countries. Are they as circumscribed as we? The Controller replied that we are in an exceptional position. We are exceptionally situated, and because of recent history we have to avoid anything in the nature of a civil disturbance and all that that involves. Mr Smyllie – 'Am I to say there is nothing to choose between both sides?' The Controller – 'As regards the War, yes'.[6]

In his memoir Connolly recounted that Smyllie 'made no secret of his objections to censorship in any form. He protested his right to express his views on the war and everything connected with it'.[7] In an interview published in *The Bell* in 1941, Smyllie declared that while a certain degree of censorship was necessary – 'for security reasons as well as to guard against breaches of neutrality'; it 'ought *not* to be allowed to interfere with a newspaper's honest opinions'.[8] Achieving this balance proved impossible, and the censorship was to place an intolerable burden on both the paper and Smyllie. As his obituary was to record, the censorship regime 'cramped his style in both the narrower and wider sense ... serious journalism was almost impossible for a man who held strong views in opposition to those of the censorship, and the incessant frustration robbed Smyllie's pen of much of its sting'.[9]

A FRIENDLY NEUTRALITY?

Despite the censorship, during the early days of the war the paper continued as though nothing had changed. It published adverts for engineering vacancies in the British admiralty, the king's wartime message to the navy and the army – which the censor noted should have been 'British Navy' and 'British Army' – and readers' letters that referred to 'Our Tommies'.[10] In addition, Smyllie continued to express his opinions freely, directing all his ire at Germany. He questioned whether neutrality would last; as the censor put it, 'a suggestion of impermanence ran through [the *Irish Times*'] earlier articles, the threat to [the neutrality policy's] permanence coming from one of the belligerents – Germany'.[11] When a substantial number of German citizens left Ireland to return to Germany, Smyllie expressed surprise that 'so many admirable citizens should feel themselves compelled to abandon their posts, their property and their homes precisely as if they had been living in a belligerent country'. Was it possible, he wondered, that the 'German Government does not believe in the permanence of Irish neutrality?'[12]

The paper also highlighted the large number of Irishmen who had signed up to the British armed forces. Indeed, Smyllie's younger brother Donald, who later became chief sub-editor of the paper, joined up, as did some younger employees. In one editorial it urged readers to sew shirts for the soldiers to see them through the winter campaign. It did not view neutrality as a bar to such activity; even 'if there were no Irish soldiers fighting on behalf of the democracies, the task still would be laid upon us; but there are many thousands of Irishmen from North and South in the ranks to-day who have a right to claim our services in this matter'.[13] Another editorial argued that it was 'absurd to pretend that the people of this country can remain as indifferent to the fortunes of Great Britain as, say, the inhabitants of Nicaragua. For one thing, there can be very few families in Éire that have not some relatives or friends in one or other of the British services.'[14] In October 1939 it ran the headline 'Cork Squadron-Leader Hero of Fight: Five RAF Machines against Fifteen Germans', under which it recounted the exploits of an unnamed Cork pilot whose squadron of five RAF reconnaissance planes were attacked by fifteen German fighter planes.[15]

From October to December 1939 the paper continued to express its opposition to Hitler and his regime. When, in early October, Hitler described Poland as an aggressor that had been dealt with, it reacted with an editorial that could hardly be described as neutral. It was Hitler, not Poland, who had 'resurrected [sic] the gospel of brute force in Europe'. The conquest of Poland was, it declared, 'one of the most cynical acts of aggression in history, excelling in brutality even the treatment of the Poles by Frederick of Prussia and Maria Theresa'.[16] At the end of October 1939 it published an extract from the London *Times* that dealt with 'ghastly tyranny of the Nazi *regime*'. The article noted that while it was 'common knowledge that the political prisoners flung into concentration camps in the first frenzy of the Nazi revolution in 1933 and 1934 were treated with barbaric cruelty … it was not generally realised that the same brutality was being deliberately continued five and six years afterwards'.[17] In December it prophesied that 'much water will flow down the Vistula before Herr Hitler and his friends will admit that the invasion of Poland was one of the greatest blunders, as well as one of the greatest crimes, in history'.[18] Nonetheless, all of the above resulted in nothing more than 'verbal warnings about the publication of unneutral matter'.[19]

Summing up the paper's policy early on in the war, the censor concluded that it 'appeared to be to ignore the censorship, publish what they wanted, and explain or apologise afterwards'.[20] But the censor's patience finally ran out at the end of December 1939 when the paper did not submit its reports on the IRA's raid on the Irish army's Magazine Fort which relieved the army of its ammunition supply. This was in direct defiance of a specific directive to submit any matter relating to the raid, and, as the reports carried details not contained in the official government statement, it was seen as a direct challenge to the censor. The chief press censor, Michael Knightly, suggested to his boss that this incident 'should be availed of to make them [the *Irish Times*] realise that they cannot ignore the Censorship with impunity'.[21] But while Jospeh Connolly saw the advantages of prosecuting the paper on a 'home issue', he believed that any advantage gained would be outweighed by the prolonged publicity of the raid and by the government's embarrassment that any prosecution would involve. Nonetheless, in a report to the minister with responsibility for censorship, Frank

Aiken, Connolly noted that the paper had a tendency 'to sail very close to the line and occasionally cross it' and that the censor's leniency might make Smyllie believe that the censorship staff was 'either weak or timid in going after him'.[22]

One group not timid in going after newspapers was the IRA. During the war, the censor banned news of the executions or hunger strikes of IRA members. This did not sit well with the IRA, which, in April 1940, sent a letter to the managements and staffs of all the national papers to warn them that it would ensure that 'if newspapers are to appear at all, they will be representative of all shades of thought'. If the papers accepted 'a censorship that is calculated to mislead the public and impair the right of all the people to live in freedom', it would have 'no alternative but to intervene'. As a consequence, the Garda Commissioner ordered that Gardaí be stationed at the various printing works to ensure that publication continued unhindered.[23] In mid-January 1940, the paper again locked horns with the censor in a report of a speech at UCD by Senator Frank McDermott condemning the 'wild beast of Nazi-ism' and suggesting that Ireland would do much 'for civilisation, and for Irish unity, if we put our ports at the disposal of the French and British Fleets for the duration of the war'. Hitler had, he declared, 'made cruelty and persecution and contempt for law leading features of his Government', just as he had made 'treachery and violence leading features of his code of international behaviour'. Such talk was, McDermott noted, 'doubtless very unneutral', but he made no claim to neutrality since there was 'no glory in it'.[24] The censor was furious: the paper was immediately served with an order to summit all matter prior to publication. In a letter to the company secretary, Arthur Burgess, the chief press censor, Michael Knightly, declared that the order represented 'the mildest action that could be taken in the circumstances'.[25] This development prompted a special meeting of the board of directors, after which Burgess wrote to Knightly to assure him that in future 'great care will be taken to comply with the chief censor's orders'. He also passed on the board's request that Knightly station one of his staff at the paper to minimise disruption to the paper's production process – a request rejected by Knightly as unfeasible.[26]

Smyllie immediately made a direct appeal to de Valera in which he denied that the paper had been 'persistently flouting the authority of the Censorship'. It had, he declared, 'certain traditions, of which, rightly or wrongly, it is proud' and admitted that 'inevitably we have not concealed our sympathies vis-à-vis the belligerents, but to expect us to do that would be to expect us to abandon all claims to be an organ of public opinion'. He was also concerned about the financial strain that the order would put on the paper; he feared a loss in sales due to the delays in publication that the order would inevitably cause. He also pointed out that the paper was in direct competition 'from the political point of view' with the *Daily Mail* and the *Daily Express*, both of which published 'blatant propaganda for one of the belligerents' and were allowed to circulate freely within the state. It was not fair, he concluded, 'to muzzle the *Irish Times*' while such newspapers were 'allowed to circulate without let or hindrance'.[27] This led Knightly to observe that Smyllie appeared to 'contend that a leading Irish newspaper should be allowed to compete with two English newspapers in "blatant propaganda" for one of the belligerents'.[28]

To resolve the situation Smyllie met first with de Valera and Frank Aiken and then with the controller of censorship, Joseph Connolly, and the chief press censor, Michael Knightly. The impasse was resolved when Smyllie gave an undertaking to co-operate fully with the censor's office and to submit 'doubtful matter' to the censor. The order seemed to have the desired effect: the censor recorded that 'the operation of our Order imposed a strain on the staff but it effected the purpose we had in view and since its suspension the "Irish Times" have been most careful to submit doubtful matter'.[29] The order was revoked on 1 February 1940, and in mid-1940 the censor recorded that Smyllie had 'adopted an offensive attitude towards the censorship staff and said frankly that he was out "to break the censorship" so far as editorial comment was concerned'. In July Smyllie complained to Knightly that one of his editorials had been altered when 'some bright boy cut out the following sentence – "The witches' cauldron is beginning to bubble with a vengeance"'. He stated that, while he had no complaint against intelligent censorship, 'frivolous blue-pencilling is hardly fair to men who are slaving night after night in an effort to keep the newspapers alive in these hard times'.[30] The delay in returning proofs, which he also complained about, was attributed by the censor to his persistence in discussing each deletion at inordinate length over the phone.[31] Nonetheless, the interference with the newspaper's editorials caused some concern within the censor's office. In a letter to Frank Aiken, the assistant controller of censorship, Thomas Coyne, outlined his view that, given the well-known political position of the paper, it should be given a greater degree of latitude in the expression of editorial comment:

> In the case of a paper like the Irish Times, which is known to be pro-British in its outlook on world affairs and which is invariably referred to in the foreign press as the anglophile Irish Times, I feel that anything they write on foreign politics is discounted by this fact and that they can safely be given liberty to write freely on world events, including the war, even in a sense favourable to the British point of view provided they say nothing which could or might involve this country in any international dispute ... I select Smyllie for special mention because the Irish Times is really the only paper that devotes a principal leader every day to foreign politics and is, moreover, the paper which by reason of its outlook and the people it caters for, most likely to get us into trouble. Of course the easy road would be to recognise that the Irish Times is pro-British and to tell them bluntly that this very fact

constituted a disqualification for writing about foreign affairs at the present time and that we would not let them do it.[32]

Despite Coyle's plea, both Connolly and Aiken were determined to follow the 'easy road'. In a letter to Aiken, Connolly pointed out that while the position of the paper was well known in Ireland and Britain, it might not be so well known in Germany; and even if it were known, Germany might claim ignorance of the fact if it needed an excuse to interfere with Irish neutrality. As the paper was the only Irish newspaper allowed by the British government to go through neutral countries to Germany, the censor had to be 'specially careful in regard to what the Irish Times may be permitted to publish'. All things considered, he concluded that the 'preservation of neutrality and the determination to give no possible excuse for complaints by either of the belligerents far outweigh any temporary intellectual starvation that newspaper readers may suffer'. Great danger could arise if the censor became 'too solicitous of the interests of the newspapers and the editors'.[33]

'A CERTAIN COMPLEXION'

By this stage, concerns over the supply of newsprint resulted in the paper reducing its size to eight pages during the week, and, with the addition of the books page, sport reportage and property advertising, to twelve pages on Saturdays. Circulation fluctuated during the war. In 1939 average daily sales stood at 25,500, in 1941 at 26,500, in 1942 dropping to 19,500 and then gradually rising to 27,000 in 1945.[34] In the summer of 1940, the paper submitted a photograph of a Local Security Force recruitment rally at College Green, Dublin, in which could be seen the emblem of the royal coat of arms on the old parliament building opposite Trinity College. The photograph was sent back to the paper with the emblem scratched out by the censor. Later that year, Sir John Keane mentioned this incident in the course of a Seanad debate on censorship. In response, Frank Aiken stated that the excision was 'done quite deliberately' because the photograph 'was taken deliberately in order to get that emblem in, and to put it over the L.S.F. meeting to try and attribute a certain complexion to the L.S.F.'. According to Aiken, the government was not 'going to let the editor play the little game that he had in mind'; Smyllie had 'quite a number of photographs to publish of the same thing if he wanted' but he had chosen not to.[35] However, the censorship files record that it was not the censor but rather the Irish Press that took exception to the emblem appearing over the LSF: 'The "Irish Press" phoned to say that, in their picture of the rally, the British emblem in the background was shown prominently. They were informed that if, in their view, it was objectionable it was an easy matter to remove it. The Censor on night duty, without consulting the Chief Press Censor, gave a similar instruction to the "Irish Times".'[36]

Thus it was a case of one newspaper suggesting censorship to the censor rather than the *Irish Times* trying to pull a fast one on the censor. The paper gave extensive coverage to the Seanad debate and also published the photograph concerned to let readers make up their own minds. It described Aiken's charges as 'baseless' and 'unworthy of an Irish minister' and stressed that the photograph (like the *Irish Press* one) had been taken from the front of Trinity College 'in order to convey the best possible impression of the large crowds in College Green'. It also pointed out that it had previously published photographs of Aiken taking the army salute on St Patrick's Day 'standing underneath the Royal Arms on the Bank of Ireland' without any reprimand.[37] The incident had its lighter side in a banned report on a debate on the freedom of the press held by a student debating society. The Revd E. Savell Hicks, who chaired the debate, recounted the photograph story and told of how the paper had suggested to the censor's office that, in the interests of fairness, the figure in the photograph giving a Nazi salute should also be scratched out. 'Who on earth is that?' asked the censor. 'Grattan' came the reply – a reference to the statue of Henry Grattan with an upraised arm that stood opposite the old parliament building.[38]

During the Seanad debate Aiken also defended the intellectual abilities of the censors, noting that they 'may not scatter Latin and German words around so freely as the leader writer of the *Irish Times*, but they are quite competent to censor a leading article or any item of news'.[39] While this may have been so, the paper questioned the efficiency of the censorship, in that the controller of censorship, his deputy and the chief press censor worked the normal nine-to-five civil service hours – something that did not gel with the nightly process of producing a newspaper. This meant that the paper had to deal directly with 'subordinate officials, who, however efficient or helpful they may happen to be, have not the authority to take important decisions, and, as is the way of their kind all over the world, have been trained always to play for safety'. It suggested that 'a senior official, with more or less plenary powers, ought to be on duty throughout the night' and that 'no subordinate official ought to be empowered to sit in judgment on leading articles, written by trained men of long and wide experience'.[40] In January 1941, the chief press censor, Michael Knightly, took up night duty for the duration of the war.

But despite this concession, every so often Smyllie did not submit articles that he knew would not escape the censor's pencil. One censorship provision that Smyllie consistently battled against was the prohibition of any mention of

Irish persons serving in the British forces. When, in February 1941, Winston Churchill mentioned that many of the top allied commanders came from Ireland, north and south, the following paragraph appeared in Smyllie's 'An Irishman's Diary' under the headline 'Nippon Go Brath':

> In his broadcast on Sunday night, Mr Winston Churchill, the British Prime Minister (N.B. Britain is an island to the east of Éire), mentioned by name nine military and naval commanders who had gained fame recently in North Africa and in the Mediterranean. I append the names of the gallant nine:

General Wavell	English
General Mackie	Australian
General Wilson	Japanese (North Island)
General O'Connor	Japanese
General O'Moore Creagh	Japanese
General Dill	Japanese (North Island)
General Brooke	Japanese (North Island)
General Cunningham	Japanese
General Somerville	Japanese

> As that venerable member of the samurai, San Tiok Eli [Sean T. O'Kelly, then Tanaiste] might or might not have put it: "Quae regio in terra plena laboris?" Gimmemewhip![41]

Smyllie was reprimanded by Knightly for not submitting the piece and in response declared that 'It was not a _very_ serious offence, and you will admit that it gave a few people a much needed laugh in these gloomy times.'[42] The various headings that the paper used for death and anniversary notices came under scrutiny shortly afterwards. For many years it had inserted memoriam notices for Irish personnel killed in the First World War under the heading 'Roll of Honour' and, in consultation with the department of external affairs, had adopted another heading – 'Killed on Active Service with His Britannic Majesty's Forces' – for those killed in the current conflict.[43] However, when it later began to incorporate the anniversary notices of such individuals under the 'Roll of Honour' heading, the censor demanded that such notices be inserted in the ordinary memoriam columns.[44] When the censor began to blue-pencil the heading 'Roll of Honour' from such anniversary notices, the paper and its readers reacted angrily. In a note to the assistant controller of censorship, Thomas Coyne, Knightly outlined a telephone conversation he had with Smyllie's deputy, Alec Newman, about the new policy:

> He argued that this did not infringe our neutrality. I asked him if he received such notices in respect of men killed with German, Russian, Spanish or other foreign forces, would he announce them under the heading 'Roll of Honour' and he replied that he would. I said that we had allowed it in respect of men killed in the Great War for the reason that they

had been asked to fight by the Irish leaders of the day, that these men believed they were fighting for their own country, but that to apply it to every Irishman who fought as a mercenary in a foreign army was going too far and that as in my opinion it was being used now as an expression of unneutral tendencies I should like to see it stopped.[45]

The new policy prompted letters of complaints, the writers of which were instructed by Smyllie to redirect them to the censor's office. It was through one of these complaints that the censor discovered that the 'Roll of Honour' heading had never been confined to those killed during the First World War and that for over twenty years the paper had used the heading for any Irish personnel killed while serving in the British armed forces. This revelation infuriated Coyne, who declared that he had 'been led up the garden path in this matter and have led the Minister up in turn'. He instructed Knightly to warn the paper 'that there must be no more Roll of Honour stuff or special segregation of British army obituaries or in memoriam notices except in respect of the 1914–18 war and that we are seriously thinking of stopping this'.[46] Having discussed the issue with Frank Aiken, Coyne informed Knightly that because of:

> the disclosure that the Irish Times has been featuring a Roll of Honour in respect of the death of British Army men in peace time for the past twenty years and, in view of the sharp practice generally of the Irish Times in the way they have handled this matter, the Minister has decided that we should prohibit the heading Roll of Honour altogether including the 1914–18 period, and also the heading Killed on Active Service with His Britannic Majesty's Forces as well as all similar headings and any special segregation of announcements relating to persons who have served in any of the British armed forces. In other words, the present practice must cease altogether lock, stock and barrel and any future announcements must be inserted in the ordinary death notices and in memoriam column in alphabetical order.[47]

The order was served on the paper by telephone and delivered in writing two days later. Its 'Court and Personal' column, which reported the goings on in high society under the royal coat of arms, also came in for scrutiny. As early as December 1939 Joseph Connolly had described the column as 'an irritant provocative to many in the state' and 'an absurd anachronism'. He was careful to stress that it appeared that 'such items are paid for at special advertisement rates and that by interfering with this column we may not only be offending the sensibilities of these readers "who dearly love a Lord" but be cutting off a source of advertising revenue from the paper concerned'.[48] After much discussion between Aiken and Connolly – during which the latter contended that the column 'merges the State and its personnel in a subordinate way with the British Court as though the State were part of the life and government of Britain' – the censor finally took action.[49] In March 1942 the paper was served with an order that prohibited it from printing the emblem of the royal coat of arms, the heading 'Court and Personal' and reports of 'the social or other activities of other foreign citizens, not ordinarily resident in Ireland'.[50] From then on the column listed the activities of Irish people only, and when the censor's restrictions were lifted in May 1945, the goings on of titled people in Britain returned, though this time under the heading 'Social and Personal'. The royal coats of arms emblem was never used again.

RELATIONS DETERIORATE

As the war progressed, relations between the paper and the censor worsened. In April 1941 it published an editorial critical of the defence of Athens, which was about to fall to German-Italian forces. Noting that 'Enough forces were withdrawn from North Africa to weaken the British chances of resisting the German onrush; yet not enough have been withdrawn to stay the assault upon Greece', it declared that the British military command had been 'caught napping'.[51] This prompted the assistant controller of censorship, Thomas Coyne, to reprimand Smyllie by declaring that 'the worse the British fortunes fare in this war the more we in the censorship feel they are entitled to the charity of our silence'. The same principle applied to the other side: the censor was 'just as much concerned to respect the feelings of the Germans and to ensure that in their case too the ebb and flow of the fortunes of war are not used as a peg on which to hang unfriendly comment'.[52] In June the paper published a review of a book called *Offensive against Germany,* which was 'an eloquent plea for a stronger British policy through which she could take the leadership of the democratic world'. Such a policy would involve 'stronger action against France, Spain, even against Ireland'. The reviewer replicated the author's view that 'in the modern world there is not, and there cannot be, such a thing as a neutral. "He that is not with us is against us" – and must abide by the consequences.'[53] This jab at neutrality was viewed as 'highly objectionable' by Joseph Connolly who wrote to the secretary to the government, to enquire whether de Valera would support the censor if strict measures were taken against the paper:

> I would propose that I should write Smyllie giving him a definite warning that if he persists in this type of conduct there will be no course left to us but to make him submit all his material. I do not want to do this unless I feel certain that in the event of such Order being passed on the Irish Times we here will be supported in our action. I would be glad if you could have a word with An Taoiseach and ascertain his views as soon as possible. Personally, I think the review headed 'Britain and the Neutrals' highly offensive and we

have already prohibited publication of much less objectionable books submitted by other papers.[54]

The final straw came in August 1941 when the paper supported the British–Soviet invasion of Iran by noting that 'It was inevitable that some belligerent would seize control of Iran sooner or later; for, both commercially and strategically, the country is of the highest importance'.[55] The parallels with Ireland, as a strategic location for the protection of shipping conveys, were obvious. Frank Aiken viewed the editorial as 'most objectionable' and issued a instruction that the paper be ordered to submit all leading articles and editorial matter for censorship. He also told the assistant controller of censorship, Thomas Coyne, to be 'as "sticky" as possible with the Irish Times stuff in future … even if it meant cutting their leading articles, including the captions, to ribbons'.[56] A few days later, the censor deleted a comment that Japan was possibly bluffing with its threat to sink American ships carrying supplies to the Soviet Union. This prompted an irate Alec Newman to remonstrate with Coyne. 'Evidently', he wrote, 'we are in danger of invasion by Japan, and evidently bluffing forms no element in the diplomatic technique.'[57] In response, Coyle described the Iran editorial as 'humiliating and contemptible' and declared that 'the war is indivisible and that the Battle of Britain is being fought at the moment by the Russians at Velikiye and elsewhere'. So far as possible, the censor was determined to prevent 'newspapers transferring the fight to our doorstep'.[58]

A short time later, Joseph Connolly retired as controller of censorship and was succeeded by Coyne. This change in personnel resulted in two of the paper's editorials being stopped. The first stated that the paper was not sorry to see Connolly go, that journalists were 'just as patriotic as any civil servants' and that since they were independent of all parties, they could be 'trusted to defend the national interests at least as stoutly as any politician'. When this was spiked, the paper took a different approach. As the censor put it, 'the Editor sneeringly wrote that they were sorry to learn that Mr Connolly was retiring from his post in Dublin Castle'. The editorial declared that 'Our newspapers have become so neutral that we defy any foreigner to discover what their policy is; and for this notable achievement full credit must be given to Mr Connolly and his team of devoted adjutants'. This editorial too was stopped.[59] One of Coyne's first tasks was to try to persuade Smyllie to stop printing troublesome book reviews. While Coyne conceded that the reviews themselves were inoffensive, he thought it 'wrong that anti-German or anti-Italian publications should be noticed at all, even for the purpose of condemning them'.[60] In his reply, Smyllie pulled no punches:

> This newspaper is, and must continue to be, pro-British. Apparently the Censorship is determined that it shall be as pusillanimous as its contemporaries, except of course, The Standard, which is steeped in anglophobia. In these circumstances, you would be the first to despise me if I should knuckle under to a Censorship for which I have no respect. I suppose that we shall have to submit all our proofs; but I would be dishonest, and unfair to you personally, if I should pretend to be willing to co-operate actively in the suppression of views that are shared by the readers of the Irish Times, to whom, having disposed my conscience – and, curiously enough, I still have one – my first duty is owed. I believe that the people of this country have a right to free thought. I believe that it is part of my job to encourage them in the exercise of that right. Evidently, it is your job to stop me, and you have the power. So there it is.[61]

Smyllie continued to publish book reviews without submission to the censor and in October 1941 the paper was ordered to submit its book page in full.[62] But as 1941 ended, Smyllie pulled off yet another deception by circumventing the ban on any mention of Irish people serving in the British forces. In mid-December a former staff member, John A. Robinson, who had joined the British navy, sent a cable to the paper announcing his survival after a torpedo sunk his ship. Smyllie immediately published a photograph of Robinson announcing that 'The many friends in Dublin of Mr John A. Robinson, who was involved in a recent boating accident, will be pleased to hear that he is alive and well … He is a particularly good swimmer, and it is possible that he owes his life to this accomplishment.'[63] When the double meaning of the caption became known to the censor, Smyllie was warned that if he attempted such a trick again the paper would be ordered to submit in full for censorship before publication.[64] The story about Smyllie's manoeuvre travelled far and wide over the following months, as evidenced by the censor's exasperation:

> Your jeu d'esprit about 'The Boating Accident' to the *Prince of Wales* in which your pal Robinson was involved is still going round the world to the tune of a hymn of hate against this country and is doing us (not the censorship but the old country which we both love so well, etc. etc. greatness and dignity and peace again) a hell of a lot of harm. Hardly a day passes without a variation of the theme being obtruded on my notice from some obscure corner of the globe.[65]

'AT DAGGERS DRAWN'

Throughout 1942 a shortage of newsprint resulted in the size of the paper fluctuating between four to six pages during the week and six to eight pages on Saturdays. Despite this reduction in size relations with the censor deteriorated rapidly. In May the paper submitted its 'Birth, Marriages and Deaths' column to the censor's office which, on Aiken's instructions, changed the names of Maryborough, Queen's County and Kingstown, Co. Dublin to Portlaoighise,

Co. Laoighise and Dun Laoghaire, Co. Dublin. When Smyllie telephoned to complain, he was informed by the chief press censor, Michael Knightly, that the paper's 'insistence on repudiating the legal names was subversive'.[66] This provoked Smyllie to write to Coyne to ask whether 'political censorship acting under the aegis of the Gaelic League' now existed. To submit newspapers to 'such ignorant tyranny' was 'a crime against common decency as well as against common sense'.[67] Smyllie did not have a high opinion of the censorship staff: he referred to one staff member as 'the poor cawbogue who sees in his blue pencil his only title to literacy', to another as a 'moronic clodhopper', and to Coyne's subordinates as 'troglodytic myrmidons'.[68]

The latter part of 1942 was not much better. In October the paper's use of inverted commas around the word 'Axis' became an issue. In his defence of the practice Smyllie pointed out that for nearly four years the paper 'in common with other literate, or semi-literate, newspapers has put the word "Axis" in inverted commas' because the word was 'an entirely bastard word, particularly when used as an adjective'. The use of inverted commas had, he contended, 'no kind of political significance'.[69] However, Coyne believed that Smyllie was 'trying this Axis business on' and that there existed a material difference when the word was 'printed with or without inverted commas and the difference is a political and not a grammatical one'. The use of inverted commas was, he concluded, 'bad from the point of view of the interests of the State', and he demanded that the paper adopt 'an objective rather than a subjective approach to the question of foreign politics in a time of special danger to the state'.[70] Throughout the third week of November the paper continually highlighted the fact that Lady Montgomery, 'mother of General Montgomery, Commander of the British Eight Army in the Middle East', was visiting Ireland. In a letter to Smyllie, Coyne accused him of 'cynical indecency' and noted that she had been coming to Dublin for fifty odd years without any mention in the paper. The reports were, according to Coyne, 'an unwarranted intrusion into the private life of an old lady for the gratification of the degenerate appetites of your West British readers'.[71]

In December the paper submitted a report of the inaugural meeting of the Literary and Philosophical Society, University College, Cork, at which a speech on censorship was delivered. Three-quarters of the report was devoted to the remarks of Smyllie in which he described the censorship regime as a 'Frank Aikenstein Monster'.[72] Needless to say, the censor excised the remark. The very final straw came shortly afterwards when the censor took exception to the publication of three items that had not been submitted for clearance. On 21 December the paper published, under the heading 'Service to Empire', a report on a speech day at a school in Northern Ireland, and under the heading 'King's

Broadcast', a reminder of the monarch's Christmas Day broadcast. The following day it published, under the heading 'We are Turning the Corner', remarks on the war made by the British home secretary, Hubert Morrison. When questioned about the non-submission of these articles, Smyllie replied that he saw no reason why Morrison's statement should have been submitted. He asserted that if it had been made by Dr Goebbels 'there would have been no question either of submission, or of complaint on the censorship's part'. The announcement of the king's broadcast 'was a simple statement of fact, without any kind of political implication', and the report of speech day at Portora Royal School was 'an unbiased report of a function outside the jurisdiction of Éire' that again involved no political issue.[73] Aiken subsequently directed that the paper be ordered to submit all material in duplicate proof form before publication.[74] This order was served on the paper on 29 December 1942 and lasted for the duration of the war.

In January 1943 Smyllie and the censor again came to loggerheads after the paper submitted an innocuous review of a book entitled *Worralls Carry On* by W.E. Johns. The book dealt with the adventures of two female members of the Women's Auxiliary Air Force in England and France and was described as 'youthful stuff, full of most thrilling and impossible adventures of two WAAFs, both in England and France' but was stopped by the censor. Surprised at the decision to suppress so innocuous a review, Smyllie re-titled the book *Trudel Carries On* by Hans Lubbe and re-wrote the review as a book dealing with 'the most thrilling and impossible adventures of two Luftwaffe auxiliaries, both in Germany and in France'.[75] One week later he re-submitted this version of the review. When this version was passed for publication, Smyllie wrote to Coyne to declare that the episode demonstrated that 'the censorship in its workings is utterly one sided, and, if not actively pro-German, at least is definitely anti-British'.[76] In his internal review of the incident Coyne claimed that the censorship had adopted a policy of stopping stories relating to particular services and thus the first review was stopped. In the case of the second review the 'forgery was included in a batch of innocuous proofs dealt with while the Chief Press Censor was engaged on more important matter and was inadvertently passed'.[77] In a letter to Smyllie, Coyne accused him of having set a trap for the censor. He also criticised the paper's habit of re-submitting material that had already been stopped, and threatened Smyllie with the prospect of having to submit page proofs or indeed the paper in full printed form for clearance in the future:

> the practice of re-submitting over and over again (in one instance at least six times) matter which has already been censored without notifying the censors that this is the case, in an

attempt to get one censor to pass what another has rejected or vice versa, causes so much needless inconvenience and is such a waste of public money that I am obliged to do something about it. I have, therefore, asked the Press Censor to consider requiring you to submit page proofs of your paper in future and, if necessary, the complete issue and to refuse to deal with matter piecemeal as heretofore.

Coyne advised Smyllie to 'say as little as possible about this affair' to avoid prosecution under the Emergency Powers Act.[78] Smyllie rejected the accusation of deliberate re-submission of material and added that, since the proposal to force the paper to submit either page proofs or the complete issue for clearance would amount to suppression, he would welcome 'a clear statement of our alleged breaches of the law'.[79] In a follow-up letter he rejected Coyne's accusation of having set a trap as 'just a damned lie' but admitted that he had acted with 'malice prepense [premeditated malice], mainly because the banning of the notice was so abysmally stupid'. Coyne's threat to 'close down the Irish Times' was, he continued, 'sheer vindictiveness, and petulant and perverse vindictiveness at that'; the paper had been 'humiliated by the ineptitude and bias of the Censorship times without number'. The depth of Smyllie's frustration can be gauged from his challenge to Coyne:

> I feel passionately on this subject. I feel deeply ashamed that my own country should be playing, via the Censorship, the part of national poltroon. I feel sick at heart that I should be forced to connive at such pettiness as the banning of the WAAF paragraph ... And all at a time when grand men are getting killed for something in which they and I – and for that matter yourself – believe with passion. I am not a bit ashamed of it. I should be ashamed if I felt otherwise; and I am glad to think sometimes that when all this filthy business is over, I at least will be able to walk through the streets with my head up, even if you do put me into gaol, fine me whatever you can extract from a harassed bank-manager and/or put me and my colleagues of the Irish Times on the bread line. And I mean that, as I never have meant anything before.[80]

In the heel of the hunt, Coyne blinked first. He accepted Smyllie's denial about the deliberate re-submission of material, and the censor's files record that a 'return of letters was agreed on and the matter was regarded as at an end' with Smyllie 'undertaking not to make any public use of the matter'. The files also indicate, however, that the story appeared in an unnamed English daily newspaper and that the censor expressed concern about the story being told in Dublin social circles.[81]

In February 1944 the censor prevented the paper from reporting that a number of shops on Dublin's Grafton Street were 'daubed with two-foot squares of yellow paint and the word "Jews" written across them'. Neither was it allowed to mention that the windows of the same shops had later been littered with adhesive stickers 'upon which the words "Perish Judah" had been printed with a rubber stamp'.[82] But despite its battles with the censor the paper vigorously defended the government the following month. In preparation for the D-Day landings, American troops arrived in Northern Ireland and the US government requested that de Valera expel the German and Japanese representatives from Dublin. His refusal to do so was supported by the paper. Noting that the war was 'being fought, inter alia, for the maintenance of the right of small nations to live their own lives in their own way' it deplored the actions of the US towards a state which, 'while neutral, has done so much since the outbreak of war to demonstrate its attitude of good neighbourliness towards the sister island'. While it could not pretend that 'the section of the Irish people whom we claim to represent is wholly indifferent to the outcome of the war', it could say with 'complete sincerity that it is wholeheartedly loyal to its own Government'.[83]

A little over a month later, however, Frank Aiken declared that the government was 'at daggers drawn' with the paper. The paper, he claimed, had 'a different outlook from the outlook of the vast majority of the Irish people on many things'. This had become manifest in 'the completely insulting manner' whereby when mentioning the president, Douglas Hyde, in reports, the paper failed to follow protocol by putting his name first. As Aiken put it, Hyde 'sometimes came after every hyphenated person in the country'. Citing an example, Aiken observed that Hyde was 'at the bottom of the list in the social and personal column' and that the only precedence he received was 'over an advertisement for corsets in one of the down-town shops'.[84] In its response the paper expressed the hope that its outlook differed 'not only in many things, but in all things' from that of Aiken. It described the insult to which Aiken had referred as 'purely accidental – a mistake such as happens in every newspaper office every night of the week'. Aiken's comments had, it contended, 'revealed in all its ugly starkness the condition of affairs that unhappily exists between the Censorship and the *Irish Times*'. The paper also let it be know that it was the only newspaper that was 'requested to submit to the Censorship every line of matter that appears in its columns, from the leading articles down to the humblest small advertisement'.[85]

The latter part of 1944 saw the censor and the paper clash several times. In September it submitted a photograph of the pope with the caption 'Pope Pius XII' which the censor altered to 'The Pope'. Intrigued, the paper enquired why it was more neutral to use 'The Pope' than 'Pope Pius XII'. In a reply the censor noted that there was only one pope. Could, the censor asked, the paper imagine the walls of Portadown being painted with the slogan 'To Hell with Pope Pius XII' or the Orangemen's historic war cry being altered to 'No Pope Pius XII. No Surrender'?[86] In October an editorial submitted for clearance was censored but the published article did not correspond with what had been submitted. As a result, the paper was ordered to submit page proofs in future. This would have delayed it going to press, especially if changes needed to be made. The explanation offered by the paper was that the editorial had been sent to the censor without the editor's amendments and that these were added inadvertently when the proof arrived back from the censor. The explanation was accepted and the direction to submit page proofs was withdrawn.[87]

In November, the censor deleted from an editorial its contention that 'Ireland's neutrality and consequent psychological isolation from the rest of the world during five years of war has resulted in a certain amount of intellectual and spiritual inbreeding'.[88] Also that month an editorial about the assassination of Lord Moyne (Walter E. Guinness, the resident minister of state or colonial governor) in Cairo was submitted for censorship and passed for publication subject to the deletion of material commenting on the position of Arabs and Jews in Egypt. The following day, however, the paper appeared without any editorial, creating the impression that it had been, in the censor's words, 'prevented from publishing a leader on the important and sensational news of the previous day by the action of the censorship'. General news filled the space where the editorial should have been, but the absence of an editorial prompted enquires from the Associated Press correspondent in Dublin, who contacted both the censor's office and the paper to find out what had happened. Apparently, Smyllie took exception to the censor cutting the comments on the position of Arabs and Jews in Egypt and so decided not to publish the editorial at all. The controller of censorship, Thomas Coyne, sought an assurance from him that this would not happen again. In his reply Smyllie gave such an assurance and acknowledged that 'the deletions, stupid and senseless as they were, did not in any way interfere with our condemnation of the Cairo murder'. But, as if to remind Coyne of the power of the press, he asserted that the censorship's 'unreasonable and unreasoning attitude towards this newspaper's leading articles invited and always must invite such misinterpretations'.[89]

VENTING ANGER

When the war in Europe ended in May 1945, the days of the censorship were numbered. In an editorial entitled 'Curtain' the paper starkly declared: 'Adolf Hitler is dead. This tremendous news was broadcast from Germany last night, and transcends everything else in importance.'[90] The following day it reported de Valera's visit to the German minister to express his condolences on Hitler's death and reported that the 'Legation had received many messages of sympathy

and there had been a large number of callers'.[91] However, the censor prohibited
it from reporting that the flag at Government Buildings was not flown at half-
mast – as had been the case when President Roosevelt had died in mid-April.[92]
The paper was later critical of de Valera's actions, noting that the 'official call
to console with the German Minister on the death of Adolf Hitler was
diplomatically "correct", just as from the broader point of view of Ireland's
relations with the victorious Powers, it was a first-class blunder'. There were
times, it observed, 'in the affairs of men when even Protocol is not infallible'.[93]

On Victory in Europe Day Smyllie had the last laugh on the censor. All the
paper's proofs were sent as usual to the censor for clearance. The material
included an unusually high number of single-column photographs of the Allied
war leaders. Before the paper went to press however, Smyllie rearranged the
front page so that, under the headline 'Peace Today in Europe', the single-
column photographs formed the shape of a page-size 'V' for victory. Starting on
the top left hand corner of the page the photographs of King George VI,
General Eisenhower, Field-Marshal Alexander, Marshal Stalin, Field-Marshal
Montgomery, Prime Minister Churchill, and the late President Roosevelt spread
down to the bottom of the page and back up to the right hand corner.[94] Four
days later, when the censorship regulations were abolished, it began its 'They
Can be Published Now' series of photographs that had been banned during the
war. The first picture was that of air raid damage in London. A later one was
that of P.J. Little, the minister for posts and telegraphs, skating on the ice in
Herbert Park during the spring of 1943 when a freeze had hit the city. That
photograph had been banned because of the censor's fear that it would
communicate meteorological information to the warring parties. But, of course,
with no censor to interfere with his editorials, Smyllie was now free to vent his
anger publicly at the system that he had raged privately against for so long.
Describing the censorship regime as 'draconian and irrational as anything that
was devised in the fertile brain of the late Josef Goebbels', his editorial outlined
the paper's treatment at the hands of the censor:

> This newspaper was singled out for particular attention. Its views already were well known.
> For years before the war we had made no secret of our hatred and contempt for the foul
> growths of Fascism and National Socialism that were stifling all freedom of thought and
> decency of living in the countries of their origin ... We respected, and acquiesced in, the
> Irish Government's policy of neutrality. Nevertheless, our sympathies from the start were
> with the opponents of tyranny and injustice; and our fervent prayer for long years of
> mental torture was that, in the fullness of time, God, in His goodness, would give final
> victory to Allied arms. Throughout those horrifying years, the *Irish Times* was forbidden
> to express, or even to hint at, its convictions. The censorship had plenary powers which it
> always was ready to employ ... It is difficult – indeed, it is impossible – to write with
> moderation about the treatment which this newspaper has received from the censorship

during recent years. Alone among the Dublin dailies, we have been compelled to submit to the autocrats of Dublin Castle every line that we proposed to print, from the leading article down to the humblest prepaid advertisement. We always were careful to say nothing that might prejudice either the Government's policy of neutrality or the maintenance of public order; yet it was seldom, indeed, that our leading articles were not hacked and mutilated in such a way as to make them almost meaningless.[95]

Following the ending of censorship, Frank Aiken, whom Smyllie described as having 'smelt treason and conspiracy against the state in every sentence', invited the editors of the major newspapers to a celebratory dinner.[96] As remembered by Todd Andrews, Smyllie was 'the "clou" of the party. All the schemes devised to defeat the censorship were revealed and all the counter ploys recounted. Smyllie was hilarious, and the evening was hilarious, too. Frank smiled benignly on the proceedings'.[97] The lifting of censorship also meant that Irish readers could now be informed of the horrors of the Nazi concentration camps. Such information had been suppressed during the war, and in its immediate aftermath some people dismissed the evidence of the camps as British propaganda. This prompted one reader to write to the paper to express her horror at 'how much the general public here doubt the truth of the articles and photographs which have been published in all the leading British newspapers about the atrocities committed by the Germans in concentration camps in Europe'. She suggested that a party of representatives from the Dáil, the army, trade unions, local government and all religions be sent to Europe to verify the existence of the concentration camps.[98] Another reader replied that such was the 'monumental and immovable ignorance' of the facts that 'The average Dubliner would not be persuaded even though all the ghosts of Hitler's victims were to rise from the dead; he would only pour himself out another drink, muttering "British propaganda".'[99] For the record, it is only fair to point out that even Smyllie himself had some difficulty believing the revelations about the horrors perpetrated in the camps. Having heard details during the war, Smyllie had remained sceptical because of his own experiences of living in a German camp during the previous war. He only fully believed the details after having had a conversation with the BBC war correspondent Denis Johnson:

For some time past I have been bothered in my mind regarding the behaviour of the Nazis to their victims in their concentration camps. Newspaper men are not easily impressed by propaganda: and I must confess candidly that I took a lot of the talk about the German camps with a grain of salt. During the last war I had been in one or two of the worst P.O.W. camps and found when I got back to England that conditions had been grossly exaggerated ... But, now that I have heard the facts from Denis Johnson I am afraid that I no longer am sceptical ... I shall spare my readers the ghastly details which horrified me; but having heard Johnson's first-hand evidence, I have been forced reluctantly to the conclusion that the men who were responsible for the camps in Germany must have been sadists of the most depraved type.[1]

Despite its harsh criticism of the censorship regime the paper leapt to de Valera's defence when, in his victory speech, Winston Churchill stated that Irish neutrality had done nothing but allow 'the de Valera Government to frolic with the Germans and later with the Japanese to their heart's content'. It described Churchill's remarks as 'to say the least of it, a slight over-statement' and pointed out that 'everybody, including Mr Winston Churchill, knows perfectly well that, taken by and large, Ireland's neutrality was wholly benevolent in respect of the United Nations ... The representatives of the Axis Powers in Dublin might as well have been in an internment camp; and we have a shrewd idea that this fact is not unsuspected in London and Washington.'[2] Indeed, in a front-page article some months later, Churchill's son Randolph, confirmed as much when he declared that de Valera's government had 'consistently followed a policy of being as friendly and helpful to the Allies as was possible whilst remaining neutral'; he claimed that the Irish government had confiscated the German Legation's wireless transmitter at the behest of the allies; had interned German aircrew who crash landed but had allowed British and American airmen to cross the border; had allowed the British military to station tug-boats in Irish ports to rescue merchant ships attacked by U-boats; and had passed on to the British all information derived from the interrogation of captured German agents. Churchill made these revelations 'in no desire to make propaganda for de Valera, but only so as that the true facts of the matter be known'.[3] When, in the Dáil, deputy Oliver J. Flanagan questioned de Valera on the veracity of the article, he did not substantially contradict it.[4] When de Valera made his reply in which he asked Churchill senior to 'find in his heart the generosity to acknowledge that there is a small nation that stood alone, not for one year or two, but for several hundred years, against aggression', the paper applauded his dignified response; while he had 'his faults as a statesman and as a politician ... his broadcast on Wednesday night was a model of good manners'. Still, he was 'cursed, or blessed, with a metaphysical mind and the recent war blew metaphysics, as it blew so many other things, sky-high'. One result of this metaphysical outlook was Ireland's ambiguous international position; as the paper noted, 'Éire is neither a Republic nor a Dominion of the British Commonwealth.'[5] By the end of the decade, however, the question of commonwealth membership was to be settled definitively.

CHAPTER 6

Challenging Times

The *Irish Times* is a relic of the Anglo-Irish ascendancy and while it is the most readable, most provocative and best published paper, its pro-British tone and editorials have the effect of giving the paper the authority of the kiss of death to any Irish politician whom the Victorian editor Smyllie takes to his huge bosom.[1]

US embassy review of the Irish Times

THE WAR WAS A TIME of considerable strain for Smyllie. The constant shortage of newsprint and his running battles with the censor took a toll on his health. So too did the changes at board level. In July 1940 Sir John Arnott died and was succeeded as chairman by his brother Loftus Arnott. Sir John's son, Sir Lauriston Arnott, became managing director. In January 1941 a prominent Dublin businessman, Frank A. Lowe, was co-opted onto the board 'to bring in new ideas and energy', and in 1945 Lowe became chairman.[2] According to one account, Lowe's arrival was prompted by dissatisfaction among preference shareholders, who, unhappy at the non-payment of dividends, successfully lobbied to have him put on the board as their representative.[3] Steeped in the tradition of the Protestant work ethic, Lowe was, as one reporter put it, 'purely a businessman ... the Arnotts had to bring him in with his money.'[4] Lowe began his career as an apprentice in Hely's Ltd, a prominent Dublin printing firm. He rose up the ranks to become a director and then chairman of the company. With a brief to modernise the *Irish Times*, Lowe was, as his nephew George Hetherington recalled, shocked at the mess he found:

Uncle Frank was utterly astonished at some of the things he found. For example, almost everybody on the paper either ran a loan account or a debit account. Either they were owed money by the company, and that was very few of them, or they owed money to the company. Then there were people who lived in the *Irish Times*, spend their entire days there, looking up the files, writing copy which they sold to other newspapers, people who weren't on the staff, didn't appear on any list, were never paid, but simply lived in the *Irish*

Times. People said Uncle Frank was a hatchet-man, but it wasn't a hatchet that was needed, it was a bulldozer, or possibly an atomic bomb. The first thing that he had to do was to start to clear up all that mess.[5]

Coming from the conventional business world, Lowe was perplexed at the system of duel control that prevailed in the paper, where the commercial and editorial departments worked independently of each other. As one reporter put it, 'Smyllie and Newman were editors as editors, they weren't involved in the business side of things, in fact it was totally foreign to them. News was what mattered, opinion was what mattered, readership was what mattered but the business end of it – not at all.'[6] The arrival of Lowe marked the beginning of the end of control by the Arnott family – a point not lost on Smyllie, who observed, 'Blow-ins and bloody grocers are trying to take over and run the paper'. As Lowe set about his reforms, editorial conferences were held to discuss the design and content of the paper. Smyllie reluctantly attended these conferences and 'made no attempt to conceal his frigid attitude but sat in aloof and disdainful silence surrounded by his close colleagues'.[7] But there were some innovations. The paper underwent a re-design, and on Monday 21 April 1941 the new look *Irish Times* made its debut. News items, as opposed to advertisements, now dominated the front page, and the sports pages were moved to the front of the paper where they remained until the 1980s. Another innovation was the 'Crosaire' cryptic crossword puzzle that first appeared in March 1943. At the previous year's Christmas Eve party, Derek Crozier, a Guinness employee, mentioned to a reporter that he had the unusual hobby of making up crosswords. By the end of the evening, having been introduced to Smyllie, Crozier had agreed to send in samples of his word. On 13 March 1943 the paper printed its first crossword – the 'Crosaire' cryptic puzzle that has appeared in every subsequent Saturday edition. The inspiration for the name of the puzzle came from the then common road signs bearing the Irish word 'crosaire' meaning crossroads.[8]

The post-war period saw significant changes in industrial relations and personnel at the paper. In January 1947 the NUJ and the various newspaper proprietors reached, for the first time, agreement on terms and conditions for journalists. These included: minimum wages for senior and junior staff; a working week of five and a half days totalling forty-four hours; three weeks paid holidays per year; and a day in lieu of each bank holiday worked.[9] Prior to this, Smyllie had fought a rearguard action with the Dublin branch of the NUJ and its campaign for a union rate. When complaints of underpayment were made to him, he inevitably countered them with the announcement, 'It is a privilege, gentlemen, to be on the staff of a literate newspaper.'[10] Indeed, newspaper managements had initially mounted a serious attempt to block the introduction of an eight-hour day in the belief that newspapers could not function on such a system. According to one reporter, 'the Independent and the Press fought very hard' to prevent the eight-hour day being introduced; they were concerned about whether a reporter would, 'when his time was up at four o'clock, walk out of a court and demand that another reporter take his place'. Before this innovation, reporters usually worked from 10 a.m. to 4 p.m., had a gap of two to three hours, and then spent another few hours covering an evening assignment. It was these working hours, particularly the gap between shifts, that fed the drink culture in Dublin newspaper circles at the time. There was, as the reporter recalled, 'simply nothing else to do'.[11]

There was also a shake-up in personnel. Alec Newman was firmly installed as Smyllie's deputy and took on more and more responsibility as Smyllie's health began to fade. Alan Montgomery became chief reporter (as the post of news editor was then known), and G.J.C. Tynan 'Pussy' O'Mahony became general manager. The ranks of reporters were swelled by the arrival of new graduates such as Jack White, who joined as a leader writer and then transferred to the London office to take over the 'London Letter', and Bruce Williamson, who replaced White as a leader writer and went on to become literary editor during the 1940s and 1950s. Another new arrival was Michael McInerney, who joined the paper as a reporter in 1946 having spent many years editing the *Irish Front* (the journal of the Connolly Association) and *Unity* (the paper of the Communist Party). McInerney was appointed industrial correspondent in 1951 and political correspondent in 1953, a post he held until his retirement in 1974. He was prominently involved in the NUJ; as well as organising the *Irish Times* chapel, he was at various times, general organiser, president and member of the national executive of the Irish branch of the union.[12] Other notables on the staff around this time were Patrick Campbell, the first 'Quidnunc' of 'An Irishman's Diary'; Brian Inglis, who rejoined the paper having left to join the RAF during the war and who succeeded Campbell as 'Quidnunc'; and Seamus Kelly who succeeded Brinsley McNamara as the paper's theatre critic and became a long-time writer of 'An Irishman's Diary'. In 1954, Kelly took a seven-month sabbatical to play the part of 'Flask', the third mate in John Huston's film *Moby Dick*.[13] Also on the staff were Paul MacWeeney, the paper's long-time sports editor; Gerry Mulvey who later become news editor and Cathal O'Shannon, who joined as a reporter. There were also several female reporters including June Levine, who wrote the social and personal column, and Barbara Dickson, who wrote the occasional 'An Irishwoman's Diary' under the pen-name 'Candida'. It was around this time too, May 1947 to be precise, that Brian Inglis claimed the distinction of being the first reporter in the paper's history to have his name placed above one of his reports. As the writer of 'An Irishman's Diary' Inglis was assigned to join the crew of the *Muirchu* (formally the *Helga* – the British navy ship used to shell O'Connell Street during the 1916 rising) on its final voyage from Cork to Dublin where she was to be scrapped. Off the Waterford coast, however, the old ship sprang a leak and sank. The first reports that reached the paper was that the ship had gone down with all hands, and Inglis' colleagues were plunged into mourning. In fact the crew had been picked up by a passing trawler and taken to Wales. When this news reached the paper, the mourning turned into celebrations, and the story that Inglis phoned through from Wales appeared on page one under the headline 'Muirchu Lost on Her Way to the Scrap-Heap' with his by-line attached.[14] In his autobiography, Inglis claimed that this was the first such by-line in the paper's history.[15]

MYLES NA gCOPALEEN

During the war Smyllie placed considerable emphasis on his 'Books of the Week' page, which also carried a new poem by an Irish poet every week. Such was the high standard of the poetry that he commissioned Donagh MacDonagh to compile an anthology of the best poems published in the column. The anthology, *Poems from Ireland*, was published in 1944 and featured poems from Patrick Kavanagh, Austin Clarke, Padraic Fallon and W.B. Yeats. In the post-war period, this emphasis on literature continued under literary editor Bruce Williamson, with the paper devoting more space to book reviews than any of its competitors. As one reviewer put it, 'the literary profession most quickly appreciated what it was doing; the Saturday Books Page of the *Irish Times* is now the only real focus for Dublin writers'.[16] The most successful of Smyllie's literary additions to the paper came in the guise of the columnist Myles na gCopaleen, better known as the novelist Flann O'Brien, or in his nine-to-five civil service career, Brian O'Nolan. Under the pseudonym Flann O'Brien, O'Nolan had succeeded in getting his first novel, *At Swim-Two-Birds*, published in 1939, but most of the stock was lost when the London warehouse in which it was stored was destroyed during the blitz. It had been often suggested to Smyllie that the paper should carry a column in Irish, but Smyllie had just as often rejected the idea – not from hostility to the language but from his objection to its compulsory teaching in schools. Despite such misgivings, he eventually consented to a column in Irish written by O'Nolan simply because their philosophy on the language was the same – that it stood a better chance of survival if it were not rammed down people's throats. In early 1940, before he began writing for the paper, Myles na gCopaleen had addressed a letter to 'Quidnunc', the author of 'An Irishman's Diary', on the subject of people who made a fuss about being able to speak the language:

> It is common knowledge that certain categories of Irish speakers are boors. They (being men) have nuns' faces, wear bicycle clips continuously, talk in Irish only about *ceist na teanga* and have undue confidence in Irish dancing as a general national prophylactic ... Hence some self-consciously intellectual citizens are anxious to avoid being suspected of knowing Irish, owing to the danger of being lumped with the boors.[17]

Given the paper's history, Smyllie was also reluctant to open the paper to criticism from Irish speakers that its Irish column was not up to scratch, a problem that was overcome by O'Nolan's status as a knowledgeable Gaelic scholar. Smyllie, unsurprisingly, was delighted with his find:

> I've been trying for years to run a column in Irish. But I always made one stipulation – that it must be above all criticism from the point of view of the language. Until Mr Myles na gCopaleen came along, all the Gaels had been refusing to admit that anyone knew anything about the language but themselves. But they're all agreed about Master Myles. He is the only issue on which Gaels of all types are unanimous. In that way I think he has done more that anyone else for the future of the Irish language. He is the only person, to my knowledge, who was ever funny in Gaelic. He is untranslatable. He has actually made people brush up their Irish who have forgotten it since they left school.[18]

Smyllie's discovery of O'Nolan came about by very unconventional means. O'Nolan's friend Niall Sheridan was already contributing racing tips to the paper, and in January 1939 they both instigated a controversy over the merits of a new play – *Time's Pocket* – by Frank O'Connor that had been greeted with less than critical acclaim by the paper's drama critic. When Seán O'Faoláin wrote to the paper to defend the play, O'Nolan took his cue. Writing under the pseudonym Flann O'Brien, he gleefully proclaimed that 'What Mr O'Faoláin wants is a sound spanking – that, or five minutes with Mr Sears [a drama critic] or myself behind the fives court'.[19] This prompted O'Faoláin to advise 'the man in the Gaelic Mask to note that, when ever he feels inclined to address his spleen to me, if he would breathe through his nose, it would keep his mouth shut'.[20] O'Connor also wrote a letter in which he asked Smyllie whether or not Flann O'Brien was a real person, and if not, was the person behind the letter known to Smyllie, O'Faoláin and O'Connor himself. He also asked how long had 'the publication of violent personal abuse and challenges to fisticuffs been part of the duty of a responsible editor.' The answers to these questions would, he concluded, allow readers 'to rest secure as to the absolute detachment of the *Irish Times* and its freedom from the methods of literary gangsters and hooligans'. Smyllie's response confirmed that he knew the identity of the letter writer but that he not could say whether O'Faoláin or O'Connor knew the person.[21] O'Connor's letter was only fuel to O'Nolan's fire, and he immediately dispatched a letter from a pained 'Francis O'Connor', asking Smyllie whether he was aware that someone was writing letters 'all about artists and the Abbey Theatre' to the paper and signing his name to them. Declaring that he would 'never meddle in politics or any sort of argument', this Francis O'Connor announced he was 'becoming a laughing stock' among his family and friends on account of the letters.[22]

June 1940 saw another bout of letters from Flann O'Brien, Lir O'Connor and numerous other O'Nolan pseudonyms. This correspondence began when a reader wrote in expressing surprise at the low attendances at the Chekhov play, *The Three Sisters*, playing in the Gate Theatre.[23] The prompt for O'Nolan came when another reader, 'H.P.', suggested that Irish intellectuals had become 'so increasingly Gaelic and anti-foreign that possibly by now they have convinced themselves that Chekhov never existed'. The remedy was simple: 'less, much less, Gaelic and much less religion'; but, 'H.P.' concluded, anyone with 'the temerity to suggest this remedy in public would be howled down at once by patriots from every corner of the twenty-six counties'.[24] This longing for a more open artistic environment prompted a memory in Flann O'Brien, who generously recalled living in the cultural utopia of Manchester:

> Heigho for the golden days I spent as a youth in Manchester! In that civilised city we had Chekhov twice nightly in the music halls; the welkin rang all day long from non-stop open-air Hamlets in the city parks, and the suicide rates reached an all time high from the amount of Ibsen and Strindberg that was going on night and day in a thousand back-street repertory dives ... Nowhere in the world outside Sheffield could the mind glut itself on so much buckshee literary tuck.

There was, he concluded, little that he or 'H.P.' could do 'to stem the tide of Gaelic barbarism in Dublin'.[25] From there on, the correspondence descended into detailed name-dropping literary reminiscences and counter reminiscences between O'Nolan's alter-egos Flann O'Brien and Lir O'Connor.[26]

The following month O'Nolan turned his sights on Patrick Kavanagh. In 1935 the paper had published a series of his poems, and when Kavanagh relocated from Monaghan to Dublin, Smyllie commissioned him to write a series of five feature articles on rural Ireland that appeared in the latter half of 1939.[27] In July 1940 Kavanagh, in the course of a book review, criticised the boy-scout movement as 'civilisation at its lowest' and the jamboree as 'the academy of illiteracy'.[28] This prompted a round of letters from indignant readers questioning Kavanagh's literary criticism skills. One reader declared that the paper was not bought 'by guttersnipes or the type of individual who enjoys strolls through the sewers conducted by Mr Patrick Kavanagh and his ilk' and that readers 'with reasonably clean minds are growing weary of the cesspool-in-the-backyard style of writing'.[29] The following week the paper printed Kavanagh's poem, *Spraying the Potatoes,* and O'Nolan took his cue. Writing as Flann O'Brien, he suggested that the paper, which he described as the 'tireless champion of our peasantry', continue to oblige its readers 'with a series in this strain covering such rural complexities as inflamed goat-udders, warble-pocked shorthorn, contagious abortion, non-ovoid oviducts and nervous disorders among the gentlemen who pay the rent'.[30] A few days later, under the pseudonym Lir O'Connor, O'Nolan posed as a landlord whose farming tenants – 'a gaggle of earnest young men, whose bizarre attire, together with the heavy beards which they affected, immediately betrayed them as pals or butties of some literary bun-fighting faction or other' – had asked him to write to the paper to defend Kavanagh. But O'Connor had never heard of the poet, and, when he finally read some of his work, he was not impressed and so could not defend Kavanagh:

> ... Butterley, my librarian, and I have searched every shelf and combed every catalogue in quest of some of this Mr Kavanagh's work. I have skimmed through the 'Utility of the Horse' by Paul Kavanagh; 'What to do with your Pulsocaura' by Pietro Kavana; 'Yoga and Rheumatism' by Pav Ka Vanna; 'I Was Stalin's Chamber Maid' by Pamela Kay Vanagh, and a score of others by authors whose names approximate to that of the man whom I set out to vindicate ... Butterley has just drawn my attention to some lines, entitled, 'Spraying the Potatoes' which appeared in Saturday's issue of the *Irish Times*, purporting to issue from his nib (or should I say 'his nibs?'). This hardly could be said to help the case of Mr Kavanagh himself. The phrase 'potatoes', which recurs in his little burlesque, may be good Runyon, but, believe me, it is very poor Kavanagh, and smacks more of pool-room, crap game and pin table than does it of the Blackrock Literary Society. No, Mr Kavanagh, I am afraid you have no claim upon my patronage. Until, such a time, therefore, as you or some of your admirers can furnish me with convincing literary proof of your existence, I cannot in all conscience take up your case.[31]

Smyllie eventually asked Kavanagh to write a letter to bring closure to the topic, in which he dismissed the 'undergraduate-magazine writers who reached the heights of epic literature in a balloon filled with verbal gas'. The correspondence was, he thought, 'very adolescent, though at times faintly amusing'.[32] Smyllie thought the letters were hilarious, and through an intermediary – Niall Sheridan – arranged for O'Nolan to come to the Palace Bar for a meeting, at which he hired O'Nolan to write a satirical column in Irish for the paper. The column – 'Cruiskeen Lawn' (brimming jug) – first appeared on 4 October 1940 and continued intermittently, in Irish and then in English, with the odd sprinkling of Latin and Greek, for over twenty years. The first column took as its topic the contents of an editorial on the Irish language published a few days previously. It had questioned the use of Irish in the home and had concluded that 'Parents who confine the family mealtime discussions to conversations in Irish must find it very difficult to explain such words as air-raid warden, incendiary bomb, non-aggression pact, decontamination, and Molotoff bread-basket'.[33] O'Nolan's column was a parody of the editorial – an imaginary mealtime conversation between a mother and a son as they try in vain to construct an Irish equivalent of 'Molotoff bread-basket', with the son finally exclaiming in frustration, 'Why can't we speak English in this house?' This first column was signed 'An Broc' (the badger), a name assigned by Smyllie. By the time his second column appeared on 10 October, O'Nolan had adopted the pseudonym Myles na gCopaleen.[34]

The new column, which one reviewer described as 'flippant, far superior in style, execution, accuracy and idiom to anything of the sort in the other supposedly pro-Gaelic dailies', provoked a flurry of anonymous letters to the paper.[35] One condemned the 'skits on the Gaelic language' and accused the paper of 'spewing' on the language. Another charged it with 'following a set policy in an attempt to sabotage (as they say nowadays) the propagation of the language and things Irish'. Others however, were delighted with the column. One praised its 'mature humour and graceful diction'; another, the column's demonstration of the language's 'elasticity and adaptability'. Yet another pointed out that in all his years of reading Irish columns in other newspapers he could not remember 'having ever seen an article which called forth a single comment, be it praise or blame, from the readers'. That, he pointed out, 'should be a sufficient defence for your contributor – if indeed he needs any'. The sight of language enthusiasts disagreeing over a column in impeccable Irish gave Smyllie much pleasure. So too did the very nature of the column, which, alert to the subtleties of Dublin speech, was a mixture of satire, fantasy and puns. Through the use of literary devices such as the 'Plain People of Ireland', the 'Research Bureau', 'The Brother', 'Bores', the 'Catechism of Cliches' and the adventures of Keats and Chapman it poked fun at and assaulted the sacred cows of the Ireland of the 1940s and 1950s.[36] Myles often suggested solutions to problems that beset the country such as this ingenious solution to wartime shortages and rationing:

> We all go to bed for a week every month. Every single man, woman and child in the country. Cripples, drunks, policemen, watchmen – everybody. Nobody is allowed to be up. No newspapers, buses, pictures or any other class of amusement allowed at all. No matter who you are you must go to bed for a week. You see, when nobody is up you save clothes, shoes, rubber, petrol, coal, turf, timber and everything we're short of. And food, too, remember. What makes you hungry? It's work that makes you hungry. If nobody's up, there's no need for anybody to do any work. In a year you'd save a quarter of everything, and that would be enough to see us right.[37]

However, it was not all plain sailing. Given the satirical nature of the column and its high-profile targets, the issue of libel was ever present. In 1942 Myles poked fun at the Institute of Advanced Studies, the head of which, the physicist Erwin Schrodinger, gave a talk entitled 'Science and Humanism' in which he said there was no logical basis for the belief of a first cause or divine creator. Another luminary of the institute, the Celtic scholar, T.F. O'Rahilly, outlined his theory that there were two different Christian missionaries to Ireland – Palladius and Patrick – who had been confused historically as one figure, St Patrick. Summing up the proceedings, Myles concluded that the 'fruit of this Institute, therefore, has been an effort to show that there are two Saint Patricks and no God'. There was a risk, he alleged, that the institute would 'make us the laughing stock of the world'. When the directorate of the institute issued a writ for libel, the paper settled out of court for £100.[38] Nonetheless, the column became so popular that in 1943 the paper published a collection set out in a double-column format with Irish on one side and English on the other. The cardboard cover was a mock-up of an *Irish Times* front page, the headlines of which included 'Myles na gCopaleen Crowned King of Tara', 'Dáil Dissolved by Royal Decree' and 'Royal Honours List Issued'![39] The popularity of the column also led to an invitation from a publisher for O'Nolan to write a Myles na gCopaleen novel that was duly published in 1941. Dedicated to Smyllie, *An Béal Bocht* (the poor mouth) was 'a biting satire on the Irish language movement written in perfect Irish' and was hugely successful.[40]

THE REPUBLIC

In the insular environment perpetuated by literary censorship, many people still viewed the paper with some suspicion. In his autobiography Frank McCourt recalled this wariness. When he applied for a job with the distribution branch of Easons, the manager warned him about the dangers inherent in the job: 'We distribute The Irish Times, a Protestant paper, run by the freemasons in Dublin. We pick it up at the railway station. We count it. We take it to the newsagents. But we don't read it. I don't want to see you reading it. You could lose the Faith and by the look of those eyes you could lose your sight. Do you hear me McCourt?'[41] When McCourt's delivery bicycle slipped on ice and the papers fell on the wet ground, shop owners complained that 'The Irish Times is coming in decorated with bits of ice and dog shit.' His manager was unconcerned, and muttered 'That's the way that paper should be delivered, Protestant rag that it is.' Despite his employer's warning, McCourt began to read the paper on a regular basis but worried about whether such activity constituted 'an occasion of sin'.[42] By the late 1940s the paper had moved beyond its traditional Protestant base to incorporate liberal thinkers from across the religious divide. In the words of one writer, it was 'the only morning paper in Ireland in which independent views are represented every day'; proof of this lay in the fact that if it 'had to depend on the five per cent minority of the republic it would have long ago collapsed'. Thus it was obvious that it circulated 'widely among Roman Catholics who like to think for themselves'.[43]

One such Roman Catholic was the archbishop of Dublin, John Charles McQuaid, with whom Smyllie had a wary acquaintance. McQuaid invited Smyllie to the archbishop's house for dinner at least once, and Smyllie thought nothing of consulting McQuaid on matters of mutual concern.[44] On one occasion, Twitchy Doyle, an elderly reporter who literally lived in the *Irish Times* building, took a turn for the worst and needed to be placed in a nursing home. Apparently Smyllie rang McQuaid seeking help and told him that Twitchy Doyle was 'one of yours'. Through McQuaid's direct intervention, Doyle was placed in a retirement home run by an order of nuns.[45] During the prolonged teachers' strike of 1946 Smyllie wrote to McQuaid to express his criticism of the minister for education's (Tom Derrig's) rejection of his (the archbishop's) offer to act as a broker between the government and the teachers' unions. Smyllie went so far as to ask McQuaid for advice in respect of 'future policy':

> I was extremely pleased, however, to learn last night that you had consented to arbitrate in the teachers' dispute and correspondingly disappointed and disgusted to find that the Minister had rejected the idea. Do you think there is any chance of an intelligent settlement? So far as I can see, Derrig is the type of man who, having stuck his heels into the ground, prides himself of his ability to keep them unstuck. Unhappily, we seem to have many such in this distressed and distressful country. I should be grateful for any advice that you might care to give me in respect of future policy. You will understand that the *Irish Times* is in a delicate position, being suspect on all sides; but I am genuinely anxious to do whatever I can to prevent a drift into an impasse ... I need not tell you that an invitation to your new abode in Killiney will be treated as a Royal Command.[46]

Indeed, the paper's coverage of the strike came in for criticism from its old nemesis, Frank Aiken, who accused it of biased reporting. Aiken noted that the minister for education had demonstrated how his settlement terms ensured that female teachers would have more take-home pay than their counterparts in Northern Ireland, and that male teachers would, after pension deductions, have only slightly less than their northern counterparts. The paper had, he argued, 'carefully left out, in regard to the women teachers, the fact that they would have more here', just as it would 'suppress everything of advantage to this country and will try to put into their papers everything that rebounds to our disadvantage'. This bias was, he concluded, part of 'a campaign steadily pursued by the *Irish Times* ... trying to convince our people that there is a better land not so far away and that they are being ground down and made slaves of in this country'.[47] Such was Aiken's animosity towards the paper that in a later debate he declared that its journalists 'not only regard themselves as Sudetan-British but they regard themselves still as active Black-and-Tans ... carrying on the fight upon the honour of this country'.[48]

During the 1948 general election the paper recommended a change of government. On polling day it declared that, while 'Mr de Valera has been a good leader in difficult times', Fianna Fáil had become 'so much accustomed to power that it has tended towards total autocracy'. Many voters, it contended, would 'feel instinctively that the time has come for a change'. For its part, Fine Gael had 'much to recommend it to law-abiding citizens, who, while vaguely dissatisfied with the existing *regime*, have no desire for radical changes'. It had 'taken an open stand in respect of the Commonwealth', and this would appeal to voters who 'prefer honesty of purpose to expediency'. As regards Clann na Poblachta, while the paper sympathised with Sean MacBride's 'declared ambition to break the vicious circle of Irish politics', it could not 'compliment him on many of the candidates who are standing under his auspices'. Ultimately, the paper was 'unable to recommend any party unreservedly' but dismissed the idea that 'nobody but Mr de Valera can form a Government'.[49] Seven months after the first inter-party government took office, Taoiseach John A. Costello declared that the state was to leave the commonwealth and become a republic. It was here that the paper finally parted company with Fine Gael, which, it reminded readers, had contested the election on a pro-commonwealth platform and thus had 'no mandate of any kind to take such a far-reaching step'. Its fury was compounded by the fact that it had advised its readers 'to vote for Fine Gael on the ground that it was the one party in the Twenty-Six Counties that was committed to membership of the Commonwealth'.[50] As the paper saw it, 'many thousands of Fine Gael electoral supporters are thoroughly disgusted at the whole business – not, indeed, that they have any great love for the External Relations Act or even of the British Crown; but simply because they cannot understand Mr Costello's sudden change of front'. Given that 'ninety-nine out of every hundred voters believed that Mr Costello and his associates were committed to a Commonwealth policy', the decision to leave the commonwealth represented 'a flagrant breach of political faith'.[51]

Fianna Fáil took great satisfaction at the paper's predicament. Sean Lemass declared that he had 'no sympathy whatever with the *Irish Times*, or with any of the people who were induced by the *Irish Times* to give their political support to Fine Gael'. The paper had advocated the formation of the inter-party government because its one merit was, 'in the view of the editor of the *Irish Times*, that its formation put Deputy de Valera out of office'. Even when the idea of a republic was first mooted, there was 'very little evidence of perturbation on behalf of the *Irish Times* because they thought it was merely a Coalition stunt to dish "Dev"; and so long as the aim was to dish Deputy de Valera, then the editor of the *Irish Times* was prepared to shout "Up the Republic" as loud as any Deputy opposite'. Now that the republic had been declared, 'the *Irish Times* and all those who take their guidance from it are getting exactly what they deserve'.[52] When the republic officially came into existence in April 1949, the paper outlined its own position in no uncertain terms:

> This newspaper never has been of favour of an Irish Republic, either within or without the British Commonwealth. We have believed, and still believe, that the destinies of this island are linked up inseparably with those of our neighbours; that Irish unity is the ideal towards which all patriotic citizens should strive, and that such unity never can be achieved on the basis of a State which holds itself aloof not only from Great Britain, but also from the Commonwealth.[53]

While it observed that it was 'far more honest to have a real Republic than a mere sham', it believed 'that the standard of political honesty in Ireland has been lowered grievously by the action of Mr Costello and his Fine Gael colleagues'.[54] The break with Fine Gael added to the paper's independence. Given its heritage, it always had a greater degree of independence and greater scope for critical thinking than its competitors. The *Irish Independent* was traditionally deferential to the Catholic church, and the *Irish Press* was essentially the mouthpiece of Fianna Fáil. Now that it had parted company with the political movement it had supported since 1922, the *Irish Times* was the only national daily paper free to criticise the church, the government and the opposition at any given time.

THE LIBERAL ETHIC

In January 1950 the paper's letter page provided the forum for a public discussion that became known as the 'liberal ethic controversy'. It arose after the paper published a report of a public lecture entitled 'The Liberal Ethic' by a Catholic priest, Felim O'Briain, during which he asserted that one of the points of agreements between socialists and liberals was 'a free morality – the ethics of free love'. This free morality postulated that 'the ten Commandments, original sin, and inclinations to sin were impositions of a crafty priesthood on ignorant and superstitious medieval people or, as in the Socialist version, the tricks of the capitalist to maintain wealth in the hands of the exploiters'. It also postulated that 'freedom of love was as essential as any other freedom, as necessary as eating and drinking'. This entailed 'artificial prevention of births ... , freedom of abortion, divorce and the State education of the children, who, in the new free society, were an obstacle to the pleasures and fun of the parents'. This liberal ethic 'met everywhere and in all points of its programme one obstinate opponent – the Catholic Church'. In countries such as Ireland, 'the discipline of the Church was accepted willingly by the people', but there were also advocates 'of free love in rebellion against the system and blaming the Church and her teachers'. According to O'Briain, such sentiment 'appeared as an occasional letter in the *Irish Times* about "priest-ridden Ireland" or "the domination of the clergy"'; at its 'most ruthless it found its most vigorous expression in the 34 prelates imprisoned behind the Iron Curtain or exiled from there'.[55]

Not surprisingly, liberals begged to differ, and two days later the paper published the first challenge to O'Briain's views. In a letter, Owen Sheehy Skeffington declared that O'Briain's beliefs deserved 'a place beside the view, still clung to, so I am told, by some fervid souls, that it is part of the Catholic religion to drink the blood of Protestant babies'. Denouncing O'Briain's 'fantastically sweeping generalisations', he pointed out that O'Briain had placed himself in the extraordinary position 'of having to believe that when, thirteen years ago, the Soviet Union decided to make abortion illegal and divorce more difficult, she was gradually swinging away from sinful Socialism and "the liberal ethic" and nearer to their "one obstinate opponent, the Catholic Church"'. There were some people in Ireland, he concluded, 'who would have us considerably more papal than the Pope' and whose religiosity only found 'expression in uncharitable and misinformed attacks on any who dare to hold differing views, be they Socialist or Liberal'.[56] O'Briain defended his views as being a representative summary of the main tenets of liberal writers, and then letters flooded into the paper, discussing such topics as the essence of liberalism, literary censorship and article forty-four of the constitution (which, while according a special position to the Catholic church also granted religious liberty).

Although most contributors signed their names, some chose to use pen-names. Brian Inglis noted: 'There have been liberals who have rationalised their appetites into a belief that everyone should indulge himself as freely as he likes; but they are no more to be considered representative than the sects at another extreme, who claim that everyone who does not share their faith is irrevocably damned to hell-fire'.[57] 'Emilius' observed: 'Most liberals, even Protestant ones, are ready to acknowledge the almost invaluable kindness, selflessness and goodness of the Catholic clergy of Ireland, but they cannot allow this claim to superior wisdom, which is so often and arrogantly made. Does not dogmatic assertion always provoke its opposite? Was not Stalin a theological student?'[58] Another contributor asked O'Briain 'whether the knowledge that there were as many illegitimate children in Ireland as in other countries led him to believe that there was a subversive liberal element in the country? Or was it not just conceivable that non-liberal Irishmen took liberties whilst cloaking themselves behind a façade of clericalism?'[59] The peculiar Irish attitude towards all matters sexual was succinctly summarised by another contributor, Patrick Hefferan, who concluded that the real problem in Ireland was 'sexophobia': Irish people were 'terrified of sex and everything sexual'. It was 'because of this dread of sex that our marriage rate is low, that women often do not marry until too old to bear children, that the Irish countryside is full of middle-aged bachelors, stalking like old billy-goats through the land, and soured spinsters who make every Irish village a "valley of squinting windows"'.[60]

The special position of the Catholic church became a topic within the wider discussion after Westmeath county council passed a resolution calling on the government to 'amend drastically Article 44 of our Constitution, thereby putting the one true Church (founded by our Divine Redeemer) on a plane above the man-made religions of the world'.[61] One reader congratulated the council on 'their stand for the social rights of Christ the King', while another wrote that the council's resolution merely asked 'the Government to place truth on a higher plane than error'.[62] These letters prompted a Canon Bateman to observe that such letters 'could only have been written by those whose minds have been "conditioned" by totalitarian training'. Was it not recognised, he asked, 'that the Papacy is the father and mother of totalitarianism, and that Hitler merely transferred to the political and social spheres the principles which Rome has developed through centuries of autocracy?' Rome was 'fighting a battle to the death with Communism to-day, simply because there is not room on the earth for two totalitarian systems, both of which claim world domination'. As far as human liberty was concerned, he concluded, 'the victory of either would be disastrous'.[63]

Putting the case for the Catholic church, J.P. Ryan, secretary of the ultra-conservative lay organisation, Maria Duce, wrote that 'For a Catholic, religion is a matter of dogmatic certitude. For him there is only one true religion. In consequence, all non-Catholic sects, as such, are false and evil, irrevocably so.' The ideal situation was for the state to extend 'full liberty and official recognition to the Catholic Church alone' and to suppress all other religions as 'inimical to the common good'. Ryan concluded that 'the liberalism of Article 44' deserved to be 'unequivocally condemned for giving equal recognition to all forms of religious belief, since it is contrary to reason and revelation alike that error and truth should have equal rights'.[64] In response, another correspondent declared that there was 'no difference between this uncompromising attitude on the part of the Catholic Church, if such be really the case, and that of Soviet Russia, for instance, which is daily being universally denounced by Rome, for its attempts to suppress and persecute those (Catholic and non-Catholic) who profess a creed other than that of Karl Marx'.[65] On 15 March the paper published the last letter on the controversy and the following June the company published the correspondence, edited by Smyllie, in a booklet entitled *The Liberal Ethic*. Reviewing this booklet for *The Bell*, Seán O'Faoláin remarked, with tongue firmly in cheek, 'My main feeling is that this cannot have happened in 1950. Surely this is a reprint of the *Irish Times* of 1850?'[66]

Despite its commitment to democracy and freedom of expression, there were some, other than the Catholic right, who viewed the paper with suspicion. In an intelligence dispatch to Washington, which described the paper as 'the newspaper of the Anglo-Irish, Protestant, well-to-do minority, (about 150,000), most of whom are strongly pro-British', a diplomat from the US embassy in Dublin criticised Smyllie's attitude towards America's involvement in the Korean War. It noted that, while 'Smyllie's editorials and other unfriendly comments about the United States have little influence on the vast majority of the Irish public, … the effect of his attacks cannot be brushed aside altogether since a great many people in Ireland are critical of the United States and enjoy reading clever and satirical diatribes against Americans'. The memo attributed Smyllie's supposedly 'anti-American statements' to the fact that at the outbreak of the First World War Smyllie had experienced 'some disagreeable personal dealings with Americans on the Continent'. This, perhaps, was a reference to the summer of 1914 during which Smyllie toured Europe working as a tutor to the son of an American businessman. Things did not go well: Smyllie later told one confidant that he had once been sacked as a teacher.[67] From then on, the diplomat mused, Smyllie 'retained a hatred for Americans in general', and on the subject of the Korean War had written 'many editorials ridiculing American foreign policy, the American soldier and General MacArthur'.[68] The real problem for the diplomat was not that Smyllie was anti-American but that he felt as free to criticise America as he did Russia. In one editorial he questioned 'whether, in all the circumstances, the Korean incident has been worth all the fuss that it has created', and criticised President Truman's assertion that America was not at war:

> President Truman, after his admirable statement on Tuesday, announced on Thursday that the Americans were not at war; they were taking 'police action' against 'a bunch of bandits' in North Korea, who had attacked their inoffensive fellow-countrymen in the Southern Republic. If the North Koreans are nothing more than 'a bunch of bandits', it surely ought not have been necessary to stage such a mighty display of force against them … In the meantime, the 'bunch of bandits' seem to have been making short work of the Southern Koreans.

But in the same editorial, Smyllie was critical of Russian posturing and denials of any involvement in the conflict:

> Up to the present the Russians have acted with characteristic cunning. They have done precisely nothing. Naturally, they have disclaimed all responsibility for the launching of the civil conflict in Korea, which, they assert, was started by the Southern Republicans ... An official statement from Moscow announces, with nauseating unctuousness that Russia's policy, now as heretofore, is to mind her own business, keeping out of the affairs of other nations.[69]

The intelligence memo also recorded how its author met Smyllie at a function and 'asked him what motivated his views on the Korean War'. Smyllie explained his position in detail, and if the intelligence memo is an accurate record of the conversation that took place one can only conclude that either Smyllie was a fully-fledged communist or that knowing his comments would be referred upwards he decided to wind the diplomat up:

> During the Versailles Conference, he said, the Soviet Government had made overtures to the Western Powers requesting participation in the new world realignment. The allied powers failed to recognise the importance of this gesture, and the United States, especially, remained violently opposed to Russia. If Russia's original proposal had been accepted, Smyllie said, he was certain that the present hopeless condition of the world would not exist. In 1919 Russia was forced to face the world alone, but it gradually developed a system which has proved so successful that it has already won the world revolution. Asked whether he didn't believe that Russia was being contained in Western Europe and in the Far East, he replied that it was not being contained anywhere. He said that the world revolution was now accomplished and that it was merely a matter of time before Russia exercised universal domination. Asked whether he did not believe that it was worth trying to fight to contain Russia, he said that it was not worth it because he did not subscribe to the theory that life would be intolerable under the Russians. He said that morally life under the Russians would be more congenial to everyone than life under the Americans.

According to the diplomat, Smyllie 'never expressed open approval of Communism' in his editorials because he knew that 'the newspaper would be ostracised at once'.[70] But given Smyllie's perennial denunciation of totalitarian governments everywhere and his role in facilitating the liberal ethic controversy, it is hardly credible to suggest that Smyllie was a closeted communist.

'CONTRA MUNDUM'

Whatever about communists, Smyllie had no time for clerical interference in the governing of the state. The growing tension between conservative and liberal Ireland, evident in the liberal ethic controversy, finally boiled over in the conflict concerning the mother and child health scheme introduced by the minister for health, Noel Browne. The scheme proposed education in respect of motherhood and free medical care for all mothers and children up to the age of sixteen without a means test. Browne's proposal met with resistance from the Irish Medical Association, which, seemingly concerned at the lack of resources available to the state, called for the inclusion of a means test. It also met with resistance from the Catholic hierarchy, which objected to the state becoming involved in sex education and to the possibility of non-Catholic doctors treating Catholic mothers-to-be or offering them reproductive advice. Negotiations failed to achieve any compromise with Browne refusing to incorporate a means test or to concede on any point to the hierarchy. By April 1951 Browne had lost the support of his cabinet colleagues and was forced to resign.

Just before he resigned, Browne sent a civil service friend to deliver to Smyllie the confidential correspondence between himself, the Taoiseach and the hierarchy. Browne had previously met with Smyllie and had secured a promise from him that he would publish the letters. As Browne recalled in his autobiography, he had 'been warned that the Government might attempt to put an embargo on their publication, but Smyllie, an editor with genuine liberal beliefs, had promised me that should such an embargo be attempted, then, at the risk of going to prison, he "would publish and be damned"'.[71] True to his promise, and at the risk of prosecution under the Official Secrets Act, Smyllie published the correspondence, thus forcing the other national dailies to do likewise. On 12 April 1951, under the headline 'Minister Releases Correspondence', the paper reproduced the full texts of the letters, the most telling of which was the initial letter of objection from the hierarchy to Taoiseach John A. Costello. It described Browne's scheme as 'a ready-made instrument for future totalitarian aggression' and outlined the church's position on health provision, on the state's imposition of a health system that did not include a means test and on the possibility of non-Catholic health professionals providing sex education:

> The right to provide for the health of children belongs to parents, not to the state. The state has the right to intervene only in a subsidiary capacity, to supplement, not to supplant ... It is not sound social policy to impose a state medical service on the whole community on the pretext of relieving the necessitous 10 per cent from the so-called indignity of the means test ... Education in regard to motherhood includes instruction in regard to sex relations, chastity and marriage. The State has no competence to give instruction in such matters. We regard with the greatest apprehension the proposal to give to local medical officers the right to tell Catholic girls and women how they should behave in regard to this sphere of conduct at once so delicate and sacred. Gynaecological care may be, and in some other countries is, interpreted to include provision for birth limitation and abortion. We have no guarantee that State officials will respect Catholic principles in regard to these matters. Doctors trained in institutions in which we have no confidence may be appointed as

medical officers under the proposed services and may give gynaecological care not in accordance with Catholic principles.[72]

The manner in which the government dropped the scheme rather than counter the hierarchy's objections infuriated Smyllie. In an editorial entitled 'Contra Mundum' he came all with all guns blazing. He questioned the church's insistence on a means tests, deplored the way in which Browne had been deserted by his cabinet colleagues, castigated the government for its subservience to the hierarchy and asked how a united Ireland could ever be achieved if the elected government allowed itself to be dictated to by the Catholic church:

> A Mother and Child scheme, embodying a means test, is in accordance with Christian social principles; a Mother and Child Scheme without a means test is opposed to them! So much, if we read them correctly, emerges from the documents which the Hierarchy contributes to the discussion. For ourselves, we cannot pretend to follow the reasoning, and we doubt if it will be followed by the puzzled and disappointed people of this country ... This is a sad day for Ireland. It is not so important that the Mother and Child Scheme has been withdrawn, to be replaced by an alternative project embodying a means test. What matters more is that an honest, far-sighted and energetic man has been driven out of active politics. The most serious revelation, however, is that the Roman Catholic Church would seem to be the effective Government of this country. In the circumstances, may we appeal to Mr Costello and his colleagues to admit the futility of their pitiful efforts to 'abolish the border' – their Mansion House Committees, their anti-partition speeches at international assemblies, their pathetic appeals to the majority in the Six Counties to recognise that its advantage lies in a united Ireland? To that majority, the domination of the State by the Church – any Church – is anathema, and from now onwards it can plead some justification for its fears. It seems that the merits of a theocratic Twenty-six Counties outweigh those of a normally democratic Thirty-Two.[73]

In the debate on Brown's resignation, Taoiseach John A. Costello declared: 'I am not in the least bit afraid of the *Irish Times* or any other newspaper. I, as a Catholic, obey my Church authorities and will continue to do so, in spite of the *Irish Times* or anything else, in spite of the fact that they may take votes from me or my Party, or anything else of that kind.'[74] Likewise, the minister for defence, Tom O'Higgins, declared that he did 'not care twopence' if the government's policy of consultation with the hierarchy 'offends to the core of his soul, Bertie Smyllie of the *Irish Times*'. Smyllie's views were, he maintained, not shared by his co-religionists who regarded him 'as the "nigger in the wood-pile" who is causing irreparable damage to them and to this nation'.[75] In a report on the controversy to the papal nuncio, Archbishop McQuaid was trenchant in his criticism of the paper, although he agreed with Smyllie's assessment of the impact of the controversy on the prospects for national unity:

> Concerning the *Irish Times*: it has surpassed itself in injustice, first of all in writing a most
> unfair editorial, at once when only one side, Dr Browne's side, has been published. (And
> the Times forgot or did not know, that Dr Browne in publishing my letters without my
> permission has gravely violated our civil law.) Secondly, the *Irish Times* has opened its
> columns to very bitter letters and has kept up the disturbance by articles of unfair comment
> ... But what many fail to see is that the Protestants now see clearly under what conditions
> of Catholic morality they would have to be governed in the Republic. The political
> enticements held out to them are now judged by them to be only snares to trap them in a
> Republic dominated by the Catholic Church. Thus, the arguments of the liberal Catholics,
> who seem to put national unity before the interests of the Faith, have been discarded in the
> eyes of Northern Protestants.

McQuaid also reported that 'representative' Protestants had condemned the
actions of the paper and that 'these Protestants and Freemasons mean to deal
with the Editor of the *Irish Times* in their own way'.[76] However, it was not
Smyllie but rather the writer of the weekly 'Report to Housewives' column –
Mary Francis Keating – who took the fall for the paper's stance on the issue.
The column had always dealt with household issues but then turned its attention
to the state of the public health service, which it described as 'something to be
shuddered over as a searing experience' as patients suffered 'a series of indignities,
of delays, and often culpable and harmful neglect'. The medical profession's
treatment of public patients also came in for criticism, with the columnist stating
that 'For one "free" doctor who is polite, painstaking, sensible of his position and
of the function which he is paid to undertake, there are ten indifferent, over-
bearing, incompetent people who represent the medical profession to those
unfortunates whose circumstances relegate them to waiting for hours in draughty
corridors in the hopes that the doctor "will see him" if he has time'. If the medical
profession viewed public patients 'as an unmitigated nuisance', the solution was
simple: 'the return of the witch doctor – who, at least, if he could not cure his
patient; poisoned him off with very great dispatch and little expense to the
community in general'.[77] This provoked an angry response from the master of the
Coombe maternity hospital, Dr William O'Dwyer, who accused the paper of
'indulging in a campaign of organised propaganda in favour of Dr Browne's
Mother and Child Scheme'. Referring to the 'Report to Housewives' column, he
accused the columnist of jettisoning 'all the principles of decent journalism' and
writing 'a concoction of lies and slander against the medical profession'. The
column was 'one of the most flagrantly vicious and immoral articles published in
an Irish newspaper in recent times' and 'nothing less than a wicket and deliberate
distortion of the truth'. Surely, O'Dwyer asserted, 'an editor has some responsibility for the ethics of journalism as practised by those on the pay-roll of his
paper'. In a comment that set a few minds in the higher echelons of the paper
thinking, O'Dwyer concluded by noting that:

In these eventful days we read some very high-minded pronouncements in other columns of the *Irish Times* with homilies to all manner of people as to how they should behave in their various walks of life. All this would be the more impressive if we could be certain that the *Irish Times* does not expect a higher standard of professional integrity from statesmen, doctors, and indeed, churchmen, than that which it expects from practitioners of journalism.[78]

Shortly afterwards, the columnist, Mary Francis Keating, the second wife of Alec Newman, the deputy editor, was dropped from the paper. This prompted Sean O'Casey to write to Keating to express his incredulity that 'The "Irish Times" should get rid of you for writing such a clear article'. He could 'understand the "I. Press", or the "I. Independent" showing you the door; but such a paper as the "Irish Times", one would imagine, could afford to keep a brave writer on its Staff'.[79] Another consequence of the mother and child saga was that the paper found itself excluded from receiving Archbishop McQuaid's annual Lenten pastorals. Reporters were forced to get the Lenten address from colleagues working at the *Cork Examiner* or the *Irish Press* as Smyllie insisted that the pastoral be published every year.[80] The boycott did not stop the paper asking the archbishop's office for the pastorals; in February 1957 the chief reporter Alan Montgomery wrote to the archbishop's office, noting that in former years he had been good enough to let the paper have, in advance, a copy of his Lenten pastoral. Scrawled across the letter in McQuaid's handwriting is the comment, 'I doubt if this is accurate.'[81] A debate on the merits of sending the pastoral to the paper then ensued. A memo written to McQuaid by one of his aides noted that he 'would be inclined to give the Irish Times the Pastoral. They will get it in any event: I doubt the value of not giving it to them: we will certainly not convert them – whatever chance there is of inducing them to be more friendly, I do not believe refusing them the Pastoral will help'. In his reply McQuaid wrote, 'Let them have it: nothing else.'[82]

A 'TRADITION OF EPISCOPOPHAGY'

But Smyllie himself did not get off scot-free. His 'Contra Mundum' editorial prompted a backlash in the Catholic press, most notably in *The Standard*, wherein Professor Alfred O'Rahilly, president of UCC, wrote a series of articles criticising the paper. In his first article he declared that the *Irish Times* had a 'tradition of episcopophagy' demonstrated by the fact that, when Catholic bishops objected to legislation, it represented 'the domination of the State by the Church', but when the paper made 'pontifical pronouncements on sociology, as it constantly does, this is not – nor would it be even if it were listened to –

domination of the State by the *Irish Times*'. As O'Rahilly saw it, the hierarchy's 'claim to record ethical criticisms, in public or in private, concerning government measures' was a right 'equally applicable to religious minorities'; the issue involved 'the right of citizens, through their religious associations, to pass moral judgements on the State'. Thus it was 'actually suicidal, for a Protestant organ such as the *Irish Times* to launch an attack on this right', and it was 'illogical and even intolerable that a small clique of journalists and Leftists should deny the right of our Catholic bishops to pass an ethical-social verdict on legislation'. Hence, as O'Rahilly saw it, the 'utterly nonsensical position that the *Irish Times* claims the right to subject the Government to a daily barrage of schoolmasterish scolding, while denying to the Catholic Episcopate the right to an occasional restrained intervention purely on matters of principle'.[83]

The following week, having provoked no reply, he compared the tactics of Smyllie to those 'of a malicious urchin who throws a stone at a church window and then runs away, watching from a safe hiding place the ensuing commotion'. Having published 'an editorial of shallow bigotry', the paper had followed this up by devoting space 'to correspondents (many anonymous) to assail their Catholic fellow-citizens with venomous scurrility'.[84] When Smyllie eventually did respond, he recommended 'to the professor the following extract from *Proverbs*: "Answer not a fool according to his folly, lest thou also be like unto him".'[85] It was, however, the exchanges between Myles na gCopaleen and O'Rahilly that caught the public imagination. The tit-for-tat exchanges between the two began when Myles described *The Standard* as 'a small pious weekly taken by the innocent to be the voice of the Catholic Church and as such very profitably sold at church doors'. Describing O'Rahilly as 'a self-licensed demagogue', Myles dismissed his articles against the *Irish Times* as 'a tirade saturated with insolence, arrogance and ignorance'. Interestingly though, Myles observed that Smyllie, 'in writing the leading article in question, lacked prudence' and that the bishops while 'making a perfectly legitimate intervention on a vital matter, should have done so overtly'.[86] In his response O'Rahilly noted that Smyllie had released his 'professional jester to emit a stream of irrelevant and stupid personal invective'. To Myles' dismissal of *The Standard* as 'a small pious weekly' O'Rahilly pointed out that it had twice the circulation of the *Irish Times*. 'Cocksure of their own omniscience', he continued, 'some members of the Dublin intelligentsia tried to browbeat us into deserting our bishops and to stampede us into running away from our social principles.'[87] Describing this response as 'a farrago of scurrility, falsehood, ignorance and illiterate writing', Myles wrote a series of articles that nit-picked O'Rahilly's article paragraph by paragraph. The funniest observation made by him was that

O'Rahilly's initials – AOR – formed an Irish word meaning 'a personal attack in prose or verse: a curse'.[88]

Given the strain it was under, the inter-party government finally dissolved itself in May 1951 and the country went to the polls. Unsurprisingly, it was Fine Gael that incurred the wrath of Smyllie's editorials. He directed particular criticism at John A. Costello, who had 'disappointed, and even disgusted, many of Fine Gael's staunchest supporters when he decided quite gratuitously to take the country out of the British Commonwealth'. He also blamed Costello for the mother and child affair, noting that 'The Taoiseach's conduct – and he must shoulder the responsibility for the behaviour of the Cabinet as a whole – was to say the least of it inept'.[89] The net result of Fine Gael's actions in government was that 'it forfeited the respect of not alone the Protestant minority, which has no monopoly of political integrity, but of all citizens who still believe in fair and square dealing'. As Smyllie saw it, the party had 'put political expediency before national honour, thereby setting a grievous example to future generations'.[90] A Fianna Fáil administration took office until 1954 and during that year's election campaign Smyllie adopted the same stance as that of 1951, reminding readers that Costello's 'subservience as Prime Minister of the State to the hierarchy was pathetic'.[91] On polling day the paper declared: 'We have pronounced ourselves in favour of Fianna Fáil'. Its support for Fine Gael had ended because of the paper's 'inability to trust in its good faith'. The party had 'sacrificed principle under pressure during the inter-Party experiment of 1948–51 [and] the chances are that it will sacrifice principle under pressure if occasion rises again'.[92] When the second inter-party government took office, Smyllie observed that it was only 'a "caretaker" Government'.[93] By this time too, Smyllie had become something of a caretaker editor whose days at the helm of the paper were coming to an end.

CHAPTER 7

Holding the Fort

It was a marvellous interlude, that period with Smyllie, but it was no way to run a
newspaper, and certainly, as time went by, it became clear that this enclave of
magnificent bohemianism was totally unsuited for a modern newspaper. The thing
that always surprised me was that the paper survived.[1]

Bruce Williamson on Smyllie's editorship

TOWARDS THE END OF his tenure and indeed his life, Smyllie was
increasingly ill and absent from the paper. As one reporter recalled, 'by
1952 his health was poor, he was in and out of hospital, and his judgement,
always arbitrary, had become increasingly erratic'.[2] Worse was to follow. On 17
September 1951 a huge fire engulfed the section of the *Irish Times* building
connecting the D'Olier Street and Fleet Street parts of the premises. The two
street-front parts of the building had been rebuilt over the previous two years,
but the connecting section, formally the linotype hall, was awaiting recon-
struction when a fire broke out. The hall had wooden floors that over the years
had become saturated with ink and oil and quickly became a furnace. Although
no one was injured, the fire destroyed the company's two rotary presses, and its
linotype machines suffered severe water damage. On a more positive note, its
stock of newsprint was stored off-site and its brand-new Hoe Superspeed
printing press was located in a different section of the building. It fell to Jack
Webb, the general manager, to arrange for the paper to be set by the *Irish Press*
and printed by the *Evening Mail*. The following morning, the *Irish Times* hit the
streets as a four-page 'emergency issue' with the news of its own misfortune the
lead story.[3] In an editorial it declared its intention to resume normal production
within a day or two and to return with 'a newspaper which, in respect of
physical form, will be superior not merely to our old self, but to all except the
wealthiest and most modern journals'.[4] But, given the damage, full production
did not return to its own premises until November, and eight months later an
industrial dispute with print unions halted publication of all national
newspapers for seven weeks.[5]

The fire prompted a brief surge of energy from Smyllie as he supervised the production of the paper at the *Evening Mail's* offices. The fire had its lighter side in cartoon form; an advert for Odearest Mattresses featured Smyllie fleeing the burning building with a typewriter in one hand and a Union Jack in the other! Afterwards, however, things settled back into the routine of journalists and editors visiting him at his home for instructions and him dictating his weekly 'An Irishman's Diary' column from his bed. The column, modelled on the chatty gossip column of the 1920s, consisted mainly of memories of days gone by. As one reviewer put it, 'Garrulously, Nichevo reminisces about Sligo schooldays, contemporaries in Trinity, internment in Ruhleben prison camp, and the balmy days of reporting during the Troubles [but] For all his clichés, its "by-the-ways", and its "a-little-bird-tells-me"s, Nichevo happens to be immensely readable: and he is certainly read'.[6] Others took a different view, nicknaming the column 'Famous People Who Know Me'.[7]

It was around this time too that the board of directors became concerned about Myles na gCopaleen's 'Cruiskeen Lawn' column. In the latter half of 1951 Myles noted that the clock outside the offices of a Pearse Street coal supplier had stopped. Andy Clerkin, a Fianna Fáil senator and lord mayor of Dublin, owned the business, and Myles affected to be concerned at Clerkin's lack of civic duty in fixing the clock so that passers-by might know the time. He immediately began mentioning in his column that 'Andy Clerkin's Clock Is Still Stopped', which, in time, was abbreviated to 'ACCISS'. This became something of an in-joke among Dubliners because Clerkin had a domineering wife named Cis, and anytime he was unsure about anything he would say, 'I'll axe [ask] Cis'.[8] Myles also invented the 'ACCISS' salute – one arm extended vertically and the other horizontally to symbolize a stopped clock – that readers were encouraged to give Clerkin on public occasions. In October 1951 the paper published various pictures of the stopped clock and, later still, Myles kept the issue alive by affecting sneezes in his column along the lines of 'ACCISSOO! (Bless me!)'.[9]

All this came to a head in February 1953 when Myles took offence at the fact that while Dublin Corporation was asking Dubliners to clean up their gardens and streets for the Tóstal (springtime) festival, the clock on the lord mayor's business premises was still stopped. Myles complained: 'When the gentleman responsible has the nerve to tell us to paint our houses, put out flags and window boxes, and so on … I say it is not good enough.' Observing that Clerkin was paid a salary by the city's ratepayers, Myles delivered his tour de grace: 'Surely to goodness he can AFFORD to take his own advice?'[10] He also took a swipe at the festival itself, the aim of which was to bring tourists to Ireland but which, according to Myles, would only result in 'rocketing prices' for native Dubliners. If, he declared, the 'expected inundation of aliens' materialised, then the festival's motto – Ireland at Home – would take on 'an ironical significance ... for the good reason that Ireland will not be able to afford to go out'. Irish people would have to peep out 'from behind soiled lace curtains to see its streets and towns taken over by the scruff and sweepings of Britain and America'. But there was one positive possible outcome: if some tourists stayed and had children, it was possible that in the future there could be 'a fair sprinkling of negro and Euroasian deputies in the Dáil'.[11]

Shortly afterwards, Myles resigned from the civil service and, as time went by and drink took its toll, 'a 'vindictive streak in his writings led to constant problems with the paper' with the net result that 'columns that offended were chopped ruthlessly or thrown into the wastepaper basket'. This situation led to many acrimonious rows and 'more than once Myles announced his positively last appearance'. According to then features editor, Jack White, the board 'would have seen him go with no regrets: they found him something of an embarrassment'. But since the column was so popular, White was always dispatched to make peace with Myles and restore the supply of copy.[12] Myles continued to write intermittently for the paper until his death in 1966, and in all probability – given the numerous biographies and books written-about him and his work – holds the distinction of being Ireland's most written about journalist. Incidentally, it was also White who, in 1954, commissioned a series of articles on the subject of the national finances from a young Aer Lingus employee, Garret FitzGerald, who wrote under the pen-name 'Analyst'. FitzGerald continued to write on economic subjects for the paper until he became minister for foreign affairs in 1973, and he returned to the paper as a columnist after he retired from active politics.

A NEW EDITOR

Smyllie's reign ended when he died suddenly in September 1954, and Alec Newman 'by unwritten law, had traditional right of succession – regardless of the misgivings felt in several quarters'.[13] As one reporter put it, Newman 'was a nice man but desperately old fashioned, good at writing leaders and editing the letters page, a highly literate man but he didn't have the right sort of personality to broaden the paper's appeal, he was of another age'.[14] But, to the staff Newman's succession was like the 'apostolic accession'.[15] Shortly after Smyllie's death there was a major shake-up of the board when the Arnott family sold the majority of their ordinary shares to a group of Dublin businessmen led by Frank Lowe. This sale was facilitated by a 1946 amendment to the company's articles of association that restricted the market for ordinary shares to other ordinary shareholders or to someone approved by the board.[16] In late 1954 the bulk of the Arnott family's ordinary shares was sold in equal proportions to Lowe, his nephew George Hetherington, Ralph Walker and his brother Philip Walker, all of whom, at one time or another, were on the board of Hely's Ltd. According to Lowe, the move was prompted by the Arnott family's wish 'that the policy which has distinguished the *Irish Times* as a newspaper, tolerant, critical and liberal, shall remain unchanged'. The latter three men joined the board in December 1954, and, while Sir Lauriston Arnott retained a significant number of ordinary shares and remained a director, he relinquished the position of managing director to George Hetherington.[17]

All three new directors had extensive business experience. Hetherington was raised by his uncle, Frank Lowe, and having served a printing apprenticeship in London eventually became managing director of Hely's.[18] The two Walker brothers had inherited their father's business – Walker's Ltd – a bicycle and pram shop. During the Second World War, Philip Walker served with the Royal Inniskilling Fusiliers in Burma and later became managing director of the family business before it was amalgamated with Hely's Ltd. Ralph Walker was a senior partner of Hayes and Sons, Solicitors, the paper's legal advisors and was, at various times, president of the Royal Horticultural Society of Ireland and the Boys' Brigade.[19] During the 1950s the paper made modest profits – £19,514 and £19,392 for the years ending September 1953 and 1954 respectively. In July 1957 the Walker brothers brought onto the board John J. McCann, the publisher of the hugely successful *Radio Review*, which the *Irish Times* published under contract. After purchasing one-seventh of the ordinary shares, McCann became managing director with the brief to oversee the launch of a Sunday newspaper, the *Sunday Review*.[20] McCann's short time at the company was not a happy one. He and the chairman, Frank Lowe, did not see eye-to-eye, and McCann resigned from the board in June 1959, selling back his ordinary shares to the other directors in roughly equally amounts. Another newcomer to the board, in May 1959, was Howard Waterhouse Robinson, a director of the Brown Thomas Group. Sir Lauriston Arnott died in 1958, and control of the Arnott block of ordinary shares passed to Sir John Arnott, then the paper's London editor.[21]

By the time Alec Newman became editor, the paper averaged ten to twelve pages during the week and fourteen pages on Saturdays. Costing three pence a copy, it now carried a photograph on page one every day and a cartoon – 'By-Line' – below the fold. The main features of the paper throughout the mid-to-late 1950s included 'An Irishman's Diary', 'Cruiskeen Lawn', 'Television Review', (useful for those wealthy enough to own a television), 'Motor Notes',

'Diary of a Farmer's Wife', 'Radio Review', 'Economic Comment' by Garret FitzGerald, and 'Eurocomment', which examined events in the common market. Although 'An Irishwoman's Diary' appeared occasionally, women's journalism was still confined to columns such as 'Around the Shops', 'Good Food', and 'Home Dressmaking'. Newman initiated a farming page on Thursdays and continued the 'Books of the Week' page, which was edited by Terence de Vere White. Despite the economic hardship of the 1950s, advertising was relatively buoyant, with advertisements for Aer Lingus, Arnotts, Pims Department Store, Guinness, Player's Cigarettes, California Syrup of Figs, Aga Cookers, Chivers Jelly, Hoover, Esso Motor Oil, and the very popular Kodak 'Brownie' camera being among the most prominent. The cartoon adverts for Odearest Mattresses with their catchy Limericks also featured throughout the 1950s.

As editor, Newman continued where Smyllie had left off and maintained the paper's strong opposition to sectarianism and censorship. In May 1956 two Jehovah's Witnesses were set upon by a mob in the village of Clonlara, Co. Clare. Led by the local parish priest, the mob ran the two men out of town after assaulting them and burning their pamphlets. The subsequent court case saw a Fr Patrick Ryan and ten locals charged with assault and malicious damage. The charges were not denied, and during the case the bishop of Killaloe made a submission to the court declaring his support for the actions of his curate. Counsel for the defence claimed the two men had committed blasphemy by propagating the notion that the holy Trinity was a pagan belief. Ultimately the judge agreed and, although finding that the charges were proved, he dismissed the case under the Probation of Offenders Act and bound the two victims to the peace on sureties of £200 each.[22] The *Irish Times* was the only newspaper to raise the civil libertarian angle by noting that 'these men have the same right as any other religious sect, whether Christian, Jewish, Mahommedan, Taoist or Hindu, to propagate their faith by peaceful means; and any denial of that right is a reflection of the state of freedom of this country'.[23]

The paper also called for reform of the censorship laws which, as Sean O'Casey put it, involved 'bishops, priests and deacons, a Censorship Board, vigilant librarians, confraternities and sodalities, Duce Maria [sic], Legions of Mary, Knights of this Christian order and Knights of that one, all surrounding the sinner's free-will in an embattled circle'.[24] In December 1957 the former chairman of the censorship board, Professor J.J. Piggott, released a statement on the reasons for his resignation the previous September. Two new members had been appointed to the board in June 1956 and had taken a more enlightened view on censorship; and as two dissenting votes were enough to frustrate a decision to ban a book, only books that were purely pornographic were banned. This situation came to a head when the question arose of banning omnibus volumes – volumes containing two or more unabridged books, one of which was already banned. The two new members refused to automatically ban such volumes, and Piggott subsequently resigned after a stand-off with the minister for justice, Oscar Traynor.[25] In an editorial, Newman supported the approach to censorship taken by the two new members: to 'confine it to its proper and reasonable function, which is the prohibition of "indecent and obscene" – or as Professor Piggott prefers to call them, "purely pornographic" – books'.[26] Piggott declared that while there had been unanimity on banning purely pornographic books that 'openly deride chastity and advocate such sexual license as trial marriages and the like' such unanimity disappeared when the board came to deal with 'Freudian-inspired fiction which delights to portray, in the name of realism, details of seductions, adulteries and free-love orgies'. Books had to be judged 'by purely moral standards' and not literary merit, and it was 'a habit with the *Irish Times* to go off the deep end when criticising the Censorship Board'.[27]

Newman adopted a similarly critical stance during the Fethard-on-Sea boycott of 1957. In May of that year the Catholic population of the Co. Wexford village decided to boycott Protestant businesses after Sheila Cloney, the Protestant wife of a local Catholic farmer, left the village with their two young children so that they would receive an Anglican education. In a report, the paper noted that the Catholic community, believing that she had left the village 'with the financial assistance and connivance of local Protestants', declared its intention to boycott Protestant businesses until the children were returned to their father. Such claims were, it noted, vigorously denied by the Protestant community, which considered the issue 'a domestic affair and none of their business'.[28] In an editorial, Newman argued that there was not 'one jot of evidence to indicate that any member of the Protestant community assisted in, or even sympathised with, her flight' and described the behaviour of the local Catholic community as 'the sort of conduct which, while official practice in the nations under Communist yoke, has no place in a 20th century democracy'. The affair, he concluded, created the impression 'that the vaunted religious tolerance of the Twenty-Six Counties is little more than skin deep'.[29] The boycott eventually ended when the local parish priest entered a Protestant owned shop and bought a packet of cigarettes.

'CHRONIC EPISCOPOPAGY'

For the most part, the board was happy enough to concentrate on the business side of things and let Newman take care of editorial content. There were, however, a few occasions when board members expressed reservations. Two such occasions were the Suez Canal crisis of 1956 and the Dublin Theatre Festival controversy of 1958. In 1956 a crisis developed over control of the Suez Canal, which connects the Mediterranean and Red Seas, and which, until 1954, had been protected by British armed forces. In July 1956 Egypt announced that it intended to nationalise the canal. Although compensation was promised to the British and French shareholders of the Suez Canal Company, British prime minister Anthony Eden rejected the idea, and the following October, British and French forces seized control of the canal. In his editorial the following day, Newman described the invasion as 'one of the most deplorable acts of aggression in post-war history'.[30] This description of events, as Newman later recalled, did not go down well with some members of the board:

> During the Suez crisis there was some difference of opinion on the Board concerning our editorial attitude. Some members were pro-Eden, some anti-Eden. This was one of the rare occasions on which editorial policy has been discussed on the Board and opinion was divided. Lowe, I think, had felt some qualms about the policy of the *Irish Times* – certainly some of his friends had given him what-for about it – but on the conclusion of my defence, he passed judgment: 'All things considered, Mr Editor', he said, 'I think you have probably taken the right attitude. But' – I waited with some trepidation as he added very slowly – 'I personally should suggest that you would do better to avoid the word aggression'. It was a small concession.[31]

Despite this small concession Newman did not abandon his criticism of Britain's actions. When Eden was forced to back down and subsequently resigned as prime minister, Newman noted that he had 'clouded the end of his long political career by a blunder of the first magnitude [and] weakened his country's authority to speak even as a diminished Great Power'.[32]

The following year the paper clashed with Archbishop John Charles McQuaid. The occasion was the ill-fated second Dublin international theatre festival. The festival had been launched in 1957 and the inaugural festival had been marred by the attempted prosecution of Alan Simpson of the Pike Theatre on charges of indecency for producing Tennessee Williams' *The Rose Tattoo*. Given that the only evidence presented by the state consisted of assertions by members of the Garda Síochána that the play was indecent, and given that the play's script was not a banned publication, the state's application for Simpson's prosecution was eventually throw out of court – though not before bankrupting the Pike Theatre. Although the *Irish Times* reported Simpson's arrest and his subsequent release without trial, it did not editorialise on the case, probably because of the sensitivities involved: at one stage the state supposedly considered banning daily papers that reported evidence given by Gardaí to prove the play was indecent.[33] It did, however, publish a page-one photograph of Simpson being arrested by no less than four detectives, and gave details of the fund launched by his friends to pay his legal costs.[34]

The second Dublin international theatre festival, for which two major plays had been secured, was equally controversial. The two plays were *The Drums of Father Ned*, by Sean O'Casey, and *Bloomsday*, an adaptation of Joyce's *Ulysses* by Alan McClelland. The controversy began when Archbishop McQuaid withdrew his permission for a votive mass to mark the opening of the festival because he considered the two plays as inappropriate for a Catholic audience. Proposed changes to O'Casey's play resulted in him withdrawing it, and the organising committee subsequently cancelled the production of *Ulysses*. In protest, Samuel Beckett withdrew three of his plays and eventually the festival itself was cancelled. Newman accused the organising committee of having 'kissed the rod' and observed that 'No evidence has been adduced that either of these productions contains a hint of obscenity or of blasphemy'. In future, the organisers would 'be well advised to submit its programme to the Archbishop of Dublin in advance of publication if it is to avoid a similar waste of money and effort'.[35] The cancellation prompted a flurry of letters to the paper, including one from 'Grace Abounding', who noted that, although clergy were prohibited from theatres because of their supposed lewdness, 'the busty beauties of the cinema are considered safe and suitable for clerical entertainment'. In contrast, another reader declared that Dublin was 'suffering from an overdose of arty-boys and pseudo-intellectuals who are striving to appear smart'. Another reader suggested that the cancelled plays be replaced by *Peter Pan*, which centred around 'people who never grow up, and a never-never land', while yet another condemned the 'crude travesties of Faith and Fatherland' that were written by 'pseudo-liberals, apostates, or repulsive offsprings of souperised slum-dwellers'.[36]

McQuaid's response to Newman's editorial was one of fury, and that fury was directed at the company's board of directors. Some clerics alerted McQuaid to the differences of opinion that existed at board level between Frank Lowe and John McCann. After the editorial was published Monsignor Joseph Deery (a one-time chairman of the censorship board) withdrew a series of articles on Lourdes from McCann's *Radio Review* – a move supported by McQuaid, who declared that 'The Directors are responsible and they are grown up men. They must accept the consequence of an attack that is unjust and public.'[37] However, McCann protested to Deery and in a letter to McQuaid, Deery concluded that McCann was 'endeavouring to make amends in the sections of the Irish Times publications which are in his complete control'.[38] As proof of this Deery enclosed a clipping of the *Sunday Review* editorial of 23 February 1958, which, in contrast to that of the *Irish Times*, supported McQuaid's action:

To request the benediction of the Church on (inter alia) the works of two men who have not failed to conceal their hostility to that Church, was an improper, if not impertinent suggestion. To have acceded to such a request would have been an impious mockery of the Faith … At best, the presentation of such plays meant the misuse of taxpayers money for the satisfaction of the vociferous few; at worst the prostitution for gain of the national conscience … For the past week, we have been subjected to the customary clap-trap of the free-thinking 'liberals' who 'license mean when they cry liberty'. They shame the word of freedom and stand discredited by the very claims they urge … A minority group of self-appointed dictators of 'culture' have sought to impose their will on the long-suffering majority. Whatever freedom means, it carries no charter for that.[39]

McQuaid's own response to Newman's editorial was to request Sir Lauriston Arnott to do him 'the favour of calling at the Archbishop's House'.[40] In his notes of this meeting McQuaid recorded that Arnott 'expressed disgust at the things that have appeared in the last 15 years in the *Irish Times* and great regret for the Tóstal leader and letters'. McQuaid declined Arnott's invitation for him to meet with Newman; he noted that 'he was without excuse, for a journalist and a gentleman would first have ascertained the facts'. Arnott stated that 'he would do all he could to have the controversy stopped and to prevent any future cause for worry'.[41] In a letter to McQuaid, Monsignor Deery claimed that, in the greater scheme of things, Arnott was 'a figure-head, with Mr Lowe as the real master'; but, he contended, when 'Mr Lowe learns of your Grace's action he will surely receive a severe shock. The next board meeting should be interesting, and should give a splendid opening to Mr McCann, if he is on his mettle.'[42] Whatever happened at board level, Arnott had a word with Newman, who wrote to McQuaid explaining his position:

Sir Lauriston Arnott gives me to understand that my newspaper's reporting of the Theatre Festival has misrepresented your conduct and has provoked your reasonable anger. May I assure that any comment which this newspaper made was not directed against your Grace, but against the tactlessness of the Tóstal Council? I would beg you to believe that such reference to your Grace as occurred in the columns of the *Irish Times* was not deliberate, and that no disrespect was intended to your Grace in person or to your sacred office. May I assure you of my deep and continued respect?[43]

In his reply McQuaid stated that he never associated Newman 'with the unfair leader' as Monsignor Deery had assured him of Newman's 'honourable attitude'. McQuaid also denied he was angry, and invited Newman to meet him if he 'did not find it inconvenient', although there is no record of such a meeting.[44] The paper's old nemesis, the by now ordained, Alfred O'Rahilly – known to reporters at the paper as 'the voice of Catholic Ireland' – also got in on the act.[45] In an article in *The Standard,* O'Rahilly accused the paper of having 'a fatal defect which is a hangover from the old Ascendancy days'. That hangover was 'chronic episcopopagy', or in layman's terms the 'disease of bishop-baiting', which resulted in Catholic readers constantly having 'their convictions flouted and ridiculed'. The paper, he declared, was 'unique among our dailies for intolerance and bigotry' and gave publicity to 'all kinds of cranks and scoffers, sabbatarians, secularists, grouching intellectuals, subjects of persecution complex'. The current situation was no different; the 'editor fired the first shot and then opened his correspondence columns to the waiting crowd of snipers, who began to squirt mud and acid from their toy-pistols'. As O'Rahilly saw it, some people 'who should have known better than to kowtow uncritically to this Protestant organ's garbled version, hastened to register themselves in the *Irish Times* as outraged highbrows'.[46] Such malevolence towards the paper was not unusual. As one reporter remembered, the paper was 'seen as the devil incarnate by a lot of Catholics; we were the people who read banned books. To be in the *Irish Times* was almost an occasion of sin.'[47]

Regarding the plays themselves, O'Rahilly declared that *Ulysses* 'was a drama – or what purported to be such – which, though expurgated, gave publicly financed publicity to a book, written by an apostate, which is not only grossly obscene but quite exceptionally blasphemous (especially as regards the Mass)'. The other play was no better having been written 'by a playwright – now advocating Communism and allowed to advocate his Communism in the pages of the *Irish Times* – who has become more and more obsessed with anti-Catholicism and has come to utilise the stage as a vehicle for mocking our faith'. He also accused the paper of 'a dishonest attempt to put on his Grace the onus of the fiasco' and claimed that McQuaid had 'made no claim to exercise dramatic guidance or censorship'; he had merely 'declared that, in the context of the proposed dramas, he would not provide a religious inauguration'. It was an 'unwarranted impertinence on the part of the *Irish Times* to decry the moral judgment and to mock the spiritual jurisdiction of our Archbishop'. 'A-la-carte' Catholics also came in for criticism; they had been 'influenced by the *Irish Times* and its propagandists to adopt, superficially and unwittingly, the philosophy which denounces any invocation of natural law or religious authority in public life'. Anyone 'objecting to lubricity in literature or to offensiveness in drama is to be regarded as a moronic philistine' and Catholics were encouraged by the paper 'to put their religion in their pocket, to cultivate the itch to be risky, to keep up to date with the Joyces and the O'Caseys'. It was, O'Rahilly concluded, 'high time for these timid Catholics to cease to be the stooges of a vociferous and hostile minority'.[48] This article was reproduced in leaflet form, presumably for distribution to churches and Catholic organisations around the country.[49]

ALL CHANGE HERE

But despite its crusading ethos, the paper was not impervious to the economic stagnation of the 1950s, a decade described by one reporter as one of 'repression, emigration, clerical domination, spurious patriotism and an education system that seemed to train people to be physically fearless and morally cowardly'.[50] The policy of economic protectionism was well past its prime, and between 1951 and 1961 over 400,000 people emigrated, depriving Ireland of much of its young population. Most worrying for the paper, between 1946 and 1961 the Protestant population in the republic declined five times faster than the overall population.[51] The preliminary report of the 1956 census recorded the lowest population figure since the inception of the state, and the paper warned that if such trends continued 'Ireland will die – not in the remote unpredictable future, but quite soon'.[52] The following year unemployment figures reached a record 78,000 and the country was on the brink of destitution. During the 1957 general election, the paper called for 'long-term government'; in other words 'a merger of Fine Gael and Fianna Fáil'.[53] When Fianna Fáil returned to government, it declared that it would have 'greatly preferred an inconclusive verdict which would have forced the two major parties – even at the cost of a second general election – first to merge, and then to regroup into the elements of a clearly defined Right and Left, with the philosophically differing approaches towards national problems that are the essence of parliamentary democracy in most countries'.[54] Shortly afterwards the Whitaker Report, which advocated the adoption of free trade, was presented to government, and in November 1958 the first programme for economic expansion was put before the Oireachtas.

In 1959 Eamon de Valera declared his candidacy for the presidency, the election for which coincided with a referendum, proposed by Fianna Fáil, to replace proportional representation with the first-past-the-post system. The paper was critical of the fact that both polls were to be held on the same day, but had no doubts about where it stood on either issue. Describing de Valera as 'the most important Irishmen of our times', it declared that Fine Gael 'did wrong, even for political reasons, to offer a candidate [Sean MacEoin] in opposition to him'.[55] On the referendum it declared that Fianna Fáil was 'not concerned either with democratic principle or with the good of the country'. Raising the spectre of perpetual Fianna Fáil government, it concluded that the 'solitary result of the "straight" vote can be to establish Fianna Fáil in office – on a disproportionately small vote – for a full term of office – possibly for two'.[56] In the middle of the campaign the paper printed a series of six articles entitled 'PR in Ireland', by Proinsias MacAonghusa. Such was the demand for re-publication of the series – described as 'a highly authoritative case-history of the single transferable vote in action' – that the paper reprinted the articles in pamphlet form a fortnight before polling day.[57] 'Quidnunc' of 'An Irishman's Diary' also regaled readers with a witty remark made in the Seanad by Owen Sheehy Skeffington, who noticed that the Fianna Fáil speakers had been furnished, presumably by party headquarters, with a large bundle of notes that was passed from hand to hand as each of them contributed to a debate on the referendum. When Sheehy Skeffington stood up to speak, he announced that while he was aware that Fianna Fáil was committed to the principle of the single transferable vote, he was unaware that the party members were committed to the single transferable speech![58] On polling day, the paper declared that no compelling reason had been 'adduced why a system which has served Ireland well for almost forty years should be abandoned'.[59] When de Valera was elected president and proportional representation was retained, it observed that 'a proper sentiment, and a decent sense of respect to a great man, have prevailed in the case of the Presidential election, whereas logic and clear thinking have been dominant in the referendum on PR'.[60] When Sean Lemass succeeded de Valera as Taoiseach, it observed that he was the 'head of the "practical" as opposed to the "traditional" wing of the Fianna Fáil Party'. He was 'an "economics" man, pure and simple', a man 'entirely divorced from some of his colleagues of the "old brigade" and inclined to make rapid changes with many of the policies which have handicapped and hindered the economic progress of the Irish nation for a great many years past'.[61] Lemass lived up to this billing and the first programme for economic expansion that ran between 1959 and 1964 led to a very changed Ireland.

NEW ARRIVALS

Change was also on the cards at the *Irish Times* with the arrival of Douglas Gageby who joined the board in July 1959. Born in Dublin in 1918, Gageby was the only son of Thomas Gageby, a Belfast-born civil servant who had come south to seek his fortune, and Ethel Smith, a national schoolteacher from Co. Westmeath. In 1922 the family moved back to Belfast where Gageby senior took up a position in the new Northern Ireland civil service. His paternal grandfather, Robert Gageby, a Protestant from the Shankill Road, was a mill worker who formed his own trade union – the Flax Dressers' Union – and was one of six trade unionists to win a seat in the Belfast municipal elections of 1898 under the banner of the Independent Labour Party. When, in 1910, he stood as a Labour candidate in one of the two general elections held that year, he became, as Gageby recalled in an interview, public enemy number one:

Overnight pious, non-smoking, non-drinking, Church of Ireland, old Robert Gageby
became an enemy of the people. The Unionist press descended on him: he was leading the
decent Belfast working man down the slope to communist. *The Telegraph* and the
Newsletter rent him. I have all the cuttings – which partly explains some of my views about
the Unionists! Overnight, my grandfather had horns and could not be tolerated. He was
consorting with people like Keir Hardie.[62]

Growing up in Belfast, Gageby showed an aptitude for languages and visited
Germany several times during the 1930s. Having studied languages at Trinity
College, he joined the Irish army during the Second World War and, because of
his proficiency in German, served in military intelligence, acting as an
interpreter between army authorities and captured German airmen and spies.
While at Trinity he met his future wife, Dorothy Lester, whose father, Sean
Lester, a former news editor of the *Freeman's Journal,* had the distinction of
being the last secretary-general of the League of Nations. (Gageby later wrote a
biography of his father-in-law, who, before his term as secretary-general of the
League of Nations, had been its high commissioner in the then-free city of
Danzig, now the Polish city of Gdansk.) When the war ended, he joined the
Irish Press as a reporter and in late 1946 was dispatched to post-war Germany
to report on conditions in that devastated country.[63] In 1949 he was appointed
deputy editor of the new *Sunday Press* and in 1952 became editor-in-chief of
the ill-fated Irish News Agency, set up by the first inter-party government at the
behest of the minister for external relations, Sean MacBride, to supply Irish
news material to the international press. It was here that Gageby first met John
Healy, with whom he established a lifelong friendship. In 1954 Gageby returned
to the Irish Press Group as managing editor to launch the group's new title, the
Evening Press, of which he was founding editor.

Gageby's reputation did not go unnoticed at the *Irish Times*. On at least one
occasion Robert Smyllie tried to recruit him to the paper. Meeting him in the
Pearl Bar one night, Smyllie remarked that he should be working for the *Irish
Times,* to which Gageby replied that he did not want to work for a paper that
was divided into gentlemen and players. As Gageby remembered it, Smyllie
took offence and did not speak to him for months.[64] In 1959 the company was
more successful in wooing him, when the managing director, George
Hetherington offered him the post of managing editor. Gageby replied that he
would accept the post only if he were to sit on the board of the company. In his
own words he 'did not want to be a hired editor [he] wanted a real say in
running the paper'. This was a distinction he had learned at the Irish Press
Group: when he had received his contract for the post of editor of the *Evening
Press,* he noticed that it contained a provision that Vivion de Valera, then
controlling director of the Irish Press Group, would be editor-in-chief of the

paper; when he raised this ambiguity with de Valera, he was told that the provision meant that as editor he 'would run the paper' and that as editor-in-chief de Valera would 'provide the necessary resources'.[65] The ambiguity rankled with him and when Hetherington made his offer Gageby took care that such ambiguity would not be repeated at the *Irish Times*. He was also careful to inform Hetherington and the other board members that he 'was a nationalist of a certain kind, largely in favour of Fianna Fáil'.[66] This did not deter the board, and Hetherington later returned to offer him the post of joint managing director and a directorship. Gageby joined the company on 1 July 1959, having purchased 2,064 ordinary shares.[67] Interestingly, he harboured a desire to edit the *Irish Press* and considered Burgh Quay his 'spiritual home'.[68] Given what he achieved with the *Sunday Press, the Evening Press* and the *Irish Times,* it is interesting to ponder how different the fate of the Irish Press Group, and indeed, that of the *Irish Times*, might have been if Gageby had been given a free hand in reinventing the *Irish Press*. But while religion was probably not a factor, the thought of a Protestant editing de Valera's *Irish Press* would probably have been akin to a red revolution in Burgh Quay.

Three weeks after Gageby was co-opted onto the board, Frank Lowe died and was succeeded as chairman by Ralph Walker. In May 1962 George Hetherington relinquished his position as joint managing director and Gageby became the sole managing director. That same month saw another new arrival – Major Thomas Bleakley McDowell – to the company. Born in Belfast in 1923, McDowell joined the Royal Inniskilling Fusiliers in 1942 and was commissioned as an officer in 1943. He became a regular officer of the Royal Ulster Rifles in 1946, studied law at Queen's University Belfast, and, after qualifying as a barrister, served in the department of the Judge Advocate General – the British army's legal department. He resigned his commission in 1955, came south to find his fortune and turned his hand to management consultancy, working for many of the large, Protestant-owned businesses in Dublin, including Pims Department Store and Burton's Tailoring. In the late 1950s his company, Management Directors Ltd, was contracted to carry out an overview of the structures and business operation of the *Irish Times*. In May 1962 the board decided upon 'a complete re-organisation of the Company and its workings' and appointed McDowell as a director with the specific brief 'firstly to place the Company on an economic basis and secondly to maintain it in that position'.[69] By the following November, McDowell was vice-chairman of the company.

NEW TITLES

All these changes prompted a burst of energy in the company. Circulation was still comparatively low; in 1954 its certified daily sales figure stood at 35,960 compared to 167,244 for the *Irish Press* and 195,588 for the *Irish Independent*.[70] Despite this, the paper received almost the same amount in government advertising revenue as its competitors – in 1955, £6,719 compared to £7,573 for the *Irish Press* and £7,705 for the *Irish Independent*.[71] But it also received a substantial amount of its advertising revenue from many Protestant-owned businesses in Dublin, something that could not be relied upon indefinitely. There was a realisation also that the company had stood still for too long and suffered from a lack of diversification. Its printing press was idle for most of the week, although the company did have two other small publishing interests – the *Times Pictorial* and the *Irish Field*.

The *Times Pictorial* dated from 1941, although it was, in fact, a revamp of the *Weekly Irish Times* that had first appeared in 1875. It was, its last issue claimed, Ireland's first tabloid newspaper, and the rational behind the 1941 revamp was simple. Given the shortage of newsprint during the war years, the *Irish Times* was unable to find sufficient space for the one hundred or so weekly photographs that would have appeared in pre-war days. Rather than dismiss the dozen staff employed in the photographic, engraving, developing and printing departments, the company transferred these workers to the weekly title, which then became a picture-based publication.[72] Its unique selling point was documentary photographic features on topics as diverse as the harsh life of Irish emigrants in Britain, life in the Irish navy, Dublin's seedy underworld, the conditions of school buildings and the coronation of Queen Elizabeth II in 1953. The paper survived in various guises until 1958, although it too had its tussles with the wartime censorship. In October 1944 it was reprimanded for publishing a picture of the actress Lana Turner with a caption saying that she had 'recently received a request for her picture to be painted, half life-size, on a U.S. Army bomber'.[73] The censor also killed an article by Smyllie on 'his experiences in a German prisoner-of-war camp in 1914–18 with Russian prisoners and of their attempts to escape'.[74] Circulation-wise, the *Times Pictorial* grew from 7,500 copies in 1941 to 38,000 copies in 1948.[75]

The paper was re-titled *The Pictorial* from June 1955 to August 1957 and the *Irish Pictorial* from then until its closure in March 1958.[76] Know popularly as 'The Pic', the sixteen-page tabloid had a circulation of 57,975 in 1953, but this declined substantially as the *Radio Review*, re-titled as the *Radio and Television Review* and carrying the listings for BBC television, grew in popularity.[77] Perhaps the most famous incident concerning the *Irish Pictorial* was its inadvertent publication of details of the 1952 budget on the morning of budget day. Two days previously, the minister for finance, Sean MacEntee, had posed reading his budget speech for the paper's photographer Dermot Barry. This cover picture appeared on the morning of the budget, and the detail of the print showed that the government proposed to end the rationing of tea and to end butter subsidies.[78] The paper had also put the offending photograph in its window display in Westmoreland Street. This prompted a rather contrived adjournment debate on budget leaks during which one opposition deputy declared that any TD could 'walk down Westmoreland Street and look into the photograph display window [where] if his eyesight is normal, he will read part of the Minister's Budget speech in the display window of the *Irish Times*'. MacEntee rejected the predictable calls for his resignation.[79] The company also published the *Irish Field* – a weekly sports paper devoted to horse racing and bloodstock breeding. It dated from 1895, had been acquired by the company in 1903, and in 1953 had a circulation of 11,493.[80] It too had strayed into intermittent trouble with the wartime censorship; in February 1945 it published weather details at a race meeting in Naas – an incident that resulted in a strong rebuke from the censor.[81]

But in contrast to its competitors the *Irish Times* had been left far behind. Both Independent Newspapers and the Irish Press Group had established strong Sunday and evening titles – the *Sunday Independent* (1906) and the *Evening Herald* (1891) and the *Sunday Press* (1949) and the *Evening Press* (1954) respectively – to maximise the use of their printing presses and to boost advertising revenue. To counter this imbalance, the *Irish Times* diversified into the Sunday and evening markets by launching the *Sunday Review* in November 1957 and by purchasing the *Evening Mail* in September 1960. Neither paper was a commercial success.

The *Sunday Review* made its debut on 3 November 1957 as a twenty-eight-page tabloid as different from the *Irish Times* in style and content as is possible to imagine. It was, one reporter remembered, 'a hard-hitting, tough little paper, but it had the misfortune to arrive on the Irish scene before Irish readers were ready for that kind of journalism'. The paper's philosophy was simple: 'if you had a good story you hit the reader with it by professional use of print and clever illustration. And you were not afraid to say what you meant.' Such an approach was 'regarded as vulgar, brash and irresponsible by many Irish journalists, not least those working in the *Irish Times*'.[82] The paper was, perhaps, before its time, and the economic climate was not ideal for launching a new paper, a fact illustrated by a story that appeared on page three of the first edition. Under the headline 'Taoiseach's Cousin an Emigrant', the story told how Eamon de Valera's cousin was emigrating to Canada with his wife and eight children so as 'to give them a future'.[83] Edited by John Healy, the paper's news editor was Ted Nealon, and under their command the paper adopted an irreverent style of reporting. Among the main features were 'London Diary' by Donal Foley, which reported on the Irish community in London; 'The Week as I Saw It' by Charles Orr, which was an irreverent look at the week's news; 'Purely Personal' by Marion Fitzgerald, which consisted of a detailed interview with prominent individuals; and 'The John Gunn Diary' which, located on the back page, consisted of snippets of gossip and news that are common in contemporary Sunday newspapers. Later additions to the paper included a four-page cut out comic strip for children and a social diary written by Patsy Dyke.

Its chief innovation was John Healy's 'Inside Politics' column, which he wrote under the pseudonym 'Backbencher'. This irreverent and sharp column quickly 'evolved from a loose collection of anecdotes about politicians into an irreverent, hard-edged and demotic treatment of the political process characterised by inside information of a type and quality that journalism had not known until then'.[84] Such irreverence was a shock to the body politic. In 1963 an independent TD, Frank Sherwin, unsuccessfully sued the *Sunday Review* and the *Irish Times* for libel. In a debate that year Fine Gael TD Oliver J. Flanagan informed the Dáil that there was a rumour circulating that the Fianna Fáil government had secured the support of Sherwin in return for him qualifying for a backdated IRA pension. In response, Sherwin claimed he was entitled to the pension because during the civil war he had been 'tortured five times in jail and crippled for life'. In reporting these exchanges in his 'Backbencher' column, Healy declared that 'Mr Sherwin rides a bike with the best, posts his own bills like an expert, he has fathered a large family raging in age from 26 to a mere four year old – so there's nothing wrong there.' The paper also published a picture of Sherwin mounted on a bicycle with the caption 'Crippled for Life – Mr Frank Sherwin, TD'. A few days later the *Irish Times* published an article entitled 'Plain Words – by Sean O Riada' in which new definitions were ascribed to some old words; 'Bribe – a pension; Cripple – a cyclist, a Sherwin; Perjurer – an expression of affection used by politicians; Politician – a perjurer, a corrupt person'. In his case for libel Sherwin argued that these references brought his reputation into public scandal, contempt and ridicule, but after a five-day hearing the jury found in favour of the papers.[85]

In September 1963 the *Sunday Review* became a forty-eight-pager with the addition of a twenty-eight-page 'Woman's Review'. This substantial addition, which included fashion, beauty, health, travel, motoring (with a female reviewer), theatre, gardening, books and shopping, was an attempt to woo a female readership. The following week it hailed this new addition as 'an outstanding success' and noted that it was 'publishing many thousands extra to

1 Lawrence E. Knox, founder and proprietor of the *Irish Times*, 1859–73.   2 Sir John Arnott I, proprietor of the *Irish Times*, 1873–98.   3 Sir John Arnott II, chairman, Irish Times Ltd, 1900–40.   4 John Healy, editor 1907–34. Healy saw the paper through the 1916 Rising, the war of independence and the civil war.

5 Charles E. Kelly's *Dublin Opinion* cartoon of the *Irish Times* newsroom.
The cartoon dates from sometime in the 1920s.

6 The front page of a special Sunday edition, 1939, on the eve of the
outbreak of the Second World War.

7 Robert Smyllie, editor 1934–54, who gave the paper a new lease of life
and was the bane of the censor during the Second World War.

8 How the paper looked when adverts dominated the front page.

9 How the paper looked after its re-design in 1941.

10 Smyllie's famous 'V for Victory' front page, May 1945. Smyllie submitted the photographs in random order to the censor but rearranged them on their return.

The original caption read, "Quidnunc, in the depths of depression, to firemen made humble confession: 'You must please get it out — For I can't write without ODEAREST — my cherished possession!'"

11 Odearest advert based on the *Irish Times* fire, 1951. Note the caricature of Smyllie leaving the building with newsprint, typewriter, and a union jack flag. The caption reads: 'Quidnunc, in the depths of depression, to firemen made humble confession, "You must please get it out, for I can't write without, Odearest, my cherished possession"'.

12 The paper's front page on the Mother and Child story, 1951. Note the headline just above the fold, 'Minister Releases Correspondence' under which the paper published the correspondence between the cabinet and the Catholic hierarchy.

13 The paper's front page reports the fallout from the Mother and Child crisis. The inter-party government dissolved itself shortly afterwards.

14 Frank Lowe, chairman, Irish Times Ltd, 1945–59. Lowe was charged with putting order on Smyllie's organised chaos.   **15** Alec Newman, editor 1954–61. Newman was Smyllie's deputy for many years and caused a storm with the paper's coverage of the cancellation of Dublin's second international theatre festival.   **16** Alan Montgomery, editor 1961–3. Monty, as he was known to his friends, left the paper to become the public relations officer for Guinness & Co.   **17** Donal Foley, news editor and later deputy editor, played a central role in the re-invention of the paper during the 1960s.   **18** Louis O'Neill, MD, 1977–99. O'Neill played a central role in the commercial development of the paper.

19 Major Tom McDowell & Douglas Gageby. Both men played a
central role in the creation of the Irish Times Trust in 1974.

20 Douglas Gageby at a presentation to mark his retirement as editor
in the *Irish Times* newsroom.

21 Brian O'Nolan (Myles na gCopaleen) who wrote the infamous 'Cruiskeen Lawn' column for over twenty years.

22 Odearest advert based on Myles na gCopaleen's ability to satirise establishment figures. The *Catholic Standard*, Alfred O'Rahilly, *Time Magazine,* and others are having their legs pulled while the figure of Smyllie pays homage in the bottom left corner.

Omniscient omnipotent Myles,
Writes a column in multiple styles,
While chastising the nation
He gets inspiration
From **ODEAREST** —*a Buddha all smiles*

23 *(left)* John Healy ('Backbencher') whose 'Inside Politics' column was the bane of Irish politicians for many years. **25** Fergus Pyle, editor 1974–7. Pyle had a torturous time as editor but is remembered for the 'Heavy Gang' exposé of 1977.
24 Some of the female journalists who worked at the paper during the 1970s: *Back row (l-r):* Gabrielle Williams, Maeve Donelan, Mary Cummins, Caroline Walsh. *Front row (l-r):* Christina Murphy, Renagh Holohan, Mary Maher, Geraldine Kennedy.

THE IRISH TIMES

Price 15p (incl. 10% VAT)   DUBLIN, MONDAY, FEBRUARY 14, 1977   No. 37,634   CITY

Gardai using North-style brutality in interrogation techniques

BRUTAL interrogation methods are being used by a special group of gardai as a routine practice in the questioning of suspects about serious crimes. This group uses physical beatings and psychological techniques similar to some used in Northern Ireland, to obtain information and secure incriminating statements.

By Don Buckley, Renagh Holohan and Joe Joyce

TODAY, and for the next two days, we are publishing a series of articles on Garda brutality, written by a team of Irish Times reporters which has spent some weeks looking into allegations against methods of police interrogation in this country. Background article and a case history appear today in News Focus, page 11; editorial comment in page 9.

High Court bid to get Dugdale marriage

Counsel urges independent investigation

By Martin Cowley

A CALL for the establishment of an independent procedure to investigate allegations against gardai of the police force...

don't
lying
down—
make a stand with
spare Rib

Members of the feminist group, Irishwomen United, lead a vociferous demonstration at Connolly Station in Dublin

Trapped cattle taken off freighter

By Michael McConnell

---

26 The paper's exposé of Garda brutality, 14 February 1977. The 'Heavy Gang' story caused serious tension between the paper and the government.
27 Continued coverage of the 'Heavy Gang' story, 15 February 1977.

THE IRISH TIMES

Price 15p (incl. 10% VAT)   DUBLIN, TUESDAY, FEBRUARY 15, 1977   No. 37,635   CITY

'Heavy gang' used new Act to intensify pressure on suspects

By Don Buckley, Joe Joyce and Renagh Holohan

LEGAL safeguards for people in custody have been abused and ignored by the group of Garda interrogators known as the "heavy gang" since the introduction of the Emergency Powers Act last October. Despite the Minister for Justice's assurances in the Dáil debate on the new law and the emphasis placed on traditional rights by the Supreme Court, members of the "heavy gang" have used the new powers to expand and intensify their interrogation methods.

Crosland: condition worsens

A STORY security not connected to British Foreign Secretary Mr Anthony Crosland...

No unit using violence – gardai

Irish Times Reporters

THE GARDA Press Office in Dublin yesterday said that there was no section or unit in the force "which as a matter of practice or policy inflicts physical violence on persons in custody."

WORST FOOT FORWARD: the Fianna Fáil leader, Mr. Lynch, at his home in Dublin yesterday, where he is recuperating from an operation on his right foot — (Photograph by Peter Thursfield).

Government likely to consider

£100m a

Newspapers plan

28 Martyn Turner's cartoon on the 'Heavy Gang' story, 1977.
29 Martyn Turner's cartoon on Charlie Haughey's resignation, 1992, which was not published due to libel concerns.

30 Martyn Turner's cartoon on X-Case saga, 1992.
Turner later presented 'Miss X' with the original drawing.
31 Martyn Turner's cartoon on Eamonn Casey's troubles, 1992,
which was not published due to the sensitivity of the story.

THE IRISH TIMES

PRICE 75p (incl. VAT) 65p sterling area   DUBLIN, THURSDAY, MAY 7, 1992   No. 43,285 CITY

Dr Casey resigns as Bishop of Galway

By Andy Pollak, Religious Affairs Correspondent and Conor O'Clery, in Washington

DR EAMONN CASEY has resigned "for personal reasons" as Bishop of Galway, according to a statement issued on his behalf by the Catholic Press Office late last night. The Pope has accepted the resignation.

Dr Casey travelled to Rome last weekend and tendered his resignation to the Vatican's Congregation of Bishops on Monday. In last night's statement Dr Casey said

he intended to "devote the remainder of my active life to work on the missions".

He was expected to return to Ireland on Tuesday but was delayed in Rome because of the Vatican's reluctance to accept his resignation immediately.

Dr Casey arrived back in Galway from Rome yesterday and is understood to have had discussions with a solicitor from Arthur O'Hagan and Son, the Dublin law firm which advises the bishops.

It is understood that before travelling to Rome, Dr Casey had

spent several days in Malta considering his position. The Papal Nuncio, Archbishop Emanuele Gerada, who would have been informed of his intention to resign, comes from Malta.

The bishop, normally one of the most outspoken and visible members of the Hierarchy, has been keeping a noticeably low profile recently. Earlier this week *The Irish Times* made unsuccessful efforts to set up an interview with him, having heard reports of his possible resignation, in order to discuss matters which might have

a bearing on the reasons for his decision.

One of these included payments amounting to $115,000 to a woman in Connecticut and a lawyer in New York on July 26th, 1990, and other regular payments to the woman over a period of 15 years since the mid-1970s.

The woman involved instructed a solicitor with the Dublin firm of Kenny, Stephenson and Chapman, to take legal proceedings against Bishop Casey last summer. Counsel was also instructed but the woman withdrew her instructions

to pursue the case earlier this decision.

It is also understood that a lawyer representing Dr Casey in the United States was involved in recent negotiations for a possible further payment of up to $150,000 to a relative of the woman in Connecticut, but that these also come to nothing.

Earlier this week Dr Casey was also forced to cancel a meeting with the executive of Trócaire, the Catholic Third World aid and development agency which he has

headed since its foundation 19 years ago.

It is understood that the events which precipitated Dr Casey's resignation go back to the period in the early 1970s when he was Bishop of Kerry. He became Bishop of Galway in 1976.

Dr Casey, who was 65 last month, has been a popular figure among the bishops for many years for his commitment to campaigns for the poor and underprivileged. He started campaigning for the homeless in Britain in the 1960s and was a co-founder of the hous-

ing lobby, Shelter.

The following is the full text of a statement issued last night on behalf of Dr Casey by the Catholic Press and Information Office.

"Dr Eamonn Casey, the Bishop of Galway, has offered his resignation to Pope John Paul II. His Holiness has accepted it. Bishop Casey is retiring for personal reasons.

"The diocesan chapter has elected Monsignor James McLoughlin as diocesan administrator. Monsignor McLoughlin is the Vicar-General of the diocese and parish priest of the cathedral parish. He has served as secretary, Bishop Michael Browne. He will oversee the administration of the diocese until a successor to Bishop Casey is appointed.

"In a statement last night, Bishop Casey said: 'I have been extremely happy as Bishop of Galway for the last 16 years. In the first place I thank the priests and religious for their wholehearted acceptance of me as their bishop and for their generous co-operation at all times.

'I ask them to continue to support me in their friendship and prayers. I shall always remember them in mine.

'It has been an immense privilege to have served the people of Galway diocese. The kindness and affirmation I have received will always remain with me.

'My faith has been immeasurably strengthened by their faith. I pray they will continue to build the local Christian community. I thank in particular those who have helped me in so many ways in responding to the many needs of our community.

'My greatest joy in my ministry has been the celebration of the Sacrament of Confirmation. I would add here a special word of acknowledgement to all the teachers of the diocese.

'As a member of the episcopal conference for almost 23 years I shall remember with special warmth the friendship and solidarity I have always experienced among my brother bishops and in particular the bishops in the West.

'I wish also to express my appreciation of the individuals which I have shared with the Bishop and the members of the Church of Ireland and the members of the Methodist and Presbyterian traditions.

'As chairman of the executive of

New talks likely in postal dispute

By Ed O'Loughlin and Patrick Nolan

WHILE BOTH SIDES in the postal dispute have said that they are willing to negotiate without preconditions, it is thought unlikely that any direct talks can begin before next Monday.

The director of letters and services at An Post, Mr John O'Callaghan, and the general secretary of the Communications Workers' Union, Mr David Begg, both declared yesterday that they were prepared to negotiate without preconditions to end the dispute.

However, it is believed that both sides may have differing beliefs on what the agenda of such a meeting should be and that this is likely to take at least until the weekend to clarify. Direct negotiations before then are ruled out by the timing of the CWU's annual conference in Tralee, Co Kerry, which ends tomorrow.

The chairman of the Labour Relations Commission, Mr Kieran Mulvey, said last night that it was too early for direct intervention but the commission's conciliation

The CWU's general secretary, Mr Patrick Nolan, said that An Post's action was a calculated attempt to escalate the dispute beyond the Central Sorting Office in Dublin but that the CMU would resist all such pressure.

The dispute began on April 27th when about 100 temporary employees began work at the Central Sorting Office in Sheriff Street. About 600 permanent employees have been suspended for refusing to co-operate with them.

International mail has been paralysed, while mail volumes in Dublin and rural areas are down to three and 33 per cent respectively.

Addressing the CMU conference yesterday the union's general secretary, Mr Begg, alleged that An Post wanted to reintroduce a radical "visibility plan" which the former Minister for Communications, Mr Brennan, dropped last year. He claimed that the company wanted to "develop a new angle" by taking on the industrial strength of the union. The management also wanted to reduce the workforce by 1,500 and to replace them by casual workers, he said.

See also pages 4 and 5

THE IRISH TIMES

PRICE 75p (incl. VAT) 65p sterling area   DUBLIN, FRIDAY, MAY 8, 1992   No. 43,286 CITY

Woman who was paid money by bishop says she is 'relieved' by his resignation

By Conor O'Clery and Andy Pollak, Religious Affairs Correspondent.

THE WOMAN who received payments from Dr Eamonn Casey said in a statement over a period of years has issued a statement to *The Irish Times* in which she says she is "relieved" that matters have come into the open and she believes Dr Casey was right to resign.

Speaking from her home in Connecticut, Ms Annie Murphy, 44, reacted to the news of Dr Casey's resignation with the words "I'm happy. I knew that sounds harsh but that's my feeling." Ms Murphy lives in the town of Ridgefield, Connecticut, with a companion, Mr Arthur Pennell, and her 17-year-old son, Peter.

Dr Casey travelled from Shannon to New York yesterday. An Aer Lingus spokeswoman confirmed that he had arrived at Kennedy Airport at 9.45 pm Irish time last night.

There was no further elaboration of Dr Casey's "personal reasons" for his resignation as Bishop of Galway from the Catholic Press and Information Office in Dublin yesterday. The director, Mr Jim Cantwell, said he had nothing to add to Wednesday night's statement.

The Primate, Cardinal Daly, in London yesterday for a meeting between the four Irish Church leaders and the British Prime Minister, Mr Major, refused to comment on Dr Casey's reasons for resigning. He said it was "neither the place nor the time".

Cardinal Daly said that the matter is in touch with opinion at home and I would prefer not to talk about

in New York the Bishop of Galway had paid over a sum of $115,000, $90,000 of which went to her and $25,000 to her solicitor. Mr Peter McKay, She said that at the same time she had signed a release relinquishing all personal legal claims on Dr Casey.

Subsequently there were discussions about a further payment of $100,000 to $150,000. The discussions involved Dr Casey's legal representative in New York, but came to nothing.

"I didn't want that $150,000," Ms Murphy said yesterday. "He did come to realise it was best that he resign. This was the best way to go."

Friends of Dr Casey said yesterday that he was likely to want to go to work as a missionary priest or project leader in South America, possibly in Chile, Peru or Equador.

Dr Casey has been to Central and South America many times in his capacity as chairman of the Catholic aid agency, Trócaire, and began learning Spanish two years ago. He had been telling people for some time before his resignation that he did not see himself living out his active life in Ireland, but in a Latin American or other Third World country.

There was a sense of shock in Galway yesterday at the news of Dr Casey's surprise resignation. The Archbishop of Tuam, Dr Joseph Cassidy, said the events were the cause of deep sorrow. "I suppose it's not so much that he resigned but that his resignation is surrounded by allegations and speculations in the media."

See also pages 4 and 5

Flew to New York: Bishop Eamonn Casey

Relieved: Ms Annie Murphy of Ridgefield, Connecticut. Photograph: Matt Kavanagh.

---

32 The paper's front page announcing the resignation of Bishop Eamonn Casey.
33 The paper reveals the connection between Bishop Casey and Annie Murphy.

34 Conor Brady, editor 1986–2002. Brady oversaw the development and
expansion of the paper throughout the late 1980s and 1990s.
35 Geraldine Kennedy, who became the first female editor of the paper in 2002.

meet the increased demand'.[86] But this innovation was too late and the *Sunday Review* published its last edition on 24 November 1963, reporting on the killing of John F. Kennedy in Dallas; its 'Woman's Review' was replaced with a twenty-page magazine on the life and death of Kennedy. The paper's demise was caused by a simple lack of advertising. As one executive put it:

> It suffered from a lack of advertising; I can't remember precisely the figure but I think when it closed down it had a circulation of 190,000. It sold very well; had it had colour – and some people say it had colour but this was colour that was printed somewhere else, brought in and fed into it, a very expensive thing to do. It didn't grab the advertisers, let's put it that way and it just didn't make money at a time when the *Irish Times* didn't have an awful lot of money anyway and couldn't afford to have a further drain on its outgoings.[87]

The huge popularity of the *Sunday Press* and the *Sunday Independent*, their strong reputations with advertisers, and the advent of television advertising hampered the *Review*'s chances of survival. The paper left one major legacy though; John Healy's 'Inside Politics' column was transferred to the *Irish Times*.

The company also tried its hand in the evening newspaper market by purchasing the *Evening Mail* in September 1960 for £220,000.[88] The *Mail*, which first appeared in 1823, was a Protestant-owned Dublin-orientated broadsheet paper. Its circulation had been declining long before the arrival of the *Evening Press,* and in most respects the rot had gone too far to be reversed.[89] Despite this, the board went ahead with the purchase of the paper from Henry Tivy, a move that was viewed by some as religious solidarity rather than commercial sense.[90] Apparently, Douglas Gageby opposed the purchase on such grounds but was persuaded by the other directors to vote for it so as to make the decision unanimous.[91] As one executive remembered, 'It was more, I think at the time, a decision made by Tivy's friends who were directors of the *Irish Times* ... I got the impression it wasn't a commercial decision at all.'[92] Nevertheless, a revival was attempted. Redesigned by Ken Gray, and edited at various times by Alan Montgomery and John Healy, the paper turned into a twenty-four-page tabloid in a bid to halt the slide in sales. But this meant trying to woo readers away from the *Evening Press,* which, under Gageby's editorship, had established itself as the dominant evening paper. In heel of the hunt, continued losses led the board to decide to cease publication and the last edition of the paper appeared on 19 July 1962. As one reporter remembered, 'the resultant drain on the company's finances dragged down their Sunday paper, the *Sunday Review,* and went close to destroying the *Irish Times* itself'.[93]

EDITORIAL CHAIRS

Given these unsuccessful attempts at diversification, the company was left economically shaken and apprehensive about the future. Indeed, there was a recognition that substantial change at the *Irish Times* title itself was desperately needed. By the late 1950s, the natural constituency towards which the paper had been principally aimed was a negligible minority. As one reviewer put it, the paper had 'rendered a service to this class by finding for it compromise formulae, which have made the passage from Unionist to ex-Unionist to Fine Gael supporter to Fianna Fáil or Labour supporter seen natural and honourable instead of a hideous betrayal of tradition'.[94] But it had not spread its appeal outside this strata to a sufficient extent to ensure its survival as a viable business. Times were changing, and the paper ran the risk of being left behind. Commonwealth membership was no longer an issue; relations with Britain were amicable enough; and there was a growing recognition that the country's future would be forged within a wider European framework. Major technological changes were also afoot. The arrival of television in 1961 concentrated the board's attention on the paper's future and in particular Newman's editorship, which, as one reporter put it, had not resulted in any innovative changes at the paper:

> Newman was a thinking editor, very much in the *Irish Times* style, very much of the Trinity style, but on the other hand not well supported by the board. There was a smooth unruffledness about Alec's tenure in the *Irish Times*. It wasn't distinctive, it wasn't outstanding; it was sort of continuously, gently, moving along. He was effectively pushed because he wasn't very effective as an editor. He was too easy going and too much in the style of Smyllie. He wasn't business orientated though it was never said that Alec was sacked.[95]

This was by no means an uncommon view. Another reporter recalled that:

> The paper was going down and circulation was falling. Alec made no changes. The population that supported it in the past was getting smaller and no effort was being made to get new readership. Alec had no head for business or circulation. He wanted a quality newspaper but times were changing; the Protestant population was declining and this was reflected in the circulation. The board wanted to shove Alec aside, to make him editor-in-chief over all the titles but Alec wouldn't have it. George Hetherington saw that the paper was doomed unless something was done to get readership, and advertisers at the time wanted readership.[96]

Newman was aware that the board was watching him and became more cautious in the views he allowed into the paper, a policy that did not sit well with Myles na gCopaleen. In a letter to Brian Inglis, who was then editor of *The Spectator*, Myles wrote:

I am most anxious to leave the dirty *Irish Times*. It was an odd enough paper in Smyllie's day but it has now become really quite intolerable. I need not discourse to you on their shocking notions of pay but in addition much of the material I send in is suppressed and for that work they pay nothing whatever. Other articles are mutilated and cut, often through sheer ignorance. The paper has in recent years bred a whole new herd of sacred cows and, cute as I claim to be, I have never been certain of their identity. In any case they are always being added to. I wrote stuff about the Irish Army's Imperial exploit in the Congo but this was all utterly killed. Alec Newman is a perfect gentleman but a complete weakling ... accepting instructions on petty matters from certain directors who make prams [the Walker brothers] and who should properly be in them (and who don't like me, think I'm dangerous).[97]

In April 1961 Newman declined to publish a letter from Sean O'Casey that would have ignited yet another war of words with the paper's ardent critic, Fr Alfred O'Rahilly. In his letter O'Casey took issue with O'Rahilly's defence of Archbishop McQuaid's ban on Catholics attending Trinity College – under pain of mortal sin – without his prior permission. Referring to O'Rahilly as 'that curious little ecclesiastical cuckoo-clock', he contradicted O'Rahilly's assertion that it was Trinity College that had prevented Catholics from attending the university. O'Casey quoted from the memoirs of a Maynooth professor, Walter McDonald, in which he outlined a scheme agreed in 1905 between Trinity College and 437 Catholics 'whose social position were such as to make each of them ready and eager for University Education'. It was then, O'Casey countered, that 'the Voice of Maynooth spoke from a pillar of ecclesiastical cloud, saying, "Be off with yous, the lot of yous; this scheme holus bolus is not for us"; and the 437 distinguished were shoo-ed away like sheep into the pen of silence'.[98] Newman declined to publish the letter and wrote to O'Casey to say so. In his reply, O'Casey acknowledged that it would 'be dangerous to let the phrase of "that curious little ecclesiastical cuckoo-clock, Dr O'Rahilly" to be bannered in the *Irish Times*'. Criticising the Protestant community as 'a poor spineless lot', he told Newman that he had 'an unenviable job sitting in an editorial chair in the midst of these cuckoo-clocks'.[99] In another letter, O'Casey recounted how Newman had told him that he 'couldn't dare publish them [his critical comments] because those in power, big shareholders, objected to anything by O'Casey in the paper'.[1]

Eventually, a number of factors ensured Newman's departure. A drop in circulation – from 36,267 copies in 1956 to 35,033 copies in 1960 – was not helped by a printers' strike in October 1960 which put the paper off the street for two weeks. In November 1961 Newman was summoned before the board and instructed to resign. In a show of solidarity, assistant editor Bruce Williamson and the editorial secretary Marion Fitzgerald both walked out in protest at the board's action.[2] A settlement was arranged for Newman by the

NUJ's father of the chapel Dan Duffy and Newman spend the rest of his career writing leading articles and a current affairs column for the *Irish Press*.[3] Newman's successor was former chief-reporter and assistant editor Alan Montgomery; he 'was not the greatest of editors; nor, indeed, was he the best player of office politics'; an extremely affable man, he had an instinct for newsgathering but found 'the Editor's chair an uncomfortable throne, far removed from the comradely hurly burly of the newsroom'.[4] Montgomery had made his mark as an able chief-reporter but, as one colleague recalled, that did not necessarily translate into being a capable editor:

> Monty was a very capable writer and had a great facility for spotting news rapidly. He was great for the fast news story and organising things. As an administrator he would have been all right but his business acumen would not have been outstanding. He hadn't been to Trinity and both Smyllie and Newman were Trinity graduates. So I think that the board's idea at the time was that Monty would somehow bring it out of the Trinity college intellectualism into a practical 1950s newspaper because the *Irish Independent* and *Irish Press* were hugely successful at the time whereas the *Irish Times* was not. If the board had wanted to change the *Irish Times* and make things different then they chose the wrong man. His capabilities were not of the great editorial style. He hadn't got the intellectual capacity for it. He was a newsman pure and simple.[5]

Indeed, one reporter recalled that Montgomery wrote no editorials while he was editor.[6] After two years in the editor's chair Montgomery was asked by Arthur Guinness & Co. to sit on an interview board to appoint that company's new public relations officer. Montgomery sat on the panel and made his recommendations, but the board eventually asked him to take the position. As the post paid far more than the *Irish Times,* he took up the offer and was, as one colleague recalled, 'highly criticised for leaving the editorship of the paper [although] Monty in many ways was lucky and certainly right to leave because his legacy to the *Irish Times* would not have been a great one'.[7] With the company still licking its financial wounds from its unsuccessful attempts at diversification (it reported losses of £20,632 and £8,053 for the years ending September 1962 and 1963) it was unable to pay any dividends to shareholders for the four years 1960–4.[8] The board now appointed one of its own – Douglas Gageby – to bring the company back from the brink. The time had arrived for the paper to yet again reinvent itself for a changing Ireland.

CHAPTER 8

The Paper of Record

When I was asked by George Hetherington to join the *Irish Times*, I told them that I was a nationalist of a certain kind, largely in favour of Fianna Fáil, and that if they found me acceptable I could not join them unless I had a seat on the board and thus a say in overall policy. When, eventually, I met the board, I told them this and they said, 'That's fine'. They were broadly national and if I did not like anything that was going into the paper I could do something about it.[1]

Douglas Gageby on joining the Irish Times

WHEN DOUGLAS GAGEBY became editor in October 1963, the paper's circulation stood at roughly 35,300. By the time he finished his first term as editor in July 1974, circulation had increased to 69,500 and it was a very different newspaper. Gageby presided over the transformation of the *Irish Times* from being the newspaper of the Protestant minority, albeit one with a liberal Catholic readership, to being a truly national newspaper. Gageby was the right man in the right place at the right time: a hugely talented journalist, he took over as editor at a time of huge social change. The move towards free trade resulted in an economic boom as the republic, branding itself as the gateway to Europe, attracted foreign capital with the lure of a low-cost but well-educated English-speaking workforce and a low corporation tax rate. Throughout the 1960s exports grew, unemployment fell, emigration declined, women entered the workforce in greater numbers, living standards increased and the sale of consumer goods increased dramatically. From mid-1959 to mid-1960 alone, the volume of national output grew by 8 per cent and the value of the country's exports rose by nearly 35 per cent. This led to an unprecedented surge in prosperity and a parallel surge in public confidence. As one chronicler of the period put it, 'the blinds were let up, the windows were thrown open, the doors were unlocked; and good, bad or indifferent, the modern world came in among us at last'.[2] A new generation of politicians emerged, and the pictures of Charles Haughey, Donogh O'Malley and Brian Lenihan became a familiar sight in the columns of the *Irish Times* and on the programmes of the new television service, Telefís Éireann, which arrived in 1961. The visit of John F. Kennedy, 'a local boy who made good', enthused the whole country and added to the optimistic mood of the time.[3] The Second Vatican Council, which ran from October 1962 to December 1965, encouraged critical debate about, and ultimately altered, Catholicism. Even literary censorship was radically amended amid the paperback revolution in publishing; in 1967 the permanent ban was replaced with a twelve-year ban, which released thousands of previously banned titles and effectively ended the censorship of serious literature.

In contrast to the de Valera-dominated *Irish Press* and the piously Catholic *Irish Independent*, the *Irish Times,* already the organ of liberal thought among the political, academic and artistic sectors was ideally positioned, under Gageby's leadership, to reflect the new Ireland. In a country that was changing beyond recognition, it could afford to rock the boat and reap rewards rather than odium for doing so. With the backing of the board, Gageby assembled a team of journalists that sometimes reflected but also sometimes led the process of social change throughout the 1960s. The result was a vibrant, socially aware and critically informed newspaper that appealed not only to the political and intellectual sectors but also to the newly affluent and critically thinking Catholic middle class. Gageby was, remembered one reporter, the 'first of the business-like editors ... a much more hands-on editor than Newman or Smyllie – he was constantly in the newsroom, was constantly almost over your back looking at stories and what was going on'.[4] Another reporter remembered him as 'a hard taskmaster, but scrupulously fair':

> He was a strict disciplinarian who, as leader, laid down the rules and watched to make sure that they were followed to the letter. He had an eagle eye and nothing ever got past him in the paper without him querying it. You could always detect the old army training in him: it was reflected in his whole demeanour. The staff was fully aware of his style and stuck by his policy. He was always in total command and he did not tolerate any insubordination. He sought ideas and said he was open to suggestions, but if he had his mind made up there was no point in going against him.[5]

Unlike any previous editor, Gageby sat on the board of the company, a position that strengthened his hand considerably in terms of securing resources. In an interview, Gageby acknowledged that being a director-editor ensured he had 'a great deal more backing from the board than an editor who is not on the board'.[6] Important elements of his contact stated that the editorial staff was responsible for its own budget and that the editor, not the advertising manager, decided the size of the paper.[7]

MAN BITES DOG

With a new editor came a change in personnel. Almost immediately, Gageby arranged for the return of Bruce Williamson, who had resigned from the paper over the treatment of Alec Newman. Williamson returned as a leader writer and would eventually become a deputy-editor. Gageby also promoted the then news editor, Matt Chambers, to the position of deputy-editor. This vacated the position of news editor – a position for whom Gageby had the ideal person in mind – the paper's London reporter, Donal Foley. Born in Waterford in 1922, Foley emigrated to London in 1944 where he worked a variety of jobs including a position in the London office of the *Irish Press*. He joined the London office of the *Irish Times* in the mid-1950s and worked under the paper's London editor, Sir John Arnott.[8] The main task of the London office was the compilation of the 'London Letter', a commentary on life in Britain in terms of social, political, economic and cultural developments. One day in September 1963 Foley received a telephone call from Gageby to tell him Major McDowell, the managing director, would be calling to see him. The following day an unenthusiastic Foley received McDowell, who surprised him by offering him the post of news editor.[9] Although he had been away from Ireland for nearly twenty years Foley's love of the Irish language, Gaelic games and traditional Irish music made him the ideal candidate to help Gageby transform the *Irish Times* into a newspaper that would reflect a modern Ireland. He would, as his obituary put it, play 'a key role in adapting the style, content and appeal of the *Irish Times* in the period of rapid economic and social change in the 1960s'.[10] As Foley noted in his memoir, the Ireland he came back to was very different to the one he had left in 1944:

> Ireland was changing. Truths learned at Mother's knee and at school had begun for many people, to take on a new meaning. Religion was no longer for many a subject for discussion in dark side chapels or confessional boxes, but a philosophy that should influence people's lives. It was a time for questioning: How? Why? When? This was why the year 1963 in fact, was a great time to come back to Ireland as news editor of the *Irish Times*. It was a time for extending the frontiers, and the advent of Radio Telefís Éireann was an important milestone in this development. People were looking for new answers. Even children were not put off by their parents' impatience. Young people were kicking over the traces, frustrated about the inanities of their own lives. They were not satisfied with the old society in Ireland with its easy acceptance of poverty and injustice as part of the will of God.[11]

To Foley, the role of the paper in such a society was clear: it was to be 'a forum for discussion, a mouthpiece for all minorities as well as the majority, and a paper with a clear-cut radical viewpoint'.[12] Remembered by one colleague as being 'brilliant with ideas', Foley frequently left the administration of the news desk to his deputy, Gerry Mulvey, while he concentrated on ideas for features that had a strong social content.[13] Another reporter also recalled that Foley was 'a great ideas man':

> He had a fine inquiring mind, a natural curiosity, was constantly asking questions. He loved originality and liked to get away from the day-to-day running news stories and to suggest and get involved in feature articles. These often had an important social content. He also liked to encourage his staff to come up with ideas. He thrived on generating exclusives. He took a tremendous pride in breaking a good story or instigating a successful series of articles. He had a sharp instinct for what would make a good feature and seemed to get a bigger buzz out of a well written feature than from a strong news story. He preferred the freedom of comment and 'colour' in features than the discipline and sometimes the boredom of straight reports.[14]

As well as being news editor Foley also wrote the popular 'Man Bites Dog' column, which was a satirical overview of the week's news. Although it never reached the same heights of satire and absurdity as Myles na gCopaleen's 'Cruiskeen Lawn', the column was so popular that it was published annually in book form. Foley also wrote the 'Saturday Column' and initiated 'Tuarascáil', an Irish-language current affairs column. Three regular columnists – Séan Ó Ríordáin, Breandán O hEithir and Donall MacAmhlaigh – wrote the weekly half-page column, the mandate of which was deal with contemporary issues through the medium of Irish. Foley was also responsible for an innovative attempt to build up the paper's circulation among university students that paid dividends later on. By increasing coverage of the emerging student movement – in particular the student protests in UCD that occurred in late 1968 and early 1969 – and distributing free or discounted copies of the paper in UCD and TCD, Foley hoped to get students into the practice of buying the paper. The plan was that the young readers would take the habit of buying the paper with then when they joined the workforce. This initiative was, remembered one reporter, 'a big factor in building the circulation' of the paper.[15]

THE NEW WAVE

Throughout the 1960s Gageby and Foley assembled a team of reporters that changed the face of Irish journalism. Both men embraced the concept of specialised correspondents, whereby reporters were assigned to specific news areas and encouraged to develop an expertise and sources in these particular areas. They appointed specific reporters to specialised fields such as education, industrial relations, diplomacy, religion, business, the north and agriculture. With these appointments came the use of by-lines that heightened public awareness of the paper's correspondents. This is turn brought its own problems: as one reporter recalled, while Foley initially believed that specialist correspondents were a good idea, he later had second thoughts and declared that 'As soon as they [specialists] are appointed they start building up their own little empires, try to become personalities and won't do any general reporting.'[16] In 1964 John Horgan was appointed religious correspondent and was dispatched to Rome the following year to cover the final session of Vatican II. Up to that point the paper had simply published news agency dispatches. Thrown into 'the cultural and theological maelstrom that was Rome in 1965', Horgan wrote 1,000 words a day, six days a week for six months on debates that centred on lay involvement in the liturgy, the use of vernacular languages and ecumenism. While in Rome, Horgan experienced 'the novelty – shock, almost – of the Mass in English, and the curiously mixed feelings engendered by the sight of a row of bishops, gift-wrapped in their scarlet belly-bands, kneeling in a queue for confession in a side-aisle of St Peter's basilica like so many altar boys'.[17]

Gageby and Foley also appointed reporters from Britain and the United States, a move that saw some *Irish Times* journalists approach Irish social problems with an outsider's critical distance and perspective. One such appointment was that of Michael Viney, an English-born journalist who arrived in Ireland from London's Fleet Street in 1961. Working as a freelancer under Alan Montgomery – for whom one of his first series of articles, 'Ireland for Sale?', dealt with the tensions in rural Ireland between locals and non-nationals who bought land – Viney came into his own under Gageby's editorship.[18] Another early series, 'Last Chance for the Language?' in 1963, gave the paper its first-ever street poster in Irish.[19] A series on unmarried mothers, 'No Birthright', followed in 1964, and in that year also Viney was dispatched to Northern Ireland for two weeks to conduct research for a series and encountered one John Hume, then a 27-year-old teacher and community activist.[20] Shortly afterwards, Hume wrote two articles for the paper entitled 'The Northern Catholic', which essentially laid out the political philosophy that would later become the cornerstone of the SDLP.[21] For the most part though, Viney picked his own topics and tackled them with the critical distance of an outsider's eye:

> Single mothers (then 'unmarried'), young offenders, the mentally ill, the alcoholic, the drug-addicted – so many of my subjects can sound wearily familiar today. But in the Ireland of the 1960s, where most academic sociology was bounded by the papal encyclicals, such researches often amounted to the raw material of social science; this was all a new approach. Reprinted in booklets, the series became student texts. They brought Catholic affairs and institutions into the *Irish Times* and its letter columns, and helped to show (I hope) the newspaper's determination to be fair. A series on Protestants in the Republic, 'The Five Per Cent', proved uncomfortable for many in that community, but Douglas, reading my copy, found it 'Great stuff!', which set me up for days.[22]

Female journalism was also dragged into the twentieth century. Moving away from the confines of cookery and fashion, Eileen O'Brien's 'A Social Sort of Column' examined social issues that were mostly ignored by society. The elderly in nursing homes, the homeless, the wives of alcoholics, a crèche run for working mothers, the traders of Moore Street, and a retraining programme for newsboys were just some of the topics examined by O'Brien in early 1967. With series such as 'Unmarried Mothers' by Margaret Boleyn and 'A Short History of the Pill in Ireland' by Mary Maher, the paper began to cover social and political issues that directly affected women.[23] A dedicated space for such journalism, 'Women First', was proposed by Donal Foley but initially rejected by Mary Maher. Maher had begun her journalism career at the *Chicago Tribune*, but, tired of the restrictive scope of female journalism there, she moved to Ireland and in April 1965 found herself on a three-month probation at the *Irish Times* – the 'small liberal, eccentric newspaper, which was bursting with ideas'.[24] When Foley suggested a dedicated women's page, Maher was 'vehemently opposed' to the idea since in her experience 'women's pages were designed by male editors with the advertising department, for housewives whom they imagined had only one interest: to buy things to bring home'.[25] But when Foley suggested a 'woman's page with serious articles, scathing social attacks and biting satire', Maher agreed, and 'Women First' was born:

> There were articles on censorship, slum poverty, the housing shortage, the class bias of education, exploitation of factory girls, corporal punishment, and a few initial attempts to raise the matter of equality along the order of 'Women Drive Better then Men' and 'When Will the Unions Fight for Equal Pay?' It was a beginning. Contraception, unmarried mothers, deserted wives, family law, children's courts, prison conditions – all the issues that didn't exist out loud in 1967 – were to follow, faster than we perhaps imagined.[26]

The page was a first for Irish journalism and the other national dailies followed suit within a few months. Maher edited the column for eighteen months before handing over the reigns to Maeve Binchy, another Foley recruit. Binchy had contributed articles to the paper while working as a teacher and was offered the post of women's editor in 1968. She edited the 'Women First' page until 1972 when she moved to the paper's London office, and she was succeeded by Christina Murphy. 'Women First' ran for another two years and was retired from the paper in October 1974. In a farewell article, Murphy, who then became education correspondent, noted that women's affairs had become mainstream and was now 'legitimate news in its own right'. The women's liberation movement had, she concluded, 'grown from a frowned-upon, suspect fringe into an important, multi-pronged lobby, and in the process has pushed women's affairs out of the cosy confines of the women's page, and onto the front pages of the newspapers where it belongs'.[27]

In 1967 Fergus Pyle was dispatched to Belfast as the paper's first northern editor. Prior to this, the paper, like all others, simply depended on a stringer who worked for a northern newspaper to sell it relevant stories. Under this system most news stories centred on unionist reaction to speeches about partition and the occasional rioting that erupted between the two traditions. There was little or nothing about the ordinary day-to-day life of northerners or the happenings at the Stormont parliament. But, with Sean Lemass' visit to Northern Ireland prime minister Terence O'Neill in January 1965 and O'Neill's reciprocal visit to Dublin the following month, it was clear that a new era in north-south relations was emerging. The *Irish Times* was the first national newspaper to establish a full-time office in the north, a move that puzzled so many people that Gageby found himself justifying it in almost every interview he did:

> And isn't it an appalling commentary on all of us in the Twenty-Six Counties that it should be so remarkable for us to have a full time office in Belfast ... All Irish newspapers had been largely sleeping for decades. We began to give good coverage to Stormont, which surprised a lot of people in the North ... Perhaps not many people eventually read it, but we were determined to have it ... All this wasn't done to sell more in the North. The aim was, if I can put it crudely, equally to show the so-and-sos down below what was going on ... It was part of our thing to say: this is a paper for the whole of Ireland. Stormont was an Assembly of Irish men and women debating on Irish soil. We were inviting people to read what they had to say. It was a slice of Irish life.[28]

While Gageby may have believed that the north was newsworthy in its own right, the reporters dispatched there did not necessarily share this view:

> Gageby also had the view that Stormont should be given the same extensive coverage as the Dáil. He felt that it should be treated with the same respect. This was a view I most certainly did not hold, as I was usually the person who had to travel to Belfast to help out. I had to spend tortuous hours listening to the most dreadful debates in the North's so called 'parliament' and then send reams of copy to Dublin. It was only a glorified county council. Yet, our circulation in the North at the time was only miniscule. That didn't deter Gageby: we had to show ourselves to be fair and impartial to the people on both sides of the border.[29]

The paper's devotion to northern issues prompted much comment. Such was its reputation for devoting copious amount of space to Stormont debates and Fergus Pyle's very lengthy reports that one unionist politician quipped that he 'preferred Hansard to Pyle. It's shorter.'[30] As one reporter remembered, 'when his copy used to come in we would watch while reams and reams came off the telex machine, and we'd go "Oh, it's Fergus." But it was all very good-humoured because he was liked and respected.'[31] Nonetheless, the appointment of a northern editor was an ingenious if unintended move, in that the north would dominate the news agenda from the late 1960s. As the unionist government clashed with the civil rights movement and the north descended into violence, the paper had a head start over its Dublin competitors. Gageby also sent reporters to other global hotspots; in 1968 Dermot Mullane was dispatched to Paris to cover the student riots, and John Horgan was dispatched to Nigeria to report on its civil war, while in 1969 Dennis Kennedy was dispatched to South Africa to report on the apartheid regime.

Gageby and Foley also set about redesigning the paper, and although each page was still printed as eight columns of single type, photographs were more boldly used on page one. Its size increased to sixteen pages on weekdays and eighteen pages on Saturdays, and the content was also radically reorganised. The sports pages remained on pages two to four, and coverage, particularly that of the GAA, was expanded, even though Gageby, unlike Foley, had no interest in sport. In an interview he expressed his belief that 'all the Irish papers give too much space to sport'.[32] Still, as one reporter recalled, 'Gageby had no interest in sport himself but knew that sport was important to a newspaper'.[33] All foreign news was placed on one page under the heading 'News from Abroad', and coverage was enhanced by subscriptions to additional international news services and the appointment of Sean Cronin as the paper's New York stringer. All financial news was grouped together into a new two-page 'Business and Finance' section edited firstly by Nicholas Leonard and in later years by Hugh O'Neill, Valentine Lamb, Andrew Whittaker, Richard Keatinge and Bill Murdoch. The editorial page was also rearranged with the leading articles being set as a double-column to make them more distinctive. 'An Irishman's Diary', written by Seamus Kelly, was also relocated to this page and, in an honour rarely accorded in print journalism, the paper began reprinting a selection of articles from 'Cruiskeen Lawn' entitled 'The Best of Myles'. It is a mark of Gageby's and Foley's success that while sales of the *Irish Independent* fell from 174,005 in 1962 to 166,890 in 1973 and sales of the *Irish Press* fell from 116,552 to 94,115 over the same period, sales of the *Irish Times* jumped from 33,300 to 67,976.[34]

BACKBENCHER

Another key ally of Gageby's was the columnist John Healy, who began his journalism career in his native Co. Mayo in 1948 as a reporter on the *Western People*. A stint in the Irish News Agency followed and after its disbandment in 1953 Healy moved to the Irish Press Group. When Gageby joined the *Irish Times* in 1959, Healy moved with him and was, at various times (as we saw), the editor of the *Evening Mail* and the *Sunday Review*. When the latter title folded in November 1963, Healy's 'Inside Politics' column, which he wrote under the pen-name 'Backbencher', moved to the *Irish Times*. This column was to many people the most influential political column of the 1960s. It was distinctive for two reasons; it contained information, sometimes on government policy, sometimes political gossip, derived from cabinet leaks that was not available to other political writers; and it was written in a daring and irreverent style that treated politicians as ordinary mortals who were not above the temptations and mistakes of everyday life. In the words of one reporter, the column helped dispel the air of reverence that had, to some extent, up to then, pervaded political journalism:

> The best service that Healy did for journalism and newspapers was that, back then ministers were sacrosanct, but he made ministers answerable. He treated them as ordinary Joe Soaps, calling them by their first name. The Fianna Fáil ministers immediately post-war were arrogant beyond belief; Lemass was the only one that was approachable. You dare not ring a minister, they were sacrosanct; but Healy broke that down. He made fun of them in many ways, broke down the whole aloofness, so that they had to talk. Politicians today are galloping to get on every micky-mouse programme.[35]

Healy also fronted the current affairs programme *The Hurler on the Ditch* on Telefís Éireann. The programme consisted of a weekly overview of political events by journalists – such as Michael Mills of the *Irish Press* – who were not afraid to speak their minds. Such critical analysis did not sit well with many politicians. In February 1965 Sean Lemass expressed his disquiet at 'a growing disposition on the part of some of our newspaper commentators, led by the *Irish Times,* to present a picture of Irish politics in which the only motivating force is represented as self-interest'. Such a picture was 'fundamentally false' and the press should, he concluded, 'seek to present a more reliable picture of Irish political life and of our political motivations than is now current'.[36] The following year, in a Seanad debate on broadcasting, Senator Patrick Quinlan spoke out against the prominent coverage given to the views of journalists like Healy and Mills. He declared that 'the political commentators who have appeared in GAA clothes, "The Hurler on the Ditch", have been given a place of importance in this country altogether out of keeping with a democratic country'. No other democracy would allow 'a small group to get into their hands the power to make and break politicians and to make and break Governments that Telefís Éireann have given to the political commentators here'. There was, he concluded, 'far too close a tie-up between this and the "Backbencher" column in the *Irish Times*'.[37]

It is generally acknowledged that Healy's main sources of cabinet information were the young guns that Lemass had appointed to cabinet. Healy was, remembered one reporter, 'very close to Donogh O'Malley, Brian Lenihan and Charles Haughey – but more to O'Malley'.[38] But O'Malley was not above criticism; Healy published details of O'Malley's drink-driving court case that had been held outside of normal court hours to spare him any embarrassment.[39] When, in September 1966, O'Malley announced the introduction of free post-primary education, Healy declared that he was 'not going to join in the current national adulation contest surrounding Mr Donogh O'Malley'; in fact, he was 'appalled at the lack of critical assessment of the new scheme'. Why, he asked, 'did O'Malley spring the bonanza on an unsuspecting country, an unsuspecting Oireachtas, an unsuspecting Fianna Fáil Party, and indeed without the full assent of all his Cabinet colleagues and without any consultation with the interests involved?' Detecting Lemass' hand in the affair Healy opined that 'behind O'Malley's plan for which he will have the money (you may take my word on that) lies the first part of Mr Lemass' last Will and Testament to ensure the success and future of the Fianna Fáil party when he retires'. Healy speculated, wrongly, that the party would call an election in 1968, several months after the free education scheme was up and running, to reap the electoral thanks of a grateful public.[40] When, in March 1968, O'Malley died suddenly the paper described him as 'at once a visionary and an innovator [who] wore himself out in the service of his country'.[41] Healy wrote a 'Backbencher' column in the course of which he had an imaginary conversation with O'Malley about the news coverage his death had received, his obituaries and his political career. O'Malley was, Healy concluded, 'a political saint ... larger than life'.[42]

But Healy also had sources within Fine Gael and at least one commentator hinted that his insider within the party was Patrick Lindsay, the long-time Co. Mayo TD.[43] Whoever his source was, in May 1964 Healy noted cryptically at the end of his column, 'I share with Mr Declan Costello a passion for discretion just now, but I can be depended upon to speak at the appropriate time.'[44] The following week Healy was the first journalist to reveal the new 'Just Society' policy programme that Costello had confidentially circulated within Fine Gael.[45] In the late 1960s Healy devoted his energies to examining how, in the midst of the economic boom, the west of Ireland was still ravaged by emigration. The prosperity of the 1960s was so disproportionately concentrated in the east and south of the country that, as emigration declined around the rest of the country, the counties of Connacht and Co. Donegal were still losing nearly 4,000 people per annum.[46] As the young population left for the east coast, a sense of gloom and hopelessness pervaded western communities and it was this sense of hopelessness that Healy captured in his series of articles, 'No One Shouted Stop', which appeared in October 1967 and were later published in book form under the title *Death of an Irish Town*. Besides writing his 'Backbencher' column, Healy also wrote a daily 'In the Dáil' column, and, as one reporter recalled, he 'always managed to pick up the choice little tit-bits of a debate. Even if was a dreadfully boring debate he could latch on to some quote and build a sketch around it'. Such was Healy's skill at picking up throwaway quotes that went over the heads of the paper's Dáil reporters that occasionally Gageby would enquire as to why the quotes only appeared in Healy's copy. Healy eventually agreed to a request from the reporters to show them his copy before he sent it to the paper so that they could include any quotes that they may have missed.[47]

Gageby and Healy were, as one reporter put it, 'a journalistic odd couple: one a quizzical Belfast Protestant and Trinity graduate, the other a professedly hard-nosed chaw from small-town Mayo'. Both men had a love of nature and fishing and 'through many political crises, what the *Irish Times* thought about things was distilled as the two men fished for trout on a midland lake or river'.[48] As another reporter recalled:

> John and Gageby were very close friends. John was briefing him on what was happening in the Dáil almost on a daily basis. They were always talking on the phone. Each held the other in very high professional esteem. Gageby had great respect for John's views and delighted in him 'stirring things up', while Healy liked what Gageby was doing with the paper and his overall policy. They complimented each other very well and it worked out successfully for the paper. Nevertheless, there were rumours that some people on the board felt the paper was carrying too much on politics, that political coverage should be cut back. This was never done, as the editorial belief was that Irish people, more than people of other countries, are infatuated by political manoeuvrings and love to read every tittle-tattle emanating from Leinster House.[49]

While news editor Donal Foley and political correspondent Michael McInerney were ardent supporters of the Labour Party, Gageby and Healy leaned towards Fianna Fáil – although Gageby always denied this. In one interview, when asked if the perceived Fianna Fáil leanings of the paper was a legacy of his days working for de Valera's Irish Press Group, he replied that the *Irish Times* had simply changed 'with the country'.[50] Healy was particularly enamoured with fellow Mayoman Charles Haughey and often referred to him in his 'Backbencher' column as 'The Golden Boy'. One reporter recalled that 'until the day he died, he believed in Haughey'. It was believed by many that Healy's admiration for Haughey rubbed off on Gageby – that Healy was, in effect, Gageby's blind spot. The reporter summed it up thus: 'I don't thing Gageby accepted that Healy would be wrong; it's a fair comment.'[51] During the 1960s, Haughey's lifestyle evoked intense gossip (particularly during the 1969 general election) and Michael Viney's suggestion to Gageby that, with six months' assistance from a solicitor and an accountant, he might arrive at something safe to print was rejected. As Viney remembered it, his 'attempt at a biographical series on Haughey was taken away by him [Gageby] and John Healy and largely rewritten by them'.[52]

Whatever about the paper being pro-Fianna Fáil, Sean Lemass was not pro-*Irish Times*. In the midst of an election campaign, the paper published a spoof editorial, entitled 'Staggering', on 1 April 1965, which informed its readers that, if re-elected, Lemass intended to ban alcohol. It quoted Lemass as having said, 'If I make it on April 7, the boozer will have to go abroad for his drink in future. He won't get it here.' At the bottom of the editorial the paper took the opportunity to remind Lemass and caution its readers that it was 1 April.[53] However, Lemass did not see the funny side of things and in a speech he declared:

> The *Irish Times*, which seems to have passed under the control of a group of crypto-reds, supporting left wing elements in the Labour party, has now, for the first time in this country, introduced the Communist tactic of attributing to its political opponents, statements which they never made. Needless to say, the words quoted in this leading article were never used by me. The suggestion is so absurd that, on this occasion, nobody is likely to believe it, but I must expect this tactic to be repeated in some other context before polling day. The Fianna Fáil government liberated the licensing laws and that is our policy. The freedom of the press is a great principle and I personally will fight for its preservation even when it is abused in this fashion.

The following day the paper acknowledged that Lemass had never advocated the prohibition of alcohol, but also observed that he had 'temporarily lost his sense of humour'.[54] On polling day it concluded that Fianna Fáil was 'the party which at the present time seems fittest to govern the country' and called on readers 'to give Mr Lemass a firm mandate'.[55]

LOSSES, PROFITS AND STRIKES

Having sustained losses during the late-1950s and early-1960s the company returned to profitability in 1964 posting a profit of £30,526. From the mid-to-late 1960s the company continued to return a profit – £25,237 in 1965, £18,040 in 1966, £49,928 in 1967, £76,834 in 1968 and £36,969 in 1969. However, it was not all plain sailing. Throughout the 1960s numerous factors affected the company's trading position. In the 1966 annual report, the chairman, Ralph Walker, mentioned the low cover-price of the paper, the huge dependence on advertising revenue, rising production costs and increased levels of taxation as major issues facing the company. He estimated that, while each copy of the paper cost 14p to produce, the company received 4$^{1}/_{2}$p of the 6p cover price for each copy sold. This meant that sales of the newspaper accounted for just one-third of the company's revenue, with advertising sales accounting for the other two-thirds. A downturn in the demand for advertising could, he warned, be disastrous for the company. Despite representations by the newspaper industry, the government had included newspaper sales in the new turnover and wholesale taxes, which the paper tried to offset by increasing its advertising rates. On a more positive note, circulation increased by 30 per cent between 1962 and 1966 to over 44,000 copies per day.[56] The booming economy brought with it challenges as well as benefits. As profits rose, so too did demands for wage increases. A plethora of strikes occurred during the 1960s, one of which closed down all national newspapers for thirteen weeks between early July and mid-September 1965. The strike resulted from a 33 per cent wage-increase demand from the Irish Graphical Society, which represented printers. Newspaper managements pleaded inability to pay and when, on 2 July 1965, the two weeks' strike notice expired, all staffs were put on protective notice. In a pre-strike editorial the paper declared that, while 'a fair call for a fair share of the cake' would not be rejected, 'pavement pounding and placard waving' would not achieve anything.[57]

When the national newspapers finally resumed publication, the paper informed readers that rumours of its demise had been greatly exaggerated. Alongside a 'cruel and vicious attempt to alarm the television authorities into announcing the false news that the President, Mr de Valera, was dead', many other 'mindless idle tales' had done the rounds in the absence of the national newspapers. The paper itself had figured in many of these tales. Rumours circulated that it would not resume publication when the strike ended or that it had been bought by, depending on the rumour, Lord Thomson, the Beaverbrook Press, Bing Crosby or the Guinness family. None of these tales was true; it had 'suffered heavily through the strike' but was in 'good fettle, not bought out by anyone, not going to be bought out by anyone'.[58] As one reporter recalled, it was the 'worst time' of the year for the printers to go on strike, because, with a dearth of news during the 'silly season' of the summer months, the newspaper managements could hold out longer for an agreeable deal to be reached.[59] The Dublin Newspaper Managers' Committee had a 'one out, all out' policy, whereby, if one newspaper title ceased production through industrial action, all titles ceased production. From the proprietors' point of view this lessened the risk of any union starting a round of wage increases by picking on the weakest newspaper first. Less than four months after the strike ended, a separate strike at Dublin Port prevented vital newsprint supplies from reaching all the city's newspapers, which consequently shrank in size.[60] Working conditions at the paper also improved. It was the first to drop the old 'grace and favour' method of retirement – whereby people worked for a pittance until they literally dropped dead – in favour of a non-contributory pension. The paper's political correspondent Michael McInerney and the NUJ were instrumental in securing this improvement, although they received a sympathetic ear from the managing director, Major McDowell.[61]

MYLES, BACKBENCHER AND THE ARCHBISHOP

In October 1965 Myles na gCopaleen unwittingly began his last controversy in the paper. In the course of an article that centred on the lack of green space within the city centre, he made passing reference to the fact that some years previously it had been rumoured that Merrion Square had been bought by the Catholic church for the construction of a Catholic cathedral, but he concluded that this rumour was probably untrue.[62] This innocuous comment prompted a long missive from the newly appointed director of the Dublin Diocesan Press Office, Ossie Dowling, who confirmed that the site had indeed been purchased with such an intention. The project had been abandoned when John Charles McQuaid was appointed archbishop and 'decided to concentrate first on the needs of the faithful in the parishes, which included social services, schools and churches'. The letter then went on to exalt the record of McQuaid, who in his first twenty-five years as archbishop, had set up 26 new parishes and had overseen the building of 34 new churches, 67 secondary schools and the opening of Our Lady's Hospital for Sick Children. While Dowling bemoaned the fact that there was 'no fine cathedral' to celebrate the upcoming silver jubilee of his appointment, he concluded that McQuaid's first concern was for the poor of Dublin.[63]

This glowing tribute to McQuaid, in response to such a throwaway comment, prompted John Healy to observe in his 'Backbencher' column that Dowling's letter make McQuaid look like 'a Minister without Portfolio'. With tongue firmly in cheek, he remarked that it was rumoured Eamonn Andrews thought that Dowling's letter came 'uncannily close to a draft script for "This is Your Life" to be screened on the 25th Anniversary in December. The lump in the throat bit is when Eamonn pulls back the curtain to reveal the surprise: one gleaming new cathedral. Fade up angelic music and roll the credits … '[64] It also provoked an irate letter from Myles na gCopaleen who promised a longer letter that would 'show that the Archbishop has more able-bodied persons of both sexes in personal attendance on him than anything attempted by the Holy Father'. He also promised a full statement on McQuaid's palaces and private transport and asked that 'any further letter in coarse praise of himself should be signed by himself and not by (still another) paid servant'.[65] This missive prompted Dowling to deny that his letter had been written on behalf of McQuaid, who, he asserted, was in Rome and knew nothing of the correspondence. His letter had been written 'not for the sake of publicity, but in the interest of truth'.[66] This provoked Myles to ask on whose behalf – given that the letter had originated from the Dublin Diocesan Press Office – it had been written. In due course, he continued, he would want to know 'what the Archbishop's income is and what he pays in rates and taxes'. The list of good works attributed to McQuaid, had, according to Myles, the effect of making his predecessor, Archbishop Byrne, look like 'a workshy layabout'. Dowling would, Myles concluded, 'do his boss a lot of good by keeping quite'.[67]

This letter brought the issue to a close, but only so far as the letters page was concerned. Behind the scenes the fallout from the squabble continued. McQuaid did not take Myles' comments about his lifestyle lightly, and sought legal advice as to whether any action could be taken against the paper. In a letter from the legal firm Arthur Hagan & Son, a solicitor, Edward G. Gleeson, expressed his horror at 'the unjust and unwarranted personal attacks in the letters in the I. Times' but concluded that there was 'no positive step – "overt" or otherwise which can usefully or wisely be taken'. Gleeson added that if Myles persisted in his letter writing, then he would review the situation because 'sooner or later a stand may have to be made against this insidious type of thing'.[68] The possibility of Myles making good his threat of writing a detailed letter to the paper about McQuaid's lifestyle was also prepared for: McQuaid was sent a draft reply, written by Dowling, that would be used in the event of Myles 'writing his threatened letter in the Irish Times'.[69] When the draft reply was returned to Dowling, the conclusion recorded was that Myles had 'indirectly called for a truce in his last letter'.[70] There was no love lost between McQuaid and Myles, who, around this time, wrote three articles on McQuaid that were rejected by the paper. As Anthony Cronin recounts in his biography of Brian O'Nolan, Douglas Gageby had assured O'Nolan that he himself would read O'Nolan's copy, sub it and, unless there were concerns over libel, publish it in full. This agreement, Cronin recounts, broke down straight away because the first three articles O'Nolan presented were about McQuaid and 'they contained, according to Gageby, gross errors of fact which Myles refused to acknowledge'.[71]

But it was not only Myles na gCopaleen who worried Archbishop McQuaid with his throwaway comments. John Healy's 'Backbencher' column also came in for scrutiny. In the run-up to the 1966 presidential election Erskine Childers proclaimed that young people of all political affiliations would recognise that

Eamon de Valera had continuously altered the social and economic structures of Ireland so as to provide greater opportunities in life. This god-like invocation led Healy to observe that Childers' view of de Valera was like 'the idea of a politically immaculate conception allied to a sort of divine Godhead, from which issued all political and economic graces at the one time'.[72] This comment rankled with McQuaid who, in a letter to Ossie Dowling, stated that although he did not wish to make an issue of what was not 'intentional blasphemy', he had a duty to intervene. The approach adopted this time was more low-key. McQuaid asked Dowling to meet with Healy and 'exhort him from me never in all his life to speak in any disparagement of the Mother of God'.[73] Dowling responded by stating that, while he did not think Healy would 'intentionally blaspheme', he found Healy's use of language 'rather frightening' and thought McQuaid's 'restrained comment' would have an effect.[74] In a follow-up letter, Dowling reported that he had met Healy in the Dáil and that he had been 'genuinely shocked that he should have offended, even inadvertently, in this manner, the more so since his ill-judged phrase had obviously pained Your Grace, whom he admires'. Healy asked for time to think about the matter – 'presumably to see if he can make amends in some way' – and Dowling suggested to McQuaid that Healy would benefit by having 'a private conversation' with him.[75] McQuaid recorded that he would be glad to meet Healy, although no record was made of such a meeting.

CHALLENGING SACRED COWS

April 1966 marked the fiftieth anniversary of the 1916 rising, and to commemorate the event the paper published a sixteen-page supplement that critically examined the event and its significance in Irish history. The supplement, *1916: A Historical Review of the Men and the Politics of the Easter Rising,* included contributions from distinguished scholars such as F.S.L. Lyons, Nicholas Mansergh, Owen Sheehy Skeffington, Basil Chubb, Conor Cruise O'Brien and Owen Dudley Edwards.[76] In an editorial Gageby implicitly criticised the role of the Catholic church in the republic's legislative process, by noting that that there existed an 'irritating grain of truth' when northern unionists claimed that 'some of the provisions of our laws down here and many of our attitudes are far from Tone's liberal and revolutionary ideas of the rights of man'. He also criticised southern attitudes towards the north – the way in which 'for forty years and more, we, Government and people, have done our damnedest to write off mentally about a million of those same Irishmen or to pretend that they do not exist, or worse, to bathe in the rosy idea that some day, by some transformation, they will again become the United Irishmen of 1798'.[77]

Shortly afterwards, Eamon de Valera stood for re-election as president. Fine Gael decided to contest the election and put forward Tom O'Higgins. The idea of Fine Gael opposing 'The Chief' for the presidency in the same year as the golden jubilee of the 1916 rising greatly irritated many within Fianna Fáil. Some members of the party blamed the *Irish Times*, which had insisted that the electorate be given a choice of candidates. In November 1965 it had declared that 'the spirit of 1916 would be well borne out if next year were to see a Fine Gael President. For the other side of the old Sinn Féin house has still its part to play and that party is not lacking in men who could with dignity and vigour fill the office'.[78] It also welcomed O'Higgins' candidacy by noting that electoral contests were 'the essence of a healthy democratic system'.[79] Not everyone saw it that way, and Fianna Fáil's Micheál Ó Moráin denounced the paper:

> For a time it appeared that there would not be any candidate opposing the President. The *Irish Times* spoke, however, demanding that Fine Gael oppose the President ... We all know the *Irish Times* is the mistress of the Fine Gael party and mistresses can be both vicious and demanding. Now it may be necessary for the Fine Gael party to jump to the crack of the *Irish Times'* whip and gather the relics of the old ascendancy around them. It would, however, be a sad day for our people if the outlook of the President of the Irish people was forged and shaped by the occupants of a back room in Westmoreland Street.

O'Higgins responded: 'I do not know that the *Irish Times* is the mistress of our party, and I certainly do not know anything about the vicious demands of mistresses. On these questions I bow to the superior knowledge of Mr Moran.'[80] On polling day the paper reviewed the election campaign and noted that, while de Valera's old age and failing sight could not justify the electorate in voting against him, the manner of his candidature was a 'strong argument' for so doing. It believed that, being the serving president, de Valera should have nominated himself instead of accepting 'the nomination of the political party which he led since its inception'. In contrast, O'Higgins' appeal to young voters was praised, as was his 'new conception of the office which one would hope would use 1916 as an eminence to look out from, rather than as a monument from which stones are to be picked for throwing when better arguments are not available'. But it did not make a recommendation to its readers; it noted that it was 'a matter which adult voters will decide for themselves'.[81] The election was a close one, with O'Higgins coming within 10,500 votes of beating de Valera.

Some months later Sean Lemass announced his resignation as Taoiseach – leading to a flurry of activity that looked like turning into a bitter and divisive succession race between Charles Haughey and George Colley. Lemass' intervention in persuading Jack Lynch to stand as a compromise candidate was welcomed by the paper as 'the happiest solution'. Describing Haughey as 'the modern man, essentially pragmatic and business-minded', and Colley as 'a chip off the traditionalist block', it opined that Lemass was 'probably wise in anticipating a split in the ranks when he chose a compromise candidate who would act as a catalyst between bitterly opposing elements'. Lynch's nomination was a 'triumph of character', and it regretted that Colley had not agreed to withdraw from the succession race as Haughey had done. His insistence on a vote had, it maintained, 'the air of a young man in a hurry'.[82] However, John Healy welcomed the idea of a leadership contest, describing it as 'the fray that never really was'. Mocking Lynch's image as a hugely reluctant but very successful politician – 'Look lads, I didn't want to enter politics, but ... I didn't want to be a Parliamentary Secretary, but ... I didn't want to be Minister for Education, but ... I didn't want to be Minister for Industry and Commerce, but ... I didn't want to be Minister for Finance, but ... ' – Healy wondered, 'Why, this week-end, is ambition – the first ingredient of a leader – of a sudden a sin?' In Healy's eyes, Lynch's succession was 'merely decision postponed'; it was 'a compromise by a party which opted to save itself from a public eating of its entrails by electing a "safe" man'.[83] The following week he declared that 'Bland Jack Lynch will learn in the weeks and months ahead just what a bitch-goddess Democracy really is and what she can do when she suckles young ambition at the monolithic breast'.[84]

'SPIRITUAL APARTHEID'

As the 1960s drew to a close, the paper again clashed with Archbishop McQuaid. In his Lenten regulations of February 1967, McQuaid re-emphasised the fact that the Catholic church forbade, 'under pain of mortal sin', Catholics from attending Trinity College. Only McQuaid himself was 'competent to decide, according to the regulations of the Holy See, in what circumstances and with what precautions for avoiding the danger of perversion, attendance at that College may be tolerated'.[85] This prompted the paper to attack McQuaid's attitude towards ecumenism. Noting that McQuaid had contradicted a rumour to the effect that the ban on Catholics attending non-Catholic schools or universities had been relaxed, the paper retorted that 'far from complaining that an opinion has been spread abroad which indicates a relaxation in his firmly-rooted prejudices against ecumenical behaviour in his diocese, his Grace should have recognised the charity that gave him credit for breathing over here the spirit of Pope John'. To the paper McQuaid represented 'the very incarnation of all that it was believed Pope John with his loving heart was trying to rid his Church of – obscurantism, self-righteousness and spiritual apartheid'.[86] This editorial provoked a plethora of letters to the paper, some supporting its stance, others criticising it. It also prompted McQuaid to publish an article in the *Sunday Independent* in which he outlined the reasons for the existence of the ban.[87] This alone, to the *Irish Times*, justified its editorial – the aim of which was 'designed to let the air into one of the festering sores in our community life'. Reasoned debate rather than dogma were now the order of the day, and in that spirit the paper challenged many of the reasons outlined by McQuaid. Noting that, while at one time Catholics could not attend Trinity College without renouncing their religion, it observed that Catholics began to attend the university as soon as the penal laws were relaxed in the early 1800s and that from the mid-1800s scholarships were awarded to Catholics. The idea of Trinity College being 'an atmosphere dangerous to faith and morals' was, it concluded, 'a figment of imagination'.[88]

Relations between McQuaid and the paper were never destined to be harmonious, and its reporters were prepared to stand up to McQuaid in public as well as in print. In a public and much reported stand-off between McQuaid and an *Irish Times* reporter, the latter refused to hand over notes of a meeting that had been attended by reporters but which McQuaid later claimed to have been a private meeting. While a reporter from another newspaper handed over his notes when McQuaid demanded them, the *Irish Times* reporter refused to do so, causing McQuaid to lose his temper in public. The meeting in question was McQuaid's address to 300 nuns gathered for the Conference of Secondary Schools in Dublin at which he spoke about rationalisation in the schools system and the effects it would have on individual orders. In line with what he understood to be the wishes of the conference organisers, the director of the Dublin Diocesan Press Office, Ossie Dowling, had issued a press release inviting press coverage of the event.[89] For one reason or another, McQuaid took issue with the fact that reporters were present during his address. In a subsequent letter to Dowling, he explained that while addressing the nuns he 'suddenly saw two men present'. Asking to be assured that no journalists were present as the meeting was private, one of the men stood up. McQuaid asked if he had taken notes, and, when the reporter replied that he had, McQuaid asked for and was given the notes. The other reporter, Denis Coghlan of the *Irish Times,* simply left the room. McQuaid outlined how he confronted Coghlan after the meeting finished, how Coghlan publicly challenged McQuaid's assertion that the meeting was private, and how he refused to give McQuaid either his notes or his name:

> After speaking, I saw this person and asked if he were a journalist and had taken notes. He said yes. 'May I have them? I must refer to my editor. Who is your editor? Mr Gageby'.

Then he produced a sheet from the Press Office and pointed out that some things were marked private but not my address. I replied that that was your [Dowling's] mistake and that I should take it up with you. I asked his name. 'I do not see that that enters into the matter' he answered ... In effect, this journalist has retained notes of what he knew to be, after my declaration, a private meeting. I object to any use of his notes.[90]

Although the paper did not use the notes in any news story, it did report the stand-off and the fact that it was a mistake on the part of the Dublin Diocesan Press Office that led to the misunderstanding.[91]

Neither was the paper shy in criticising Fianna Fáil. In particular it criticised the party's stance, or lack of it, on the Vietnam War. In February 1968 Gageby noted that while the republic once had an independent foreign policy, by the late 1960s 'that impetus and sense of pride have gone by the board; and the impression has grown that we must say nothing to offend the American establishment – which, particularly at this moment in time, is not the same as the American people'. The government's few official pronouncements on the war were 'extracted with considerable difficulty – like a dental operation performed by an apprentice blacksmith'. The war was, he concluded, 'too important, in human and political terms, to permit any Government or individual the luxury of non-commitment, or the allusion that, somehow or other, integrity can be preserved by silence and expressions of ambiguous high-mindedness'.[92] As regards the war itself, Gageby believed that US President Lyndon Johnson viewed the conflict as 'a moral crusade' and that it was this concept that had 'twisted the American intervention from the beginning: it is what is responsible for the crisis with which the United States is now faced, and which will end by destroying a country and a people for their own "good"'. The war had, he concluded, 'involved the progressive discrediting of American judgment along the entire chain of political and military command'.[93]

The paper was also critical of the government's 1968 attempt to change the voting system from proportional representation to the first-past-the-post system. It highlighted the possibility of perpetual Fianna Fáil government by observing that 'the danger is that with the first-past-the-post system no other party might arise to challenge Fianna Fáil as far into the future as we can see – or indeed ever'.[94] In later editorials it referred to the government's drawn-out arguments in favour of change as 'The Neverendum'[95] and accused Fianna Fáil of 'eating their own tail in pouring derision on the faults of a system which the Irish electorate have more than once explicitly endorsed'.[96] Such was the paper's preference for the retention of proportional representation that in June 1968 deputy Sean Moore of Fianna Fáil accused it of publishing 'vicious leading articles advocating the retention of that archaic system'. The paper was, he contended, trying to 'influence public opinion not in the cause of the country but in the interests of maintaining the *status quo*'. The only minority that would suffer from the abolition of proportional representation was, he concluded, 'the people of the Ascendancy type who want to go on governing this country, not from Government benches or Leinster House, but from various old seats of power'.[97] On polling day the paper declared that it was 'in the country's best interests to vote "No" ... to the Government's extravagant, time wasting and potentially dangerous campaign'.[98] When the proposal was defeated, it concluded that 'many people who normally vote Fianna Fáil decided to teach them a lesson for their extravagance, for their self-indulgent waste of nearly a year's campaigning, for their insolence in foisting on the electorate a Referendum which no one asked for'.[99]

Indeed, during the general election of 1969, the paper veered towards supporting the re-invigorated Labour Party, which had proclaimed that the seventies were going to be socialist. It complimented the party's choice of candidates – such as Conor Cruise O'Brien, David Thornley, and Justin Keating – but it stopped short of explicitly urging its readers to vote for the party. On polling day it advised readers 'that the quality of the men put forward should be scrutinised and weighed up as never before' as the country needed 'legislators and leaders in the Dáil, not messenger boys'. The Labour Party's biggest contribution to the campaign was its 'courage to put forward men of distinction who would add notably to the strength of the Dáil, if elected', and a vote for the party was 'a vote for higher standards'. Hoping for the emergence of a genuine left-right dimension in Irish politics, it opined that the electorate was voting 'to set the scene for a genuine confrontation, to end Civil War politics, which, in spite of all statements to the contrary, are still firmly embedded in the two main parties'.[1] It was not to be, however; with Fianna Fáil demonising Labour's swing to the left as communism reinvented, the party went on to win an overall majority. There was no smashing of civil war politics; indeed, as the north descended into a protracted period of violence, civil war politics were to enjoy a revival in the south.

CHAPTER 9

'Have Your Cake and Eat I.T.'

McDowall [sic] is one of the five (Protestant) owners of the Irish Times, and he and his associates are increasingly concerned about the line the paper is taking under its present (Protestant, Belfast-born) Editor, Gageby, whom he described as a very fine journalist, an excellent man, but on Northern questions a renegade or white nigger.[1]

Andrew Gilchrist to London foreign office

FROM THE LATE 1960s Northern Ireland dominated the political and media landscapes. The post-war changes in education introduced by the British Labour Party led to the emergence of a generation of well-educated Catholics that allied itself to critically-thinking Protestants and liberals generally to establish the Northern Ireland Civil Rights Association. The border was not an issue; the movement demanded an end to institutionalised discrimination against Catholics in terms of housing allocation, employment and political representation. The demand for equality was anathema to the unionist government, and unionism generally misinterpreted the civil rights movement as subversive to the state. Given his background, Douglas Gageby took an immense interest in the civil rights movement; he travelled to Derry on at least one occasion to participate in a civil rights march. In one editorial he described the gerrymandering of Derry as 'a travesty of democracy'.[2] In another he declared that 'by a shameless manipulation, the majority is deprived not only of the control it would have if democracy prevailed, but even of an influential voice in the running of the city'.[3] But while Gageby viewed the civil rights movement as a latter-day version of the United Irishmen, its marches often provoked counter-demonstrations from hard-line unionists. In October 1968 Northern Ireland's minister of home affairs, William Craig, banned a civil rights march in Derry, which went ahead regardless. The outcome was described by the paper's northern editor, Fergus Pyle: 'For a quarter of an hour on Saturday afternoon, police in a Derry street punched, batoned and pursued Civil Rights demonstrators in a brutal and sickening display of what can only be called concerted violence.'[4]

The televising of the clashes between the RUC and the civil right marchers shocked viewers in Ireland and Britain, and, as Gageby put it, 'brought home to the people of Britain that there is something rotten much nearer home than Rhodesia'.[5] When, in January 1969, students marched from Belfast to Derry and encountered violence from unionists, Gageby declared that 'Once again the main source of violence in the North is seen to come from the Protestant right, and Northern Ireland is presented as a place where it is not even safe to ask for the rights which are so often proclaimed to be British.'[6] He also took issue with Taoiseach Jack Lynch's view that the sectarian strife was the result of partition. Sectarianism, as Gageby saw it, predated partition and was the result of the Conservative Party giving succour to unionists in their 1912 campaign to stop home rule, when 'the lords and lawyers made their speeches on Irish soil and then went back to their clubs in London to swap stories over brandy and port'.[7] When, at the behest of the British government, the northern premier, Terence O'Neill, announced reform of the voting system, Gageby asserted that reform of the unionist mindset was also needed. 'There still exists', he noted, 'within the Unionist Party the idea that they own the North, and that any concessions to the minority are a kindness to the tenantry.'[8]

As the Orange marching season, 'with its orgy of sham religious and deadly earnest political activity', rolled around, he declared that unionism 'with its Siamese twin, Orangeism, is wholly a sectarian and racist duality'.[9] But the advent of the civil rights movement meant things would never be the same again. As Gageby put it, 'the day is over when Orangemen can act as if the streets belonged to them alone. If Orangemen can flaunt their offensive slogans alongside their protestations of civil and religious liberty, there are now others, well organised too, who feel that they have the right to flourish their claims and desires.'[10] As the confrontations between the two sides worsened and the British government deployed troops to keep the peace, Gageby noted that Britain was 'at last alerted to the conditions its historical policies have produced in that part of the United Kingdom which nature intended to be a part of one island'.[11] These policies had, he noted, resulted in 'inequalities and injustices which would shame a Franco'.[12] Gageby's view of the Orange Order was heavily influenced by how his trade union-orientated grandfather had been, as he put it himself, 'done down by the unionists'. Gageby acknowledged this influence in a 1974 interview: 'He was, this is, I think, a key thing in my personality, he was anti-Orange – not just non-Orange, anti-Orange.'[13]

'A RENEGADE OR WHITE NIGGER'

Such editorial views did not sit well with all the directors of the paper, two of whom had served as officers in the British army. On one side stood the company chairman, Ralph Walker, his brother Philip, and the managing director Major McDowell; on the other, Gageby and George Hetherington. Apparently, Gageby did not think too highly of the Walker brothers. As remembered by one journalist, the Walker brothers were 'petty, Masonic, narrow in vision and very British empire ... Gageby would not have had time for the Dublin Masonic Protestants with their Boys' Brigade etc. ... He hated them. Whatever Gageby was he was genuinely republican and outward looking but the Walker brothers were just narrowly focused businessmen'.[14] Major McDowell took such exception to Gageby's editorials that on a trip to London he made contact with 10 Downing Street because he 'felt that he could be of some use with regard to the situation in Northern Ireland'. A discussion about McDowell's approach then ensued between the British prime minister, Harold Wilson, and Peter Gregson, one of his private secretaries. According to Gregson's account of the discussion, Wilson thought 'it would be desirable for our Embassy in Dublin to make contact with Major McDowell when he gets back. He thinks that Major McDowell's offer of assistance may relate more to intelligence than to journalistic activity.'[15] Having been informed of McDowell's approach, the British ambassador in Dublin, Andrew Gilchrist, met McDowell for lunch and sent a report of the meeting to Kelvin White at the foreign and colonial office in London:

> I had McDowell to lunch today. It is all about something he mentioned to me before, but now he is hotter under the collar about it. McDowall [sic] is one of the five (Protestant) owners of the Irish Times, and he and his associates are increasingly concerned about the line the paper is taking under its present (Protestant, Belfast-born) Editor, Gageby, whom he described as a very fine journalist, an excellent man, but on Northern questions a renegade or white nigger. And apart from Gageby's editorial influence, there is difficulty lower down, whereby sometimes unauthorised items appear and authorised items are left out. So far (except for last item) nothing new. But McDowell went on to say that he now felt a certain degree of guidance in respect of which lines were helpful and which unhelpful, might be acceptable to himself and one or two of his friends on the Board: this was what he had in mind in telephoning to No. 10. Oddly enough I had had McDowell in mind in certain conversations I had in London a fortnight ago. His present approach requires rather careful handling and I shall discuss it in London next week. I am writing this letter merely in case you wish to brief No. 10 and to assure them that we will do what we can to exploit this opening. I am destroying the correspondence.[16]

From this report it seems that McDowell had mentioned Gageby's attitude towards Northern Ireland to Gilchrist before. It also appears that McDowell had held conversations with other board members about Gageby's editorial line on the north. Interesting, in the company's annual report for 1969, the chairman, Ralph Walker, mentioned that the board determined the paper's editorial policy and that the paper's contents were reviewed at fortnightly board meetings.[17] In a follow-up letter to Kelvin White, Gilchrist suggested that McDowell 'be given a comfortable lunch by someone or other on one of his fairly frequent visits to London'.[18] In turn, White wrote to his superiors informing them that McDowell 'was seeking a degree of guidance, in the hope that he will be able to inculcate greater moderation in his own paper. Apparently he has troubles with his editor and this, not intelligence activity, was the root of the matter.' Nonetheless, White assured them that the foreign office would do what it could 'to exploit this opportunity'.[19] The first lunch took place on 30 October 1969 and White sent a detailed report to Gilchrist in Dublin:

> We had a lengthy talk over lunch, ranging over many Irish matters, and the newspaper world especially, but if I had to sum up very briefly what McDowell really had to say I think it would be that he wants to help and is willing to be used as a link. (This does not exclude the point of guidance you recorded in your letter of 2 October, but it does go rather further). I do not think he has anything specific, or dramatic, in mind; the offer is rather the result of those feelings of duty and anxiety that many who are emotionally both British and Irish must now be experiencing ... McDowell himself said he had hitherto, for obvious newspaper reasons, tried to keep free of those constraints that follow if a newspaperman forms an honourable alliance with the official world, but the present situation was so serious and so different he thought he ought to offer his services. His qualifications are his contacts in both capitals, and his acceptability in Whitehall terms through his service in the Judge Advocate General's department ... McDowell did not seek ammunition for use against his Editor, but he did, as you forecast, mention rather apologetically, that Editor's excessive zeal ... At the moment I think it would be useful, so far as we in the Department are concerned, to keep in touch with McDowell, to keep him briefed in general terms, and to encourage him to forward the moderates' cause in his paper. This is very much what you had in mind. Beyond that I cannot see a go-between role for him, but that would be a matter for you to suggest if you found doors closed to you.[20]

A subsequent lunch took place on 12 December 1969 and White again sent a detailed report to Gilchrist. He reported that McDowell lamented 'the lack of contact between prominent people in the North and in the South', and White directly quoted McDowell as stating that if some form of gathering to bring the two sides together could be contrived then 'the *Irish Times* would be happy to help, if need be contributing its name, finance, and administrative assistance'. McDowell 'made it plain that this was not a promotional stunt; the paper would be prepared to keep itself in the background if we thought that better'. White envisaged a series of seminars that avoided contentious subjects and instead focused on 'themes where inevitably North and South would find it made sense to co-operate'. As White saw it, 'McDowell might be well-placed to get things moving if both sides prove either reluctant to issue an invitation or too scared of their extremist fringes to accept an invitation from the other government'.[21] McDowell's approach to Downing Street would later result in him being accused of undermining the integrity and independence of the paper by approaching a foreign government for editorial guidance after the correspondence quoted above came into the public domain.[22] Despite his contacts with London, McDowell's actions did not interfere with Gageby's editorials on Northern Ireland affairs. As one journalist put it, 'McDowell was largely an Orangeman whereas Gageby was a republican. McDowell had the commercial side of the paper, Gageby the editorial and that functioned very well. Gageby was not open to challenge on that field. McDowell eventually saw himself as the former of Irish opinion, as the go-between for London and Dublin. But when Gageby made his mind up on anything he had an iron will and that was that.'[23] As another journalist remembered, 'The Major tolerated Gageby's nationalism and northern policy – though he hated it – because Gageby was key to the paper's prosperity, and because he himself actually believed in editorial independence. In fact the paper under Gageby was never anywhere near as nationalistic as Gageby himself was, in private, on the north.'[24] Like Gageby, McDowell did not shy away from visiting the north and despaired of the escalating violence. In 1969 he twice offered himself as a peace-broker and requested the paper's Belfast office to arrange meetings with leading members of nationalist and unionist factions. However, having arrived at the Belfast office in a white limousine, the staff 'concluded the boss was out of touch and, with some difficulty, persuaded him to drop the idea'.[25]

'AN ALIEN BACKGROUND'

Gageby also crossed swords with Fine Gael's Liam Cosgrave on the issue of Northern Ireland. In an editorial he noted that deputy John Kelly had attacked the government for 'its appalling indifference and neglect towards the north'. But, as he pointed out, Fine Gael 'had a share of office for two periods'. Had, he pointedly asked, the party 'presented the country with an alternative to the Government's non-policy towards the North?'[26] This rebuke prompted an angry outburst from Liam Cosgrave, who declared that he was 'not particularly disposed to be receptive to advice from that quarter when I look back on the comments – it is hardly necessary to repeat them or to refresh the public memory – in leading articles in the *Irish Times* going back to a number of dates in May 1916 referring to the national insurrection to assert the rights and to defend the interests of the people'. Fine Gael had, he declared, a consistent record in defending the rights of all and had 'afforded them the opportunity, whether they had an alien background or otherwise, to express freely and without restraint any comments they wished to make, recognising at the same time that they had an alien background and that their circumstances and attitudes did not, and do not, reflect the majority view of the Irish people'.[27] This prompted Labour's Conor Cruise O'Brien to observe that 'The editor of the *Irish Times* is a Belfast Protestant' and to ask, 'Is that what is meant by "alien background"?' He also noted that Cosgrave had finished his speech by reciting some words of Theobald Wolfe Tone, whose background, as O'Brien put it, 'was every bit as "alien" as that of Douglas Gageby, the editor of the *Irish Times*. It was in fact the same.'[28]

Gageby also clashed with senior figures in Fianna Fáil in the aftermath of the arms crisis of 1970. While Taoiseach Jack Lynch maintained that partition could only be undone by peaceful means, others in the party had different ideas. In December 1969 Neil Blaney declared that Fianna Fáil had never decided 'to rule out the use of force if the circumstances in the Six Counties so demanded'[29] – a declaration that led John Healy to refer to him as 'Bang Bang Blaney' in that week's 'Backbencher' column.[30] The sudden resignation of the minister for justice, Micheál Ó Moráin, raised eyebrows and on the night of 5 May 1970, the paper, like all national newspapers, received a telephone call from the government information bureau asking how late it could hold off printing the next day's edition so as to receive an important government statement. It also received a visit from an unnamed TD who was under the impression that the news had already broken.[31] The statement – that ministers Neil Blaney and Charles Haughey had been sacked from the cabinet because they did not fully subscribe to government policy on Northern Ireland and that another minister, Kevin Boland, had resigned in protest – finally reached the paper at 2.50 a.m. The country, which, as John Healy put it, 'had gone to bed arguing over whether Mick Moran had been pushed or resigned woke up with the answer: two more fired and a third departing of his own free will'.

Thus began a day of rumour and speculation. 'The Longest Political Day', as Healy aptly described it, 'had everything but sex – and, as one Fianna Fáil deputy said halfway through it, we have enough on our minds without sex'.[32] Rumours of government ministers being involved in gun-running swept the country. While Gageby supported Lynch's stance, he also made the point that the motive of those who sought to arm the nationalist minority was not necessarily 'conquest by arms of the Unionist majority'. There was, he pointed out, the stark prospect that 'if trouble should break out again, the forces of the Right would be so armed that the minority would be practically defenceless'.[33] The subsequent marathon Dáil debate in which deputies traded insults about their 'national records' nauseated Gageby. It was, he declared, 'easy to become impassioned in Leinster House, Dublin; it is cheap emotionalism, but what Northern Nationalists are aware of and what Unionists are smugly aware of is that in too many cases the words of Leinster House mask an ignorance of, and an indifference to, the soil itself of the North, and the people too.'[34] When those who had been sacked or resigned voted confidence in Lynch's leadership he noted caustically that 'They are hanging together – Fianna Fáil is a great organisation. So is the Mafia.'[35] The chaotic scenes at the party's subsequent ard fhéis were captured neatly by John Healy:

> 'Well – what did you think of the row?' 'What row? I saw no row. There was no row. There never will be a row in Fianna Fáil. Never mind the papers ... ' Of course it never happened. Kevin Boland was never incoherent with rage. Paddy Hillery, his face twisted in a rare display of the real Hillery temper, never told the faithful that they had to choose between Kevin Boland and Fianna Fáil. The Taoiseach, Mr Jack Lynch, was never booed and no-one chorused 'Union Jack, Union Jack' as he plodded manfully through his policy for Northern peace and integration. Sean MacEntee, one of the few surviving veterans of the fight for freedom, was never booed and catcalled, was never gonged by the platform party he sought to defend, and was, finally, never cut off and left to roar silently and unheard, his amplification gone, so that he was reduced to a Chaplinesque study in frustration; we never did see the punch-ups and no good republican ever told eager beaver RTÉ cameramen to go point their '—— camera' in the other direction as they chaired Kevin Boland through the Taoiseach's speech to the bottom of the giant RDS hall. A few dissident voices – yes; but no row. The Fianna Fáil Party isn't split. It was never more united.[36]

As a former army intelligence officer, Gageby was incensed that two intelligence officers, Colonel Michael Hefferon and Captain James Kelly, were made the scapegoats of the affair at the behest of the political establishment. Such was Gageby's distain for Jack Lynch that he had Lynch blackballed from the prestigious 'Murphy's Club' – a social club for the wealthy and powerful run by accountant Russell Murphy – although Lynch was later readmitted.[37] When Lynch resigned as Taoiseach in 1979, Gageby pondered about how much he really knew 'about the activities of his colleagues in that disreputable business leading up to the arms trial' and concluded that 'the last word has not yet been written about the episode'.[38] Gageby also harboured a dislike for Des O'Malley, who was minister for justice during the arms trial. At an informal 'absolutely off the record' meeting with the editors of the national newspapers in 1970, O'Malley pointed out that, under the Offences against the State Act 1939, newspapers were prohibited from using the letters 'IRA' to describe contemporary activities by militant republicans. Taken aback, the editors gave a robust defence of their reporting of the northern situation and told O'Malley that newspapers were only reporting, not glamorising, what was happening. Incensed at what he saw as an attempt to interfere with press freedom, Gageby decided that if he were ever again invited to such a meeting he could not give a guarantee that it would be off the record.[39]

'THE BÊTE NOIRE OF IRISH POLITICS – UNIONISM'

As the northern troubles worsened, Gageby continued to be critical of right-wing unionism and the British government's inaction on the north, an indication that Major McDowell's contact with Downing Street did not result in any dilution of Gageby's views. The events of Bloody Sunday saw him declare that it was as if 'Britain, shorn of her empire, has been able to concentrate in the small area of the six north-eastern counties of Ireland all that talent for arrogance, blindness and malevolence that an imperial Power in decline manifests when faced with a small but determined people'.[40] The introduction of direct rule in 1972 again saw him direct his ire at unionism that 'based its foundation on a slogan which is the very antithesis of parliamentary politics'. Its slogan of 'No surrender' had become 'something of a sick joke'. The 'unionist regime', as he called it, had 'only one major political task in order to ensure their way of life for ever more: they had to be just and generous to the minority'. Instead, it had 'preferred to stick to a sterile, stockade outlook' with the British government eventually concluding that 'Orange-Order mentality and British justice are irreconcilable'. Direct rule, he concluded, represented 'recognition of the fact that only in ultimate unity will peace come to Ireland, and only thus will relationships between the two islands be normalised and harmonised'.[41]

Just as such critical comment did not sit well with some board members, so too did some unionist politicians take offence at Gageby's editorials. In one instance the paper was criticised in a speech by A.R. Acheson, a member of the Lisburn Unionist Association. The incident that prompted Acheson's speech was Gageby's editorial on the attempted killing of the Northern Ireland junior minister for home affairs, John Taylor, shortly before direct rule was introduced. What annoyed Acheson was that, while the editorial noted the condemnations of the SDLP and the Irish and British governments, it did not itself expressly condemn the attempted assassination. In his editorial, Gageby noted that Taylor's political career had been 'dedicated to maintaining a state of affairs in Ireland which the majority of the people in this country reject'. Thus, as Acheson saw it, the paper had 'used the incident as the occasion to sneer at the mentality and political record of John Taylor, and to fire another burst at the *bête noire* of Irish politics – Unionism'. The paper's 'stock-in-trade' was, Acheson declared, to 'debunk the Unionist position'. The paper was 'dedicated to the "reunification" of Ireland, and so Unionism, which stands in the way of attaining this goal, must either be laughed out of court or rejected as an invalid position for Irishmen. Hence the sneer, the jibe, the refusal to treat Unionism seriously. And hence the *Irish Times*' failure to condemn a murderous attack on a Unionist Minister.'[42]

The paper reported Acheson's speech extensively and reprinted Gageby's editorial underneath to allow readers make up their own minds. In a later interview Gageby revealed that similar sentiments had been expressed to him by Fine Gael's John Kelly, who told him that the *Irish Times*, 'as a Protestant paper, should be a bridge to the Protestant people' of the north. Gageby responded that he did not believe 'that you talk to the unionists in those terms, after all, surely we are trying to get out of the business of where a man is judged as Protestant or Catholic. I am completely against that'. As he saw it, the paper had done a lot of good in making unionists rethink by 'saying "Look, you know, you have got to turn stones too" and we've said it toughly, very toughly, in other words you talk to a unionist, I think, I must say it crudely, you give him a clatter on the jaw first and then he says, "I see what you mean" and he talks to you.' There was, Gageby believed, 'a danger of talking too softly to unionists'.[43] As the northern parties moved towards the power-sharing agreement of 1973 and the leader of the UUP, Brian Faulkner, faced resistance from Orange Order members of the Ulster Unionist Council, Gageby declared that, of all the elements of the council, 'the Orange is the craziest'. Noting that the Orange Order described itself as a religious organisation, he asked, 'What would any of them say if 150 Jesuits or Franciscans turned up at the party conference of one of the political parties of the Republic?'[44] In welcoming the Sunningdale Agreement, which established a power-sharing executive, he noted that while it would not please every Irish nationalist the deal created 'freedom to achieve freedom from hate, from fear and violence, and thence freedom to create a better society'.[45]

But it was not to be, and as loyalist resistance to sharing power with nationalists became more militant Gageby turned his wrath on not only those who set out to wreck the agreement but also the British government which, as he saw it, stood idly by and let loyalists hijack the north in the guise of an all-out strike. As loyalists set up barricades and crippled industry and everyday life without any reaction from the police or army, Gageby described their behaviour as 'less a strike than an embryo *coup*' and asserted that 'One does not have to be particularly cynical or suspicious to wonder if Catholic/Republican intimidation on this scale would have been tolerated.'[46] He was determined that the paper would support the beleaguered power-sharing executive as its opponents grew more violent. As recalled by then northern editor, Conor O'Clery, when he filed a report indicating that the end was near he was instructed to put a more positive gloss on the fate of the executive:

> The day before the Northern Ireland Executive fell, its Unionist chairman, Brian Faulkner, issued a statement saying that the Unionist-SDLP-Alliance executive remained united,

despite the growing anarchy in the streets. It was clear however, at least in the *Irish Times* Belfast office, that Sunningdale was finished, and I wrote a story for the front page saying the executive was hours away from disintegrating. Shortly afterwards I got a call from Jack Fagan on the news desk asking me to write a more upbeat lead. I refused. Then, Henry Kelly, at that time working from the editor's office, came on the line with the same request. It was Gageby himself, I realised then, who was insisting that the *Irish Times* should not go down in history as 'abandoning' the power-sharing politicians in their darkest hour. Perhaps John Hume had been on the phone to him. I succumbed. The paper's splash headline the next day, above my name, read, as far as I recall: 'Executive Shows United Front'.[47]

When the executive collapsed under the strain of the strike, Gageby furiously declared that 'In all the shame that Britain has suffered at the hands of her departing colonials this lying-down to the bigots of Belfast ranks high in infamy; for it has been accompanied by deception of the Government in Dublin'. The British army and government had 'been routed without a shot being fired; a few hoods and masks and clubs and the UDA men put the Tommies in their place'.[48] In a subsequent editorial, he compared the events of Bloody Sunday with the passivity of the British army towards the armed loyalists who had brought down the executive: 'The British Army is willing to practise its skills on the Nationalist side. It is a different story when Loyalists are concerned. Brigadier Kitson's box of tricks is for the Catholics; Protestants can get away with organised subversion of the institutions of State and the worst they have to suffer is a string of insults over the air delivered by Harold Wilson'.[49] According to one journalist, the collapse of the executive greatly dismayed Gageby: 'He got disillusioned after all the work, all the enormous energy he put into the northern situation, he worked his guts out, he'd been in the place day and night. He was totally disillusioned with the north especially the break up of the Sunningdale Agreement. He was devastated when it all fell apart.'[50] As the northern situation worsened and internment was introduced the paper published accounts of the prisoners' experiences. Smuggled off the internment ship *The Maidstone*, these accounts were written by a Dublin journalist who had been detained because of his connections with a Sinn Féin newspaper.[51]

'LOSE YOUR CONTRACEPTIVES!'

As the north descended into two decades of conflict, life continued apace in the south. New arrivals at D'Olier Street around this time included Conor Brady, Mary Cummins and Renagh Holohan, who all joined the paper in 1969. Brady joined as a reporter and worked from Belfast at the onset of the troubles and would later become editor of the paper. Cummins had a long and distinguished career as a columnist, while Holohan was northern editor between 1974 and 1976 before returning to the news desk in Dublin. Other arrivals included Geraldine Kennedy and Nell McCafferty. Kennedy joined the paper in February 1973 and would later become its first female editor. McCafferty joined in May 1971, arriving a day late because she and Bernadette Devlin had been convicted and fined for a civil-rights offence in Northern Ireland.[52] McCafferty made her name writing a personalised diary of what was happening at the Dublin criminal courts – a change from the usual sanitised coverage that had existed up to then.[53] She also played a key role in the formation of the Irish Women's Liberation Movement, which was at the forefront of the campaign for equal rights for women and to which the paper devoted much coverage. It reported the inaugural meeting of the organisation in April 1971 and must have taken great delight in reporting the comment by one 73-year-old lady who boldly declared that there was 'nothing wrong with contraception and nothing wrong with enjoying sex'.[54] The following month it described the chaotic scenes at a thirty-minute stand-off in Dublin's Connolly Station between custom officers and members of the organisation who had travelled by train from Belfast laden with contraceptives: 'The order came: "Lose your contraceptives!" and a shower of condoms, pills and spermicidal jelly fell at the feet of Customs men and slid along the railway platform towards the waiting crowd.'[55]

Along with women's rights, membership of the European Economic Community was also current and in May 1972 a referendum on membership was held. The position of the paper was clear and succinct: 'We should join.' As Gageby saw it, 'entry to Brussels may be one of the final steps in the re-establishment of Ireland as a nation, a further approach to the day when Emmet's epitaph may at last be written'.[56] Later that year, another referendum, this time on removing the special status of the Catholic church from the constitution, was held, and the paper was equally sure about where it stood: 'A loud vote for "Yes" on the Article 44 question is mandatory for anyone who believes in a peaceful and harmonious future for Ireland.'[57] That year also saw the company launch the *Education Times*. Edited by John Horgan, who was by then also an independent Senator, it was the country's first education journal and besides covering the rapid expansion of technological education at third level it also carried features such as book reviews and a four-page section for parents dealing with curriculum developments.[58]

In 1973 a general election was held: the choice was between Fianna Fáil and a coalition of Fine Gael and the Labour Party. Given that 51 per cent of the electorate was female, the 'Women First' page devoted substantial coverage to the election and made a concerted effort to put discrimination against women on the political agenda. On one day it put forward an all-female cabinet, including Senator Mary Robinson as Taoiseach and the well-known social campaigner Sister Stanislaus as minister for health and welfare.[59] On another it profiled all sixteen female candidates running for office.[60] It also published a questionnaire on social issues and women's rights that it had distributed to all political parties and subsequently devoted two days of its column space to publishing the responses it had received, outlining the various political parties' views on issues such as equal pay, discrimination in the workplace, the legalisation of contraception and divorce and the right of women to sit on juries.[61] As polling day approached, the Dublin newspaper world was plunged into a short-lived crisis. As rumours of a takeover of Independent Newspapers grew, its 180 journalists stopped work to discuss their position. This resulted in their collective sacking and them deciding to occupy the company's premises in Middle Abbey Street. Over at the Irish Press Group, an industrial dispute erupted when the entire staff of the *Sunday Press* was sacked following its refusal to handle a column written by Gay Byrne. The staff argued that the use of such copy was in breach of a 1964 agreement on the use of material by non-staff members.[62] These incidents had an impact on the *Irish Times,* which not only shared the cost of the newspaper distribution network with the other two newspaper groups, but which also co-operated in terms of dealing with industrial disputes. All three national newspaper groups, in the guise of the Dublin Newspaper Managers' Committee, had a longstanding agreement that if one newspaper closed through industrial action then all newspapers automatically closed. As a result of this agreement the *Irish Times,* like the Independent and Press titles, did not appear on 14 March 1973. The following day however, it appeared as usual, but alone, on the newsstands thus breaking the longstanding 'one out, all out' agreement. As one journalist put it:

> Gageby decided to break the 'one out, all out' agreement. He had had enough of the lightening strikes at the *Irish Press.* On one occasion the paper was about to go to press when a call came through announcing a strike at the *Irish Press.* Gageby was furious and resolved that this was the last time we wouldn't print. About a fortnight later there was a similar occurrence but the paper went to press anyway.[63]

The board issued a statement in which it noted that this was the fourth occasion since October 1971 on which the paper was not published because of a dispute in which it was not involved directly and that the usefulness of the 'one out, all out' agreement had been under discussion for some time with the other companies. Referring to the 'gravity of the general situation in the country at the present time', the board stated that it had an obligation to the public that overrode all other considerations, and so it had decided to resume publication.

Stating that it would not seek to take advantage of the non-appearance of its competitors' titles, it informed readers that the print-run would not be increased.[64] This reassurance to its competitors was, perhaps, a virtue of necessity since there was some doubt about the capacity of the printing press to deliver additional output. The two disputes were resolved shortly afterwards: the journalists of Independent Newspapers were given assurances that there would be no job cuts or changes to working conditions under the new owner, Tony O'Reilly, while management at the Press Group rehired all the staff it had sacked when it realised that the print unions were about to become involved in the dispute.

'HAVE YOUR CAKE AND EAT I.T.'

The eruption of the northern troubles had effects other than causing boardroom differences; as the troubles worsened, more newsroom resources were devoted northwards and the paper increased in size. In the company report for the year 1969, the chairman noted that 'The events in the North added greatly to the costs of newsgathering, and resulted in no small way in the decision to publish larger issues of the *Irish Times*.'[65] Heavy taxation also hit the company's coffers; in 1970 alone it paid over £90,000 in turnover and wholesale taxes; in the 1971 annual report the chairman estimated that, being subject to four different taxes (wholesale, turnover, income and corporation taxes) resulted in the company paying £4.50 for every £1 of profit after tax. The newspaper market had also become more crowded. In 1970 a report on the newspaper industry, compiled by the Committee on Industrial Progress, found that the sector faced increased competition from British newspapers, sales of which had risen by over 60 per cent between 1964 and 1969. Also, technological innovation was likely to increase such competition and the scale of investment required to modernise production methods would make it difficult for Irish firms to compete. It also mentioned the possibility of British newspapers setting up satellite printing plants in Ireland, and the prospect of foreign take-overs of Irish newspapers.[66] Despite these obstacles, the paper continued to increase its circulation and maintain its profitability. As circulation increased from 52,313 in 1968 to 63,128 in 1972, the company returned profits of £76,834 in 1968, £29,575 in 1969, £68,028 in 1970, and £10,898 in 1971.[67]

At start of the 1970s the *Irish Times* was still a publicly quoted company with a nominal capital of £450,000 divided into 380,000 £1 preference shares quoted on the stock exchange and 70,000 £1 ordinary shares owned by the directors.[68] Preference shareholders were entitled to one vote per twenty-five shares held, while ordinary shareholders (the directors) were entitled to one vote per five shares held. This meant that the majority voting interest resided with the preference shareholders (15,200 votes) rather than the ordinary shareholders (14,000 votes). The preference shares were widely dispersed in terms of ownership. In the late 1960s the last member of the Arnott family with an interest in the company, Sir John Arnott, sold his 17,081 ordinary shares to the other directors. Shortly afterwards, he resigned as London editor to administer the Phoenix Park racecourse, in which the family retained an interest.[69] In January 1971 the company's five directors owned the 70,000 ordinary shares in equal portions. Douglas Gageby held 9,500 in his own name and another 4,500 via his company, Fetchfer; Major McDowell held 1,000 in his own name and another 13,000 via his company, Dowell Ltd; George Hetherington held 1,600 in his own name and another 12,400 via a National Bank of Ireland nominee account; and Philip and Ralph Walker jointly held 28,000 shares in an Ulster Bank nominee account.[70]

In the annual report circulated to shareholders in advance of the company's AGM in May 1972, the chairman, Ralph Walker, stated that the company's balance sheet 'did not indicate a strong position' and that the bank overdraft of £180,000 was 'much higher' than the board would like. However, he did mention that the board was expecting a £270,000 surplus arising from a revaluation of its property.[71] At the AGM he announced that the directors had 'decided that, taking into account the improved position which will be reflected in the next balance sheet as a result of the revaluation of the fixed assets, the situation can best be met by an injection of £50,000 capital'. He then proposed that the five ordinary shareholders, who were also the directors, put up the £50,000 in return for the creation and equal distribution of 50,000 £1 ordinary shares.[72] At the extraordinary general meeting held to decide this issue, one preference shareholder complained that the creation of new ordinary shares would result in control of the company passing from the preference to the ordinary shareholders, and proposed that the new capital be raised by the sale and leaseback of the company's premises. This proposal was rejected, although the directors would later propose this course of action to help defray the costs of setting up the Irish Times Trust. The creation of 50,000 new ordinary shares was approved; this boosted the voting power of the ordinary shareholders from 14,000 to 24,000 votes, giving the directors control of the company.[73] The 50,000 new ordinary shares were distributed in blocks of 10,000 to each of the five directors' companies or nominee accounts.[74]

At the subsequent AGM, in April 1973, the chairman announced that the company had broken two records in 1972; the paper had reached its highest-ever circulation by selling 63,128 copies per day, and the company had made its biggest-ever profit of £242,134. A number of other factors helped make the company's balance sheet look extremely healthy: the capital base had been increased by the £50,000 issue of ordinary shares; the value of the company's property had increased by £436,703; it had achieved rationalisation by the sale of its property on Westmoreland Street; it had paid off its £180,000 overdraft; and the substitution of VAT for wholesale and turnover taxes had resulted in a reduction of the tax rate from fifteen to five per cent. It was on such a high note that Ralph Walker retired as chairman to be replaced by Major McDowell.[75] The following month the company wrote to its shareholders to inform them that the board was considering the possibility of a re-organisation of the share capital that would 'result in some improvement' for shareholders. Discussions with advisors were continuing and, as the board put it, it wanted to 'draw attention to this possibility now, so that shareholders who may be contemplating selling are aware of the situation'.[76] In September 1973, the five directors, by virtue of an agreement that they should all act unanimously, transferred their ordinary shares into the trusteeship of a solicitor's firm.[77] That same year the company would make a profit of £427,511 – a 77 per cent rise over the record 1972 figure of £242,134.[78]

On 5 April 1974 the paper led its front page with the announcement that the company had become a trust 'to maintain the *Irish Times* as a serious and independent newspaper'. It also announced that a charitable foundation had been established to 'ultimately benefit from the profits of the newspaper'. The reason given for the change was that the directors had 'been concerned for some time lest through the disposal of stock holdings or other events' the paper might become controlled by proprietors who might not maintain its high editorial standards.[79] The trust was, as that day's editorial put it, 'an assurance that an Irish institution is completely protected from outside takeover or control'.[80] The establishment of the trust was facilitated by Investment Bank of Ireland, which purchased the ordinary shares from the five directors for £1,625,000 or £325,000 each. The bank also organised the purchase of the preference shares. The owners of the 275,000 5¹/₂% £1 preference shares were offered £1 per share, which, according to the bank's purchase document, represented a 122% capital increase on the value of such shares, given that they had a market value of 45p each before the offer was announced. The owners of the 105,000 6¹/₂% £1 preference shares were offered £1 per share, which represented an 85% capital increase on the value of such shares, which had traded at 54p each before the offer was announced.[81] *Business and Finance* magazine concluded that as the offer price for preference shares represented 'a profit of more than 100% on the present quoted stock, there is no way the preference holders can quibble at what is a very fair price'.[82] While this might sound generous, it is worth recording that the preference shares were bought at their nominal value. In contrast, the directors' ordinary shares were bought for £13.54 each. Given that the directors had created and purchased 50,000 new ordinary shares two years previously at a cost of £1 per share, this meant that they sold these shares for £677,000 or 13 1/2 times their original purchase price.

Staff reaction to the financial manoeuvres varied, as the complexities of the deal caused some confusion. As one journalist put it, 'nobody understood it; Andrew Whittaker, the business editor, was the only one who went through it piecemeal and asked questions but everyone else accepted that it was going to be like *The Guardian* – it would be the best thing that ever happened the *Irish Times*'.[83] As another journalist noted, 'the staff greeted it with astonishment, they didn't understand, some saw it as pure greed ... although they were given assurances that the same terms and conditions and benefits would continue as before'.[84] Yet another recalled that 'the staff was delighted with the trust because we believed that it would save the *Irish Times*. It meant that O'Reilly [Independent Newspapers] could not buy us up, and a trust sounded so responsible'.[85] Another recalled that it 'was regarded positively as something that did confirm the independence of the paper – that was a real plus – it was at a time of prosperity, coinciding with the House Agreement so there was a general air of well-being and good feeling'.[86] Yet another recalled that the reaction 'was generally favourable. There had been concern, and some fear, that the paper would be bought by Thomson or another multi-national, and that our great editorial freedom would be lost. It was all a bit of a mystery at the time, though some of the details caused more merriment than anguish – "instinct with Christian value" raised a smile'.[87] The business editor, Andrew Whittaker, concluded that the sale price paid to the directors was at 'the high end of an arguable price range' and expressed concern about the level of debt the company had incurred to establish the trust.[88] *Business and Finance* magazine commented that, while the price paid to the five directors 'was not over-generous, neither was it giving a great deal away'. But it concluded that 'a private individual or organisation would be prepared to pay more from a profit point of view'.[89] The *Sunday Independent* noted that the trust enabled the five ordinary shareholders to cash their shares in tax free without relinquishing control of the company and described the deal as an 'extraordinary ingenious financial exercise in having your cake and eating it'. It accused the paper of having engaged in 'a wave of public relations euphoria calculated to distract from the essentials of what is happening' and described the trust as 'a self-perpetuating oligarchy answerable commercially and financially and in every other way only to themselves'.[90]

It seems the primary reason for the establishment of the trust was to accommodate the wish of three directors (George Hetherington and Philip and

Ralph Walker) to retire and extract their investment from the company. In an interview after the trust was announced, Major McDowell stated that 'no takeover approach had been received, but [he] agreed that some directors might have wished to sell'.[91] This view was supported in an interview that Douglas Gageby gave shortly afterwards in which he stated; 'The trust came up, came about because three of the five directors said, you know, we've been here twenty-five years, we'll move.'[92] It has often been suggested that one of the factors behind the directors' decision to establish the trust was the expressed intention of the Fine Gael–Labour coalition to introduce a new tax on capital gains. After much deliberation a white paper on capital taxation was published in February 1974, the result of which was the Capital Gains Tax Act 1975. The legislation became operative in 1975 but retrospectively applied a tax of 26 per cent to assets disposed of after 6 April 1974. However, the tax applied only to whatever value accrued to the market value of the assets from that date onwards. That said, having sold their shares in September 1973 the directors avoided paying any tax at all. According to one advisor central to the establishment of the trust, Don Reid, the introduction of capital gains tax was not an issue:

> The principal object of the exercise was to prevent the possibility of the *Irish Times* being taken over and losing its independence by becoming a subsidiary of a larger group. The problem was that there were preference shares of little value quoted on the stock exchange. These, if acquired by a single owner would give virtual control at little cost and this was seen as a major vulnerability ... Because the transaction took place around April 1974 when capital gains tax was introduced various people including some financial journalists sought to identify a tax angle as being a motivating factor. However this does not stand up to scrutiny because in calculating a taxable gain an allowable cost was the market value of the asset sold as at 5 April 1974, so that on a sale say in April 1975 the taxable gain was the growth in value in that twelve months less the costs of the sale.[93]

According to one company executive, the trust came about because of a fear of takeover and a wish by some directors to realise their assets:

> What influenced that [the trust] mainly was the *Irish Times* was beginning to make commercial sense and at that time there were a lot of proprietors – like Lord Thomson – who wouldn't have minded owing and developing the *Irish Times* as a newspaper, but as a commercial entity ... So there was pressure coming on the board of directors from that point of view. The other pressure coming on them was that the Walkers and Hetherington were getting old; they had twenty per cent each of the company. If they sold to Lord Thomson for instance, that twenty per cent would have given them a nice amount of money; whereas if they didn't sell the twenty per cent would be worth very little. So there was that sort of pressure. In the heel of the hunt they decided, spearheaded by McDowell, to establish a trust.[94]

The company's articles of association stated that ordinary shares could not be sold or transferred to any person while any other ordinary shareholder or person selected by the board was willing to purchase those shares.[95] With three of the five directors wishing to sell their large quantities of ordinary shares at the same time, it was probably impossible for the two remaining directors, McDowell and Gageby, to do what had always been done up to that point – purchase the shares or find wealthy individuals whom they trusted to do so. The board also decided against a quotation of the ordinary shares on the stock market because, as McDowell put it, the paper 'would have been open to a take-over situation ... [and] ... lead to the possibility of attrition over time of the control held by the ordinary shareholders'.[96] The trust system was, it seems, the most efficient way to allow Hetherington and the Walker brothers to leave, and enable McDowell and Gageby maintain control. The Bank of Ireland also had its own motivations for advancing such a large sum of money to finance the establishment of the trust. In 1977 the bank's then managing director, Ian Morrison, told the paper's former business editor, Andrew Whittaker, that McDowell had put the trust plan to Bill Finlay, then governor of the bank. The bank's board of directors had approved the loan, knowing it was 'not a normal business investment'. According to Whittaker, Morrison told him that the bank's directors were fearful of the conjunction of high inflation rates and the activities of the IRA and wanted the paper there as 'at least one voice of sanity'.[97]

THE IRISH TIMES TRUST

The process of changing from a publicly quoted company to a private trust involved the creation of a plethora of new companies. A new entity, Irish Times Holdings, was created to buy the 120,000 ordinary and 380,000 preference shares in Irish Times Ltd. This company was created so that the bank did not purchase shares in the paper directly. Firstly, it bought the five directors' 120,000 ordinary shares for £1,625,000. This move was financed by Investment Bank of Ireland, which received 1,625,000 redeemable shares in Irish Times Holdings. Secondly, the five directors invested a total of £380,000 or £76,000 each to finance the buyout of the 380,000 preference shares. In return, each of the five directors received 76,000 redeemable shares in Irish Times Holdings. The bank and the five directors were entitled to a 7 per cent dividend on their redeemable shares. The idea of all this was that Irish Times Ltd would redeem all the shares out of future profits, thus allowing the bank and the directors to walk away from the company. At least 725,000 of the bank's shares had to be redeemed before any of the directors' shares could be redeemed.[98] Voting control of Holdings resided not with the bank or the five directors but with a new entity created to be a buffer between the bank and the paper – the Irish Times Trust, which owned the 100 voting shares in Holdings. The trust was also tasked with ensuring that the paper was published in accordance with a new charter. It did this by securing control of Irish Times Ltd, which had its shareholding changed into 500,000 non-voting shares (held by Irish Times Holdings) and 100 new voting shares which were allocated to Irish Times Trust and its governors.[99] Thus while the paper was owned by Holdings until such time as Irish Times Ltd could buy the redeemable shares, editorial control of the paper lay with the trust. According to Don Reid, this was precisely why the bank's money was put into Holdings and not Irish Times Ltd or the trust:

> In summary then we had a situation in which Trust held the voting shares of Times and Holdings but had no financial interest in either; Holdings bought the shares from the outgoing shareholders with money provided by the bank but had no voting control over Times ... The function of Holdings then was to avoid the bank or the outgoing shareholders being involved in any company dealing with the publication of the *Irish Times*. One of the functions of Trust was to have the ultimate controlling role within the group but nonetheless devoid of any financial value. Thus a potential bidder had no target for his bid and Trust itself had no power to sell [the paper].[1]

Another new entity, Irish Times Foundation, was established with the purpose of distributing money to charitable causes and was also overseen by the governors of the trust. Under the foundation's articles of association, Major McDowell was entitled to be chairman so long as he remained a governor of the trust or unless he resigned the position.[2] The objectives of the foundation (and the trust) were outlined in its extensive memorandum of association and included furthering the advancement of education, the relief of poverty and the advancement of medical, surgical and veterinary science on the island of Ireland. Since the memorandum of association mentioned financing and funding such worthy objectives and since, in its press release announcing the establishment of the trust, the board had announced that the foundation would 'ultimately benefit from the profits of the newspaper', many assumed that at some stage money would be set aside from the profits of Irish Times Ltd to enable the foundation to fulfil it objectives.

The trust secured the amendment of the memorandum of association of Irish Times Ltd so that the paper would thenceforth be published as 'an independent newspaper primarily concerned with serious issues for the benefit of the community throughout the whole of Ireland free from any form of personal or of party political, commercial, religious or other sectional control'.[3] In addition, the paper would pursue an editorial policy that would support 'constitutional democracy through governments freely elected' and seek the 'progressive achievement of social justice between people and the discouragement of discrimination of all kinds'. Further, it would encourage the 'promotion of a society where the quality of life is enriched by the standards of its education, its art, its culture, and its recreational facilities, and where the quality of spirit is instinct with Christian values but free from all religious bias and discrimination'. It would encourage 'the promotion of peace and tolerance and opposition to all forms of violence and hatred' and 'the promotion of understanding of other nations and peoples and a sympathetic concern for their well being'.[4] The trust would also ensure that news would be as accurate and as comprehensive as practicable and be presented fairly; that comment and opinion would be informed and responsible, and would be identifiable from fact; and that special consideration would be given to the reasonable representation of minority interests and divergent views.[5] In one interview, Gageby stated that these objectives 'carried on to a great extent what has been the norm for about ten years, for as long as I know the *Irish Times*'.[6] Oddly, despite the fact that the trust has responsibility for the paper's journalism, it has never issued a report on or a review of the performance of the paper in living up to the trust's objectives.

The trust was run by a board originally composed of between seven and twelve governors that would be 'representative broadly of the community throughout the whole of Ireland who are committed to the objects of the company'.[7] This board, which was later enlarged to fourteen members, was self-appointing, and ineligible to become a governor were present or former ministers of religion, those connected with other media whether employee or shareholder, those who had, in the preceding five years, been an elected member of any national or regional parliament, those who had in the previous five years, represented in national politics a political party or group, those who had connection of such a nature as to be capable of causing the belief that they were more than a mere member of a political party or group, and those whose views or actions were inconsistent with the objects of the company.[8] Also ineligible were current or past employees of Irish Times Ltd unless the chairman of that company, Major McDowell, consented to such an appointment. His consent was necessary to appoint two governors – himself and the journalist John Healy. Oddly, Healy resigned as a governor almost immediately: appointed on 10 April 1974, he resigned on 2 July 1974. McDowell, so long as he was a governor (and unless he resigned from the position) was to be chairman of the board of governors.[9] The board was entitled to appoint governors to act as directors of Irish Times Limited,[10] and all governors had to swear an oath to uphold the editorial objectives of the trust.[11]

The articles of association of Irish Times Ltd were also changed to reflect the new order. The amended articles allowed for the governors of the trust to sit on the board of the company, stipulated that the editor was to be a director, and that so long as he was a governor of the trust, McDowell was to be a director of Irish Times Ltd.[12] They also stated that so long as he remained a director (and unless he resigned from the position) he was to be chairman of the board.[13] The articles exempted McDowell from a provision that compelled a director to resign if s/he was required to do so by all the other directors.[14] They also stated that he was to be chief executive of the company unless he resigned from that position[15] and that the powers entrusted to and conferred on him as chairman or chief executive could 'not without his consent be revoked withdrawn altered or varied in any way so long as he shall continue to hold that office'.[16] According to Don Reid, the origin of much of McDowell's powers lay in the fact that the company was run by board of governors:

> The Irish Times Ltd was also a bit unusual in that it was given the powers to carry on business and so forth but a number of decision-making powers normally exercised by a board of directors were delegated to Major McDowell. Directors of Trust were automatically to be directors of Irish Times Ltd thus giving Trust control of that board. The people then appointed to the Trust board were all prominent people with leading positions in their various walks of life but not necessarily with business experience. The bank was concerned for the security of its money and looked to Major McDowell's well-established business prowess to run the business. This was the source of his unusual powers.[17]

The same ineligibility conditions that pertained to membership of the trust also applied to membership of the board of Irish Times Ltd and directors were also required to take an oath to uphold the objectives of the trust.[18] With their shares sold, George Hetherington, Ralph and Phillip Walker resigned as directors of Irish Times Ltd. In June 1974 Douglas Gageby, a little uneasy at the mixed reaction that the creation of the trust had caused, retired as editor. According to one journalist, there had come 'very quickly the realisation that a lot of money had been made by McDowell, Gageby and others in forming the trust' and a negative reaction developed.[19] Indeed, it seems that one journalist later took too critical a view of the events surrounding the establishment of the trust. In 1982 the board commissioned long-time journalist Tony Gray to write a history of the paper to coincide with its 125th anniversary in 1984. When he submitted a preliminary draft to Gageby, the project was 'dropped, due, it is believed, to sensitivities about the working of the trust set up to safeguard the newspaper in the 1970s'.[20] As remembered by one company executive, the windfall 'became a big embarrassment to Gageby with his gathering of "social" journalists and there was a sort of journalistic reaction against the trust particularly the tax-free money ... The social people on the editorial side thought this was not what the editor should have done. In himself he was very uncomfortable and he decided to resign as editor and he left the company'.[21] However, within three years Gageby was back to rescue the paper a second time.

CHAPTER 10

Troublesome Times

The 'Heavy Gang', as the group has been nicknamed within the force, physically assaults and applies severe psychological pressure on suspects. The pressure includes threats, lies, and psychological tricks and is intensified by depriving suspects of sleep, food and water over long periods ... There are also suggestions that the 'Heavy Gang' are ... forcing people to stand spreadeagled against a wall for lengthy periods.[1]

Irish Times *exposé of Garda brutality, 1977*

IN THE LAST WEEK OF June 1974, Fergus Pyle, the paper's European correspondent, received a telephone call offering him the editorship. Pyle had joined the paper in 1956 and served as the paper's first northern editor and its European correspondent, first in Paris and then in Brussels. A superb correspondent with an enviable reputation as an astute reporter, he was, nonetheless, an unlikely editor. He had been away from Dublin for seven years, and his abrupt appointment caused a degree of resentment among the staff – none of whom had been told that Gageby intended to retire. As one journalist put it, 'The appointment was a total shock ... Many people only found out when the editorial conference began at 5.00 p.m. and we found Fergus in the chair, and no sign of Gageby. Fergus had certainly been groomed for the job and had been the Major's choice for many years, but because there was no talk of Gageby going, there was no expectation of Fergus coming.'[2] Other possible successors, such as news editor Donal Foley, who had played a far more central role in the paper's reinvention and success, were overlooked. Foley's health was not the best; still, given the trust's ideals of openness and transparency, it was a strange way to effect a change of editor.

One rumour that did the rounds was that Foley was overlooked because of his religion. As one journalist remembered, 'the Major decided he [Pyle] was the one and not Donal Foley. We believed this was clearly because he was a Protestant; he was thrust into the job whether he wanted it or not and many believe he didn't. It's also true that Donal held strong socialist views which might not have been to the Major's liking.'[3] Another rumour had it that Major

McDowell 'wanted someone more malleable on the national question'.[4] But, as another journalist observed, while Pyle's view on the north was closer to McDowell's than to Gageby's, 'none of us saw any indication that Douglas was other than totally supportive of Fergus's appointment. I think both he and the Major had a clear idea of the "type" that was needed to be editor of the *Irish Times*. Protestantism was part of that, but not central; it was being highly educated, well read, cosmopolitan, intelligent, and a TCD graduate would also be a plus'.[5] While the initial hostility towards Pyle subsided, it never disappeared:

> He encountered resentment and suspicion from the start, but not because anyone thought Donal should have been editor ... The problem with Fergus was that most of the editorial staff did not know him personally. He had never been a reporter, but had gone from features to Belfast in 1965. He then transferred to Paris and later to Brussels, so when Gageby went in 1974 there were many sub-editors and reporters who knew him only as a name. He tended to deal directly with Gageby, and his copy was more or less sacrosanct. Many of the subs knew him only as the man in Belfast/Paris/Brussels whose copy was invariably too long and late. There were several individuals who never relaxed their dislike, even contempt towards him, and this certainly gave him problems ... Donal Foley, by the way, was always strongly supportive of Fergus as editor.[6]

Indeed, as another journalist remembered, 'Donal never talked about being passed over and he didn't behave like that ... What did happen to Fergus was that Donal maintained a moral authority in the place, so people gravitated to him for decisions ... Fergus had never been a news editor. He never actually had to cope with a great herd of reporters and tell them what to do. Donal was the alternative editor, the person to go to if you had a question to ask.'[7] Thrown in at the deep end, Pyle had a tortuous three years as editor. Having been away from D'Olier Street for so long, he had no power bloc within the paper. He appointed James Downey and Dennis Kennedy as assistant editors, but he still lacked the sure touch of Gageby. Some of his troubles were of his own making, but many were caused by external factors. Unlike his predecessor, Pyle was unsure of himself as editor, and his term also coincided with a steep economic recession that threatened the very existence of the paper. Pyle had been a popular reporter, but he quickly made himself unpopular as editor as his uncertainty began to annoy staff and upset the production process. As one journalist put it:

> He was an awfully nice man and a very nice editor to work under. He was just not tough enough or hard enough for the job. The problem was he debated things too much. In a daily paper you've got to move on and I always remember when I was acting news editor occasionally, I would go to him and say will we run 'A' or 'B' and he'd spend three quarters of an hour discussing it with you and you'd come out and you still wouldn't know what he

wanted; whereas with Gageby he'd say 'A' of course or he'd say that's what you're paid for, decide for yourself. The conferences were going on for ages and they held up production because you can't spend time debating things ad nauseam.[8]

As another journalist remembered, Pyle was 'the direct opposite of Gageby in terms of man-management and management in general. His conferences tended to wander along without any sign of a decision.'[9] Another remembered that, whereas the mid-day conference to decide the next day's paper would normally last thirty or forty minutes, 'when Fergus took the conference it could go on for an hour-and-a-half until it became a bit of a joke – it was the time the paper was running the newspaper in the classroom project, and Fergus's conferences were called "the classroom" in the newspaper'.[10] Pyle's uncertainty was reflected in a tendency to take the articles of the trust literally. As he saw it, everything going into the paper had to meet the strict criteria set down by the trust's articles: he 'took everything literally, particularly the articles of the trust. He would ask, "Does this accord with the articles etc?" He was very unsure of himself.'[11] Also, whereas Gageby had a good eye for the use of photographs and insisted on a lively layout, Pyle preferred the continental style that favoured slabs of print across the front page. As one journalist put it: 'It was a total mistake from the start. He was not an executive, he was a writer. He did very good stuff from Brussels and Paris but he was a foreign correspondent. An organised executive he was not. He tried to turn the *Irish Times* into a continental paper like *Le Figaro*. He had very little news sense. It was bad casting.'[12]

Sales of the paper initially remained buoyant; between January and June 1974 average daily sales stood at 69,420, an increase of 1,444 copies per day on the previous six months. But no sooner had Pyle assumed the editorship than the economy began to suffer the effects of an international recession that had begun in the latter half of 1973 when oil-producing countries in the Persian Gulf increased the price of oil from $3 to $11.50 a barrel. Given that it took two-and-a-half barrels of oil to make one ton of newsprint, the price of newsprint jumped from £63 per ton at the end of 1972 to £180 per ton in mid-1974.[13] As the effects of the oil crisis began to hit the Irish economy, companies began to cut advertising budgets. While circulation remained steady, advertising revenue plummeted, and so too did the company's profits. In 1974, the company lost £100,000, and a period of entrenchment began. Unlike Gageby, who had been able to spend heavily on resources and promotion, Pyle had to cut editorial budgets and even the size of the paper itself. In November 1975 the paper introduced a smaller typeface that enabled it to squeeze in one extra line per inch of column space. At this time newsprint was the greatest single factor in the paper's cost structure: 28 per cent of the cover price (2.82p out of 10p) went towards the cost of newsprint. Given that the cost of newsprint per copy had increased by 135 per cent in five years, it was believed that the adoption of a smaller typeface would allow it to conserve newsprint, increase advertising space and 'maintain the quantity as well as the quality and depth of news coverage'.[14]

The company also diversified its trading activities. In Britain newspapers had broadened their revenue bases by investing in TSN – tobacco, sweets and newspaper – shops; and in 1975, led by new managing director Peter O'Hara, the company purchased three such shops. But losses continued to mount and in 1975 the company lost £300,000. Given the magnitude of the loss and the fact that the company was in debt to the tune of over £2m following the establishment of the trust, alarm bells began to ring. In February 1976 the company decided to cease publication of the *Education Times*. Its circulation had not reached expectations, and the imposition of increased VAT on newspapers announced in that year's budget was the final straw. Circulation of the *Irish Times* remained relatively steady throughout 1975 but fell alarmingly during the first half of 1976. For the first six months of 1975, average daily sales stood at 68,104, while the figure for the second half of the year was 69,804.[15] In contrast, the average daily figure for the first half of 1976 was 65,938, although this improved somewhat in the second half to 66,829 copies per day.[16] But the fall in advertising revenue showed no sign of abating, and in 1976 the company lost over £400,000. This was exacerbated by the cost of establishing its chain of newsagents, retraining costs associated with the changeover to new photo-composition technology, and the adverse impact of that year's bank strike on advertising revenue.[17] Cumulative losses for 1974 to 1976 stood at £1m and this, combined with the debt the company had assumed to establish the trust, made extinction a distinct possibility. In March 1977 Peter O'Hara resigned as managing director, and the chairman, Major McDowell, reassumed direct responsibility for the profitability of the company. Another director, Louis O'Neill, was appointed general manager with responsibility for the commercial management of the company.[18]

That same month Andrew Whittaker, who had resigned as business editor and worked for O'Hara as the company's corporate development manager, visited the managing director of the Bank of Ireland, Ian Morrison. Whittaker urged Morrison to remove Fergus Pyle as editor and to reduce Major McDowell from chairman and chief executive to non-executive chairman to secure the finances of the paper and its journalism. Morrison refused; he also rejected Whittaker's idea that the bank install a receiver to the paper because it would collapse the company's credit. Interestingly though, Morrison canvassed Whittaker's opinion on whether or not he thought Gageby would be willing to return as editor.[19] Indeed, many wondered whether the bank would intervene to recover its investment. At a press conference to release the bank's annual report, Morrison stated that its financing of the trust was intended to preserve the paper as 'an independent entity in perpetuity' and noted that, although the bank was concerned about the company's losses, it was confident that 'given time and good management, the situation could be put right'. The bank's investment was, he maintained, 'at arm's length' and it was up to the trust to put things right.[20] But, as remembered by then general manager, Louis O'Neill, 'What happened was the Bank of Ireland became more and more interested in the *Irish Times* because the *Irish Times* was beginning to owe it more and more money ... There was a bit of tension beginning to build up and it sent in one or two executives from time to time to see what we were doing and where we could save money.'[21] The bank seconded a company finance expert to the paper to keep an eye on income and expenditure; this person also attended board meetings. As one advisor to the paper recalled, 'The bank continued to support the trading position of the company but it did have real difficulty in paying its way. There was a limit to the extent to which the bank would accept exposure and while there were ongoing discussions and negotiations the future did look bleak'.[22] In May 1977 the board put a survival plan to trade unions that involved the non-payment of that year's round of national wage agreement increases and twenty-two voluntary redundancies.[23] The rationalisation had the desired effect, and in 1977 the company returned a profit of £306,000.

TRIALS AND TRIBULATIONS

Throughout all these financial tribulations Fergus Pyle tried to hold the paper together as best he could, with varying degrees of success. In July 1976 the paper was summoned before the high court to answer a charge of contempt with regard to the special criminal court. The summons arose from an article, published on 11 June 1976, that centred on the death sentence passed on Noel and Marie Murray for the murder of Garda Michael Reynolds during a bank robbery in 1975. The article was written by the paper's political correspondent, Dick Walsh, and carried reaction to the sentence from the Garda Representative Association and the Association of Legal Justice. It was the latter's reaction that got the paper into hot water. It described the sentence as 'particularly reprehensible because it was passed by the Special Criminal Court, a court composed of Government-appointed judges having no judicial independence and which sat without a jury and which so abused the rules of evidence as to make the court akin to a sentencing tribunal'.[24] The director of public prosecutions sought an order of committal against the paper, Fergus Pyle and Dick Walsh for contempt of court. At the hearing, the paper's legal counsel, Samuel Crivon, stated that the paper 'deeply and sincerely regretted the publication complained of and its effect in scandalising the Special Criminal Court'. He spoke at length about, and presented to the court a copy of, the trust's objectives and submitted that the judge would conclude that the material complained of 'was reprehensible both to the Irish Times Ltd and the trust company'.

Crivon explained that on the night in question neither Fergus Pyle nor Dick Walsh was present when the statement was telephoned in at 11.15 p.m. With the print deadline already expired, the chief sub-editor, Niall Fallon, read the statement and decided to attach the most relevant pieces of the statement to the page-one article that had been written earlier by Walsh. Neither the editor-on-duty (James Downey) nor Walsh was consulted on this, and it was, Crivon submitted, purely a case of human error arising out of the rushed circumstances and because Fallon had not realised the offensiveness of the material.[25] Crivon told the court that, had they been consulted, neither Pyle nor Walsh would have allowed the statement to be published, and also stated that, following the publication, Pyle had circulated a memorandum to staff on how to deal with such matters in the future. This memo restricted the terms under which press statements giving 'political, social, legal or other views could be printed'.[26] Crivon then apologised on behalf of both the paper and Pyle and expressed their 'respect for the Special Criminal Court and their desire to maintain the prestige and dignity of the judges who compose that court'.

In their individual evidence both Fallon and Walsh confirmed the veracity of this account of events. Pyle confirmed he had not been on duty that night and that he knew nothing about the statement until he read it in the paper. He expressed his regret for the article and assured the court of his respect for the special criminal court and its judges. In his judgment, the president of the high court, Mr Justice Finlay, declared that no order of committal should be made against either Pyle or Walsh. With regard to the paper he held that publication of the statement should not have occurred, and that experienced journalists should have seen that the statement constituted contempt of court. Nonetheless, he could find no intent or malice on the paper's part. As he saw it, notwithstanding the seriousness of the statement, no servant of the paper had intended to commit the particular contempt, and so he could make no order against it.[27] But while the paper and its journalists escaped any sanction, Pyle's performance in the witness box came in for criticism. In his evidence he had not made an explicit statement accepting responsibility for the content of the newspaper whether he was physically present or not (as editors are traditionally obliged to do) and he was criticised by some of his staff for this. As one journalist put it, Pyle's performance 'caused outrage among the staff; the perception was that he was trying to lay the blame elsewhere'.[28] Another journalist recalled that Pyle's statement was 'thought by the journalists to be wrong thing to say and was seen as a failure to support his journalists'.[29]

The following year, the paper was threatened with prosecution under the Official Secrets Act when some confidential government information came into its possession. In 1976 the government decided to purchase a 24 per cent stake in Bula Mines for £9.54m, and much to the consternation of the opposition, the minister for industry and commerce, Justin Keating, refused to divulge the various independent valuations put on the mine. In early 1977 the paper's financial editor, Richard Keatinge, received an envelope containing one of the independent valuations and, having consulted Fergus Pyle, contacted the department of industry and commerce for a comment. A senior civil servant subsequently contacted Pyle and threatened him with proceedings under the Official Secrets Act. As one journalist remembered, the news conference that followed was a tense affair: while Keatinge and news editor Donal Foley pushed for the story to be published, Pyle decided that the story be dropped.[30] It later ran the story, but only after the *Sunday Independent* published similar documents on the valuation controversy.[31] This belated decision to run the story prompted Fianna Fáil's Des O'Malley to allude to the fact that one of the trust's governors, Richard Wood, was also a shareholder in Bula Mines:

> On Friday, 4 February, 1977, Mr R. Woods [sic], one of the proposed recipients of the £9.54 million visited the offices of the *Irish Times* newspaper. He was quite entitled to be there as he is one of the members of the board of trustees of the newspaper. On Tuesday, 8 February, the *Irish Times* devoted an entire page to an examination of the Bula valuations, quoting extensively from documents which the Minister has seen fit to withhold from the Dáil, the Members of this House being asked to vote this Bill into law without seeing the documents which were made available to this newspaper under circumstances which I described.[32]

However, Keatinge insisted that Richard Wood was not involved in passing any information to the paper.[33] This episode did nothing to endear Pyle to the staff, but it may have strengthened his resolve when, a week later, it came to publishing the heavy gang exposé. In late 1976, two Gardaí separately approached news features editor Conor Brady and told him that suspects were being mistreated in custody to secure incriminating statements, which in turn were used to secure convictions. Having been editor of *Garda Review*, Brady felt he could not be directly involved in any investigation by the paper. When he passed the information to Pyle, a team of reporters was assigned to dig deeper. On 14 February 1977 under the headline 'Gardai Using North-style Brutality in Interrogation Techniques', the paper began a week long series of articles by Don Buckley, Renagh Holohan and Joe Joyce that outlined the activities of a 'heavy gang' of interrogators within the Garda Síochána. The series took weeks to put together and was based on extensive interviews with victims of Garda misconduct, lawyers, doctors, social workers and concerned members of the force. The investigation concluded that brutal interrogation methods were being used by a group of Gardaí charged with the questioning of suspects about serious crime:

> The 'Heavy Gang', as the group has been nicknamed within the force, physically assaults and applies severe psychological pressure on suspects. The pressure includes threats, lies, and psychological tricks and is intensified by depriving suspects of sleep, food and water over long periods ... There are also suggestions that the 'Heavy Gang' are ... forcing people to stand spreadeagled against a wall for lengthy periods ... The psychological tactics include alternating groups of 'brutal' and 'nice' detectives, disorientating people by keeping them in rooms with blinds drawn and lights on all day and night so that they lose track of time, and confusing them by constantly giving conflicting orders. Suspects are forced to sit by fires or heaters and refused water and an atmosphere of fear is induced by loud banging, shouting, threats and sometimes screams from outside the room. All these are intended to break the suspect's resistance to reveal information or more commonly, to signing incriminating statements.[34]

The move towards these interrogation methods was, the paper concluded, in response to political pressure to secure convictions. It also informed readers that the Garda Commissioner, Edmund Garvey, had refused to grant an interview and that the minister for justice, Paddy Cooney, had not responded to its request for an interview. In its editorial the paper tried to pre-empt and neutralise the criticism that would be levelled at it by the government. Firstly, it made clear that it had 'not been taken in by subversive propaganda, which the Minister for Justice has several times blamed as the source of accusations against the Gardaí'; instead, the series was 'the product of many weeks diligent research and investigation by skilled journalists'. Secondly, it stressed that it was not accusing the Garda Síochána of 'using illegal violence on a widespread scale'; instead the accusations centred 'on a small minority of the force'. Thirdly, it declared that the investigation did not 'in any way align the *Irish Times* with the political views of any person who has been subjected to ill-treatment'. With these disclaimers out of the way, the paper questioned the extent to which the ill-treatment of suspects was 'condoned or ignored by people in authority over the force'. It expressed difficulty in accepting that the information gathered by its reporters would not have been available to the minister for justice had he gone and looked for it. Similarly, it expressed difficulty in accepting that the

Garda Commissioner could have been 'completely unaware of the very many accusations against the men under his command'. While conceding that the institutions of the state and the rule of law were under attack, it declared that Gardaí did no service to the state 'by descending to the same methods as the gunman and the criminal'. Gardaí could not, it concluded, 'take it upon themselves unilaterally to extend their powers beyond those set down by the elected representatives of the people'.[35]

As the week progressed, the investigative series dominated the front page, and detailed case histories of ill-treated suspects were printed in the 'News Focus' page.[36] In a classic case of the politics of semantics, the minister for justice, Paddy Cooney, denied the existence of a Garda squad specialising in interrogation and denied that the force was under political pressure to secure convictions.[37] The paper was not easily assuaged; it described the response as 'inconclusive and unsatisfactory ... and classically ambiguous'. It had never alleged the existence of a squad tasked with interrogation duties specifically; it had alleged that a squad within the force was exceeding its legal limitations. It also noted that Cooney was not 'prepared to say that all complaints against the Gardaí were unjustified'.[38] In a subsequent interview on RTÉ, when Cooney was asked why the journalists had believed the allegations if they were untrue, he replied that, 'although he was not saying that they were untrue, there were journalistic tricks which could be employed to make things sound something a bit different from what they were'.[39] Such was the sensitivity of the story that other Irish media were initially reluctant to pick it up. On the day the story broke, RTÉ did not mention it in its early morning news bulletins and only added the story to its news agenda after the Garda press office issued a denial to all media outlets. In contrast, as news editor Donal Foley recounted, 'you couldn't walk across the newsroom of the *Irish Times* without tripping over television cables. Both BBC and ITN have done full programmes on the Gardaí and their antics.'[40] The coincidental fact that the paper broke the story at the same time that the state was pursuing a case against Britain in the European court of human rights over the use of unorthodox interrogation methods in Northern Ireland prompted some politicians to attack the paper's heritage and question its loyalty to the state. In a speech at a Fine Gael meeting in Listowel, deputy Gerard Lynch let it be known that he believed the story was a ploy to distract attention away from the European case:

> It is no coincidence that these charges get prominence in a section of the press that has been traditionally hostile to Irish institutions and who never cease to attack the moral and political standards by which Irish people live. Neither is it a coincidence that such charges are levelled with increasing ferocity at the very time when the nation from which such organs would have us take our standards is on trial before the world for activities that more

properly belong to Cromwellian days or the era of the pitch cap for the mere Irish. Obviously the publicity given to such allegations in the British press and their allies in the Republic is designed to distract attention from the Irish case at Strasburg, and it should be see as such by all Irish people.[41]

Another Fine Gael TD, Fintan Coogan, accused the paper of 'doing the dirty work for John Bull'.[42] It fell on politicians outside the state to congratulate it on its groundbreaking investigative series; Paddy Devlin of the SDLP described the investigation as 'a job the politicians should have been doing for some time past'.[43] It was Pyle's golden hour as editor, and, despite rumours that he hesitated over the story, he was nervous about the story more so than against running it. As remembered by assistant editor, James Downey, Pyle was 'desperately nervous about it, he was like a cat on a hot brick, and while it's not good for journalists to see this he was very brave to do the story'.[44] According to deputy news-editor Gerry Mulvey, Pyle 'had no hesitation on the heavy gang; it had been running a long time and tied up several reporters for weeks. It was a huge drain on resources but he had no hesitation in running the story.'[45] Renagh Holohan, one of the reporters who worked on the story, remembered that the 'heavy gang story was one of the few things he actually went for':

> He was very brave over the heavy gang. We did it and we don't often do those things because you have to be given a lot of time to do it. You have to take someone off daily chores to do this research and then of course there's lawyers' problems and everything. It was crying out to be done and it was done. He was very supportive of it. He didn't have a problem with it at all. It might have been held up for a couple of days when we were ready to go but that's inevitable with something as controversial as that.[46]

Conor Brady, who was present at the final conference at which Pyle gave the story the go-ahead, remembered that Pyle was apprehensive and queried whether the paper should secure affidavits from the interviewees. However, he accepted Donal Foley's assertion that there was no way those who had given information, sometimes in confidence, to the paper would swear to it. As Brady put it, 'the reality was that Fergus would carry the can, not Foley or anybody else, if the story blew up in our faces. But Fergus gave the go ahead, knowing that he, and the newspaper, were largely defenceless. It was a brave decision, for which he was subsequently not given sufficient credit.'[47] Indeed, had Pyle not been editor at the time, then the series may never have been published. According to Brady, Douglas Gageby once told him that the series would not have run had he still been editor. Brady attributed this statement to Gageby's absolute belief in the supremacy of the state and its agents.[48] As another journalist put it, while Gageby wanted the paper's reporters to be liberal, he also wanted them to be part of the mainstream of Irish life, and this 'sometimes led him to be protective about the state, to be cautious about the sort of investigative journalism which could be seen to undermine the credibility of the state or its security apparatus. He was wary about criticism of the Gardaí and of course, of the Army.'[49] Not so Fergus Pyle, who, as Brady put it, made the difficult decision to publish the story 'in a climate of apprehension over the gathering strength of violent and subversive forces'.[50]

The heavy gang story was followed by another exposé, this time on the infighting within the Garda technical bureau. The controversy began over mistakes made during the investigation into the assassination by the IRA of the British ambassador, Christopher Ewart-Biggs, in Dublin in July 1976. A fingerprint expert examined a helmet that was found at the scene but found nothing on it. However, a colleague of his subsequently found a print on the helmet that he believed belonged to a member of the IRA. This discovery was communicated to the government and the British and Northern Ireland authorities and police forces. Puzzled, the first officer re-examined the helmet and found that the print was in fact his own. A third officer examined the print and concluded that it belonged to the officer who had first examined the helmet. These two officers reported their finding to a superior officer, who rejected their finding. The two officers then decided to check past cases and discovered fingerprint irregularities in several cases. A major row then ensued within the technical bureau over the activities of the two officers, and their duties were altered to less senior work.[51] Details of all this came into the possession of the paper, and it ran the story on its front page over several days. One report alleged that the two officers had discovered that fingerprint evidence was falsified in a failed attempt to convict a man of murder.[52] Another report revealed that the Garda Commissioner, Edmund Garvey, had ordered the force's intelligence unit to investigate the leaking of information to the paper.[53] In an editorial, the paper praised the actions of the whistle-blowers within the technical bureau and declared that the 'truth must be brought out, if only to vindicate the members of the Garda Síochána who have risked their careers rather than remain silent'.[54] A subsequent investigation by Scotland Yard's fingerprint department concluded that the print was not that of the IRA member who was suspected of involvement in the ambassador's murder.

THE SECOND COMING

That year, 1977, also saw Pyle's longest lasting editorial innovation – the realignment of the pagination of the Saturday edition to introduce 'The Weekend' section that is today the Saturday supplement. Edited by Brian

Fallon, the new section assembled all the feature articles – book extracts, travel and gardening columns, book reviews, Donal Foley's 'Saturday Column' and the television and radio listings – into a four-page segment that would eventually become the paper's first supplement.[55] Despite such innovation, circulation continued to slide from 66,829 in the second half of 1976 to 61,791 in the first half of 1977, and both the board and the staff began to get edgy.[56] Thus began moves – from both sides – to unseat Pyle from the editorial chair. As then father of the paper's NUJ chapel, Paul Gillespie, put it: 'The staff was increasingly unhappy with the direction of the paper, worried about the economic circumstances, increasingly unhappy with the paper's editorial management, and whether he [Pyle] was up to it. But there was a lot of sympathy for him as well. It was not all antagonistic. But towards the end it was clear that Fergus was not going to survive and then it was a question of what would happen afterwards.'[57] One senior journalist, Dick Walsh, sought a meeting with Major McDowell:

> He was told the Major felt it would be inappropriate to meet union representatives. Dick reported back to the chapel. He asked for and was given approval to assemble a group of senior staff, some of whom were on the chapel committee, to seek a meeting to discuss the critical state of the paper in an atmosphere free of the normal rules of engagement imposed by traditional industrial relations. McDowell agreed to the meeting after he had been assured that it would be informal, confidential and designed to resolve a problem which was already plainly visible. Several meetings were held. The journalists' group agreed with McDowell that it would be wise to persuade Douglas Gageby to return as editor, and the group met Gageby to discuss this proposal.[58]

The Bank of Ireland was also watching developments with concern. There existed a worry that the company was heading towards insolvency or might be accused of reckless trading if losses continued. When Gageby indicated his willingness to return, the board suggested to Pyle that he stand aside; he agreed, and on 30 June 1977 he resigned as editor. The gloss put on the change was that Pyle had resigned upon his appointment as editorial director of the company to advise McDowell on new technology.[59] Shortly afterwards, he left the paper to become information officer at Trinity College. According to one journalist, Pyle took these developments 'very well, though he was extremely hurt … His anger was directed chiefly against the Major, rather than Gageby'.[60] He returned to the paper in the 1980s and was posted to Berlin to cover the reunification of Germany, and eventually became the paper's chief leader writer.[61]

Gageby's return as editor was greeted with joy among the staff, although most also felt sorry for Pyle. As one journalist put it, 'people were pleased because Gageby was seen as such a good editor, and there was a bit of a worry that there wasn't a steady hand on the place ... but people felt desperately sorry for Fergus Pyle because being there for three years and then being ousted was pretty grim'.[62] During his 'second coming', as his return was referred to, the company was run by a triumvirate of Gageby (editorial), McDowell (chairman and chief executive) and Louis O'Neill (deputy chief executive). One of the first decisions taken was to sell off the chain of newsagent shops the company had bought in 1975. Although it had expanded into this activity with the long-term purpose of alleviating losses suffered by the paper, the subsidiary company (Irish Times Distributors) set up to manage the shops had added to the company's overall losses. Gageby also decided on a shake-up of senior personnel; Donal Foley was made deputy editor, Gerry Mulvey news editor, and James Downey night editor with responsibility for overseeing the production of the paper.

Unlike Pyle, Gageby had access to the company's purse strings and spent £100,000 on marketing the paper in his first year. He decided to make the paper's 'News Focus' page, which alternated between in-depth current affairs and magazine-style articles, the centre of the paper's promotional activities. The page's editor, Conor Brady, was promoted to assistant editor and given charge of the marketing budget. The hope was that by running a series of articles on a given topic over a number of days or weeks, readers would get into the habit of buying the paper on a more frequent basis. These series, some of which had a rural theme to broaden the paper's appeal outside of Dublin, were promoted on national radio using the tagline 'Keep up with the Changing Times'. Although some series were derided by one commentator as being 'chosen as much for ease of promotion as much for its merits' the tactic worked.[63] During the first six months of Gageby's return, circulation increased slightly to 62,325. However, circulation increased dramatically in the first half of 1978 when average daily sales hit 66,242 copies. In the second half of 1978 circulation broke the 70,000 mark for the first time, with the paper averaging 70,335 daily sales. The following year, 1979, saw circulation rise to 75,009 in the first and 77,316 in the second half of the year.[64] The company also returned to profitability; it returned a pre-tax profit of £306,000 for 1977.[65] Indeed, the newspaper industry enjoyed something of a fillip during the papal visit of 1979 and the paper published a forty-eight-page pictorial record of the visit that retailed at 30p per copy. Such was Gageby's enthusiasm for the visit – he described it as a 'potential illumination for everyone on the island' – that the office joke was that he would make history by becoming the paper's first Catholic editor.[66] As Gageby saw it, the pope was calling on Ireland, and the paper would not be beaten in its coverage of the various functions and masses. In his address to the reporters assigned to cover the visit, he warned them that he did not want any 'fashionable liberals sneering at the Pope'. As one journalist put it, he was determined 'to bury any memory of the *Irish Times* as the voice of Protestant Unionism. He wanted us to be liberal but also to be part of the mainstream of Irish life.'[67]

But it was not all plain sailing and the early 1980s saw the paper face a number of challenges. Given the depressed state of the economy, advertising revenue remained static. In addition, the introduction of a second television channel in 1979 saw the newspaper industry lose precious advertising to RTÉ. Between 1979 and 1983 the national newspapers' share of all advertising revenue fell from 52 to 34 per cent; over the same period RTÉ's share rose from 33 to 43 per cent. The newspaper industry also suffered from the highest VAT rate in Europe; while a minority of European states zero-rated newspapers or had typical rates of 9 per cent, Ireland's rate stood at 23 per cent. As a consequence of all this, the price of the paper gradually rose from 25p in July 1981 to 45p in July 1984.[68] The changeover to new technology also posed significant challenges. In the mid-1970s photo-composition technology was introduced, and the paper began the long process of phasing out hot-metal, although for quite a while both processes were used simultaneously. One major challenge was aligning the different types of printing plates to ensure that equal pressure was applied to all pages so as to avoid faintly printed pages. As remembered by James Downey, the deputy editor in charge of production, Gageby did not have much time for the delicacies involved in the technology changeover:

> He was impatient, not to say angry and ill-tempered, with the accommodations without which it would have been impossible to make the change in very difficult conditions from the old hot-metal system to the new print technology. On one bad night he panicked and said, apparently in all seriousness, that we should abandon the whole enterprise and go back to hot metal.[69]

Despite the pressures involved, the paper did not miss an edition in its gradual changeover from hot-metal to photo-composition, or indeed the later transition from photo-composition to computer-based technology. The prospect of job losses stemming from new technology was not lost on the National Union of Journalists: the May 1980 house agreement between it and the company stipulated that there would be 'be no loss of NUJ jobs whether by non-replacement or compulsory redundancy as a result of the introduction of computerised photo-composition or any other form of new technology'.[70] Concerns were also expressed about the state of the company's printing press. The paper was still produced on the Hoe and Crabtree press purchased by Frank Lowe in 1951, but as yet the company could not afford a new one. Also, after several years of growth, circulation began to decline in the early 1980s. In the second half of 1982 circulation stood at 87,433; this declined to 84,408 in the latter half of 1983.[71] Although the company stopped making its accounts public in the early 1980s, one commentator concluded that the company incurred significant losses in 1983 and 1984.[72]

THE HAUGHEY FACTOR

Shortly after returning as editor, Gageby invited John Healy to return to the paper. He had left in February 1976 after Tony O'Reilly invited him to join Independent Newspapers. Healy signed a two-year contract that was honoured even though he never wrote a word for any Independent title because the NUJ objected to his recruitment while journalists were being made redundant under O'Reilly's restructuring process.[73] Healy thus returned to the *Irish Times* to write 'Sounding Off', a twice-weekly opinion column in which he coined many of the political catchphrases – such as 'grassroots' for local party workers and 'national handlers' for Garret FitzGerald's political and media advisors – that are still used today.[74] Having been an admirer of Haughey as a minister, Healy had great expectations of him when he became Taoiseach in 1979. As one journalist put it: 'He certainly never made any secret of his admiration for Charlie Haughey. This had a huge influence on his writing and brought accusations of lack of objectivity. He took it on himself to fight all Haughey's battles for him, to snipe at Jack Lynch and Garret FitzGerald or anyone else that was not on the same wavelength.'[75] But in one of his columns Healy challenged the idea that he was unique in being on friendly terms with a prominent politician by listing the family relationships and friendships that existed between various journalists and politicians. As he put it, many journalists 'have party affiliations, and sometimes they are card-carrying members of Fine Gael, Fianna Fáil, Labour, The Stickies'.[76] Gageby also had high hopes for Haughey and expected that the 'pent-up energies of the years should now pour forth in major effort'.[77] It was not to be, and, as Gageby later put it, 'Mr Haughey's first period of office was a disappointment. Where was the man who laid out the problems of this State so clearly in a television speech in January 1980 – and then appeared to do nothing?'[78] Healy too expressed exasperation with Haughey's choice of ministers. He had, Healy opined, 'a claque of second and third-raters around him … and more than a few stupos in his Cabinet'.[79] Haughey's first administration ended in June 1981 and was replaced by a Fine Gael–Labour coalition that fell in January 1982, having tried to introduce an austerity budget. As polling day approached, senior editorial staff debated with Gageby about the virtues of giving editorial support to Fine Gael and Labour rather than Fianna Fáil, with mixed results:

> For whatever reason, at that time Douglas Gageby had a soft spot for Charlie Haughey. And he had no time at all for the 'Blueshirts', as he habitually called members of Fine Gael. Against this background, it seemed certain that the newspaper would counsel a vote for Fianna Fáil in its election-day editorial. At the time, sentiment amongst the editorial staff of the paper ran strongly against Haughey, though not necessarily against Fianna Fáil. Gageby was well aware of this, knowing also that the majority of the paper's readers were equally suspicious of the Fianna Fáil leader. He was urged to publish an editorial backing the return of the coalition. He did not denounce this impertinence out of hand. Instead, he called for a draft. And another. And yet another. The fifth and final draft embodied a lukewarm endorsement of the Fine Gael-Labour coalition, criticising their ineptitude but praising their honest effort. It was published on election day.[80]

As the editorial in question put it, 'It is live now and pay later with Fianna Fáil or pay now and live later with the Coalition.'[81] Nonetheless, Haughey returned as Taoiseach for the best part of 1982 before his administration fell and was replaced by a Fine Gael–Labour coalition that lasted until 1987. One person who did not have a soft spot for Haughey was Kevin Myers, who joined the paper as a casual reporter in 1979. Long-time 'An Irishman's Diary' columnist Seamus Kelly died that year and Myers took over the column in mid-1980. When news editor Conor O'Cleary proposed to Gageby that Myers take over the column full-time, he objected but eventually relented. Thus began many rows between Gageby and Myers over what constituted relevant material for the column. While Gageby favoured the social diary of old – name-checking events, functions, book launches and listing who attended what – Myers favoured political opinion pieces. One topic tackled by Myers was the airbrushing from history of the Irishmen who had fought in the British forces during the two world wars, a theme that brought mild rebukes from Gageby. But when Myers turned his attention to the finances of Charles Haughey, Gageby spiked two articles and strongly rebuked Myers for crossing into territory that belonged, as he saw it, strictly to the paper's political correspondents.[82] Gageby also disliked other journalists delving into Haughey's finances. According to one such journalist, Frank McDonald:

> Gageby disliked a heavily researched piece I wrote on Haughey's wealth in December 1979, after he became Taoiseach, so he 'buried' it on page eight … he basically didn't want stuff that was 'damaging' to Haughey to appear in the paper – other than the usual political stuff. He also, probably, thought it was wrong to be delving into people's personal affairs. After all, he himself had done very well out of the establishment of the Trust.[83]

But Gageby did not interfere with straight news reporting. In October 1982 the paper's security correspondent, Peter Murtagh, published two stories on the Haughey government's interference with the Garda Síochána. He outlined how Haughey's minister for justice, Sean Doherty, had attempted to transfer a Garda sergeant from his Co. Roscommon constituency. The sergeant had raided a pub owned by a friend of Doherty's and had resisted pressure from Doherty to drop charges against those found drinking after-hours.[84] It must be noted that Gageby permitted publication of this story, whereas the *Sunday Independent,* which had the story before the *Irish Times,* refused to publish it.[85] Murtagh also revealed that in an assault case against Doherty's brother-in-law a witness had been detained by the RUC, thus preventing him from giving evidence at the court case. This had happened following contact between police intelligence services on both sides of the border, contact initiated by Doherty's office.[86] Immediately after the Fine Gael–Labour coalition assumed power in December 1982, Murtagh revealed that Haughey's administration had ordered the Garda Síochána to bug the telephones of two political correspondents. The two reporters, Geraldine Kennedy of the *Sunday Tribune* and Bruce Arnold of the *Irish Independent,* had written extensively on the various challenges to Haughey's leadership, and the bugging was an attempt to identify their sources.[87]

Given that the state's intelligence agency was spying on journalists at the behest of a political party, it might be expected that Gageby's editorial would have explored the implications this had on the idea of a free press. Although his editorial criticised the 'frivolity and wastefulness' of the bugging, the bulk of it focused on the legitimate use of the procedure, the technology itself and how it was used to cope with 'a certain population of foreign spies' – a reflection, perhaps, of his obsession with all things military.[88] In a subsequent editorial he stressed that care had to be taken so that 'in cleaning up the mess, damage is not done to the whole security fabric'. Not missing the point entirely, he observed that Fianna Fáil had been 'reckless beyond belief'.[89] In the subsequent challenge to Haughey's leadership there were widespread expectations that he would be ousted. While the *Irish Press* published a two-page political obituary of Haughey, Gageby engaged in a bout of wishful thinking. He declared that Haughey would resign and 'in going he will prove that he is a better man than some of those who speak against him'; he would go 'because the stream of advice to him not to endanger the party will eventually overcome the normal pride and egoism of any man who has been called to lead his organisation'.[90] When it became clear that Haughey had no intention of resigning, Gageby described his decision to fight the challenge as 'like vaingloriousness shading into narcissism'. Haughey had 'a record of socially-conscious legislation behind him' and, he declared, it 'would be better for him and for the country if he stepped down with that still as his record, rather than continue in office and be remembered as the man who was not big enough to hand over power to his now very insistent colleagues'.[91] On the day of the parliamentary party meeting to decide the issue, John Healy cryptically predicted that Haughey would survive. While his column focused on the looming pro-life amendment debate, at the end of the column was the totally unconnected sentence; 'By the way, anyone have a job for a troupe of coffin-dancers who are free due to a last-minute cancellation?'[92]

The paper also made planning an issue in its reportage. In a report in October 1983, the paper's local government correspondent, Frank Kilfeather, wrote an article on what he saw as the over-use of section four motions that compelled the county manager to carry out the wishes of the council. He noted that, while most county councils rarely used this power, Dublin county council dealt with an average of twelve section four motions every month. Members of the council were, as Kilfeather put it, 'abusing Section 4 motions ... using it for pushing through planning applications'.[93] His article, and the fact that he listed the councillors who proposed such motions, did not go down well with some councillors. One criticised what he termed the 'defamatory, politically biased, selective, propagandistic and generally untrue, unjust and unfair report' and called on the council to consider excluding the paper's reporters from its meetings. Amid laughter, another councillor, Liam Lawlor, stated that 'in some cases the manager was in favour of Section 4 motions because they resolved some problems'. This prompted the council's principal officer for planning to get on his feet and deny Lawlor's assertion. Other councillors supported the paper. One stated that the article was accurate and that the paper had 'covered planning meetings for a long time and they did it when it wasn't popular or profitable'. The matter was ultimately referred to the council's organisation and procedure committee to consider.[94]

'THE THEOLOGICAL CONSTITUTION'

Gageby and Healy were also critical of Haughey for giving his support to the pro-life lobby in the early 1980s. As Fianna Fáil and Fine Gael fought for electoral supremacy, Catholic lay groups pushed for a constitutional ban on abortion. Although abortion was illegal, some feared that a successful constitutional challenge on the grounds of privacy would result in abortion being legalised. The political uncertainty of the early 1980s allowed these lobby groups to extract an assurance from Garret FitzGerald that Fine Gael would hold such a referendum. Not to be outdone, Charles Haughey committed

Fianna Fáil too. The end result was the 1983 referendum on the insertion of a pro-life clause into the constitution – a process by which, as John Healy put it, 'a small and unrepresentative bunch, a theological Armalite rifle in one hand and the ballot paper in the other divided this Free State society with the effectiveness of the Provies. All in Christ's name'.[95] The paper opposed holding a referendum that, as Gageby put it, would allow 'Orange voices ... to prove again that Dublin is run from Rome'.[96] So strong was his opposition that the paper proposed a resolution that it hoped the Dáil might pass to negate the need for the referendum:

> That Dáil Éireann, while affirming its total condemnation of abortion and its intention to ensure that abortion remains unlawful, considers, in the light of the views expressed by the Protestant Churches and others, and in the light of the pressing urgency of the economic and social issues of the day, that it is untimely and inappropriate, at present, to proceed with any proposal for a Constitutional Referendum in relation to this matter.[97]

As Gageby saw it, the acceptance of this resolution would be 'the practical side of ecumenism and a good deed in the cause of the whole nation'. As voting day approached, he denounced the referendum as 'The Second Partitioning of Ireland' facilitated by politicians who were 'copper-fastening Lloyd George's work every day'. He also criticised the zeal with which the pro-amendment lobby pushed its agenda by declaring that 'if God is behind some of the fanatical laymen, then the rest of us Christians are in for a horrible surprise'.[98] John Healy was equally against the referendum; in his column he took a dig at Haughey for running with the pro-amendment lobby. Where, he asked 'are all the great Republicans we had in the late sixties and in the early seventies? I reckon Honest Jack had about the measure of them.'[99] On voting day the paper unsuccessfully called for a 'no' vote and prophetically noted the irony that, while mistrust of the supreme court was a hallmark of the pro-amendment groups' argument, the amendment was so loosely worded that the supreme court could interpret it in a variety of ways.[1]

The paper took a similarly broadminded stance when the Fine Gael–Labour coalition proposed lifting the constitutional ban on divorce in 1986. As Gageby asserted in one editorial, 'a negative decision would place citizens in the Republic in the same camp as those whom they criticise for saying "No" to reasonable proposals for progress'.[2] He also took a dig at Charles Haughey, who had played for political advantage by allowing individual deputies to campaign as they saw fit. As Gageby saw it, there were some politicians 'who like nothing better than to spout about Bodenstown or Wolfe Tone' but whose republicanism was 'pathetic to observe'.[3] In another editorial he asserted that the state 'would not be true to itself if it denied to its citizens civil rights that are enjoyed by the people of the North'.[4] While this was a fair point, he soon afterwards made the ludicrous claim that a negative result could drive many constitutional nationalists 'into the arms of Sinn Féin and the IRA. The South, they would say, is play-acting; is not and maybe never was genuine about a new Ireland, about one Ireland. This could lead to more anarchy, more killings on both sides.'[5] On voting day the paper unsuccessfully called for a 'yes' vote.[6] Gageby was also critical of Haughey's claim that the Anglo-Irish Agreement of 1985 represented a sell-out of Irish unity. Such a claim was, Gageby countered, 'audacity of a high order ... by Dublin politicians, who are strong on verbiage and weak on action'.[7] Such opinion did not endear Gageby to unionists who, in any event, did not have a high opinion of the paper. When, in July 1985, the European Commission appointed the paper's deputy editor, Dennis Kennedy, as head of the commission's Belfast office, Ulster Unionist MEP John Taylor accused the commission of having 'insulted the majority in Northern Ireland' because Kennedy 'works for a republican newspaper, the *Irish Times,* which takes a pretty strong united Irish line'.[8]

In 1984 the company enjoyed a windfall of £2.7m when Reuters, the news agency in which it held shares, was floated on the stock exchange. The company put £1m towards a new press, and in February 1985 used the balance to redeem the Bank of Ireland's preference shares in Irish Times Holdings at a cost of £1.65m.[9] According to managing director Louis O'Neill, the news agency's flotation saved the day: 'Then a certain amount of money was paid to the bank, they forgave the interest and a settlement was made. I don't know if the *Irish Times* would have ever made enough profit to pay off the bank. It was like a tidal wave coming up behind them.'[10] As Irish Times Holdings did not file annual accounts, it is unclear whether or not the bank ever received dividends on its shares in Irish Times Holdings. Major McDowell's company, Dowell Ltd, received dividends totalling £31,327 from Irish Times Holdings between 1979 and 1982.[11] It is unclear whether Gageby received dividends, as his company was unlimited and was not required to file accounts.[12] It is also unclear whether Hetherington or the Walker brothers received dividends, as neither of their companies filed accounts with their annual returns.[13] However, it is likely that, since one shareholder received dividends, all shareholders did. From the records in the Companies Registration Office, it appears the shares held by McDowell, Gageby, Hetherington and the Walker brothers were also redeemed in February 1985, possibly by way of a bank loan. On the same day that the bank's shares were redeemed, the company's memorandum of association was changed to allow it to 'fund the holding thereof and the redemption of any of the shares of the company by borrowing or any other means'.[14] On that day also McDowell, Gageby, Hetherington and the Walker brothers transferred their shares from their respective companies to Irish Times Holdings. Irish Times Ltd subsequently redeemed the remaining shares: 250,000 in December 1987 and 130,000 in October 1988.[15]

In 1985 the company purchased a new printing press – a Uniman 4/2 – that could print a forty-eight page newspaper and produce 32,000 copies per hour. Costing £2.5m, the new press allowed for full colour pages; previous to this, colour adverts were pre-printed by Independent Newspapers and then inserted in the paper. This meant that every time the paper got a colour advert it boosted the coffers of its main competitor. Independent Newspapers printed the paper for five months as the old press was dismantled and the new press installed. Deputy editor James Downey oversaw production of the paper during this critical transition period. The cost of the new press and its installation came to £3m. This was paid for by a £1m loan from Bank of Ireland, a £500,000 loan from the Industrial Credit Corporation and a £500,000 re-equipment grant from the Industrial Development Authority. The company used £1m of its Reuters windfall to make up the balance. For his part, Gageby was wary of sinking the Reuters money into a new press; Conor Brady remembered him once expressing a fear that it 'could drag the newspaper and the company to the bottom'. Indeed, as managing director Louis O'Neill remembered, the board was not convinced either: 'I remember McDowell saying to me, the board wasn't convinced, and he said "be it on your head".'[16] Once the machine was operational, the paper could include colour adverts and separate supplements. Market research to test readers' reaction to supplements and colour indicated negative reactions to both, but the changes went ahead anyway, and over next few years various supplements – sport, property, and business – were added.[17]

By this time Gageby's days as editor were coming to an end. He had returned in 1977 with the intention of staying two years but had stayed for nine. He had, in the eyes of some, stayed too long and had become increasingly cantankerous. At one stage he had five deputy editors – Bruce Williamson, Jim Downey, Ken Gray, Gerry Mulvey and Dennis Kennedy – and this team did most of the day-to-day work in running the paper. It appears that Gageby did not want to retire but was eventually convinced that it was time to go. He was, as one journalist put it, 'eventually pushed out'.[18] In August 1986 the board announced that Gageby had tendered his resignation and that the post would be publicly advertised and the new editor appointed via a competitive process. This procedure had been agreed between the board and the paper's NUJ chapel following the fallout from the appointment of Fergus Pyle as editor in 1974. The process allowed for a shortlist of candidates to be drawn up by the board that would then be vetted by the paper's NUJ chapel. If the chapel felt any candidate was not acceptable as editor, then that person would be eliminated from the process.[19] Only two candidates made it to the shortlist, both internal candidates of wide editorial experience, James Downey and Conor Brady. The choice, as it became known in the newsroom, was between 'the Yuppies and the Downeys'.

CHAPTER 11

Changing Times

Perhaps to a degree that maybe irritated some journalists I did insist on very thorough levels of validation. I didn't go on the basis of supposition. I didn't go on the basis of 'Let's give it a run and see what happens' ... I think it was always important for the *Irish Times* that if we said something as a fact, then the reader was entitled to assume that we had established it as a fact and that we weren't presenting supposition as fact. The paper's lifeblood is its credibility.[1]

Conor Brady on his editorship

IN DECEMBER 1986 the board announced that Conor Brady was to be Douglas Gageby's successor. He had joined the paper in 1969 and reported from Belfast and London in the early 1970s before leaving to edit *Garda Review* from where he joined RTÉ as a radio reporter. He returned to the paper in 1976 as news features editor and was night editor when the 'Stardust' inferno claimed the lives of forty-eight people in February 1981. However, Brady had left the building before news of the disaster reached the news desk and did not turn on his car's mobile radio as he drove home. He thus missed all attempts by the news desk to contact him and awoke the next morning to read a very different paper than that he had approved the night before.[2] He left the paper again in 1981 to edit the *Sunday Tribune,* returned in 1983 as an assistant editor and in 1985 became a deputy editor. The following year he became the first Catholic editor of the *Irish Times*.[3] However, he was not the popular choice among the staff, most of whom viewed James Downey as the front runner in the Gageby succession stakes. As one journalist put it:

All the journalists expected Jim Downey to get the job. He was very much considered the journalists' favourite for the job so it was a shock when Conor Brady got it. Brady was considered too young. Downey had been there a longer time; he wrote a lot of leaders, he mixed more with the journalists and Brady was considered too young and brash for the job. When the decision was made Gageby came in and announced it in the newsroom and there was a stunned silence because it was not expected at all.[4]

Brady was well aware of this situation and acknowledged that 'if it had come to a staff vote Jim would have got it there and then'.[5] In accordance with the appointment process agreed between the company and the NUJ chapel, the editorial committee 'debated Brady and debated Downey and perhaps 90 per cent of the chapel wanted Downey and not Brady but Dick Walsh wisely said we have no grounds to disqualify him and we didn't. He was perfectly qualified and was duly appointed.'[6] The staff preference for Downey stemmed from the fact that they knew what he stood for – he was a former Labour Party candidate – and he was a gregarious colleague. In contrast, Brady was viewed as being 'politically doubtful' and as 'being too much of a development manager rather than an editor'.[7] Brady prepared for the selection process by putting together a prospectus that detailed his plans for the newspaper under various headings – news, features, the arts, sport, design – and a circulation-building strategy aimed at achieving a daily average sale of 100,000 copies over ten years. As one journalist remembered, the board was very 'impressed by Brady's plans about supplements. A lot of the developments that he oversaw were actually presaged in his presentation to the board such as modernising the editorial role and including supplements. He delivered on a lot of it.'[8] Announcing Brady's succession, Gageby told the newsroom that 'the future is bright, you're got the right man for the job'. But the day his appointment was announced Major McDowell advised him not to attend the newsroom's Christmas party that night. Brady took the advice, and managing director Louis O'Neill was left to bear the brunt of the journalists' anger.[9]

In the run-up to Gageby's retirement, a number of significant changes were made to the articles of association of Irish Times Ltd. An extraordinary general meeting in June 1986 created ten £1 non-redeemable 'A' shares, all of which were allotted to Major McDowell. The articles were also changed to stipulate that McDowell was to be a director of Irish Times Ltd for life, as opposed to the previous status that allowed him to be a director as long he was a governor of the trust.[10] Given that the articles already stipulated that he was to be chairman as long as he was a director, this new stipulation effectively made him chairman for life. The voting powers attached to the new 'A' shares copper-fastened this position: they entitled McDowell to a veto ('one vote plus such number of further votes as shall be equal to the total number of votes conferred on all other members of the company') when voting on any issues related to the 'A' shares or his new position as a director (and thus chairman) of Irish Times Ltd for life.[11] The changes were mirrored in changes to the articles of association of the Irish Times Trust.[12] According to one company advisor, McDowell's contract was reviewed and updated every few years and 'the trend was to make his position as chairman and chief executive more secure on the grounds that his commitment over the years had denied him the opportunity of taking on other occupations or pursuits'.[13]

Having settled in, Brady began to implement his plans for the paper, which, at this time, had a circulation of just over 80,000. As Brady saw it, most areas of content, apart from general news, were under-resourced and under-provided for in terms of pagination with sport, features, the arts, books, film and music all jostling for space. Almost immediately all this changed. A full-length daily digest highlighting the contents of the paper was initiated on page one, the sports pages were moved to back of the paper, and there was a shift towards increased specialist reporting in the fields of science, legal affairs, the environment, health, social affairs, the media, food and entertainment. The new printing press allowed for colour photographs and advertisements and also facilitated the introduction of specialist supplements – Working & Living (later Education & Living) on Tuesdays, commercial supplements on Wednesdays, Property on Thursdays, Business on Fridays, Sport on Mondays and Saturdays and 'The Weekend' supplement on Saturdays. Brady also appointed the first female assistant editor, Maev-Ann Wren, in August 1986. The following year Dick Ahlstrom was appointed science correspondent. In later years Brady initiated a strategy to increase readership outside Dublin by converting page two into a regional news page, with the focus alternating daily from one region to another. The paper was also profitable: in the sixteen months up to January 1988, it made a profit of £1.2m; in the year ending December 1988, it made a profit £1.7m.[14] The profits for 1989 and 1990 were £3.6m and £3.1m respectively.[15] Staff numbers also increased from 190 editorial staff in 1986 to 280 in 1996 – a sign perhaps that the journalists' doubts about Brady were misplaced. That said, it also hinted at the over-staffing problems that would arise in later years.

As Brady saw it, the paper should measure itself not against indigenous competition but against similarly sized newspapers in Europe. He became involved in the World Editors' Forum and spent time observing what was happening in comparable quality European newspapers, on which he modelled the development of the *Irish Times*. His emphasis was on developing the range of editorial services, modernising the paper, its production process, and bringing it 'into line with some of the things that were commonplace around other European newspapers at that time'. This strategy was in contrast to that of some governors and directors whose 'attitude always was "well we're so far ahead of the Independent that we don't have to worry about anything"'.[16] One crucial way of broadening the paper's (and the readers') outlook was by the appointment of foreign correspondents at international hotspots, which in turn lessened its reliance on syndicated press agency material. These bureaux gave an

Irish interpretation of major international events and opened and closed as news priorities changed. In 1987 Conor O'Clery went to Moscow to cover the dissolution of the USSR; he later moved to Washington and was replaced in Moscow by Seamus Martin, who, in 1992, discovered correspondence between the Workers' Party and the central committee of the Communist Party of the Soviet Union in the archives of that defunct party.[17] Ed O'Loughlin and Jarlath Dolan went to South Africa to report on the transition from the apartheid regime to democracy. Other overseas correspondents included (at different times) Paddy Agnew in Rome, Lara Marlowe in Paris, Fergus Pyle in Berlin and Miriam Donohoe in Beijing. While the cost of posting correspondents abroad later became an issue, reader research 'confirmed that there was an appetite and an appreciation among our readers for accurate, balanced and Irish mediated news from beyond our own shores'.[18] As Brady saw it, the *Irish Times* simply followed the example set by comparable newspapers elsewhere in Europe, and the cost was very little in the greater scheme of things:

> People's horizons were perhaps limited. Ireland was still an insular place. For example, a lot of people made a great fuss about the number of overseas correspondents we had. It was regarded as something to be wondered at. In actual fact we never had more than four or five people abroad but if you looked at comparable newspapers, for example *Jyllands-Posten* in Denmark, – the same circulation as the *Irish Times*, it had twenty people overseas, or if you looked at *Diario* in Lisbon, a smaller newspaper than the *Irish Times*, it had the same ... I suppose what we were trying to do was to bring the paper more broadly into line with the services which were being provided for readers by those European newspapers. It was costly, but in terms of the paper's overall budget it was relatively small.[19]

The paper also had to deal with the introduction of computerised typesetting. The switch from manual to electronic publishing was a slow process and involved journalists using computers to type their content before handing it over to printers who retyped it to arrange the layout and make up the pages. This costly process slowed down the transition to full electronic publishing but ensured industrial harmony. As a result, the *Irish Times,* unlike the Irish Press Group, which endured a damaging six-week closure in 1985 over the introduction of computerised technology, never missed an edition. Independent Newspapers simply granted extremely generous terms to its staff in order to facilitate the transition, a strategy the *Irish Times* could not afford.

'PISS AND VINEGAR STUFF'

Within a few weeks of becoming editor, and at the behest of John Healy, Brady had dinner with Charles Haughey who informed him of his ambitious plans –

an international finance centre for Dublin, the rejuvenation of Dublin's Temple Bar area and the reorganisation of the beef export business – to rejuvenate the country's stagnant economy. Two months into his editorship he had to decide which party, if any, the paper would support in the imminent general election. To Brady's mind 'the only prospect of rescue seemed to repose in Charles J. Haughey' because the Fine Gael–Labour coalition government was split on how to develop the economy. In the lead-up to polling day he wrote a series of editorials favouring a change of government on the basis that the coalition could not resolve the country's economic woes. These editorials prompted complaints from some readers and also displeased the paper's ardent anti-Haughey political editor Dick Walsh.[20] Brady was well aware that the paper's left-leaning journalists, most of whom were dismayed at his appointment, were watching where he was taking the paper editorially:

> Some individuals who were involved in left-wing politics were also active in the NUJ chapel. I knew they were watching their new editor with interest, especially to ensure that the newspaper did not veer too far to the right at this time of real social tension. I was aware of them. And they were aware that I was aware of them. But there was never any real trouble between us. There was a healthy and cautious respect for each other's positions.[21]

Indeed, in 1990 several of the paper's NUJ officers got embroiled in a spat with the *Phoenix* magazine over the political allegiances of one of the paper's former journalists, Stephen Hillard, who died that year. A series of obituaries of Hilliard in the paper neglected to mention his links with various republican organisations. The *Phoenix* subsequently ran a story stating that Hilliard had been an active member of both Sinn Féin and the IRA in the late 1960s and had joined the Officials (Stickies) following the spilt in the republican movement in 1970. Hilliard's widow attempted to sue the magazine for criminal libel but failed to secure the necessary permission from the high court. Several *Irish Times* NUJ officers then took an action against the magazine's editor, Paddy Prenderville, via the NUJ's ethics code, accusing him of unprofessional conduct. The complaint was initially upheld, but at a subsequent appeal hearing, during which six former IRA leaders testified that Hilliard had been a member, the appeal was successful and Prenderville was cleared of any wrongdoing.[22]

The one issue that most journalists and Brady agreed on was the mystery of Haughey's wealth. Throughout the 1980s and 1990s various journalists, including Frank McDonald, Dick Walsh, Mark Brennock and Brady himself, devoted significant time and resources to investigating the source of Haughey's unexplained wealth, but to no avail. This close focus on Haughey's finances caused much friction. While Dick Walsh 'was like a dog with a bone about

Haughey's unexplained money', John Healy dismissed the reportage as 'piss-and-vinegar stuff'.[23] Haughey himself was even more blunt: he once asked a reporter whether the paper's leading articles were written 'by an ould one in a cold bath with the water lapping around her fanny'.[24] The explanation for Haughey's wealth only emerged with the split in the Dunne family in the mid-1990s during which it was revealed that Ben Dunne had made payments to politicians. It was rumoured that Haughey was among the recipients, but his name was not mentioned in the Price Waterhouse report into the affair commissioned by the Dunne family. Although the paper could not link Dunne and Haughey, it did establish that Dunne had lodged money for Haughey to bank accounts in the name of John Furze. Everyone assumed this was a pseudonym for Haughey. However, the paper's finance editor, Cliff Taylor, put a call through to *The Guardian* in London and asked its library to check the name in its computerised clippings system. Two entries came up: an academic in America and a banker on the Cayman Islands. Taylor then dispatched a reporter, Barry O'Keeffe, to the Cayman Islands to track Furze down. O'Keeffe door-stepped Furze who, although surprised, agreed to give him an interview. However, he refused to confirm whether he had passed the money on to Haughey.[25] The paper subsequently ran a story in which it stated that the ultimate beneficiary of the money was a Fianna Fáil politician.[26] In his memoir Brady conceded that no media organisation succeeded in exposing the political corruption that was endemic in Ireland during the 1970s and 1980s but also pointed out that it was not for the want of trying. As he noted, 'it took three sworn tribunals, invested with the powers of the High Court, six judges, 20 senior counsel, approximately 40 other lawyers and any number of court-authorised officials, working over five years, to find out what we now know about Haughey, his money and the circle of people who bankrolled him'.[27] The report of the high court inspectors assigned to investigate the illegal offshore Ansbacher accounts named Richard Wood, a former governor of the Irish Times Trust, as an Ansbacher account holder.[28]

The paper had more luck in highlighting corruption among Dublin county council officials, councillors and developers. At a council meeting in February 1993, Green Party councillor Trevor Sargent produced a £100 cheque his party had received from a developer to read a rezoning submission and asked whether other councillors had received cheques. As the paper put it, 'there was a hys-terical reaction in the council chamber [as Sargent] found himself surrounded by "baying councillors" and had to be escorted from the chamber for his own protection'.[29] One councillor went so far as to grab Sargent in a headlock and attempt to grab the cheque from his hand.[30] These unprecedented scenes prompted the paper's environment correspondent Frank McDonald and political reporter Mark Brennock to re-examine the relationship between developers and councillors. McDonald, along with Frank Kilfeather, had examined this subject before; in September and October 1982 they had written a series on 'land rezoning in Co. Dublin, highlighting otherwise inexplicable decisions, but of course without being able to produce proof that money changed hands'.[31] This series prompted one councillor to accuse the paper of using 'methods of presentation which derive from propaganda techniques perfected by the Nazis'.[32] McDonald had more luck this time round. In July 1993 the paper printed a series of reports that alleged councillors had received money in brown envelopes from lobbyists and representatives of development companies for supporting controversial land rezoning schemes in Co. Dublin. One report revealed that a deceased councillor, Fianna Fáil's Sean Walsh, had left more than £237,000 in several bank accounts after his death in 1989. The report described Walsh as 'one of the most active councillors in earlier rezoning controversies'.[33]

The political establishment shot the messenger: Dublin city council passed a motion condemning the paper for 'impugning the reputation' of Walsh.[34] One Fianna Fáil TD, Batt O'Keeffe, declared that the report 'marked a new nadir in Irish journalism' and went so far as to call for the Defamation Act to be amended to allow relatives of deceased individuals to sue for libel.[35] Summing up the problem of investigating and exposing corruption, McDonald observed that 'the problem in Ireland is that you can't libel the living without being sued or libel a deceased person without being accused of speaking ill of the dead'.[36] A subsequent Garda investigation got nowhere. It was only when, in July 1995, that two barristers, Colm MacEochaidh and Michael Smith, placed an advert in the paper offering a £10,000 reward for information on corruption in the planning system that things began to happen. Among those who responded to the advert was retired building executive James Gogarty, who revealed he had participated in paying a €30,000 bribe to Fianna Fáil minister Ray Burke in 1989.[37] This success made Brady question whether the paper's policy of not paying for information was too restrictive; 'in eschewing what we saw as one evil, we may have allowed a greater one to proliferate'. But, he concluded, even those immune from libel proceedings, 'the parliamentarians, protected by absolute privilege, had been unable to crack the security screen around Haughey and his cronies'.[38]

'WRONG, TOTALLY AND UTTERLY WRONG, WRONG, WRONG'

The Northern Ireland peace process also loomed large throughout Brady's editorship. Shortly after becoming editor, Brady met the SDLP's John Hume, who told him of the possibility of a ceasefire and a new political settlement. He followed this with a round of meetings with various individuals who would play key roles in the peace process, such as Frank Millar, general secretary of the UUP, Peter Robinson, deputy leader of the DUP, secretary of state Tom King, Charles Haughey, British ambassador Nick Fenn and Sinn Féin's Gerry Adams. Brady kept the boards of the company and the trust appraised of these meetings: 'Some apprehension was voiced from time to time, especially that the newspaper might be unwittingly used to further a dangerous agenda. But in general the board and Trust were extremely supportive.'[39]

Early on he came to the view that the paper had to improve its reportage of the unionist position. He felt his predecessor Douglas Gageby 'rarely gave them much sympathy in their political predicament and very seldom gave them any credit for attempting to come to terms with a situation that was probably beyond the boundaries of their own adaptability'.[40] To this end he recruited the former general secretary of the UUP, Frank Millar, to contribute a column to the paper. In 1989 he joined the staff of the paper as its London editor. Brady was aware that this appointment would raise eyebrows, that 'it would be confirmation of the paper's subliminal unionist or pro-British tendencies', but he concluded that there was a long tradition of crossover between politics and journalism at the paper. Some staff members – Michael McInerney, John Horgan, James Downey and Geraldine Kennedy – had run for political office, and Brady reasoned that, if this crossover was acceptable from left-wing politics, then 'it should be acceptable from the right (if that was where one placed the Ulster Unionists)'.[41]

When the talks between John Hume and Gerry Adams became public knowledge the paper, particularly columnist Mary Holland, strongly supported Hume while other Dublin newspapers, particularly the *Sunday Independent*, castigated him for talking to Adams. As the peace process dragged on and encountered obstacle after obstacle, Brady believed that 'some other media delighted in excoriating the *Irish Times* for its support for the process'. Former staff members also questioned the paper's stance. In particular, former deputy editor, Dennis Kennedy was critical of the mechanics of the peace process and the paper's support of it. In one article he contended that the process was 'going to extraordinary lengths to insist that a political tradition seeking the dismantling of the State, espoused by a minority, is of equal validity to a political tradition supporting the State and espoused by a majority'.[42] In his review of Brady's memoir, Kennedy concluded that the paper 'of all southern papers, was uniquely placed to challenge the dubious thinking of both the Anglo-Irish and the Belfast Agreement, and to cry foul on the continual appeasing of terrorism'. While he acknowledged that it allowed occasional critiques of the process, he concluded that, 'where southern opinion and the North was concerned, it was the bland leading the blind'.[43]

Another critic of the peace process and the paper's support for it was the paper's long-time 'An Irishman's Diary' columnist, Kevin Myers. In one column Myers stated that he knew of no other political project that had 'received such continuous and unquestioning endorsement from the media as has the peace process'. It had 'spawned a entirely new breed of congenial, predictive journalism' and had resulted in 'a steady deterioration of journalistic standards' brought on by 'the natural desire of journalists to play a responsible role in the resolution of decades of tragic conflict' or the 'fear of being seen to be a warmonger'.[44] However, as Brady pointed out, such an allegation implicated not only all the paper's reporters and news editors but also Myers himself. When the Good Friday Agreement was signed in April 1998 Myers had retracted all his predictions that republicans would never sign up to a peace agreement by writing, 'Wrong, totally and utterly wrong, wrong, wrong. It's an unsettling, disorienting thing finally to realise that the prediction about which I have written thousands of words turns out to have been complete rubbish ... It is a fact; an undeniable and glorious fact, and I am gloriously, magnificently, totally wrong.'[45] For his part, Brady rejected the views of both Kennedy and Myers:

> We supported the Hillsborough Agreement of 1985, the Belfast Agreement of 1998 and I believe the product at the end justified that position. I would resist absolutely any suggestion that we were soft on terrorism or soft on the IRA. We were the one media organisation that absolutely insisted that there be strict adherence to the requirements of decommissioning and disarmament so much so that we were being referred to in *An Phoblacht* every week as the 'Decommissioning Times'.[46]

Indeed, just as some accused it of appeasing republican violence, others accused it of appeasing unionism. When it insisted that Sinn Féin sign up to the new policing board, it came in for flak from the Irish government, which viewed it as 'pushing the pace and supporting a "unionist" agenda'.[47] In such a long and intricate process that involved a multitude of emotive issues and stumbling blocks, it was impossible for any media outlet to please everybody all the time. Looking back, Brady concluded that 'the course of events, leading to peace and broad political agreement in Northern Ireland, vindicates the processes that flowed from the Hillsborough Agreement of 1985 and the Belfast Agreement of 1998. The *Irish Times* supported these to the full and I am proud of our stance.'[48] Interesting though, the paper's leading article on the day of the Good Friday Agreement referendum did not call for a 'yes' vote: it simply urged people to go out and vote.[49]

'ON MATURE RECOLLECTION'

During his editorship Brady presided over numerous exposés, the most controversial of which was, perhaps, the paper's revelations during the 1990 presidential election. More specifically, it was the way in which the paper made those revelations that caused a stir. As one journalist, put it, 'We got jeered widely all over the world for being the only newspaper not to print the news but to have a press conference about it, but I can understand why we did it'.[50] Fianna Fáil's Brian Lenihan, Fine Gael's Austin Currie and Mary Robinson, whose husband, Nick, had once provided cartoons for the paper, and whose father-in-law had once been a director of the company, all contested the election. Very early on it became apparent that Robinson's left-wing politics appealed to the paper's journalists and that 'every commentator on the newspaper favoured Robinson'. Brady thus 'tried to alleviate this by ensuring that news coverage of Lenihan and Currie was generous' and by imposing a moratorium on the election in the final week of the campaign.[51] But it was the paper's exposé of Brian Lenihan that made the election interesting. In May 1990, Jim Duffy, a UCD student and one-time Fine Gael member, who was writing a Master's thesis on the presidency, interviewed Lenihan who had recently undergone a liver transplant. During the interview, Duffy asked about the events of the night of 27 January 1982 when the Fine Gael–Labour coalition's budget fell and Taoiseach Garret FitzGerald sought a dissolution of the Dáil from President Patrick Hillery. Telephone calls were put through to Áras an Uachtaráin by Sylvester Barrett, Brian Lenihan and Charles Haughey to put pressure on Hillery not to grant FitzGerald a dissolution and to invite Haughey to form an alternative government. In response to Duffy's question, Lenihan told him that he had rung and spoken to Hillery and that Hillery had told him to 'lay off'. This was untrue, as the only person the politicians spoke to that night was the army officer on duty, who did not transfer the calls to Hillery. Why Lenihan told Duffy he had spoken to Hillery is unclear: some believe he was suffering the effects of heavy medication after his liver transplant; others that he simply told Duffy what he had intended doing but had not done.

With the election under way, Duffy was commissioned by the paper to write a series of articles on the history of the presidency, one of which mentioned the phone calls to Hillery. In that article Duffy wrote: 'To hammer home the point, a series of phone calls were made by him (Haughey) and, at his insistence, by Brian Lenihan and Sylvester Barrett, two close friends of Dr Hillery. The President angrily rejected all such pressure and, having judged the issue, granted Dr FitzGerald the dissolution.'[52] Lenihan's claim to have spoken to Hillery was not mentioned in the article. Co-incidentally, Duffy's article was attached to the press release issued by Fine Gael at the launch of Austin Currie's campaign. In a letter dated 4 October but received by Lenihan's office on 17 October – five months after the interview had taken place – Duffy enclosed fifteen quotes from the interview that he wished to use in his thesis. In his letter, Duffy stated that this was an opportunity for Lenihan to 'inspect them to ensure their accuracy' and to excise any quotes that he did not want used.[53] Given the frank nature of Lenihan's claim that he had actually spoken to Hillery, and given that writing a thesis is about uncovering original material, it is somewhat surprising that Duffy did not include this statement in the list of quotes to be vetted by Lenihan. Indeed, much of the subsequent controversy centred on Lenihan's interjection, halfway through the part of the interview that dealt with the phone calls, in which he stated, 'Well, between ourselves, I mean you're not going public with this?' to which Duffy replied, 'Oh, No, No'. It is possible that Lenihan interpreted this as meaning that what went before and after this interjection was confidential, whereas Duffy (and the *Irish Times*) interpreted it as relating only to the part of the discussion, which centred on Haughey's role in the phone calls, that followed.[54] In any event, as Lenihan saw it, Duffy's letter confirmed that the interview 'was confidential, and its contents were only to be disclosed in Mr Duffy's academic thesis after I had approved them'.[55]

On 16 October, Lenihan visited UCD for a questions and answers session with students. One student, Seamus Kennedy, the chairperson of UCD's Young Fine Gael branch, asked Lenihan whether he had rung the Áras on the night of 27 January 1982. Lenihan said he had not. This, in effect, was a direct denial of Duffy's newspaper article but Duffy, who was present at the session, did not challenge Lenihan on the denial.[56] On 22 October the *Irish Press* published an interview with Lenihan in which he again denied having rung the Áras. Again, this denial did not prompt any challenge from Duffy or the *Irish Times*. That evening Lenihan appeared on RTÉ's *Questions and Answers* alongside Garret FitzGerald who, the day before, had cut short a trip to Venice at the request of Fine Gael. RTÉ was informed at 4 p.m. that afternoon that Jim Mitchell, who was Currie's director of elections, was being replaced by FitzGerald. It remains unclear why the party felt compelled to recall FitzGerald from Europe to appear on the show. In the audience was Brian Murphy, former chairman of Young Fine Gael, a member of the Currie campaign team and a friend of Jim Duffy. During the programme, as part of a discussion on the powers of the president, and not as part of a pre-submitted question, Murphy directly asked Lenihan whether he had rung Hillery in January 1982. Lenihan's negative reply was immediately contradicted by FitzGerald, who stated he had been in the Áras when the phone calls came through and had heard Hillery remonstrating with

the Fianna Fáil politicians. The discussion ended with Lenihan again denying
that he had rung Hillery.

Jim Duffy took Lenihan's televised denial as contradicting his article on the
presidency that had appeared in the *Irish Times* almost four weeks previously.
The day after the programme, he rang the paper's political editor, Dick Walsh,
and told him about the taped interview with Lenihan and his wish to confirm
his article as accurate. Walsh urged Duffy to allow the paper to publish the
contents of the tape, but he refused. Walsh then suggested that Duffy give an
interview to the paper in which he would assert his article's accuracy. Later that
evening he played the tape to Walsh, the paper's political correspondent, Denis
Coghlan, and Conor Brady. They agreed on the text of a front-page article,
under Coghlan's by-line, stating that the paper had 'corroborative evidence' of
Lenihan's phone call to Hillery. This article was factually incorrect in that it
stated, 'The calls were taken by the President in Áras an Uachtaráin where he
was in the company of the resigning Taoiseach Dr Garret FitzGerald.'[57] The
paper did not approach Lenihan to establish the veracity of the account given
on the tape or to ask for a comment. As Brady saw it, this story was an attempt
to give Lenihan a 'soft landing' by forcing him to come clean. However, it had
the opposite effect: it prompted Lenihan to consult his solicitors about suing the
paper for libel.[58] The story also prompted a series of phone calls between the
government press secretary, P.J. Mara, and Brady:

> We went to very great lengths to try to protect Brian Lenihan at that stage and we
> published a very cautious story saying that we had corroborative evidence and we put that
> out and we waited for twenty-four hours. We were basically saying to Brian Lenihan,
> 'Look, we have something, would you come and give an explanation of this?' P.J. Mara
> telephoned me and he said, 'What is this corroborative evidence?' and I said, 'Look you
> better say to Brian Lenihan, tell him what it is.' Although I couldn't actually give him
> details it was quite clear that P.J. knew. He said, 'I know all about this tape and about Jim
> Duffy.' P.J.'s exact words were 'How conclusive is this?' and I said, 'If this was before a
> court then a jury wouldn't have much difficulty bringing in a verdict'. So he went back to
> Lenihan and Brian still denied it. We were absolutely astonished at this and P.J. was
> astonished at this. He said, 'I can't get him to face reality' and I said, 'Are we going to be
> into a denial situation?' and I suppose it was because we were facing into a denial situation
> – and indeed Brian did go on television and deny it – that we had to make sure that when
> we made the allegation – bear in mind we were only a few days away from the election –
> so if we were going to make this allegation against Brian Lenihan it had to be very clear
> that it was valid.[59]

On the day the story appeared, Duffy rang the paper from UCD in an
agitated state. He was being tracked down by Fianna Fáil supporters and had
taken refuge in the college chaplaincy. Duffy told Brady he wanted legal advice,
and a car was sent to collect him and bring him to Hayes and Sons, the paper's

legal advisors. It was here that Duffy decided that he wanted to release the tape to all media by way of a press conference, a decision that would lead to the paper being criticised for holding a press conference rather than publishing what it knew. But, as Brady pointed out, this was not the paper's decision to make:

> The Lenihan business was complex and we took a lot of criticism for handling it the way we did and going the press conference route rather than publishing the thing. But the explanation is really very simple and that rests with Jim Duffy. Jim's attitude was that he wanted this thing brought into the public domain. He made it very clear to us right through that he was holding possession of the tape, we didn't have possession of the tape. He let us listen to it but he wanted it broadcast so that people – and I understand why he would want it broadcast – could hear the voice for themselves and know that it wasn't a set up of some kind or other. And we found ourselves in the position where if we went with the content of the tape in print form it would have been deniable whereas his attitude was 'Well, let's get the thing heard.' The arrangement we came to with him was that a relatively small amount of the tape would be put out on the news conference but the great bulk of it then was published in the *Irish Times* the following morning.[60]

On 25 October, Duffy, accompanied by deputy editor Ken Gray and duty editor Eoin McVey, played the relevant portion of the tape to assembled journalists from all the national media. In its reportage and photography captions the paper referred to the event as Duffy's press conference, as distinct from being an *Irish Times* press conference. The rest is history. Lenihan went on RTÉ's *Six-One* news programme and 'on mature recollection' denied the veracity of the tape. Several days later he was sacked as Tanaiste, and, although he topped the poll, Mary Robinson was elected on Austin Currie's transfers. In the paper's eve of poll editorial, Brady declared that Lenihan had 'shown himself to be enmeshed in a set of attitudes and values from which this state must escape; a set of attitudes and values which ought to be consigned to history' – an editorial that offended Lenihan greatly.[61] As he saw it, the editorial 'created a stereotype of me as a dishonest politician whose values are somehow rooted in an age where dishonesty was acceptable ... The *Irish Times* made it clear that it did not consider me fit to hold the office of President as they did not view me as a person of integrity.'[62] Many people also thought that the exposé was a result of the journalists' preference for Mary Robinson, a charge that Brady rejected outright:

> ... people thought somehow it was sort of a contrivance on our part to ensure that Mary Robinson won the election. And in actual fact, although a lot of the journalists within the paper were very pro-Mary Robinson, in fact the editorial line was not particularly supportive of her. In the editorial on the day before people voted we said this woman has been re-constructed, many people say that she is now presenting an appearance which is

quite different from the person that they knew. Editorially we did not support Mary Robinson. In fact, what we said the day before the election was that if the president were to be elected on the basis of authenticity – on the basis of what you see is what you get – Austin Currie would have been the man.[63]

Lenihan later accused the paper of being 'more interested in exposing the tape to the full blast of the electronic media than it was in revealing the contents of the tape in its own newspaper columns where the impact may not have been so devastating' and asserted that the press conference 'amounted to active and unprecedented participation of a newspaper in an election campaign'.[64] Not so, according to Brady, who maintained that 'If Jim Duffy had said, "Look, you can take the whole tape and publish it and leave me out of it", I think we probably would have just published the content in the newspaper, but I would have wanted it to be on RTÉ the following day to confirm the authenticity of the voice.'[65] As for publishing Lenihan's mistaken assertion that he had spoken to Hillery on the night in question (as opposed to simply ringing the Áras as he had done), Brady stated, 'We believe now that Mr Lenihan's calls did not get through to the President. But we did not know that at the time. In the circumstances, it was necessary that the information be brought into the public domain.'[66] Given the confluence of events, many commentators believe that Lenihan had allowed himself to be entrapped by Fine Gael, a view now shared by Brady:

> I guess the whole sequence of events from the meeting at UCD to the *Questions and Answers* thing through to Jim Duffy coming to us confirms that. I'm not sure Jim Duffy was consciously part of this, I don't think he was. I think he genuinely felt that he had information which was of public significance and he brought it to us but it certainly served the Fine Gael agenda which I can see now looking back. But it wasn't as clear at the time. All we had was information which strongly contradicted Brian Lenihan's public position. We gave him every opportunity to try to come to terms with that, but in the end, far from being a soft landing, it was a very hard landing.[67]

Lenihan's biographer, James Downey, described the saga as a 'veritable crescendo of coincidences' and concluded that Fine Gael 'had laid a trap and Lenihan had walked into it'.[68] For his part, Jim Duffy has always rejected the notion that he was part of a trap for Lenihan.[69] As is often the case with a controversial story, there was no way to please everyone. As Brady put it, 'It was one of those situations I suspect where no matter what we did we were going to be wrong ... Whatever way you would look at that episode I think people would have said, "They did it wrong, they trapped the man or they went for him behind his back", which isn't true. We made every effort to make sure that he could have a soft landing on the thing, but he didn't take it.'[70]

'FORGIVE ME SINNERS'

Two years later, the paper published another major exposé, this time centred on the activities of the bishop of Galway, Eamonn Casey, who was well known for his work with Irish emigrants in Britain and for helping establish Trócaire, the third world aid agency. In January 1992 the news desk received a telephone call from one Arthur Pennell, the partner of Annie Murphy, a woman who claimed to be the mother of Casey's son. Pennell wanted to tell the story of the affair that Casey and Murphy had had in the early 1970s. They lived in Connecticut, and the paper's North American correspondent, Conor O'Clery, was instructed to interview Murphy. At some stage she showed O'Clery a videotape recording of herself and Casey meeting in a New York hotel in 1991. Murphy also provided the paper with tapes of conversations she had secretly recorded with friends in which Casey's paternity of the child was discussed. Having conducted his initial interview, O'Clery telephoned Brady and told him that Murphy appeared to be telling the truth. The problem was that there was no corroborative evidence, and the paper found it extremely difficult to verify the details of a story that was almost twenty-years-old and was a closely guarded secret. As Brady put it, 'We had the greatest of difficulty in establishing the facts in relation to Annie Murphy and her son Peter. Anything that we were going to say or report would have been deniable if we had nothing more than hearsay. A lot of the witnesses who were prepared to give us information off the record were not prepared to go on the record. It was a very, very difficult story to verify.'[71] The paper was wary of becoming involved in a blackmail attempt; it was also wary of drawing the wrath of the Catholic church by publishing a sensational story that it could not prove was true. As Lorna Siggins, a reporter who worked on the story, put it, 'It was a very difficult project, and the editor was anxious to ensure every aspect of it was verified. There was a fear that someone else would get wind and publish before us ... perhaps a subconscious wish, given that the *Irish Times* would still have been perceived as a Protestant newspaper.'[72]

Nonetheless, Brady decided to assign a team of reporters to the story to see what they could come up with. However, some reporters refused to work on the story on the basis that they 'simply felt that the whole issue was distasteful and did not want to be associated with it. One said he felt it purely a private matter and that the *Irish Times* should not intrude into Bishop Casey's private life.'[73] The reporters that persevered with the story were supervised by news editor John Armstrong and included Conor O'Clery, Andy Pollak, Lorna Siggins, Deaglán de Bréadún and Geraldine Kennedy. The team spent twelve weeks investigating the claim, and eventually O'Clery was instructed to return to

Connecticut with supplementary questions. Annoyed at the diligence of the paper, Pennell and Murphy became agitated and warned that they were thinking of taking the story elsewhere.[74] But the paper still did not have any corroborative evidence and ran the risk of Casey issuing a denial if it ran the story. As Lorna Siggins remembered, at meetings to discuss the progress of the story Brady 'encouraged people to be free and frank with their opinions and reservations. In that context, the impact of Murphy's claims on Casey and on the church was discussed but some of those who expressed most severe reservations worked extremely hard to put the final reports together.'[75]

Just as things looked stalled, Murphy directed O'Clery to a New York priest who, over the years, had been the conduit of payments from Casey to her. When he met the priest he was given details of various payments that had been made by Casey over the years and established that in 1990 a payment of £70,669 had been made out of a reserve account operated by the diocese of Galway.[76] Again, however, these payments did not necessarily prove paternity of the boy. Nonetheless, the paper decided to request a meeting with Casey to discuss the paternity allegation and the source of the money sent by him to the US. Religious affairs correspondent Andy Pollak telephoned the bishop, who had been holidaying in Malta but who had travelled from there to Rome, and arranged a meeting for when he returned to Ireland. The arrangement was that Casey would meet two reporters – Pollak and O'Clery – at the Skylon Hotel, near Dublin Airport. Casey never showed up, and that evening the Vatican announced Casey's resignation as bishop of Galway 'for personal reasons'. Brady decided the paper could only print what it had proof of: 'having given him a fair opportunity to state his side of the story, we went ahead and published what we knew we could stand over'.[77]

He was concerned that if Casey denied paternity – or indeed the relationship with Murphy – it would simply be her word against his, with the paper caught in the middle. Thus it led with a story about how it had been seeking to interview Casey about money he had paid to a woman in Connecticut.[78] However, its editorial hinted at what was afoot by calling on Casey to make 'an honest acknowledgment of the facts' that would clear the air and comfort others 'who have found themselves caught between what the law of the Church requires and what real life may actually throw up'.[79] Two days later, its editorial noted that Murphy had made serious allegations against Casey but it did not detail what these allegations were.[80] Finally, Casey acknowledged he was the father of Peter Murphy and the paper ran the story under the by-line of 'Irish Times Reporters'.[81] When it emerged that the paper had been aware of the paternity allegation all along, other media organisations accused it of timidity in its approach to the story. The point that it was an allegation, not a fact, until Casey acknowledged paternity, was lost on most critics. As religious affairs correspondent Andy Pollak, put it:

> I think Conor Brady was absolutely right to be 100% certain about the story before publishing it, and to check everything three or four times. This was the biggest story to hit Ireland for decades. It involved the Catholic Church, which was still extremely powerful (this was before the clerical sex abuse scandals which so undermined its authority). The *Irish Times,* as a traditionally 'Protestant' paper, could easily be portrayed as gunning for the Church if we got anything wrong.[82]

Brady also rejected the notion that the paper was too cautious in its handling of the story and was critical of how other newspapers took Murphy's claims at face value: 'I have to confess that when I look back at the way in which some other newspapers printed as fact that which they could not possibly have learned for themselves, I have to take a very deep breath. It took us some weeks to establish even what we could publish. Yet a number of other newspapers effectively lifted that, took it as gospel and then added their own versions to it.'[83] Soon after the exposé Casey left for a missionary appointment in Ecuador and the £70,669 of diocesan funds was repaid by his friends. In comparison to the far more serious criminal offences of other Irish clergy that emerged in subsequent years, Casey's indiscretion is now viewed as relatively insignificant. But at the time it caused shockwaves among the faithful and is seen as a point at which the Catholic church's authority began to wane. Such was the sensitivity surrounding the esposé that the paper rejected a cartoon from its resident cartoonist, Martyn Turner, which featured Casey reading a sermon with the tag-line 'Forgive me sinners, I have fathered.' Turner was told that 'it would have to be a very good cartoon indeed for me to get any comment about Bishop Casey into the paper. It was a sensitive subject.'[84] As Brady observed, 'You have to bear in mind that this was 1992. The sheer incredibility of the story at the time was on a scale that people wouldn't understand in today's world.'[85]

'DESCENT INTO CRUELTY'

That same year, 1992, duty news editor Niall Kiely got wind of a very unusual case involving the attorney general's office. A reporter, Carol Coulter, who later became the paper's legal affairs correspondent, substantiated the details of what would become known as the 'X Case'. Coulter discovered that the attorney general, Harry Whelehan, had been granted a high court interim injunction to prevent a 14-year-old female rape victim from leaving the state to have an abortion. The girl in question, who became known as 'Miss X', had been sexually abused by an adult neighbour (who was later convicted and sentenced), and her parents made a complaint to the Garda Síochána. They informed the Gardaí that they intended to take their daughter to Britain for an abortion and sought advice as to how best to ensure continuity of evidence so that charges could be preferred against her abuser. The Gardaí sought advice from the director of public prosecutions, who in turn sought advice from the attorney general's office. Whelehan concluded that, by virtue of the 1983 pro-life amendment to the constitution, there were constitutional implications in the case. He thus secured, at an *in camera* hearing at the high court, an interim injunction preventing the girl from travelling abroad. Having got wind of these proceedings, the paper faced the choice between respecting the *in camera* ruling of the court or deliberating defying that order by publishing what it knew at the risk of incurring a heavy fine or the imprisonment of its editor.

Brady sought legal advice and, having consulted with Major McDowell, decided to publish the facts of the case in the public interest. The story was published, under the by-line of Niall Kiely, as a low-key, one-column story, below the fold on page one.[86] The story had the desired effect, as other media picked it up and public unease began to grow. By the time the case proper came before the high court, the issue was a matter of huge public controversy. When the court, again *in camera*, acceded to the attorney general's request that 'Miss X' be compelled, under threat of imprisonment, to remain in the state for ten months, the public outcry was deafening. Protesters marched on the Dáil, and one Fianna Fáil TD rang Brady to berate him 'for causing the whole thing'.[87] The paper published a front-page cartoon by Martyn Turner that spoke volumes. His depiction of a schoolgirl in pigtails, standing on a map of the state with a razor-wire-topped fence surrounding the coastline with the caption '17 February 1992: The introduction of internment in Ireland ... for 14-year-old girls' was widely reproduced in other media. He later presented 'Miss X' with the original drawing of the cartoon. (Indeed, Turner's cartoons often hit the spot, much to the annoyance of many interest groups. In July 1993 a cartoon of his addressed the Israeli bombardment of Southern Lebanon with a clever play on the Steven Spielberg film *Jurassic Park*. It depicted a dinosaur wearing a Star of David helmet chasing panic-stricken people. The caption read 'Jewrassic Park, AKA Southern Lebanon: 60,000 years in the making ... One week in the destroying'.[88] This provoked a storm of protest from the Jewish community and the Israeli press.[89] In October 1995 when anti-divorce lobbyists declared that a Jewish government minister could not legislate for divorce because he did not understand the nature of Christian marriage Turner drew a cartoon of Jesus on the cross saying 'Don't quote me on Christian marriage – I was Jewish'.[90] This prompted one reader to make a complaint to the Garda Síochána on the grounds that the paper had committed blasphemy.[91]) Under the heading 'Descent into Cruelty', Brady's editorial was a damning indictment of the high court's decision:

> What has been done to this Irish Republic, what sort of state has it become that, in 1992, its full panoply of authority, its police, its law officers, its courts are mobilised to condemn a 14-year-old child to the ordeal of pregnancy and childbirth after rape at the hands of a 'depraved and evil man'? With what are we now to compare ourselves? – Ceaucescu's Romania? The Ayatollah's Iran? Algeria? – There are similarities ... It must be presumed that the politicians who sponsored and supported the 1983 Amendment did not envisage the use of crime branch detectives, judges and injunctions to enforce the completion of pregnancies by child rape victims. It was certainly not in the minds of many of those who went out in good conscience and voted for the Amendment eight years ago.[92]

'Miss X's' parents immediately appealed the decision to the supreme court which, to the shock of pro-life activists, ruled that, because the 1983 constitutional amendment guaranteed equal weighting to the lives of both the expectant mother and the unborn, when a mother's life was at risk (including suicide, as it was in this case), then a termination was perfectly constitutional. The injunction was lifted, and 'Miss X' was allowed to travel abroad. Two years later, Brady received a letter from 'Miss X' thanking him and the paper for taking a risk in breaking the story about what had happened to her. To Brady it was 'probably the most valuable and affirming letter' he ever received in his sixteen years as editor.[93] Other letters did not convey the same sentiment. Within a year of the 'X Case' the moral abyss that was endemic clerical sexual abuse revealed itself. The revelations of sexual abuse of children by priests and the church's covering up of these crimes by transferring errant priests to different parishes began in the diocese of Ferns but quickly spread. Revelations of abuse at orphanages and other religious institutions subsequently emerged. The culture of silence that had surrounded such activity was finally broken, but it was not easy to report such horrific abuse. As Brady recalled in his memoir, 'for our court reporting of the sexual abuse cases – we drew a lot of hostility'. The paper had to endure endless abusive telephone calls and threatening letters. Envelopes containing excrement were posted to the paper, and in what must – given the horrific crimes perpetrated by priests – rank as the irony of ironies, the paper was accused of seeking to destroy the moral fabric of Irish society.[94]

The 'X Case' revelations did nothing to ease the already tense relationship that existed between the paper and Albert Reynolds, who had succeeded Charles Haughey as Taoiseach in January 1992. Shortly after taking office, Reynolds sued the paper over an opinion piece written by the economist Raymond Crotty, who cited Reynolds as a minister who had benefited from

Ireland's membership of the EU, because his pet-food factory had secured EU funding. Reynolds sued for defamation on the basis that the article contained an innuendo that he had used his privileged position to his own benefit.[95] Reynolds' action was settled for a sum in the region of £75,000. Relations between Reynolds and the Labour Party were equally unharmonious. In November 1994 Reynolds appointed Harry Whelehan as president of the high court against the wishes of Labour leader and Tánaiste, Dick Spring, who then led his party colleagues out of the cabinet meeting. As attorney general, Whelehan had been criticised over his handling of the 'X Case' and the handling of an extradition request relating to a paedophile priest, Brendan Smyth. The extradition warrant for Smyth, who was wanted in Northern Ireland, had lain for seven months in the attorney general's office. The explanation for this was that the case required careful handling given that the alleged offences had taken place twenty years earlier.[96]

No sooner was Whelehan appointed as president of the high court than that explanation came unstuck. Shortly after being appointed, the new attorney general, Eoghan Fitzsimons, brought the existence of a similar previous case – involving a monk named John Duggan in 1992 – to the attention of Reynolds and Fianna Fáil ministers. The following day, in a Dáil speech on the Smyth affair, Reynolds made no reference to the Duggan case. He later stated that Fitzsimons' written advice on the applicability of the Duggan case was not handed to him in the Dáil chamber.[97] An anonymous telephone call to Dick Spring alerted him to the existence of the Duggan case, and when he established that Reynolds had known about the Duggan case before his Dáil speech, he led the Labour Party out of government. Reynolds resigned as leader of Fianna Fáil and was replaced by Bertie Ahern, with whom Spring was prepared to re-enter government. But on 5 December the paper's political correspondent, Geraldine Kennedy, reported that Fianna Fáil ministers, not just Reynolds, had been aware of the Duggan case before Reynolds' speech.[98] Spring then ended negotiations with Ahern and instead formed a coalition with Fine Gael and Democratic Left, the first time a new government was formed without an election.

NEW TECHNOLOGY

Irish Times Ltd also moved forward technologically. In 1994 it established a new media division, and in October that year it launched the paper on the world-wide-web using the web domain *irish-times.com*. This site was the first online newspaper in Ireland and the UK and brought the paper to a worldwide readership. In December 1995, a Malaysian-born Swedish diplomat living in

Stockholm won its 'click the ball' competition (based on the old newspaper favourite 'x the ball' competition).[99] As time went by, annexed sites were added – a sports news service (Sports Extra), searchable databases (Recruitment and Irish Ancestors), in-depth reports on long-term issues (Path to Peace, Eurotimes), and a supplement in Irish (An Teanga Bheo). In March 1999 the company, led by Seamus Conaty, unveiled a new portal page, *ireland.com*. This new site, although still primarily centred on the daily newspaper, allowed for new services such as a breaking news section, a free e-mail address and a searchable archive of the paper.[1] Incidentally, the paper's first satellite filing by laptop took place from halfway up Mount Everest in 1993. Reporter Lorna Siggins, with a laptop-carrying yak, accompanied an Irish team of climbers to its base camp, from where the team successfully reached the summit, and transmitted regular updates on its progress back to the newsroom in Dublin.[2]

As internet access became more widespread during the 1990s, visitor numbers to the site increased. The paper's website became the first Irish website to have its visitor numbers officially audited. ABC//electronic measured the site as having 396,000 visitors during October 1997, with more than 4m page impressions, thus making it the busiest website in Ireland at that time.[3] A year later the figures stood at 645,556 users and 6.03m page impressions.[4] In March 2007 the respective figures were 1,185,000 visitors and 17.2m page impressions. An online survey in 1999 indicated that 60 per cent of site visitors were under thirty-five-years-of-age, two thirds of visitors were male, and 80 per cent had a third-level qualification. Geographically, it was almost evenly split between Irish and overseas visitors, with the highest concentration of overseas visitors (31 per cent) located in the US and Canada.[5] All these innovations showed that the internet allowed for greater exploitation of material generated for the paper. It enabled the paper to extend its readership overseas, to create additional revenue sources and to build the *Irish Times* as a strongly branded news and information service provider across a range of media. But it was not a one-way street. Developing and maintaining the site did not come cheaply: the company spent £10m on the site and to recoup its investment made the site subscription-based in 2002. The internet also posed challenges to the newspaper in that it allowed for the entry of non-traditional publishers into the information industry. In contrast to the huge costs in establishing and running a printed newspaper, electronic publishers had lower market-entry and labour costs. The internet allowed electronic entrepreneurs to target high value advertising – property, appointments, motors – that was once the primary preserve of the newspaper industry. As the medium developed the company expanded its portfolio of websites with the purchase of the property website *myhome.ie* for €50m in 2006 and a 30 per cent stake in *entertainment.ie* in

2007 as part of its strategy of protecting its advertising revenue and developing itself as a major digital media business. In June 2008, the company reverted to a free website, *irishtimes.com*, following a redesign of the paper and the integration of the print and online news divisions.

In the mid-1990s the company deliberated long and hard about launching a Sunday title, a process initiated and advanced by Conor Brady. With its three titles Independent Newspapers had an edge when it came to offering large volumes of readers to advertisers across all or some of its titles. If the *Irish Times* had a Sunday title, it too would be able to offer a large combined readership to advertisers. That said, the paper had no problem attracting advertising though it was conspicuous by its absence in the Sunday market, a point emphasised by Brady in his argument for launching a Sunday title:

> My rationale for developing a Sunday title was simple. Sunday had become the best reading day of the week. People take time on Sundays to read about issues that have arisen during the week. They catch up on news and views that they may not have had time to engage with during the week. I felt that the *Irish Times* should be part of that process – that it should not go silent at the time when other newspapers were engaging in dialogue with their readerships. I also felt that the company was largely a one-product operation and as such was vulnerable. The Sunday title would have been a different style of newspaper. We did quite a few mock-ups and even printed test-editions on the press. We test-marketed it through 'Behaviour and Attitudes' and we got very positive responses.[6]

There were several reasons why the time felt right for launching a Sunday title. The paper's circulation hit an all-time high of 95,319 in 1995.[7] In addition, the collapse of the Irish Press Group in May 1995 left a huge void in the Sunday market (the *Sunday Press* had a circulation of 150,000 when it ceased publishing). However, there were also significant obstacles that made the company think twice. There were strong concerns that a successful Sunday title might weaken the paper on other days, notably Saturday, which was the biggest selling day for the paper. There were also concerns, advanced by managing director Louis O'Neill, that the printing press, used to full capacity for six days of the week was not capable of operating seven days a week:

> In trying to do it we would have been flogging the press from Monday to Saturday and then as soon as the Saturday paper was finished we'd start printing a Sunday paper with big pagination. So I turned against the Sunday on the basis that we didn't have the facilities to print it. And I said to Conor, 'If we launch a Sunday and three or four weeks down the road because of mechanical problems we can't get out on time or we have to reduce the pagination because we can't get the press up and running on Monday after a weekend or we lose an edition – I said, I'm not prepared to take that leap'.[8]

Some believe that the overstaffing that was to plague the company in later years was a legacy of the company's advanced plans for launching a Sunday title. As one journalist put it, 'Brady wanted a Sunday paper and the Major was equivocating – "Maybe I will and maybe I won't," so the company began staffing up. This is what we on the ordinary staffing levels believed … We were so overstaffed that it was quite incredible. We had far greater supervision than any crèche.'[9] In the heel of the hunt Major McDowell felt the development would involve 'over-exposing the paper in terms of resources and was able to carry the board with him to Brady's great disappointment'.[10] For his part, Brady stated that, although everyone 'felt that the risks were very high', personally he 'would have taken the risk'.[11] But whatever tensions existed over launching a Sunday title, they were nothing compared to the controversy that erupted in 1994 when McDowell appointed his daughter to the position of deputy managing director; a decision that sparked near-civil war in D'Olier Street.

CHAPTER 12

Madam Editor

A newspaper's first duty is, particularly at times of crisis, times of public concern and at times of public alarm, to be there telling people what has happened. It was a decision taken on grounds which did not prioritise that duty. Now, there were various technical reasons advanced for it; I have to take those at face value. But I would have argued and I did argue at the time that if we had to crawl up Fleet Street on our hands and knees with copies of the paper between our teeth and give them out to people on the street we should have done it. It was disastrous.[1]

Conor Brady on the non-appearance of the paper post–9/11

WHILE DIFFERENCES OF OPINION about a Sunday title caused a degree of tension at the company, it was nothing compared to the tensions that emerged in the run-up to the retirement of managing director Louis O'Neill. He had been at the helm of the commercial side of the house since 1977 and ran the company on a day-to-day basis. By the mid-1990s he was approaching retirement, and the issue of succession loomed large. It was in this succession race that Major McDowell made a move in November 1994 that caused consternation among staff on both sides of the house. As executive chairman he appointed as deputy managing director his daughter, Karen Erwin, a senior partner in A&L Goodbody Solicitors. Nobody ever suggested that Erwin would be anything other than an extremely able executive. A distinguished lawyer, she had extensive experience of how business operated. The problem people had with her was the manner in which she was appointed. Put briefly, it was thought that she got the job only because she was the boss's daughter. This was most unfortunate for everyone involved – not least Karen Erwin, who was otherwise well-qualified for the position. One governor, Don Reid, tried to talk McDowell out of the plan:

The first time I heard of the appointment was the night before it became public. I was uneasy about it and sought to have the terms of the appointment at least modified or postponed. But Karen had already resigned from the legal firm. Tom's [McDowell's] reasoning was that he needed somebody of ability and talent to succeed him in running the paper ... However, the board meetings were on the next day ... In any event the

253

appointment was confirmed. Subsequently the strains within the senior management became severe. My view, whether right or wrong, was that Major McDowell had probably acted within the scope of his authority and that the only chink in that argument might be based on a conflict of interest point, but this would be difficult to sustain, given that one was speaking of a senior partner in a law firm.[2]

Conor Brady recalled being summoned to McDowell's ground floor office, which the staff had nicknamed 'The Bunker', and being informed of the appointment. Brady warned him that there would be 'uproar across the organisation' and that he would be accused of nepotism, to which McDowell replied that nepotism only applied to 'the advancement of a family member who is *unworthy* of it'. But as Brady saw it, 'There was a sense across the organisation that in setting up the Trust, taking his profit in 1974 and then having been installed as chairman and chief executive, Tom had the best of both worlds. Now it seemed that he wanted to have the *Irish Times* baton pass on to the next generation of his family.'[3] As managing director, Louis O'Neill found himself caught in the middle:

> In hindsight Major McDowell was getting a bit long in the tooth and was looking at the future. He always acted as though he owned the *Irish Times* because he was in such a pivotal position. I think the Karen Erwin affair was him trying to leapfrog Karen into the top management in the hope, that with my co-operation, she would take over from me as managing director ... Now, to me that was stretching our relationship too far; it was taking my relationship with him just too far, he was impeding on our relationship to a point, you could almost say in a contemptuous way. I resented it because I had very good top managers; the other side of it was it affected my relationship with my managers. I had a great relationship with them and then all of a sudden somebody comes in between them and me and they're resentful. They weren't resentful with me because they knew I had nothing to do with it but they saw their promotional prospects gone.[4]

When the staff found out about the appointment there was immediate uproar. For many years they had fostered a benign view of McDowell and his effective control of the various *Irish Times* companies. As one journalist put it, 'He got away with it for a long time, partly because the paper, apart from the odd hiccup, was prospering, and partly because he did not interfere with editorial policy.'[5] But, to many, his latest move was a step too far:

> It was only when we hit the 1990s that things began to change. Frank McDonald began writing about the trust, and people on the other side of the house began to complain of their frustrations in dealing with this autocratic control. Information began coming out from all over and there were meetings held in pubs with people from both sides of the house united in our demand that this be stopped. Dick [Walsh] said, 'Well, we have our appointments procedure and we're going to insist that we use it.' But we needed the support of everybody in the place. So we went to SIPTU and we got the other unions

involved. We got the SIPTU lawyer in, we discussed ways and means of dealing with this, and the editorial committee decided to retain a lawyer.[6]

The paper's NUJ chapel mandated its editorial committee to seek a meeting with McDowell and passed a motion stating that it was 'gravely concerned at the manner of her appointment and by the fact that it cannot but be seen as a blatant exercise in nepotism'.[7] The committee was told it could not meet with McDowell because he had gone home sick. Later, one governor defended the appointment to the editorial committee as a progressive move because a female had been appointed to a senior position: he was bluntly told that the appointment had more to do with 'genes than gender'.[8] The committee took legal advice on the trust's memorandum and articles of association, particularly the article that stipulated that the paper should 'be free from any form of personal or party political, commercial, religious or sectional control'.[9] In the midst of this near mutiny, McDowell called a meeting of Irish Times Publications Ltd, an extended board that included the senior executives from the commercial and editorial departments, to be held at his home. He declared that there was a necessity for change, that O'Neill needed back-up, and that he had persuaded his daughter to sacrifice a promising legal career to join the paper. The speech, according to one attendee, was greeted with 'a stony silence around the table. It endured for perhaps 30 seconds but felt like an hour.'[10]

With no sign of the anger abating, Brady secured a small victory in the following days. The paper's political correspondent, Geraldine Kennedy, wrote a story about the cost of the new staff appointed by the Labour Party, many of whom were relatives of the party's TDs. This led to the party being accused of nepotism, and Brady wrote an editorial in which he accused it of 'one of the most blatant acts of political jobbery in the history of the State, when it doled out a plethora of government positions to family members and political chums on assuming office'.[11] This prompted a letter from Labour's Joe Costello, who, reminding readers of Erwin's arrival at the company, challenged McDowell to 'state publicly what special qualifications his daughter has for the job to which she was appointed, how the post was advertised and what selection process was followed'.[12] Brady telephoned the trust's vice-chairman, Donal Nevin, who was acting chairman due to McDowell's illness, to inform him of the letter. Nevin decided to issue a rebuttal to appear alongside Costello's letter. He stated that the trust's decisions on commercial matters were 'made exclusively in the best interests of the company' and accused Costello of 'an intolerable impertinence' in seeking the information about Erwin's appointment. He concluded by stating that when a vacancy for chief executive arose it would be advertised.[13] No sooner had this commitment appeared than the editorial committee demanded

an input into the selection process. A committee composed of two representatives from the board (Donal Nevin and Ken Gray) and two representatives
from the editorial committee (Mary Maher and Dick Walsh) agreed, in 1995, a
new appointments mechanism for senior positions. When a vacancy arose, it
would be advertised publicly, and an interview panel, with an external
independent assessor, would interview candidates to fill the position on merit.
Any person with a family connection to a candidate would be ineligible to sit
on the interview panel. As one negotiator put it, 'the agreement responded to
concerns in both the commercial and editorial departments. Senior executives
on the commercial side were against the attempt to introduce the daughter of
the chairman of the trust at the level and in the manner proposed; on the
editorial side the attempt was seen as evidence of determination to set the stamp
of a family firm on the *Irish Times*.'[14]

But despite the new appointment procedure, the company 'moved into a
period of unease and tension'. When Erwin took up her position as deputy
managing director, many of the commercial staff 'went into a state of ill-
concealed resentment and apprehension'.[15] It was a difficult time for all –
particularly O'Neill, who was caught between McDowell's ambitions for his
daughter and the seething anger of his senior staff. Relations between
McDowell and O'Neill virtually collapsed. As O'Neill put it, 'There was a
terrible awkwardness about the whole thing. It just didn't work. I was resentful
of McDowell taking so much for granted in our relationship and friendship.
And as it didn't work, McDowell became cross with me, he felt I should make
it work. As his friend I should make it work.'[16] As Conor Brady saw it, Erwin
herself was placed in an impossible position:

> Running a paper like the *Irish Times* requires ... in every department – whether advertising,
> editorial or production – a huge accumulated body of expertise, knowledge and skill. An
> awful lot of it is intuitive and build up over years of involvement. Most people in the *Irish
> Times* were really good at what they did and here was this individual who was perfectly
> competent and perfectly well accomplished in her own field, being parachuted in on top of
> these people. She understood very quickly that she knew not nearly enough about what was
> going on in the place. The senior staff understood that she knew a great deal less than they
> did and yet they – and in particular I have in mind the people on the commercial side of the
> house – were being told 'thus far shalt thou go and no further' because this person is
> coming in here now to take over the operation. That's how they saw it.[17]

While Erwin's appointment did not have any direct effect on the editorial
side of the house, it 'changed the atmosphere in the place completely from 1994
onwards'. Brady considered retiring as editor and 'would have stepped down
from the editorship a lot earlier had we not been left with this terribly uncertain

and unsatisfactory situation in regard to the future of the commercial side of the organisation'. The internal power play gave the paper's competitors endless gossip material and, as Brady saw it, a competitive advantage:

> The whole latter part of the 1990s at the *Irish Times* became overshadowed by the issue of what was happening on the commercial side of the organisation with the result that decisions were taken too slowly and advantages that we had in terms of technology and our product were overtaken; they were eroded by other newspapers. The *Independent*, for example, got its printing plant up and running way ahead of us, even though we had been into the colour field before them in 1986 when we set up the first colour printing press. The whole organisation became fixated on this issue of what was going to happen, and Louis felt that he had been pressured into having to accommodate the whole Karen situation, and he was getting it in the neck from his senior staff who were ambitious of succeeding him.[18]

The irony was that Erwin, despite the controversial circumstances of her appointment, was never personally disliked. An able executive, she built up good relations with many of those who had initially felt threatened by her appointment. Nonetheless, the controversy absorbed attention and energy from all sides of the company and was, perhaps, a product of the particular historical and cultural juncture at which the company found itself. As he was getting on in years, McDowell was anxious to ensure that the future on the company was in, what he saw as, safe hands. But others took a different view and saw the appointment as a new generation of McDowell rule at the paper. As one journalist put it, the editorial committee was 'concerned with the structures and independence of the *Irish Times* rather than personal disagreements. But it could not ignore the lessons learned from experience, both in the *Irish Times* and in the *Irish Press*, in the last twenty years.'[19] After Erwin's appointment and the adverse reaction it provoked, McDowell depended for support more and more on the governors of the trust, who were also members of the board of Irish Times Ltd. As criticism grew more vocal, Irish Times Publications Ltd, the outer board of senior executives was dissolved: 'After one stormy board meeting, at which editorial and commercial managers expressed their frustrations, the board ceased to meet. Later it was wound up.'[20] In March 1997 McDowell relinquished the post of chief executive but remained as chairman of Irish Times Ltd. Louis O'Neill succeeded him as chief executive. In 1998 an external corporate review of the company concluded that its management was 'institutionalised' and 'hierarchical' with executives resorting to 'personal abuse' instead of 'robust debate'. It also warned of the dangers a downturn in the economy would pose for the paper given that two thirds of its advertising revenue came from the booming appointments and property sectors.[21]

In January 1999 McDowell announced that he was to stand down as chairman of Irish Times Ltd but was to remain a board member as well as chairman of the trust. He proposed that his successor as chairman be Don Reid. The night before the crucial four-hour board meeting, all governors received a letter from the editorial committee expressing their concerns. Reid became non-executive chairman and tried to resolve the 'difficulty surrounding Karen Erwin's appointment by creating a niche role for her with group responsibility for corporate governance and all legal matters'.[22] Shortly afterwards, Louis O'Neill announced his intention to retire, and in June 1999 he refused to accept a presentation from the board of Irish Times Ltd to mark his departure. He explained his decision in a three page-letter to the directors in which he outlined the unbearable pressure under which he felt he had been placed:

> ... the past five years have been a period of great personal difficulty for me since the unexpected appointment, in 1994, by Major T.B. McDowell of his daughter Karen Erwin to senior office in the company. Day after day I had to face the difficulty of reconciling the relentless pursuit for the advancement of Karen with the understandable objections of my senior management team and what I consider to be the best interests of the *Irish Times*. Despite the commitment given at the time of her appointment that Karen's advancement would be contingent on my approval, all attempts I have made at objective assessment have been rejected out of hand. I have been accused of not doing enough for Karen when in actual fact I did more for her than I have ever done during my career; enough was never enough.[23]

In accordance with the new appointments procedure the position of managing director was advertised and interviews held. Erwin announced that she would not be seeking the position, and O'Neill's successor was Nick Chapman, a former managing director of BBC Enterprises. Chapman took over the project to establish a new printing plant and the modernisation process continued. The company ordered a new, larger capacity printing press, a Geoman 3/8, capable of printing a high-quality 64-page colour newspaper in up to four sections, to be build at a green field site outside the city.[24] New computer systems for the editorial and commercial sides of the house were purchased, and a new Saturday magazine and a new weekly entertainment supplement, *The Ticket,* were launched in late 2000. In 1999 the company reached an agreement with its printers on a voluntary redundancy scheme that included a profit-sharing scheme that allowed for 8.5 per cent of company profits to be paid out to staff.[25] The following year agreement was reached with the NUJ: in return for the introduction of new technology and changed work practices journalists received a pay increase and joined the profit-sharing scheme.[26] The estimated cost of these projects was £100m and the board decided to pay for them out of the cash reserves built up during the 1990s. While this saved the company from borrowing costs, it left nothing for a rainy day. However, a report commissioned from economic consultant Peter Bacon concluded that the favourable economic climate could be expected to continue.[27] No one could have foreseen the events of 9/11.

'THOSE LOFTY AMBITIONS'

McDowell's boardroom manoeuvres led many people to examine the workings of the trust more closely. After years of existing in the shadows, the trust, and McDowell's effective control of it, faced a forensic examination by the editorial committee. The committee was surprised and dismayed at what it found:

> When it was formed in 1974 the Trust had been described to members of the staff as a protection against take-over and a means by which those who worked for the paper would come to regard themselves as its owners. It was also presented as a charitable trust, whose surplus funds would provide for the renewal of plant and the refurbishment of premises; after which any remaining profits would go to charity. To say that these impressions were wide of the mark would be an understatement. Twenty years after the articles and memorandum were written, the editorial committee discovered that significant revision had ensured that, in practice, all authority was vested in the chairman, Major T.B. McDowell. The discovery had a profound effect on the way in which the editorial committee viewed the actions of the management and, in particular, any proposal to change structures or senior personnel in a way that could be interpreted as part of a continuing campaign to protect and promote McDowell.[28]

The trust met once a month in McDowell's office. After a private meeting of the governors, the editor would be invited in to discuss editorial matters. The trust meeting would then end, and a meeting of the board of Irish Times Ltd would begin after the executive directors had entered the room.[29] As Don Reid put it, as time went by and the company evolved, this system of governance became outdated:

> With the passage of time and the co-option of executives to the board, the need for the combination of the two offices [chairman and chief executive] and the exceptional powers granted to Major McDowell became somewhat inappropriate. There was a tendency for the trust board meetings to be held on the same day as the Irish Times Ltd board meetings as a matter of convenience. As the agendas would be similar, the view developed that the Irish Times Ltd board was acting in little more than a nominee capacity, with real decisions being taken elsewhere. In fact Major McDowell probably had the right to decide most matters himself under the articles. In any event, the structure bred unrest.[30]

Conor Brady also had reservations about how the trust operated; in his memoir he noted, that as the years passed, 'McDowell came increasingly to dominate the Trust.'[31] Indeed, during the 1990s the articles of association of Irish Times Ltd were altered to give the trust more power in running the company. A 1994 amendment ensured that no resolution before the board could be passed unless the chairman and a governor or two governors voted in favour of it.[32] A 1997 amendment gave governors five votes each compared to the executive directors' one vote each.[33] Governors also came in for criticism for their apparent reluctance to stand up to McDowell. In a farewell speech to the newsroom, Louis O'Neill stated that when he differed with the McDowell family, the trust's governors appeared to find no conflict between their support for a 'personal advancement strategy and their commitment to protect the *Irish Times* from any kind of personal, party political or other sectional control'.[34] As Brady put it, 'Some of the trust members were very strong, independent individuals, and they discharged their role with determination. Others were less so. On balance, the governors of the trust did their job well. But it can be argued that, had they taken a different stance on certain issues, some of the difficulties that emerged during the latter years of the 1990s and early into the new decade might have been avoided.'[35]

Questions also began to be asked about the 1974 commitment to 'ultimately' pass on donations from the profits of Irish Times Ltd to Irish Times Foundation for distribution to charitable causes and, indeed, about the Irish Times Trust's pledge to fund educational and charitable causes via the Foundation. Conor Brady raised this issue with McDowell several times: 'He was defensive and argued that the critics misunderstood the status of the *Irish Times* as a "charity". It did not exist to fund *charities*. It *was* a "charity" – in the same way that the Lifeboats Institution or the Red Cross, is a charity.'[36] For the record, neither Irish Times Trust nor Irish Times Foundation is registered with the revenue commissioners as a charity, and Irish Times Ltd pays corporation tax on its profits like any other company. But the changes of 1974 included a declaration that a charitable foundation (Irish Times Foundation) would 'ultimately benefit from the profits of the newspaper'.[37] As yet, this has not happened, although in 1990 the memorandum of association of Irish Times Ltd was altered to allow the company to 'make gratuitous donations at the absolute and uncontrolled discretion of the company whether by payments in cash or by the transfer of assets of any kind, to the Irish Times Foundation Ltd'.[38] In 2005 the Irish Times Trust initiated a journalism fellowship in remembrance of Douglas Gageby. But the charitable endeavours envisioned in 1974 have not yet materialised. In retrospect Brady believed that 'it might have been preferable if those lofty ambitions had not been built into the 1974 trust arrangement. Or if they weren't going to be met, it might have been better that they had been taken out along the way.' The possibility of distributing profits to charity did not arise until the 1990s, and Brady believed that it was then that the organisation should have faced up to the issue one way or the other:

I think the trust is an entirely laudable concept and it maintained the independence of the paper. It maintained the editor's independence. The more controversial bits of it – the profits ultimately going to charity – were probably well intended. You have to bear in mind that it was drafted at a time when all the world seemed bright. You had a rapidly expanding economy, you had a newspaper which was, by the standards of the time, making very significant profits, and the idea of having something that would channel off money to hospitals and educational institutions seemed entirely plausible. But then twelve months later, the organisation was on its knees, and its survival was in question, so there was no question of it giving out any money at that point. It was making a loss. As a senior executive and assistant editor I was conscious of the fact that the organisation was still paying off the debts that had been built up in 1974. So the money simply wasn't there. We began to make some sort of serious money in the mid to late 1990s, and that was the point at which the trustees should either have honoured that commitment or taken it out. But I wasn't on the trust. So I can say no more about that.[39]

By the mid-1990s the paper was making record profits. As the economy boomed, so too did sales of the paper, advertising revenue and profits. Sales rose from 105,312 copies per day in the first six months of 1997 to 111,729 in the last six months of 1998.[40] Profits rose also: £3.3m in 1994, £3.6m in 1995, £5.4m in 1996, £9.3m in 1997, and £14.1m in 1998.[41] Such large profits led many to ask why no money was ever transferred to Irish Times Foundation for distribution to charity as had been the declared intention of the trust in 1974. Some believe the answer lies in clause 2.d of the trust's memorandum of association, which states that the trust would achieve its objectives by ensuring that the paper was published 'as an independent newspaper primarily concerned with serious issues for the benefit of the community throughout the whole of Ireland'.[42] But this explanation contradicts earlier clauses in which the trust expressly pledges to finance schools and colleges, educational scholarships, to provide funds to agencies engaged in the relief of poverty, to fund medical research and to pay for the upkeep of lifeboats.[43] These clauses also contrast with the recent assertion that it was always the intention that such good causes would only benefit from the assets of Irish Times Ltd if that company were ever wound up. While there is a provision for this in the trust's articles of association, this caveat was not publicly stated in 1974.[44] In any event, the charitable foundation, Irish Times Foundation, has not, as yet, fulfilled any of its charitable objectives, a situation that jars somewhat with the introduction of a staff profit sharing scheme in 1999.

'THERE'S NO PAPER TOMORROW'

The year 2001 started off on a high note: revenue for appointments advertising reached its highest-ever peak in the first quarter before dipping and then dropping sharply in the second and third quarters as a slowdown in the computer industry began to bite. Having spent all its cash reserves on its modernisation programme, the company had to borrow money to tide itself over. Then 9/11 happened. Conor Brady was in California and found himself stranded there when, as the biggest news story in years unfolded, all US airports were shut down. Brady was in telephone contact with Dublin on the day (Tuesday) of the attacks, but then the telephone system collapsed. When he managed to re-establish contact with Dublin, a shock awaited him:

> It was a most unfortunate confluence of events. I was in San Francisco at my nephew's wedding and I was in touch for the first twenty-four hours afterwards. I was in touch with Conor O'Clery in New York and Elaine Lafferty in Los Angeles and I was in touch with Pat O'Hara, the executive editor in charge in my absence, and then the whole thing just broke down. The phones just died. And when they came back thirty hours later, I got through to Pat O'Hara and he sounded like a man who had been hit over the head with a hammer. He said, 'I just have to tell you this has been the worst day in my life: there's no paper tomorrow'. It remains today with me still a source of great sadness and regret that it should have happened on my watch. It certainly wasn't an editorial decision.[45]

O'Hara informed him that the Irish government had declared a national day of mourning for that Friday (14 September) and that the board had decided not to publish a newspaper on that day. Rumours abounded that it was purely a commercial decision as all the advertising for the Friday edition had been cancelled. But, as company chairman Don Reid recalled, it was a bit more complicated than that. While there was a run of advert and newsagent cancellations, there were also technical difficulties:

> The national day of mourning was a Friday. On the previous day various members of the senior management team came and talked to me ... They were, they said, having a rush of cancellations – both of ads and of bulk orders for the papers ... Some were making the case that we should cancel the following day's paper. Others were advancing the case for delaying the decision ... We had a long meeting. The problem was that the printing press was linked to bundling and addressing equipment and all were supposed to work as a single interdependent unit. The press was of different manufacture from the rest and all were very old and in urgent need of replacement. They were giving unbelievable trouble at the time and for some time and breakdowns and very late deliveries were the order of the day. The problem was that if there were extensive changes in the programmed orders and addresses the system was at serious risk of breaking down and it would probably not be possible to restore the system even for the next day's run. We were also told that the difficulty might last for more than one issue. We talked about all sorts of possibilities including a small run with manual distribution. Another was to print off a nominal edition which might be given out as a free sheet. But for each proposed solution there was a corresponding problem or risk, and in the end it was agreed by everyone at the meeting that we could not take the risk of publishing on the Friday and losing the Saturday run and possibly some in the following week.[46]

Immediately after the decision not to publish was taken, Reid telephoned Major McDowell to inform him; McDowell was not at all happy. When Conor Brady eventually got through to Reid, he expressed his disagreement, but Reid told him that the staff had been sent home, no pages had been prepared, and it was too late to reverse the decision:

> In fairness to the people involved, I think by the time people understood the implications of what was happening and I remember I got on the phone line from San Francisco to two or three very senior people on the corporate side of the house and I pleaded with them and explained the enormity of not coming out. I think they understood that, but by that time the whole machinery had been wound down, people had gone home, the press had been mothballed for the night, staff had been dispersed, but it was not good. And I was left in the very difficult position that I had to try to support my senior colleagues when I got back and try to deal with a very angry staff and a very angry editorial committee. I did go in and put the best case forward, but I have to say my heart wasn't in it. The fact of the matter is that you can't take that kind of a view about the publication of the newspaper on any given day. There are many days when the *Irish Times* publishes at a loss; there are many days that RTÉ broadcasts at a loss. You might as well argue that, because there's no advertising on the leader page, therefore you should pull it out of the paper. You can't take that view.[47]

It was the first time in its history that the company made a deliberate decision not to publish. The paper had not published editions before, but this had been due to the events of 1916, the national general strike in 1918, industrial disputes within the paper, or in accordance with the 'one out, all out' agreement of the Dublin Newspaper Managers' Committee. The *Irish Times* was the only national newspaper not to publish on 14 September 2001. The *Irish Independent* published as usual and declared itself 'the only source of detailed news and comment around'; it sold over 100,000 copies and announced it was donating the revenue from that day's sales to the Irish-American victims' fund. At the subsequent board meeting, Reid reviewed the decision not to publish:

> At the next board meeting of Irish Times Ltd I reviewed the position as fully as I could, including the reasons for our decision, and I asked for confirmation from the relevant executive directors in the different areas that their views were properly represented and for confirmation that everyone at the meeting on the Thursday had agreed with the decision. It was so confirmed. Tom McDowell again repeated that he would not have agreed, and Conor Brady made his comment about getting the papers out on bicycles if need be. I responded that the problem was our failure to get our equipment up-to-date on time, and that I believed that if we were confronted with the exact same circumstances again we would have little option but to go the same way. A matter that did concern me on the day, but which I did not throw open for discussion as no one else had raised it, was whether the decision not to publish put us in jeopardy with the trust. The view I took was that a decision not to publish would have to extend for more than a single issue before such a risk would arise.[48]

The paper's journalists greeted the decision not to publish with apoplexy. The editorial committee passed a motion 'deploring' the decision and described it as 'a dereliction of duty'.[49] There was also a commotion about how the paper had covered the unfolding events. While all other newspapers cleared their front sections for the 9/11 story, it was relegated (after page one) to page eight onwards of the *Irish Times*. As one journalist remembered, 'There was a big to-do that we didn't clear the whole front of the paper – we let things stay as they were and put in a few pages inside. There was a lot of anguish over that.'[50]

Worse was to follow. As advertising revenue dropped in the latter half of the year, it became apparent that the company was going to make a loss. The fact that it had spent all its cash reserves on its modernisation plan only added to the crisis. So too did the delay in getting the new printing press up and running. When it finally got running, it proved inadequate to the task of printing the high-gloss weekend magazine that had been introduced in October 2000. This printing job had to be sub-contracted out at a cost of £20,000 per week. While the circulation of the paper reached its highest level ever, 120,397, in the second half of 2001, the company, which made a profit of £7.15m in 2000, made a loss of £2.35m in 2001. When the cost of the restructuring plan that followed was factored in, the company faced a deficit of £21.7m.[51] In November 2001 it fell to Conor Brady to deliver the bad news: a reduction of 250 in staff numbers, with 112 jobs going in the editorial side of the house. He told the staff that the paper faced the real prospect of closure if the cuts were not implemented immediately.[52] Other cost-cutting measures included the closure of the Beijing and Washington bureaux, cutting back on regional coverage, the axing of the *Education and Living* supplement and the replacement of the high-gloss Saturday magazine with a newsprint version that the company could print itself. The paper also confined itself to printing one edition, abandoning the old practice of printing separate country and city editions.

Although there was to be an excess of voluntary redundancy applications, the situation caused a huge decree of resentment. The Dublin Printing Group of Unions demanded that the company finances be independently assessed and insisted that a complete overhaul of the organisation's structures be part of the restructuring process. In a statement on corporate governance it declared that 'the manner in which the Trust and the Company was administered was more appropriate to a late 19th century family business, complete with defensive and secretive structures, than to a modern business enterprise'.[53] Indeed, many commented on the invisibility of those charged with the corporate governance of Irish Times Ltd – the chairman and governors of the trust – throughout the crisis.[54]

When the staff voted to accept the restructuring programme, a number of committees composed of union representatives and management were established to implement the plan. One such committee focused on corporate governance, and it agreed that the powers of the trust should be significantly reduced so that it would no longer have a majority on the board of Irish Times Ltd. It also called for the 'A' shares that had copper-fastened McDowell's position within the various companies to be abolished. In December 2001, McDowell stood down from the board of Irish Times Ltd and also stood down as chairman and as a member of the trust. In return he became 'President for Life' of the Irish Times Group, an honorary position that carried no power or remuneration. The number of governors entitled to sit on the board of Irish Times Ltd was limited to three, a move that tilted control away from the trust and towards the executive directors of the company. Also, whereas formally each governor had five votes each, each director now had one vote. The governors retained their power to veto any decision that would impact on the 'ethos, quality and standards' of the paper.[55] In addition, the DPGU secured a position on the board to represent the interests of workers. McDowell's successor as chairman of the trust was David McConnell, a genetics professor at Trinity College. In January 2001 Maeve Donovan replaced Nick Chapman as managing director and in April that year Brian Patterson, a former chief executive of Waterford-Wedgwood, replaced Don Reid as chairman of Irish Times Ltd. In August 2002, Conor Brady announced his intention to retire as soon as a successor was appointed.

In the midst of all these troubles the paper published an interview that rocked the world of Irish sport. In May 2002 sports reporter Tom Humphries interviewed Roy Keane in Saipan as the Irish soccer team was preparing to take part in the world cup finals in South Korea and Japan. Such was the frank nature of Keane's thoughts on the team's preparations and the attitude of the Football Association of Ireland towards the competition that the article appeared as a verbatim transcript of the interview, starting on the page one. The resultant furore caused Keane to resign from the squad and to be sent home by team manager Mick McCarthy. During the controversy, sales of the paper went through the roof.[56] Humphries himself was no stranger to controversial sports stories. Several of his reports from the 1996 Atlanta Olympics dealing with the doping allegations made against Irish swimmer Michelle Smith were not published due to libel concerns, and he temporarily resigned from the paper over the affair.[57]

MADAM EDITOR

The race to succeed Conor Brady was, for the most part, an in-house affair. After two rounds of interviews the contenders were narrowed down to four applicants: Geraldine Kennedy, the paper's political correspondent; Fintan O'Toole, columnist and theatre critic; Cliff Taylor, associate editor (news); and an external candidate, John Mullin, deputy editor of *The Scotsman*. On 11 October 2002 Geraldine Kennedy became the first female editor of the *Irish Times*. Kennedy had joined the paper in February 1973 and became the first woman to chair the Oireachtas press gallery in 1975. In 1980 she joined the *Sunday Tribune* as its political correspondent and in 1982 moved to the *Sunday Press*. In 1987 she won a Dáil seat for the newly formed Progressive Democrats but lost it in 1989. She returned to the *Irish Times* as its public affairs correspondent and was appointed political correspondent in 1993 and political editor in 1999. It was, she remembered, a tough time to take over as editor:

> It was a very tough time, I think, to take over. There had been an awful lot of changes, a lot of culture shocks in the place; it was difficult and took some time to settle the place down again and bring stability, and yet at the same time we were bringing out a newspaper every day with one third less staff and trying to maintain the integrity and quality of it. So it was an unsettling period in the *Irish Times,* which we've put behind us now ... I suppose the most important thing that I had to do was to ensure that, with the financial crisis and one third of journalists gone out of the place, the biggest challenge to me was to try to maintain the authority, integrity and journalism of the paper. And without claiming any great credit, it could not have been done unless we all worked as a team, I think we did pretty well in the circumstances in which we found ourselves.[58]

Barely a year into her editorship Kennedy had to deal with a very public controversy when it was revealed that the company's thirteen directors had shared a combined payout of €3.28m in 2002, a year in which the company made a €2.8m loss and in which most of the redundancies arising from the financial crisis became effective. This revelation sparked outrage among the staff, which demanded that full details of the payments be made public. Shortly afterwards Kennedy spiked an opinion piece, written by columnist John Waters, that was critical of the large payments to directors at a time of editorial cutbacks. Waters had submitted his article and, after consultations with the page editor and some amendments had been agreed upon, it was passed for publication. Later that evening the article was spiked. At a later meeting with the journalists' editorial committee, Kennedy cited legal concerns for her decision but also stated that the timing of the article was not appropriate.[59] The article quickly leaked to other newspapers, which published Waters' comparison of the paper's professed ethos of accountability and transparency with its actual behaviour:

> For several weeks now, this organisation had been disquieted by the extraordinary remuneration packages of the company's executive directors ... in the midst of a crisis

characterised by stringent cost cutting at every other level. Had such events occurred in another comparable institution of Irish life, the *Irish Times* would have been to the fore in ventilating, judging and condemning ... Instead, the company, responsible for running a newspaper demanding openness, transparency and accountability from all and sundry claims privilege for secret deals on the basis that this is a private company, and declines to divulge information pertaining to the remuneration packages of its executive directors. Meanwhile, the editorial arm of the organisation is beset by a severe numbing of its investigative muscles, its high priests of piety paralysed into silence. So far there have been no editorials, no analysis, no opinion or commentary and only the sketchiest of backside-covering reports containing dry and scant details ... Is it seriously proposed that an organisation so delinquent in terms of the standards it prescribes for others is capable of policing itself? ... It seems not to have occurred to anyone, or perhaps they don't care, that in order to indulge in the dubious privilege of judging and censuring others, you need first to sweep your own side of the street.[60]

One journalist, speaking on the basis of anonymity, told the *Sunday Business Post* that it was 'an obvious case of double standards. If the government told us to hold off on publishing a piece, that the timing wasn't suitable, we'd tell them to go to hell. It's openness, transparency and accountability for everyone except us.'[61] The situation was made worse by many politicians bluntly telling the paper's reporters to get their own house in order before demanding accountability from other institutions. Speaking on RTÉ radio about Kennedy's decision to spike his article, Waters said: 'You would not meet a straighter person; you will not meet a more ethical person; but Geraldine Kennedy is compromised, I believe, by the situation she has inherited, by the structures and culture of the *Irish Times*.' Kennedy subsequently sent Waters a letter terminating his contract.[62] The NUJ responded by stating that normal procedures of due notice and due process had not been followed. Breach of contract proceedings loomed large, and so Waters was reinstated after he withdrew the claim that Kennedy had been compromised as editor. Several days later the company released full details of the directors' remuneration.[63]

In mid-2004, the paper again became the centre of news coverage after the discovery of the so-called 'white nigger' letter (see chapter 9) that the British ambassador to Dublin, Andrew Gilchrist, had written to his superiors in London in October 1969. In 2000 the Public Record Office in London had released the letter under the thirty-year rule. Upon its release only one person, Professor Ronan Fanning, who was reviewing that year's release of files for the *Sunday Independent*, saw it. However, Fanning did not include the letter in his reports of the releases for the *Sunday Independent* because he did not think it was particularly newsworthy in the larger scheme of things: 'there were much more important things going on in 1969', such as the resignation of Northern Ireland prime minister Terence O'Neill and the battle of the Bogside. While he knew some of the other journalists and exchanged some opinions with them, he operated alone and not as part of the media file-sharing pool. Neither did he restrict himself to the files that were highlighted for journalists but, as a historian, also examined other files that were released. He came across the letter and photocopied it along with hundreds of other documents. He viewed the letter as a bit of historical gossip or an anecdote. He did, however, send it to Gageby, whom he knew slightly, with a covering note that he could make what use of it he wished. He received no reply from Gageby, who by that time was ill.[64] No reporter from the *Irish Times,* the *Irish Independent* or the *Irish Examiner* saw the letter. However, the *Irish Times* reporter did see correspondence dated 7 November 1969, which made detailed references to the contentious letter.[65] The November letter, and a subsequent letter dated 29 December 1969, formed part of the paper's coverage of the releases in 2000.

In 2002 Jack Lane from the Aubane Historical Society saw the October 1969 letter and sent a copy to Geraldine Kennedy on 10 January 2003. Kennedy replied five days later, stating that she was 'unable to confirm the veracity of the letter'. Lane then sent copies of the letter to various newspapers and magazines, one of which, *Irish Political Review,* published it.[66] The *Sunday Independent* then ran a front-page story on the letter.[67] The following day the *Irish Times* printed an un-by-lined article in which McDowell denied having used the racist terminology. He also denied that he sought to interfere with editorial policy at any time; his 'only interest at that time was to help solve the problems in Northern Ireland'.[68] As Jack Lane saw it, McDowell's denials effectively meant that 'for some reason, the British Ambassador in Dublin told a pack of lies in a secret, confidential letter to Whitehall'.[69] The denials prompted Ronan Fanning, in an article in the *Sunday Independent,* to ask the serving British ambassador, Sir Ivor Roberts, what the likelihood was of an ambassador attributing such words to an informant if the informant had not spoken the words in question: the answer was 'Nil'.[70] There the matter rested until May 2004, when, in a letter to the *Irish Times, The Guardian*'s Roy Greenslade accused the paper of 'self-censorship' by not having published the contents of the letter upon its release in 2000. He also criticised the paper's lack of action in 2003 until the *Sunday Independent* made an issue of it. As Greenslade saw it, 'By any objective journalistic criteria, the involvement of a newspaper controller in affairs of state, especially in talks with the representatives of a foreign country, required much greater candour from a paper of record.'[71]

This accusation of self-censorship prompted a strong rebuke from Conor Brady, who was editor when the contentious letter was released in 2000. He asked whether anyone seriously believed that 'if such a letter had been uncovered by Irish journalists at this time and "covered up" by someone else, that this would not have become instantly known throughout the various newsrooms?'[72] As he later put it, 'The letter was not seen by our reporter – or by the reporters for the other newspapers who were present – when the archives were opened. It is as simple as that. She had no knowledge of this letter. Neither had the London editor, Frank Millar, or any other editorial executive. It is simply incredible, were its existence known among the senior journalists of the *Irish Times*, that it could have been suppressed.'[73] However, the paper's delay in dealing with the letter – almost two weeks after its existence was made known to it – and the fact that it only dealt with the letter after the *Sunday Independent* had published it placed the paper in an embarrassing position. As one former journalist put it, the saga was 'a monumental mess up of the type that happens three times a day in every daily newspaper. The paper should have made a clean sweep of the thing in one issue.'[74] Whatever about looking for editorial guidance from Downing Street, most media coverage focused on the language used in the intelligence report. McDowell categorically denied having used the abusive phrase and, in fairness, Gilchrist had a non-diplomatic way with words in his intelligence reports. In one dispatch to London, he noted that the then minister for finance, Charles Haughey, was 'aping the ways of the English ascendancy'. In the same dispatch, he noted that there would be a Protestant backlash in Northern Ireland by London's 'open dickering' with Dublin if the British government agreed to talks about the border.[75]

RECOVERY AND EXPANSION

In early 2005 the paper strayed into another storm of controversy. This time it was courtesy of long-time 'An Irishman's Diary' columnist, Kevin Myers, who picked up on a exchange between academic Ed Walsh and representatives of lone parents. In a public lecture Walsh claimed that the social welfare allowances given to unmarried mothers encouraged young teenage girls to become pregnant – a claim rejected by lone parent representatives. Into the fray stepped Myers, who pointedly asked, 'How many girls – and we're largely talking about teenagers here – consciously embark upon a career of mothering bastards because it seems a good way of getting money and accommodation from the State?' He later referred to lone parents as 'mothers of bastards' (MoBs) and 'fathers of bastards' (FoBs). The term 'bastard' and its various acronyms appeared sixteen times in the column, and the life of a single parent was described as 'crushingly limiting, with little sense of achievement or personal ambition, and no career to speak of, other – that is – from cash-crop whelping'.[76] It is anyone's guess how this article satisfied the trust's requirement that comment and opinion be informed and responsible. The following day was, in the words of columnist Fintan O'Toole, 'one of the worst days in the history of the *Irish Times*'.[77] The public backlash to Myers' column dominated talk radio shows. The paper was also inundated with letters of protest from outraged readers: one condemned the 'unchristian cruelty of his language'; another asked 'When can we expect the tabloid *Irish Times*?'[78] Another columnist, Eddie Holt, described Myers' column as 'verbal pornography'.[79] As Geraldine Kennedy remembered, while she initially had strong reservations about the article, she still gave it the go ahead:

> It caused great controversy. I think that was a mistake. You know by instinct and you're best always to follow your instinct. My initial instinct was negative and then I said to myself, 'If these are his views and he's going to be writing about this issue, then the readers should know where he's coming from' ... I was completely wrong to publish that. In retrospect it shouldn't have happened. It caused great hurt to people: you shouldn't call innocent children bastards. It just was wrong.[80]

Two days after his column appeared Myers apologised for his choice of language, but reiterated the broad thrust of his column.[81] The paper itself was slower to apologise. Initially it noted that, while Irish society had 'become less willing to tolerate the passing of casual, cruel judgment on the lives of others, less willing to ignore the pain thoughtless slights and name-calling inflict on the vulnerable', the paper remained 'committed to free speech and the promotion of robust debate even if, at times, odious things are said which are offensive to some readers'.[82] With the controversy showing no signs of abating, Kennedy eventually expressed regret for allowing the column be published and apologised for the offence caused.[83] Myers ultimately parted company with the paper in May 2005.

As the advertising sector stabilised post 9/11, so too did the company's finances. In 2003 it made a profit of €8.5m, with €675,000 going to staff through the new profit sharing scheme. The company also sold the *Irish Field* for €2.4m.[84] In 2004, the company made a profit of €15.3m – with the staff again enjoying a share in the profits and six executive directors sharing €3.2m between them.[85] A letter from senior staff to the trust described this remuneration as 'extravagant, disproportionate and indefensible', declared that the 'inflated salaries being paid to those at the top make a mockery of the paper's very identity' and expressed concern that 'the whole thrust and meaning of the enterprise has now been turned upside down and that our work and standing as journalists have been seriously undermined'.[86]

That same year, a proposal to make the editor subordinate to the managing director – thereby changing the equal status they had in terms of reporting to the board – was accepted by company chairman Brian Patterson but rejected by Kennedy.[87] As she observed, this equal status 'is a very unusual structure but in a way it guarantees the independence of the journalism and I think it is very important and certainly I would not countenance a change in that status on my watch'.[88] The trust, the body charged with protecting the independence of the paper, eventually rejected the proposal – but only after a heated debate on the future of the company. Some argued that it had to expand into ancillary business activities to ensure the paper had alternative revenue streams to safeguard its viability. Other saw this policy as relegating the paper in terms of spending priorities. They pointed out that the trust's main purpose is to ensure the publication of the paper and, while ancillary business activities may be necessary to ensure the survival of the company, they should not develop at the expense of the paper. A proposal to create a separate private company to take ownership of the €70m printing complex, paid for out of the paper's profits, was seen by many on the editorial side as a threat to the long-term independence and viability of the paper. While the sale of the plant would net the paper a considerable sum, in the longer term it would starve the paper of a profitable revenue stream that could sustain it in difficult times.

In any event, outward expansion continued. In 2005 the company acquired a 45 per cent interest in Fortunegreen, a joint venture with Associated Newspapers and Metro International to publish *Metro*, a commuter free-sheet. In May of that year, the company began printing an international edition in London and Barcelona for distribution throughout Britain and Spain. According to Kennedy, when the board studied circulation figures it noted that sales dipped during holiday periods; thus the decision to follow readers by launching an international edition.[89] The company made a profit of €14.1m in 2005, and circulation remained buoyant at 117,456 copies per day.[90] In 2006, a year in which it made a profit of €22.7m, the paper left its home of 124 years.[91] It sold its D'Olier Street – Fleet Street buildings and took a twenty-year lease on a modern office building on Tara Street. It also acquired a 50 per cent stake in *The Gloss*, a new woman's monthly magazine. In 2007 it purchased a 43 per cent stake in the Gazette Group, which published several weekly local newspapers in the greater Dublin area.

'BERTIEGATE'

But the paper still continued on with its main function – exposing the underbelly of Irish political life to public scrutiny. On 21 September 2006 a front-page story by public affairs correspondent Colm Keena revealed that the

Mahon Tribunal was investigating a number of payments from businessmen to Bertie Ahern in 1993 while he was minister for finance.[92] The story was based on information from a tribunal letter to one of the contributing businessmen. This information came, via an anonymous and unsolicited leak, into Keena's possession.[93] A subsequent editorial noted that, while Ahern's coalition partner and leader of the Progressive Democrats, Michael McDowell, had accepted Ahern's explanation that the payments were loans to see him through his marital separation, he had 'provided himself and his party with wriggle room in the event of other disclosures'.[94] It is believed that this mention of 'other disclosures' prompted Ahern to mention other money he had supposedly received from Manchester businessmen in 1994: he 'believed the *Irish Times* had information about it but was unable to publish the details'.[95] However, the story did not seem to have any significant effect on public opinion: an opinion poll showed that while two-thirds of voters believed that Ahern was wrong to accept the payments, Fianna Fáil's overall support had jumped eight points since the previous May. As far as the paper was concerned, this demonstrated that the 'culture of nods and winks and looking the other way is alive and well in Irish democracy'.[96]

While the public might not have been fazed by the story, the Mahon Tribunal was incensed; it accused the paper of undermining its investigation by publishing confidential information it believed should not have been circulated in advance of a public hearing. In reply, Kennedy stated that paper had 'received an unsolicited and anonymous communication that I considered an important matter in the public interest for this newspaper to verify and publish'. During the process of verification it emerged that the payments were facts, not allegations, and that Ahern was moving in the high court to stop the tribunal from proceeding with its investigation into these payments.[97] Summoned to appear before the tribunal and ordered to produce the documentation on which the story was based, both Geraldine Kennedy and Colm Keena informed the tribunal that, on legal advice, the documentation had been destroyed. The penalty for non-compliance with the tribunal's order was a fine of up to €300,000 and/or two years in prison on conviction under the Tribunals of Inquiry Evidence Act. In her evidence Kennedy stated that the story was published in the public interest and that the payments would never have come to light had the paper not published the story because the payments did not relate to planning matters and so fell outside the tribunal's remit. She defended her decision to order the destruction of the documentation, and refused to answer any questions on it in case any answer might help the tribunal identify the source. She also took the opportunity to remind the tribunal that it would not have been set up had it not been for leaks to journalists.[98] In his evidence,

Colm Keena stated he had written the story because it was in the public interest, and declined to answer any questions relating to the documentation on which it was based for fear of 'narrowing fields and assisting towards the identification of sources'.[99]

Having got no satisfaction, the chairman of the tribunal, Judge Alan Mahon, requested the high court to compel Kennedy and Keena to produce the documentation on which the story was based and to reveal their sources. By the time the high court case was heard, the tribunal had changed tactic. In the wake of the story several government ministers, in an attempt to make the leak the main story and take the attention off Ahern, had inferred that the tribunal was responsible for the leak. The tribunal now simply wanted Kennedy and Keena to confirm that the leak had not come from the tribunal. This, the argument went, would restore public confidence in it and allow it to get on with its investigation. It all boiled down to whether or not the documentation that Keena had seen had a harp and signature on it. If it did, then the leak could not have come from the tribunal, as all its documentation was devoid of insignia and signatures. Amid a flurry of legal argument centred on the freedom of the press and the protection of journalistic sources, the president of the high court, Mr Justice Richard Johnson, stated that the court accepted that the story was 'a matter of public interest'. Counsel for the paper, Eoin McGonigal, told the high court that neither Kennedy nor Keena would obey an order to return to the tribunal and reveal their source.[1] For her part, Kennedy had no regrets about publishing the story and would rather go to gaol than reveal any sources:

> It was a good story; anybody would have published it if they'd got it. It was in the public interest and there's absolutely nothing to be defensive about. And a lot of time has been spent by other journalists trying to figure out where did we get the story or where did we not get the story, and I'm just not going there. Sure you couldn't. It would undermine the newspaper. And also we're in the position with this one, where, even if we wanted to, as I have said in the tribunal, the source is anonymous. So we have extra difficulties. But even if we did know who the source was, we wouldn't reveal it. Nobody would want to go to gaol, but if that's what you have to do to carry out journalism, I would do it.[2]

In October 2007 the high court criticised the 'reprehensible' destruction of the documentation on which the story was based, and ruled that Kennedy and Keena return to the tribunal and provide answers to its questions. In a somewhat qualified judgment, the court noted that, if the questions could lead to identification of the source, then the journalistic privilege against disclosure could be invoked. However, it noted that this was not the situation because the source had been stated to be anonymous and because the relevant documentation had been destroyed. Thus answers could simply indicate that the tribunal itself was not the source and therefore preserve its integrity.[3] However, such answers might narrow the field of potential sources and help identify the source; shortly afterwards the paper was given leave to appeal this decision to the supreme court. After having made several appearances at the Mahon Tribunal in relation to his financial affairs, Bertie Ahern resigned as Taoiseach in May 2008.

FUTURE TIMES

What the future holds for the *Irish Times*, or indeed any newspaper, only time will tell. The digital revolution continues apace; in 2007 the entire back catalogue of the paper became available on the internet via a government subsidy of €1m. Whether there is a future for the printed edition of the newspaper remains to be seen. As Geraldine Kennedy sees it, there will always be a demand for the printed as opposed to the electronic word:

> If you were to listen to some of the nay-sayers in the World Association of Newspapers or the World Editors' Forum, they would have you believe that television would do away with newspapers, that the web would do away with newspapers, that everybody had to go compact size or there would be no future for newspapers; and in all of these issues they've been wrong. But what you have now is people getting their information from various and different platforms, and I think the difference now is that what we produce is that information and independent analysis, the context so to speak, and when you're looking at the world out there you have to give the people the information in the format that they want it. But I believe that a sufficient number of people will want to read the written word. I believe that there will be a future for print journalism for a long, long, long time. I can't ever imagine a newspaper being replaced by an electronic screen. It's a completely different experience, even though I do recognise that a lot of young people spend hours on their computers.[4]

What the future holds for journalism is also uncertain. A society rises and falls on the quality of its journalism. In a consumer society obsessed with trivia, sensationalism, titillation and banal celebrity culture, quality and investigative journalism is being squeezed more and more as a radically transformed news cycle places an increasing emphasis on getting news first rather than getting it right. The proliferation of inexpensive hybrid-newspapers from Britain (the bulk of whose content is produced in Britain for a British readership) has also put pressure on indigenous titles. Although the paper needs to make a profit to maintain its existence, the trust structure of the company protects it somewhat from such pressures. As Kennedy put it, 'the memorandum and articles of association – an independent newspaper for the island of Ireland, free from commercial, party political or other control – sets out the whole vision for our journalism, for the practice of journalism. It's great to have it there, and it's very important that it has been there, especially at a time when newspapers have become more commercial. It gives us our mandate.'[5] Given the radical transformation of the republic's economy and the huge changes in Irish society, many commentators have accused the paper of becoming part of, rather than challenging, the establishment.[6] However, as Kennedy put it, Irish society itself has changed, and the paper has also changed to remain relevant:

> I have read that the paper has moved to the right under my editorship. I have also had criticisms that we are a left-wing rag. So I suppose if you're getting it from both sides, you must be doing something right. But I think what you have to do is move with the society that you serve, and it's now not the 1960s or the 1970s. It's beyond 2000. And you have to keep in touch with your community of readers and serve their interest. If you're looking back on the history of the *Irish Times*, you will see changes at particular times. You have to change, as my predecessors did. You have to change with your readers; otherwise you wouldn't be providing for them and writing on issues that they're interested in.[7]

The Ireland, and indeed the world, that the paper nowadays reports on is a very different one than even Kennedy's most recent predecessor had to deal with. A plethora of issues that once dominated political discourse – such as the power of the Catholic church, the northern conflict, and divorce – have been resolved and replaced by a host of new but equally contentious issues for the paper to report on and for Irish society to grapple with. According to Kennedy, the Northern Ireland peace settlement, multiculturalism, the refusal of political parties to legislate in accordance with the supreme court judgment in the 'X Case' and balancing the recent surge in wealth with the provision of services are the issues that are most pertinent for the paper today.[8]

Having reached 150 years of age, the *Irish Times* has travelled a path of self-transformation. Established to defend the union of Ireland and Britain, it sought to prevent the return of a parliament to Dublin, but, ironically, it was, and for many years remained, a voice of logic and reason when that parliament was finally established. It constantly challenged the double standards that existed in Ireland, where the majority of the population professed themselves devout Catholics but exempted themselves, though not others, from the church's teachings. It campaigned against the imposition of Catholic doctrine on issues such as literary censorship, divorce, health care and sexual matters at a time when politicians seemed determined to prove the validity of unionism's old claim that 'home rule is Rome rule'. It is only in recent years that these issues have been resolved, although issues such as the church's influence on health care and primary school education, and political cowardice in relation to matters sexual, remain to be resolved. Put most simply, the function of journalism is to question the power brokers (including media) within society and to hold them accountable to the public. Any list of the stories that shook up Irish society would have a high concentration of *Irish Times* exclusives on it. Controversies surrounding the trust aside, the paper's contribution to Irish journalism has been immense. The *Irish Times* has helped open up and transform Irish society and will continue to do so for many decades to come.

Notes

CHAPTER ONE
'A First Class Daily Paper'

1 IT untitled leader, 8 June 1909, p. 8.
2 IT untitled leader, 25 Jan. 1873, p. 5 &
   'The Late Major L.E. Knox' 27 Jan. 1873,
   p. 3.
3 H. Oram (1983) *The newspaper book*, p. 68.
4 Moloney, P. (1952) 'A survey of the
   development of Dublin daily newspapers',
   p. 5.
5 IT 'Publications' 8 June 1859, p. 1.
6 Moloney, 'A survey of the development',
   p. 67.
7 IT untitled leader, 29 Mar. 1859, p. 2.
8 Ibid.
9 Ibid.
10 Moloney, 'A survey of the development',
   p. 82.
11 IT 'Letters to the editor' 23 Nov. 2001,
   p. 17.
12 IT 'The late Rev Dr GB Wheeler' 25 Oct.
   1877, p. 5.
13 IT 'New daily paper' 7 June 1859, p. 2.
14 IT 'Transport troubles' 8 June 1959
   (supplement p. vi).
15 IT 'Newspaper production in the 19th
   century' 8 June 1959 (supplement p. v).
16 IT 'Our jubilee' 8 June 1909, p. 5.
17 Moloney, 'A survey of the development',
   pp 46–7.
18 Cullen, L.M. (1989) *Eason & Son*, p. 56.
   Eason bought the Irish branch of the
   company in 1886.
19 IT 'The new year – the *Irish Times*' 1 Jan.
   1867, p. 2.
20 Cullen, *Eason & Son*, p. 75.
21 IT untitled leader, 7 Mar. 1867, p. 2.
22 IT 'Letters to the Editor' 15 Mar. 1867,
   p. 3.

23 IT untitled leader, 7 Mar. 1867, p. 2.
24 Devoy, J. (1929) *Recollections of an Irish
   rebel*, pp 369–70.
25 IT untitled leader, 25 Jan. 1873, p. 5.
26 IT 'Funeral of the late Major L.E. Knox'
   30 Jan. 1873, p. 6.
27 IT 'Our Jubilee' 8 June 1909, p. 5.
28 Nesbitt, R. (1993) *At Arnotts*, p. 7 &
   Findlater, A. (2001) *Findlaters*, p. 23n.
29 IT 'Sir John Arnott' 29 Mar. 1898, p. 5.
30 IT 'To Newspaper Proprietors & c'
   22 November 1873, p. 9.
31 IT untitled leader, 27 May 1873, p. 5.
32 IT 'To the readers of the *Irish Times*'
   27 May 1873, p. 5.
33 Moloney, 'A survey of the development',
   p. 135.
34 IT untitled leader, 20 Mar. 1882, p. 4.
35 UCDA; Moloney Papers: P95 79,
   circulation ledger.
36 IT untitled leader, 22 Nov. 1873, p. 9.
37 IT untitled leader, 3 July 1874, p. 5.
38 IT untitled leader, 1 Aug. 1877, p. 4.
39 IT untitled leader, 22 Oct. 1879, p. 8.
40 Dunlop, A. (1911) *Fifty years*, p. 137.
41 Ibid., pp 166–71.
42 IT untitled leader, 22 Aug. 1881, p. 4.
43 IT untitled leader, 14 Oct. 1881, p. 4.
44 IT untitled leader, 4 May 1882, p. 4.
45 IT 'Appalling murders in the Phoenix
   Park' 7 May 1882, p. 1.
46 IT 'Mr Michael Davitt and the murders'
   11 May 1882, p. 6.
47 Moloney, 'A survey of the development',
   p. 82.
48 UCDA; Moloney Papers: P95 79,
   circulation ledger.
49 Moloney, A survey of the development,
   p. 115.
50 Cullen, *Eason & Son*, p. 76 & p. 78.

51 Ibid., p. 79.
52 UCDA; Moloney Papers: P95 53–71, 'Under the Clock' Mar. 1952, p. 4.
53 IT 'Details of Mr James A. Scott' 29 Nov. 1899, p.4.
54 IT untitled leader, 18 Dec. 1885, p. 4.
55 IT untitled leader, 19 Dec. 1885, p. 3.
56 IT untitled leader, 9 Apr. 1886, p. 4.
57 NL; Arnott J. (1886) *A second alternative policy for Ireland*.
58 IT untitled leader, 8 June 1886, p. 4.
59 IT 'O'Shea Divorce Case' 17 Nov. 1890, p. 5.
60 IT untitled leader, 18 Nov. 1890, p. 4.
61 IT untitled leader, 4 Dec. 1890, p. 4.
62 IT untitled leader, 8 Dec. 1890, p. 4.
63 IT untitled leader, 8 Oct. 1891, p. 4.
64 IT untitled leader, 17 June 1892, p. 4.
65 IT untitled leader, 2 Sept. 1893, p. 4.
66 Moloney, 'A survey of the development', p. 82.
67 Ibid., p. 115.
68 IT untitled leader, 29 Mar. 1898, p. 4.
69 IT 'Prospectus: The Irish Times Ltd' 26 Nov. 1900, p. 7.
70 Irish Times Ltd, memorandum and AoA, articles 22 & 30.
71 Ibid.
72 IT untitled leader, 6 Jan. 1900, p. 4.
73 *The Times*; 'Irish gifts for Irish regiments' 10 Feb. 1900, p. 14.
74 UCDA; Moloney Papers: P95 79, circulation ledger.
75 Ibid., P95 53–71 'Under the Clock' Dec. 1950, p. 2.
76 IT 'Obituary: Mr W.A. Locker' 6 June 1930, p. 4.
77 Moloney, 'A survey of the development', p. 154.
78 IT 'Obituary: Miss A.B. Maguire' 2 Mar. 1937.
79 IT 'From the college races to modern olympics' 14 June 1984 (supplement, p. xii).
80 Ellman, R. (ed.) (1966) *Letters of James Joyce*, p. 27, Joyce to mother, 8 Feb. 1903.
81 Ibid., pp 31–2, Joyce to father, 26 Feb. 1903.
82 Ibid., p. 32, mother to Joyce, 2 Mar. 1903.
83 IT 'The motor derby' 7 Apr. 1903, p. 5.
84 IT 'The Playboy of the west' 29 Jan. 1907, p. 5.
85 IT 'Playboy of the west' 30 Jan. 1907, p. 8.
86 IT untitled leader, 30 Jan. 1907, p. 6.

CHAPTER 2
Tumultuous Times

1 IT 'Obituary Mr John E. Healy' 31 May 1934, p. 6.
2 Ibid.
3 IT untitled leader, 8 July 1911, p. 6.
4 IT untitled leader, 10 Oct. 1911, p. 4.
5 IT untitled leader, 11 Oct. 1911, p. 6.
6 IT untitled leader, 9 Apr. 1912, p. 4.
7 IT 'Ulster Day' 28 Sept. 1912, p. 6.
8 IT 'After Ulster' 30 Sept. 1912, p. 6.
9 IT 'The old year' 1 Jan. 1913, p. 6.
10 IT 'The Ulster amendment' 2 Jan. 1913, p. 6.
11 IT 'The Lords' decision' 31 Jan. 1913, p. 6.
12 IT 'Ulster's resolve' 14 July 1913, p. 6.
13 IT 'The second rejection' 16 July 1913, p. 6.
14 IT 'The threatened tramway strike' 26 Aug. 1913, p. 6.
15 IT 'The tramway strike' 27 Aug. 1913, p. 8.
16 IT 'Dublin's own fault' 29 Aug. 1913, p. 6.
17 IT 'The Dublin riots' 1 Sept. 1913, p. 4.
18 IT 'Dublin's labour problem' 4 Sept. 1913, p. 6.
19 Ibid.
20 IT 'Church Street accident fund' 5 Sept. 1913, p. 7.
21 IT 'Letters to the Editor' 8 Sept. 1913, p. 6.
22 IT 'On reading much etc … ' 8 Sept. 1913, p. 7. The poem was later re-titled 'September 1913'.
23 IT 'The art gallery' 8 Sept. 1913, p. 6. The paintings were later bequeathed to the National Gallery, London, although before he died on the Lusitania, Lane donated thirty-nine paintings to Dublin. After much litigation, Lane's collection is now divided into two sets that rotate between London and Dublin every five years.
24 IT 'The labour crisis' 13 Sept. 1913, p. 6.
25 IT 'To the Masters of Dublin' 7 Oct. 1913, p. 6.
26 IT 'The end of the strike' 3 Feb. 1914, p. 4.
27 IT 'Irish Times Limited' 10 Nov. 1914, p. 9.
28 IT 'Rank paganism' 1 July 1913, p. 6.
29 IT 'Letters to the Editor' 7 Nov. 1913, p. 8.
30 Ibid., 8 Nov. 1913, p. 7.
31 IT 'Mr Walton's case' 8 Nov. 1913, p. 6.
32 IT 'Letters to the Editor' 10 Nov. 1913, p. 7.
33 CB (1913) 'Editorial', 3:12, 857–867. See also 'A challenge to the *Irish Times*', 981–4.

34 IT 'Letters to the Editor' 10 Nov. 1913, p. 7.
35 Ibid., 11 Nov. 1913, p. 6.
36 Ibid., 14 Nov. 1913, p. 8.
37 Ibid., 14 & 15 Nov. 1913, p. 8.
38 Ibid., 12 Nov. 1913, p. 5.
39 CB (1913) 'Editorial', 3:12, 861 of 857–7.
40 CB (1913) 'A challenge to the *Irish Times*', 3:12, 984 of 981–4.
41 IT 'The exclusion of Ulster' 19 Feb. 1914, p. 6.
42 IT 'The government and Ulster' 21 Mar. 1914, p. 6.
43 IT 'The army and Ulster' 23 Mar. 1914, p. 6.
44 IT 'The army resignations' 24 Mar. 1914, p. 4.
45 IT 'The Ulster crisis' 27 Apr. 1914, p. 6.
46 IT 'Danger and duty' 27 July 1914, p. 4.
47 IT 'The government and Ireland' 28 July 1914, p. 4.
48 IT 'United Ireland' 4 Aug. 1914, p. 4.
49 IT 'Mr Redmond's call to arms' 17 Sept. 1914, p. 4.
50 IT 'Danger and duty' 26 Sept. 1914, p. 4.
51 IT 'Ireland and the war' 25 Sept. 1914, p. 4.
52 IT 'Recruiting in Ireland' 29 Sept. 1914, p. 4.
53 IT 'Obituary Mr John E. Healy' 31 May 1934, p. 6.
54 IT 'The Trinity College war list' 15 Apr. 1916, p. 4.
55 IT 'Sedition in Ireland' 12 Apr. 1916, p. 4.
56 IT 'The Outbreak' 25 Apr. 1916, p. 4.
57 IT 'Irish Times Tuesday 25 April 1916' 16 May 1916, p. 4.
58 UCDA; Moloney Papers: P95 53–71, 'Under the Clock' Sept. 1950, p. 4.
59 *The Times* 'From within the cordon' 1 May 1916, p. 9.
60 Ibid.
61 IT 'Martial law' 27 Apr. 1916, p. 2.
62 WIT 'Incidents of the rebellion' 29 Apr., 6 & 13 May 1916, p. 3.
63 WIT 'Echoes from the firing line' 29 Apr., 6 & 13 May 1916, p. 4.
64 The Irish Times, (1917) *The Sinn Féin rebellion handbook.*
65 UCDA; Moloney Papers: P95 79, circulation ledger.
66 IT 'The Insurrection' 28 & 29 Apr. & 1 May 1916, p. 2.
67 IT 'The Arms Act' 3 May 1916, p. 2.
68 IT 'Mr Birrell's resignation' 5 May 1916, p. 4.
69 IT 'Rebellion and after' 6 May 1916, p. 4.
70 IT 'Letters to the Editor' 9 May 1916, p. 6.
71 Ibid., 16 May 1916, p. 6.
72 IT 'Sir John Maxwell's position' 10 May 1916, p. 4.
73 IT 'Rebellion and settlement' 13 May 1916, p. 4.
74 O'Hegarty, P.S. (1998) *The victory of Sinn Féin*, p. 3.
75 IT 'The state of Ireland' 5 July 1917, p. 4.
76 IT 'The east Clare election' 12 July 1917, p. 4.
77 IT 'Ireland and conscription' 23 & 24 April 1918, p. 4.
78 Oram, H. (1983) *The newspaper book*, pp 136–7.
79 IT 'Death of Mr R.M. Smyllie' 13 Sept. 1954, p. 6.
80 *The Times*, 'Irish players at Ruhleben' 8 Jan. 1917, p. 11.
81 IT 'British prisoners at Ruhleben' 31 Dec. 1918, p. 2.
82 IT 'Death of Mr R.M. Smyllie' 13 Sept. 1954, p. 6.
83 IT 'Foreign journalists and Sinn Féin' 30 Jan. 1919, p. 5.
84 IT 'The state of Ireland' 22 Jan. 1919, p. 4.
85 IT 'No surrender' 11 Mar. 1920, p. 4.
86 IT 'The state of Ireland' 3 Jan. 1920, p. 6.
87 IT 'The lord mayor of Cork' 26 Oct. 1920, p. 4.
88 IT 'The campaign of crime' 3 Nov. 1920, p. 4.
89 IT 'The Dublin murders' 22 Nov. 1920, p. 4.
90 IT 'Respice-Prospice' 1 Jan. 1921, p. 6.
91 DE; vol. 1. Debates on reports – publicity (May 1921)
92 IT 'The dispatch Childers censored' 22 June 1976, p. 10.
93 IT 'An Irishman's Diary' 17 Nov. 1945, p. 3.
94 IT 'The dispatch Childers censored' 22 June 1976, p. 10.
95 IT 'The Choice' 9 Dec. 1921, p. 4.
96 IT 'Ireland and the treaty' 10 Dec. 1921, p. 6.
97 IT 'The Dáil and the people' 22 Dec. 1921, p. 4.
98 IT 'Dáil Eireann's duty' 3 Jan. 1922, p. 4.
99 IT 'The Dáil decides' 9 Jan. 1922, p. 4.

CHAPTER 3
A New Order

1 IT 'An aspect of nation building' 23 Feb. 1925, p. 4.

2 Stanford, W.B. (1944) 'Protestantism since the treaty', *The Bell*, 8:3, 218–32.

3 UCDA; Moloney Papers: P95 79 circulation ledger.

4 IT 'The Four Courts' 1 July 1922, p. 2.

5 IT 'Premier-elect Mr W.T. Cosgrave' 9 Sept. 1922, p. 9.

6 NA D/T; S 1394 – Acting secretary of provisional government to newspaper proprietors, 3 July 1922.

7 Ibid., Memorandum on censorship.

8 Ibid., Publicity report July 1922, PG decision 6 July 1922.

9 Ibid., Publicity report July 1922, PG decision 7 July 1922.

10 MA; S 12275 (General press file).

11 IT 'Obituary Mr John E. Healy' 31 May 1934, p. 6.

12 IT 'Work and pay' 21 Sept. 1922, p. 4.

13 DE; vol. 1, col. 797 (Sept. 1922).

14 NA D/T; S 1394 – Complains against the press 15 Nov. 1922. Thomas Derrig was a prominent anti-treaty republican.

15 NA D/T; H180/30 – Death notices of Irregulars, publication in press, Grehan to Lester, 11 July 1924.

16 Ibid., Lester to ministry of home affairs, 12 July 1924.

17 IT 'The Elections' 16 Aug. 1923, p. 6.

18 IT 'The Irish language' 7 Mar. 1922, p. 4.

19 IT 'A new chapter' 1 Feb. 1922, p. 4.

20 IT 'Irish in the schools' 25 June 1924, p. 6.

21 IT 'Quis Custodiet?' 13 Nov. 1926, p. 6

22 IT 'Compulsory Irish' 17 Nov. 1926, p. 6.

23 IT 'Compulsory Irish' 11 Dec. 1926, p. 6.

24 CB (1927) 'Editorial', 17:1, 7.

25 DE; vol. 26, col. 1456 (Nov. 1928)

26 DE; vol. 10, col. 158 (Feb. 1925).

27 IT 'Divorce in the Free State' 11 Feb. 1925, p. 6.

28 IT 'The Dáil and divorce' 12 Feb. 1925, p. 6.

29 CB (1925) 'Editorial', 15:3, 200.

30 IT 'The Free State elections' 16 Feb. 1925, p. 4.

31 IT 'The Free State elections' 20 May 1927, p. 6.

32 IT 'The fight for votes' 30 May 1927, p. 6.

33 IT 'Constitution or chaos' 4 June 1927, p. 8.

34 IT 'Public safety' 21 July 1927, p. 6.

35 IT 'Fianna Fáil to go into the Dail' 11 Aug. 1927, p. 7.

36 IT 'Taking the oath' 12 Aug. 1927, p. 7.

37 IT 'Fianna Fáil's decision' 12 Aug. 1927, p. 6.

38 Gaughan, J.A. (1980) *Thomas Johnson*, p. 310. See also IT 'A scoop that never was' 12 Dec. 1979, p. 14.

39 IT 'Forecast of Labour leader's shadow cabinet' 15 Aug. 1927, p. 7.

40 IT 'A narrow escape' 17 Aug. 1927, p. 6.

41 IT 'The absence of Mr Jinks' 17 Aug. 1927, p. 7.

42 IT 'Why Mr Jinks abstained' 18 Aug. 1927, p. 7.

43 Fleming, L. (1965) *Head or harp*, p. 154.

44 Mikhail, E.H. (ed.), (1977) *W.B. Yeats*, p. 324.

45 IT 'Irish poet honoured' 15 Nov. 1923, p. 7.

46 O'Connor, G. (1988) *Sean O'Casey*, pp 198–9. See also IT 'Abbey Theatre scene' 12 Feb. 1926, p. 7.

47 IT 'Cant and facts' 13 Feb. 1926, p. 6.

48 Fleming, *Head or harp*, pp 160–1.

49 IT 'Obituary of Mr John E. Healy' 31 May 1934, p. 6.

50 Andrews, C.S. (1982) *Man of no property*, pp 135–6.

51 IT 'Nearly 70 years in newspaper work' 25 June 1949, p. 7.

52 IT 'Newspaper production in the 19th century' 8 June 1959 (supplement p. v).

53 CRO; IT Ltd, annual reports 1921–4.

54 UCDA; Moloney Papers: P95 79, circulation ledger.

55 IT 'An Irishman's Diary' 21 July 1938, p. 4.

56 IT 'Text of the evil literature bill' 13 Aug. 1928, p. 5.

57 IT 'Censorship of films' 6 Mar. 1924, p. 6.

58 IT 'Good-will and censorship' 13 Aug. 1928, p. 6.

59 IT 'The Censorship Bill' 29 Sept. 1928, p. 6.

60 IT 'The Censorship Bill' 18 Oct. 1928, p. 6.

61 IT 'The Censorship Act' 14 May 1930, p. 6.

62 DE; vol. 38, col. 356 (Apr. 1931).

63 IT 'Banned books' 19 Nov. 1942, p. 3.

64 IT 'A Critical election' 30 Jan. 1932, p. 8.

65 Ibid.

66 IT 'Danger and duty' 13 Feb. 1932, p. 8.

67 Ibid.

68 IT 'To-day's election' 16 Feb. 1932, p. 6.

69 IT 'Mr de Valera's prospects' 23 Feb. 1932, p. 6.

70 IT 'Mr de Valera's challenge' 23 Mar. 1932, p. 6.

71 IT 'The real issue', 8 July 1932, p. 6.

72 IT 'Religion and politics' 25 June 1932, p. 8.

73 IT 'Aeroplanes over the park' 27 June 1932, p. 7.

74 IT 'Million minds with a single thought' 27 June 1932, p. 7.

75 IT 'Governor-General and Mr de Valera' 11 July 1932, p. 7.

76 IT 'The Governor-General' 12 July 1932, p. 6. The paper published the correspondence on 12 July 1932, p. 7 under the headline 'Governor General demands apology'.

77 IT 'The haunted house' 1 Nov. 1932, p. 6.

78 IT 'General O'Duffy' 16 Mar. 1933, p. 6.

79 DE; vol. 46, col. 799 (Mar. 1933).

80 O'hEithir, B. (1986) Begrudger's guide, p. 67.

81 IT 'Danger and duty' 19 Aug. 1933, p. 6.

82 IT 'Proclaimed' 23 Aug. 1933, p. 6.

83 IT 'The only way' 26 Aug. 1933, p. 8.

84 IT 'The new party' 9 Sept. 1933, p. 8.

85 IT 'The Free State' 9 Dec. 1933, p. 8.

86 IT 'Mr de Valera's choice' 24 Mar. 1934, p. 8.

87 IT 'Towards dictatorship' 28 Apr. 1934, p. 6.

88 IT 'Senate and constitution' 29 May 1936, p. 8.

89 IT 'Back to work' 2 Oct. 1934, p. 6.

90 IT 'Of great price' 18 Oct. 1934, p. 6.

91 IT 'Fine Gael's chance' 30 Oct. 1934, p. 8.

CHAPTER 4
Smyllie's Reign

1 Campbell, P. (1960) *Come here till I tell you*, p. 105.

2 IT 'Obituary Mr John E. Healy' 31 May 1934, p. 6.

3 Anon. (1941) 'Meet R.M. Smyllie'. *The Bell*, 3:3, 185 of 180–8.

4 IT 'Death of Mr R.M. Smyllie' 13 Sept. 1954, p. 6.

5 Anon. (1941) 'Meet R.M. Smyllie'. *The Bell*, 3:3, 185 of 180–8.

6 IT 'Death of Mr R.M. Smyllie' 13 Sept. 1954, p. 6.

7 Anon. (1941) 'Meet R.M. Smyllie'. *The Bell*, 3:3, 185 of 180–8.

8 Fleming, L. (1965) *Head or harp*, p. 168.

9 Inglis, B. (1990) *Downstart*, pp 86–7.

10 Brown, S. (1937) *The Press in Ireland*, pp 168–71.

11 Andrews, C.S. (1982) *Man of no property*, pp 136–7.

12 UCDA; Moloney Papers: P95 79, circulation ledger.

13 IT 'George V' 21 Jan. 1936, p. 8.

14 IT 'Irish Times Ltd' 25 Nov. 1937, p. 12 & 8 Dec. 1938, p. 12.

15 Sheridan, N. (1973) 'Brian, Flann and Myles', p. 44.

16 Fleming, *Head or harp*, pp 144–5.

17 Quinn, A. (2001) *Patrick Kavanagh*, p. 127.

18 Fleming, *Head or harp*, p. 148.

19 IT 'Alec Newman dies after long illness' 7 Mar. 1972, p. 9.

20 Orr, C. (1989) *Splash!*, p. 31.

21 IT 'Alan (Monty) Montgomery' 17 Oct. 1996, p. 15.

22 'Style in the *Irish Times*' – courtesy of Gerry Mulvey.

23 Campbell, (1967) *My life and easy times*, p. 122.

24 Inglis, *Downstart*, p. 85.

25 Bundock, C. (1957) *The National Union of Journalists*, pp 110–11.

26 Ibid., p. 122.

27 Fleming, *Head or harp*, p. 127.

28 Inglis, *Downstart*, p. 81.

29 Ibid., pp 83–4.

30 Fleming, *Head or harp*, p. 128.

31 IT 'The Challenge' 22 June 1936, p. 6.

32 Fleming, *Head or harp*, p. 39.

33 O'Donovan, D. (1998) *Little old man cut short*, p. 32.

34 Orr, *Splash!*, p. 41.

35 Gray, T. (1991) *Mr Smyllie, Sir*, p. 45.

36 NA D/J; OCC 1 – No 3 (2) 'The New Germany' published Oct. 1929.

37 IT 'Germany's verdict' 7 Mar. 1933, p. 6.

38 IT 'Germany's fascism' 11 Mar. 1933, p. 6.

39 IT 'Art in Germany' 24 Apr. 1934, p. 6.

40 IT 'After three years' 31 Jan. 1936, p. 6.

41 IT 'Germany under Adolf Hitler' 2–17 Nov. 1936.

42 Ibid., 7 Nov. 1936, p. 6.

43 Ibid, 10 Nov. 1936, p. 4.

44 IT 'Jewry's Lot' 14 Nov. 1938, p. 6.

45 IT 'Honour for Irish journalist' 27 Mar. 1939, p. 5.

46 NA D/T; S 9805 – Robert M. Smyllie, 13 & 21 June 1938.

47 Bowyer Bell, J. (1969) 'Ireland and the Spanish Civil War 1936–39', *Studia Hibernia*, 9, 140 of 137–63.

48 IT 'The Spanish problem' 5 Aug. 1936, p. 8.
49 IT 'The Spanish tangle' 11 Aug. 1936, p. 6.
50 IT 'The People's government' 4 Aug. 1936, p. 6.
51 Fleming, *Head or harp*, p. 169.
52 IT 'Spain's agony' 19 Aug. 1936, p. 6.
53 IT 'Unhappy Spain' 26 Aug. 1936, p. 6.
54 Fleming, *Head or harp*, p. 170.
55 DDA; Blackrock Papers; Allen to McQuaid, 27 Aug. 1936.
56 Ibid., James Staunton to McQuaid, 23 Sept. 1936.
57 Ibid., Allen to McQuaid, 5 Sept. 1936.
58 McGarry, F. (1999), *Irish politics and the Spanish Civil War*, p. 165.
59 II 'Giants of the Press' (Inglis, B.) 9 Nov. 1991, p. 18.
60 Anon. 'Profile: Mr R.M. Smyllie', *The Leader*, 7 June 1952, 52:11, 22 of 21–2.
61 IT 'Ich Dien' 4 Dec. 1936, p. 6.
62 IT 'The King's farewell' 11 Dec. 1936, p. 8.
63 IT 'King and president' 12 Dec. 1936, p. 8.
64 DE; vol. 62, col. 647 (May 1936).
65 DE; vol. 63, col. 1080 (July 1936).
66 DE; vol. 80, col. 214 (May 1940).
67 DE; vol. 82, col. 1958 (May 1942).
68 IT 'Volunteers' 19 Feb. 1937, p. 6.
69 IT 'Ireland and Spain' 22 Feb. 1937, p. 6.
70 IT 'Éire' 1 May 1937, p. 8.
71 IT 'Gentlemen, the King!' 12 May 1937, p. 6.
72 IT 'Freedom of the press' 13 May 1937, p. 6.
73 DE; vol. 59, col. 876 (Nov. 1935).
74 IT 'Freedom, Farewell!' 4 June 1937, p. 6.
75 IT 'L'Etat c'est moi' 5 June 1937, p. 8.
76 IT 16 June 1937, p. 1.
77 IT 'To-Morrow's poll' 30 June 1937, p. 8.
78 IT 'Journey's end?' 29 Dec. 1937, p. 6.
79 IT 'An appeal to Ulster' 18 Jan. 1938, p. 6.
80 IT 'An eventful week' 23 Apr. 1938, p. 8.
81 IT 'An act of faith' 26 Apr. 1938, p. 6.
82 IT 'To-Morrow's poll' 16 June 1938, p. 6.
83 IT 'L'enfant terrible' 13 June 1938, p. 6.
84 IT 'Mr de Valera's victory' 21 June 1938, p. 6.
85 IT 'The next war' 21 Nov. 1935, p. 6.
86 IT 'The next war' 12 Feb. 1936, p. 6.
87 IT 'The northern problem' 16 Jan. 1937, p. 8.
88 IT 'If war comes' 22 Feb. 1939, p. 6.
89 IT 'The temple of Janus' 17 Apr. 1939, p. 6.
90 IT 'Ireland in war' 3 May 1939, p. 8.
91 IT 'Neutral or –?' 13 June 1939, p. 6.
92 IT 'Germany's error' 4 July 1939, p. 6.
93 IT 'Where do we stand?' 26 Aug. 1939, p. 8.
94 IT 'Éire the unready' 28 Aug. 1939, p. 6.

CHAPTER 5
'Nippon go Brath'

1 IT 'Out of the shadows' 12 May 1945, p. 3.
2 See Smyllie, R.M. (1946) 'Unneutral Neutral Éire', *Foreign Affairs*, 24, 317–26.
3 IT 'Commonwealth at war' 6 Sept. 1939, p. 6.
4 NA D/J; OCC 5 – PCMR 1939–42 (Sept. 1939).
5 NA D/T; S 11306 – Connolly to de Valera, 19 Sept. 1939.
6 NA D/J; OCC 3 – Notes on press conferences (19 Sept. 1939).
7 Gaughan, J.A. (1996) *Memoirs of Senator Joseph Connolly*, p. 399.
8 Anon. (1941) 'Meet R.M. Smyllie', *The Bell*, 3:3, 184 of 180–8
9 IT 'Death of Mr R.M. Smyllie' p. 4.
10 NA D/J; OCC 1 – No. 3 (1) various proofs.
11 NA D/J; OCC 7 – RPC: *Irish Times*.
12 IT 'Humanity in war' 12 Sept. 1939, p. 4.
13 IT 'A Winter campaign' 12 Sept. 1939, p. 4.
14 IT 'Éire's position' 28 Sept. 1939, p. 6.
15 IT 'Cork squadron-leader hero of fight' 2 Oct. 1939, p. 5.
16 IT 'Pax Germanica' 7 Oct. 1939, p. 6.
17 IT 'A terrible indictment' 31 Oct. 1939, p. 6.
18 IT 'Poland's future' 14 Dec. 1939, p. 6.
19 NA D/J; OCC 7 – RPC: *Irish Times*.
20 Ibid.
21 NA D/J; OCC 1 – No 3 (1), Knightly to Connolly, 30 Dec. 1939.
22 Ibid., Connolly to Aiken, 30 Dec. 1939.
23 NA, D/J; S164/40 – IRA to staffs, IRA to managements, 6 April 1940 & Commissioner's office to D/J, 9 Apr. 1940.
24 IT 'Ireland and British empire' 13 Jan. 1940, p. 8.
25 NA D/J; OCC 1 – No. 3 (1) Knightly to Burgess, 15 Jan. 1940.
26 Ibid., Burgess to Knightly, 14 Jan. 1940.
27 Ibid., Smyllie to de Valera, 15 Jan. 1940.
28 Ibid., Knightly to Connolly, 20 Jan. 1940.
29 NA D/J; OCC 5 – PCMR 1939–42 (Jan. 1940).

30 NA D/J; OCC 1 – No. 3 (1) Smyllie to Knightly, 5 July 1940.
31 NA D/J; OCC 7 – RPC: *Irish Times*.
32 NA D/J; OCC 1 – No. 3 (1) Coyne to Aiken, 13 Sept. 1940.
33 Ibid., Connolly to Aiken, 18 Sept. 1940.
34 UCDA; Moloney Papers: P95 79, circulation ledger.
35 SE; vol. 24, col. 2564–2611 (Dec. 1940).
36 NA D/J; OCC 7 – RPC: *Irish Times*.
37 IT 'Arms and the ban' 6 Dec. 1940, p. 5.
38 NA D/J; OCC 2 – R/14 – Irish church dignitaries.
39 SE; Vol. 24, col. 2564–2611 (Dec. 1940).
40 IT 'The Censorship' 4 Dec. 1940, p. 4.
41 IT 'An Irishman's Diary' 11 Feb. 1941, p. 4 (Where else in the world would you get such hard work?).
42 NA D/J; OCC 1 – No. 3 (2) Smyllie to Knightly, 14 Feb. 1941.
43 MA; OCC 2/68 – Coyne to Aiken, 20 Aug. 1941.
44 Ibid., Coyne to Aiken, 20 Aug. 1941.
45 Ibid., Knightly to Coyne, 20 Aug. 1941.
46 Ibid., Coyne to Knightly, 22 Aug. 1941.
47 Ibid., Coyne to Knightly, 23 Aug. 1941.
48 NA D/J; OCC 1 No. 3 (1) Connolly to Aiken, 23 Dec. 1939.
49 Ibid., Connolly to Aiken, 7 Aug. 1940.
50 NA D/J; OCC 1 No. 3 (3) Censor's order to *Irish Times*, 13 Mar. 1942.
51 IT 'The battle For Athens' 24 Apr. 1941, p. 4.
52 NA D/J; OCC 1 – No. 3 (2) Coyne to Smyllie, 25 Apr. 1941.
53 IT 'Britain and the neutrals' 14 June 1941, p. 5.
54 MA; OCC 2/58 – Connolly to Moynihan, 16 June 1941. Moynihan's response is not recorded.
55 IT 'Into Iran' 26 Aug. 1941, p. 4.
56 NA D/J; OCC 1 – No. 3 (2) Coyne to Knightly, 26 Aug. 1941.
57 Ibid., Newman to Coyne, 28 Aug. 1941.
58 Ibid., Coyne to Newman, 29 Aug. 1941.
59 NA D/J; OCC 5 – PCMR 1939–42 (Sept. 1941).
60 MA; OCC 2/58 – Coyne to Smyllie, 27 Sept. 1941.
61 Ibid., Smyllie to Coyne, 28 Sept. 1941.
62 Ibid., Coyne to Aiken, Oct. 1941.
63 IT 'A happy escape' 17 Dec. 1941, p. 5.
64 NA D/J; OCC 1 – No. 3 (2) Coyne to Knightly, 18 Dec. 1941.
65 NA D/J; OCC 3 – CC; Coyne to Smyllie, 16 Feb. 1942.
66 Ibid., Knightly to Coyne, 15 May 1942.
67 Ibid., Smyllie to Coyne, 16 May 1942.
68 Ibid., Smyllie to Coyne, 27 Nov. 1942.
69 Ibid., Smyllie to Coyne, 30 Oct. 1942.
70 Ibid., Coyne to Smyllie, 30 Oct. 1942.
71 Ibid., Coyne to Smyllie, 23 Nov. 1942.
72 NA D/J; OCC 5 – PCMR 1939–42 (Dec. 1942).
73 NA D/J; OCC 1 – No 3. (3) Smyllie to Knightly, 24 Dec. 1942.
74 Ibid., Knightly to board of *Irish Times*, 29 Dec. 1942.
75 NA D/J; OCC 3 – CC; Page proofs 1 & 11 Jan. 1943.
76 Ibid., Smyllie to Coyne, 15 Jan. 1943.
77 NA D/J; OCC 7 – RPC: *Irish Times*.
78 NA D/J; OCC 3 – CC; Coyne to Smyllie, 16 Jan. 1943.
79 Ibid., Smyllie to Coyne, 18 Jan. 1943.
80 Ibid., Smyllie to Coyne, 18 Jan. 1943.
81 NA D/J; OCC 7 – RPC: *Irish Times*.
82 NA D/J; OCC 5 – PCMR 1944 (Feb.).
83 IT 'The American demand' 13 Mar. 1944, p. 3.
84 DE; vol. 93, col. 1535–1536 (Apr. 1944).
85 IT 'A different outlook' 27 Apr. 1944, p. 3.
86 NA D/J, No. 3 *Irish Times*, Sept. 1944.
87 NA D/J; OCC 7 – RPC: *Irish Times*.
88 NA D/J; OCC 5 – PCMR 1944 (Nov.).
89 NA D/J; OCC 7 – RPC: *Irish Times*.
90 IT 'Curtain' 2 May 1945, p. 3.
91 IT 'Herr Hitler's death' 3 May 1945, p. 1.
92 NA D/J; OCC 5 – PCMR 1945 (May).
93 IT 'Aftermath' 15 May 1945, p. 3.
94 IT 'Peace today in Europe' 8 May 1945, p. 1.
95 IT 'Out of the shadows' 12 May 1945, p. 3. See also 'An Irishman's Diary' 19 May 1945, p. 3 and 2 June 1945, p. 3.
96 IT 'An Irishman's Diary' 19 May 1945, p. 3.
97 Andrews, C.S. (1982) *Man of no property*, p. 124.
98 IT 'Letters to the Editor' 14 May 1945, p. 3.
99 Ibid., 17 May 1945, p. 3.
1   IT 'An Irishman's Diary' 26 May 1945, p. 3.
2   IT 'Aftermath' 15 May 1945, p. 3.
3   IT 'In spite of neutrality Éire helped Britain' 13 Nov. 1945, p. 1.
4   DE; vol. 98, col. 1249 (Nov. 1945).
5   IT 'Turning away wrath' 18 May 1945, p. 3.

CHAPTER 6
Challenging Times

1   US embassy report on political coverage in Irish newspapers: Dept of State: RG59 1948–64, box 1, no. 3079, c1950.

2   IT 'Profile gallery: Frank A. Lowe' 6 June 1959, p. 8. See also IT 'Death of Mr Frank A. Lowe' 20 July 1959, p. 9.

3   Gray, T. (1991) *Mr Smyllie, Sir*, pp 196–7.

4   Interview with Gerry Mulvey, 31 Jan. 2006.

5   Gray, *Mr Smyllie, Sir*, p. 198.

6   Interview with Cathal O'Shannon, 30 Jan. 2006.

7   Orr, C. (1989) *Splash!*, p. 35.

8   IT 'He's a Diamond Man of Letters (7)' 12 Mar. 2003, p. 15.

9   Bundock, C. (1957) *The National Union of Journalists*, p. 222.

10 Campbell, P. (1967) *My life and easy times*, p. 178.

11 Interview with Gerry Mulvey, 31 Jan. 2006.

12 IT 'Death of Mr Michael McInerney in Dublin' 28 Jan. 1980 p. 8.

13 IT 'Seamus Kelly, "Quidnunc"' 11 June 1979, p. 11.

14 IT 'Muirchu lost on her way to the scrap-heap' 9 May 1947, p. 1.

15 Inglis, B. (1990) *Downstart*, pp 157–60.

16 Mercier, V. (1945) 'The Times (Irish)', *The Bell*, 9:4, 293 of 290–7.

17 Quoted in Ó Conaire, B. (1986) *Myles na Gaeilge*.

18 Anon. (1941) 'Meet R.M. Smyllie', *The Bell*, 3:3, 187 of 180–8.

19 IT 'Letters to the Editor' 11 Jan. 1939, p. 5.

20 Ibid., 13 Jan. 1939, p. 5.

21 Ibid.

22 Ibid., 16 Jan. 1939, p. 5.

23 Ibid., 30 May 1940, p. 7.

24 Ibid., 3 June 1940, p. 2.

25 Ibid., 4 June 1940, p. 4.

26 See IT 8 June p. 8; 10 June, p. 6; 12 June, p. 4; 13 June p. 4.

27 Quinn, A. (2001) *Patrick Kavanagh*, p. 82 & p. 125.

28 IT 'Fiction: Maurice Walsh's new novel' 20 July 1940, p. 5.

29 IT 'Letters to the Editor' 25 July 1940, p. 4.

30 Ibid., 29 July 1940, p. 2.

31 Ibid., 30 July 1940, p. 6.

32 Ibid., 7 Aug. 1940, p. 6.

33 IT 'Irish in the home' 28 Sept. 1940, p. 6.

34 This pen-name was taken from Dion Boucicault's play *The Colleen Bawn*, which was partly based on Gerald Griffin's novel *The Collegians*. In the novel the character Myles na gCopaleen makes a brief appearance; in the play he has a leading role in which the character represents the 'Stage Irishman' in his most stereotypical form.

35 Mercier, V. (1945) 'The Times (Irish)', *The Bell*, 9:4, 297 of 290–7.

36 See Hogan, T. (1943) 'Myles na Gopaleen', *The Bell*, 13:2, 129–40.

37 Orr, *Splash!* p. 53.

38 Costello, P. & Van de Kamp, P. (1987) *Flann O'Brien*, pp 93–4.

39 Cronin, A. (2003) *No laughing matter*, p. 139.

40 Costello & Van de Kamp, *Flann O'Brien*, p. 77.

41 McCourt, F. (1996) *Angela's Ashes*, p. 394.

42 Ibid., p. 414.

43 Butler, H. (1996) *In the land of nod*, p. 28.

44 O'Donoval, D. (1998) *Little old man cut short*, p. 103.

45 Interview with Gerry Mulvey, 31 Jan. 2006.

46 DDA; Communications 59; IT Correspondence; Smyllie to McQuaid, 24 Apr. 1946.

47 DE; vol. 99, col. 2605 (Mar. 1946).

48 DE; vol. 104, col. 1376 (Feb. 1947).

49 IT 'Polling day' 4 Feb. 1948, p. 5.

50 IT 'Up the republic' 13 Nov. 1948, p. 7.

51 IT 'End of an epoch' 25 Nov. 1948, p. 5.

52 DE; vol. 113, col. 485 (Nov. 1948).

53 IT 'Republic and pact' 13 Apr. 1949, p. 5.

54 IT 'Looking ahead' 20 Apr. 1949, p. 5.

55 IT 'Liberal ethic condemned by professor' 24 Jan. 1950, p. 3.

56 Irish Times (1950) *The liberal ethic*, pp 9–10.

57 Ibid., p. 20.

58 Ibid.

59 Ibid., p. 40.

60 IT 'Letters to the Editor' 25 Feb. 1950, p. 9.

61 Irish Times (1950) *The liberal ethic*, p. 73. Only six members of the council were present when the resolution was passed and it was repudiated at a later meeting.

62 Ibid., p. 77.

63 Ibid., p. 78.

64 Ibid., pp 80–2.

65 Ibid., p. 85.

66 Sheehy Skeffington, A. (1991) *Skeff*, pp 143–4.

67 Fleming, L. (1965) *Head or harp*, p. 118.
68 US embassy to US Dept of State; political views of R.M. Smyllie, editor of the *Irish Times*, 7 Nov. 1950.
69 IT 'Falling temperature' 1 July 1950, p. 7.
70 US embassy to US Dept. of State; political views of R.M. Smyllie, editor of the *Irish Times*, 7 Nov. 1950.
71 Browne, N. (1986) *Against the tide*, p. 186
72 IT 'Minister releases correspondence' 12 Apr. 1951, p. 1. Bishop of Ferns James Staunton (secretary to hierarchy) to Taoiseach John A. Costello 10 Oct. 1950.
73 IT 'Contra Mundum' 12 Apr. 1951, p. 5.
74 DE; vol. 125, col. 784 (Apr. 1951).
75 DE; vol. 125, col. 940 (Apr. 1951).
76 Cooney, J. (1999) *John Charles McQuaid*, pp 273–4.
77 IT 'Report to housewives' 14 Apr. 1951, p. 5.
78 IT 'Mother and child' 19 Apr. 1951, p. 5.
79 Krause, D. (1980) *The letters of Sean O'Casey*, vol. 2, pp 787&794; O'Casey to Keating, 4 May 1951.
80 Interview with Gerry Mulvey, 31 Jan. 2006.
81 DDA; Communications 59; IT Correspondence; Montgomery to McQuaid, 25 Feb. 1957.
82 Ibid., Memo to McQuaid, Feb. 1957.
83 *The Standard* 'Mother and child scheme' 20 Apr. 1951, pp 1&9.
84 Ibid., 'The political question and the theological issue' 27 Apr. 1951, pp 1&16.
85 IT 'An Irishman's Diary' 12 May 1951, p. 7.
86 IT 'Cruiskeen Lawn' 2 May 1951, p. 6.
87 *The Standard* 'No answer' 11 May 1951, p. 9. O'Rahilly later returned to the topic in *The Standard* on 17, 24 and 31 Aug. 1951.
88 IT 'Cruiskeen Lawn' 16 May 1951, p. 4 (See also IT 17–19, 21 & 23 May 1951).
89 IT 'Dissolution' 5 May 1951, p. 7.
90 IT 'Begging the question' 23 May 1951, p. 5.
91 IT 'To-Morrow's choice' 17 May 1954, p. 5.
92 IT 'Polling day' 18 May 1954, p. 5.
93 IT 'The party lines' 25 May 1954, p. 5.

CHAPTER 7
Holding the Fort

1 Gray, T. (1991) *Mr Smyllie, Sir*, p. 221.
2 White, J. (1973) 'Myles, Flann and Brian', p. 73.
3 IT 'Serious Fire in the *Irish Times*' 18 Sept. 1951, p. 1.
4 IT 'The *Irish Times*' 18 Sept. 1959, p. 3.
5 UCDA; Moloney Papers: P95 53–71, 'Under the Clock' Sept. 1951, p. 1. See also IT 'Work resumed in printing trade' 12 July–30 Aug. 1952, p. 1.
6 Anon. (1952) 'Profile: Mr. R.M. Smyllie' *The Leader*, 52:11, 22 of 21–22.
7 Gray, *Mr Smyllie, Sir*, p. 220.
8 Cronin, A. (2003) *No laughing matter*, p. 181.
9 IT 'Cruiskeen Lawn' 26 Oct. 1951, p. 3 & 3 Feb. 1953, p. 4.
10 IT 'Cruiskeen Lawn' 5 Feb. 1953, p. 4.
11 IT 'Cruiskeen Lawn' 7 Feb. 1953, p. 8.
12 White, J. (1973) 'Myles, Flann and Brian', pp 70–4.
13 Orr, C. (1989) *Splash!*, pp 78–9.
14 Interview with Brian Fallon, 10 Oct. 2006.
15 Interview with Gerry Mulvey, 31 Jan. 2006.
16 CRO; IT Ltd, AoA, (article 24) dated 9 Dec. 1946. The amendment stipulated that 'No Ordinary share shall be transferred to a person who is not an Ordinary shareholder while any Ordinary shareholder or any person selected by the Directors as one whom it is desirable in the interests of the Company to admit to membership is willing to purchase same'.
17 IT 'The Irish Times Ltd: AGM' 14 Dec. 1954, p. 8. In the 1957 shareholders' register the 70,000 ordinary shares were held as follows: Lauriston Arnott 6,073; George E. Hetherington 9,392; Frank A. Lowe 503; New Ireland Assurance Co., the investment vehicle of the Arnott family 11,008; National Bank, the investment vehicle of Frank Lowe and later George Hetherington 11,400; Philip Walker 10,648; Ralph Walker 10,648; John McCann 10,320. The balance of 8 shares was owned by a miscellany of individuals.
18 IT 'Former director of the *Irish Times*' 24 Nov. 2001, p. 16.
19 IT 'Mr Ralph Walker dies in Dublin' 12 Nov. 1980, p. 4 & IT 'Death of Philip Walker' 29 Nov. 1982, p. 5.
20 CRO; IT Ltd, annual report 1957.
21 CRO; IT Ltd, annual report 1959.
22 Corless, D. (2004) *GUBU Nation*, pp 133–8.

23 IT 'Case dismissed' 28 July 1956, p. 7.

24 IT 'Letters to the Editor' 8 June 1957, p. 7.

25 IT 'Chairman explains why he resigned' 6 Dec. 1957, p. 5.

26 IT 'Law and disorder' 6 Dec. 1957, p. 7.

27 IT 'Letters to the Editor' 7 Dec. 1957, p. 9.

28 IT 'Village boycott of school and shops' 27 May 1957, p. 1.

29 IT 'Fethard-On-Sea' 11 June 1957, p. 5.

30 IT ' Invasion' 1 Nov. 1956, p. 7.

31 IT 'Death of Mr Frank A. Lowe' 20 July 1959, p. 9.

32 IT 'Sir Anthony Eden' 10 Jan. 1957, p. 5.

33 See Whelan, G. & Swift, C. (2002) *Spiked*, p. 352n.

34 IT 24 May 1957, p. 1 & 10 June 1958, p. 4.

35 IT 'Final curtain' 15 Feb. 1958, p. 7.

36 IT 'Letters to the Editor' 19 Feb. 1958, p. 6.

37 DDA; An Tostal 1953–60; McQuaid to Derry, 21 Feb. 1958.

38 Ibid., Derry to McQuaid, 23 Feb. 1958.

39 Ibid., *Sunday Review* clipping; 'Impertinence' 23 Feb. 1958.

40 Ibid., McQuaid to Arnott, 21 Feb. 1958.

41 Ibid., Notes of Meeting, 24 Feb. 1958.

42 Ibid., Deery to McQuaid, 25 Feb. 1958.

43 Ibid., Newman to McQuaid, 28 Feb. 1958.

44 Ibid., McQuaid to Newman, 3 Mar. 1958.

45 Interview with Gerry Mulvey, 31 Jan. 2006.

46 *The Standard* 'An Tostal' 28 Feb. 1958, pp 1&7.

47 Interview with Cathal O'Shannon, 30 Jan. 2006.

48 *The Standard* 'An Tostal' 28 Feb. 1958, pp 1&7.

49 DDA; An Tostal 1953–60; Leaflets of O'Rahilly's article.

50 O hEithir, B. (1986) *Begrudger's guide*, p. 122.

51 Ferriter, D. (2004) *The transformation of Ireland*, p. 582.

52 IT 'The vanishing Irish' 2 June 1956, p. 7.

53 IT 'Order of merit' 5 Mar. 1957, p. 5.

54 IT 'The new Dáil' 8 Mar. 1957, p. 5.

55 IT 'No' 17 June 1959, p. 7.

56 IT 'PR' 5 June 1959, p. 7.

57 IT 'PR in Ireland' 1 June 1959, p. 1. The articles appeared between 20 and 25 April 1959.

58 IT 'An Irishman's Diary' 14 Feb. 1959, p. 8.

59 IT 'No' 17 June 1959, p. 7.

60 IT 'No and de Valera' 20 June 1959, p. 9.

61 IT 'To-Morrow' 24 June 1959, p. 7.

62 Kenny, I. (1987) *In good company*, pp 173–4.

63 See Whittaker, A. (ed) (2006) *Bright brilliant days*.

64 Kenny, I. (1987) *In good company*, p. 185.

65 Interview with Douglas Gageby, 11 Aug. 1998.

66 Kenny, *In good company*, p. 187.

67 CRO; IT Ltd, annual report 1959.

68 Interview with Douglas Gageby, 11 Aug. 1998.

69 IT 'Irish Times Ltd AGM' 22 Dec. 1964, p. 10.

70 DE; vol. 149, col. 660 (Mar. 1955).

71 DE; vol. 155, col. 716 (Mar. 1956).

72 NA D/J; OCC 1 – No. 3 (2) IT to censor's office 24 Oct. 1941.

73 NA D/J; OCC 1 – No. 156 – *Times Pictorial*.

74 NA D/J; OCC 5 – PCMR 1943 (Sept.).

75 UCDA; Moloney Papers: P95 79, circulation ledger.

76 The paper had four editors 1941–58: George Burrows, Tony Gray, Ken Gray and Peadar Ward.

77 DE; vol. 137, col. 651–4 (Mar. 1953).

78 *Irish Pictorial* 'Ireland by Dermot Barry' 29 Mar. 1958, p. 8.

79 DE; vol. 130, col. 1565–74 (Apr. 1952).

80 DE; vol. 137, col. 651–4 (Mar. 1953).

81 NA D/J; OCC 1 – No 175 – *Irish Field*.

82 Foley, D. (2003) *Three villages*, p. 113.

83 SR 'Taoiseach's cousin an emigrant' 3 Nov. 1957, p. 3.

84 Horgan, J. (2001) *Media in Ireland*, pp 63–4.

85 IT 'Jury rejects libel claim by Dublin TD' 7 Nov. 1964, p. 7.

86 SR 'Public hail the three-in-one Review' 6 Oct. 1963, p. 1.

87 Interview with Louis O'Neill, 21 Sept. 2007.

88 CRO; IT Ltd, balance sheet to 30 Sept. 1961.

89 See IT 'An Irishman's Diary' 20 July 2002, p. 15.

90 Henry Tivy, had acquired the paper in 1915. See IT 'Mr H.F. Tivy' 13 Oct. 1960, p. 7.

91 Downey, J. (2006) 'Irish Catholic's favourite Protestant editor', p. 23.

92 Interview with Louis O'Neill, 21 Sept. 2007.

93 Downey, J. 'Irish Catholic's favourite Protestant editor', p. 23.

94 Mercier, V. (1945) 'The *Times (Irish)*', *The Bell*, 9:4, 293 of 290–7.

95 Interview with Cathal O'Shannon, 30 Jan. 2006.

96 Interview with Gerry Mulvey, 31 Jan. 2006.

97 Cronin, *No laughing matter*, p. 218; Myles to Inglis, 17 Aug. 1960.

98 Krause, D. (ed.) (1992) *The letters of Sean O'Casey*, vol. 4, pp 208–9; O'Casey to *Irish Times*, 12 Apr. 1961.

99 Ibid., pp 212–13, O'Casey to Newman, 15 Apr. 1961.

1 Ibid., pp 245–6, O'Casey to B. Miles 18 Sept. 1961.

2 Orr, *Splash!* p. 103.

3 Interview with Gerry Mulvey, 31 Jan. 2006.

4 IT 'Alan (Monty) Montgomery' 17 Oct. 1996, p. 15.

5 Interview with Cathal O'Shannon, 30 Jan. 2006.

6 O'Donovan, D. (1998) *Little old man cut short*, p. 106.

7 Interview with Cathal O'Shannon, 30 Jan. 2006.

8 IT 'Irish Times Ltd AGM' 16 Dec. 1963, pp 10 & 22 Dec. 1964, p. 10.

CHAPTER 8
The Paper of Record

1 Kenny, I. (1987) *In good company*, p. 187.

2 Tobin, F. (1984) *The best of decades*, p. 8.

3 IT 'John F. Kennedy' 26 June 1963, p. 7.

4 Interview with Cathal O'Shannon, 30 Jan. 2006.

5 Kilfeather, F. (1997) *Changing times*, p. 35.

6 Hurley, P. (1966) 'Ireland's Newspapers'. *The Word*, June 1966.

7 Kenny, *In good company*, p. 189.

8 IT 'Donal Foley dies after a distinguished career as journalist' 8 July 1981, p. 6. Sir John Arnott was the last Arnott to have an association with the paper. He served as London editor between 1954–1973.

9 Foley, D. (2003) Three Villages, p. 118.

10 IT 'Donal Foley dies after distinguished career as journalist' 8 July 1981, p. 6.

11 Foley, *Three villages*, p. 121.

12 Ibid.

13 Interview with Gerry Mulvey, 31 Jan. 2006.

14 Kilfeather, *Changing times,* pp 36–7.

15 Interview with Gerry Mulvey, 31 Jan. 2006.

16 Kilfeather, *Changing times,* p. 37.

17 Horgan, J. (2006) 'Aggiornamento', p. 63.

18 See IT 'Ireland for sale' 4–7 Sept. 1962

19 See IT 'Last chance for the language' 29 Jan.–8 Feb. 1963.

20 See IT 'No birthright' 12–19 Sept. 1964 & 'Journey north' 4–9 May 1964.

21 IT 'The Northern Catholic' 18 & 19 May 1964, p. 8.

22 Viney, M. (2006) 'Y', p. 157. See also IT 'The five per cent' 22–26 Mar. 1965.

23 See IT 31 May–2 June 1966 & 14 Mar. 1968, p. 8.

24 Oram, H. (1993) *Paper tigers*, p. 50.

25 Gillespie, E. (ed.) (2003) *Changing the Times*, p. 11.

26 Ibid., p. 12.

27 Ibid., p. 248.

28 Kearney, R. & Moran, D. (1984) 'Public responsibility and the Press', *Crane Bag*, 8:2, 13–23.

29 Kilfeather, *Changing Times*, p. 34.

30 Anon. (1974) 'Inside Back', B&F, 10:42, 36.

31 Interview with Mary Maher, 18 July 2007

32 Hurley, P. (1966) 'Ireland's Newspapers', *The Word*, June 1966.

33 Interview with Gerry Mulvey, 31 Jan. 2006.

34 Brady, C. (2005) *Up with the Times*, p. 109.

35 Interview with Gerry Mulvey, 31 Jan. 2006.

36 DE; vol. 214, col. 585 (Feb. 1965).

37 SE; vol. 60, col. 1492, (Feb. 1966).

38 Interview with Gerry Mulvey, 31 Jan. 2006.

39 Coogan, T.P. (2003) *Ireland in the twentieth century*, p. 447.

40 IT 'Mr O'Malley and his new scheme' 17 Sept. 1966, p. 10.

41 IT 'The burden of office' 11 Mar. 1968, p. 11.

42 IT 'O'Malley: A figure bigger than life' 16 Mar. 1968, p. 10.

43 O'Dea, T. (1984) 'The Great Khan of Cortoon', *Magill*, 7:10, 24–33

44 IT 'Inside Politics' 9 May 1964, p. 12.

45 IT 'Inside Politics' 16 May 1964, p. 10.

46 Tobin, *The best of decades*, p. 102.

47 Kilfeather, *Changing Times*, pp 42–3.

48 Viney, M. (2006) 'Y', p. 155.

49 Kilfeather, *Changing Times*, p. 43.

50 Hurley, P. (1966) 'Ireland's Newspapers', *The Word*, June 1966.

51 Interview with Gerry Mulvey, 31 Jan. 2006.

52 Viney, M. (2006) 'Y', p. 157.

53 IT 'Staggering' 1 Apr. 1965, p. 9.

54 IT 'What politicians are saying about the *Irish Times*' 2 Apr. 1965, p. 1.

55 IT 'The choice' 6 Apr. 1965, p. 9.

56 CRO; IT Ltd, annual report 1966. By this time the ownership of the company's 70,000 ordinary shares had undergone another shake-up as indicated by the January 1964 shareholders' register. John Arnott held 17,081 shares, Douglas Gageby held 12,520, George Hetherington held 1,503 in his own name and 11,400 in the guise of the National Bank of Ireland, Philip Walker held 12,712, Ralph Walker held 11,714 in his own name and another 1,000 jointly with Thomas McDowell and Howard W. Robinson held 2,064. The balance of 6 shares was held by a miscellany of smaller shareholders.

57 IT 'Starting from To-Morrow' 1 July 1965, p. 7.

58 IT 'The secret history of the *Irish Times*' 13 Sept. 1965, p. 11.

59 Interview with Gerry Mulvey, 31 Jan. 2006.

60 IT 'Marathon' 25 Jan. 1966, p. 7.

61 Interview with Gerry Mulvey, 31 Jan. 2006.

62 DDA; Communications 28; DPO Oct. 1965. See also IT 'Cruiskeen Lawn' 6 Oct. 1965, p. 10.

63 IT 'Letters to the Editor' 8 Oct. 1965, p. 9.

64 IT 'Inside Politics' 16 Oct. 1965, p. 10.

65 IT 'Letters to the Editor' 18 Oct. 1965, p. 9.

66 Ibid., 19 Oct. 1965, p. 7.

67 Ibid., 20 Oct. 1965, p. 9.

68 DDA; Communications 29; DPO Nov.–Dec. 1965, Gleeson to McQuaid 9 Nov. 1965.

69 Ibid., James Ardle McMahon to McQuaid, 11 Nov. 1965.

70 Ibid., McMahon to Dowling, 14 Nov. 1965.

71 Cronin, A. (2003) *No laughing matter*, p. 242.

72 IT 'Inside Politics' 30 Apr. 1966, p. 10.

73 DDA; Communications 34; DPO Mar.–Apr., 1966, McQuaid to Dowling, 30 Apr. 1966.

74 Ibid., Dowling to McQuaid, 3 May 1966.

75 Ibid., Dowling to McQuaid, 5 May 1966.

76 See IT 7 Apr. 1966 for 1916 Supplement.

77 IT 'Call of the past' 7 Apr. 1966, p. 7.

78 IT 'The park' 17 Nov. 1965, p. 9.

79 IT 'June engagement' 4 Feb. 1966, p. 9.

80 Tobin, *The best of decades*, pp 142–3.

81 IT 'Our President' 1 June 1966, p. 9.

82 IT 'Disengagement' 4 Nov. 1966, p. 9

83 IT 'Inside Politics' 5 Nov. 1966, p. 8

84 IT 'Inside Politics' 12 Nov. 1966, p. 10

85 DDA; Communications 40; DPO Trinity Ban 1967.

86 IT 'Lent' 6 Feb. 1967, p. 9.

87 SI 'Reason for the ban on Catholics going to Trinity College' 12 Feb. 1967, p. 8.

88 IT 'Lent – II' 13 Feb. 1967, p. 9. The ban was finally lifted in June 1970. See IT 'Be Thankful' 26 June 1970, p. 11.

89 DDA; Communications 43; DPO Apr.–June 1968.

90 Ibid., McQuaid to Dowling, 28 June 1968.

91 Ibid., press clippings.

92 IT 'Where do we stand?' 26 Feb. 1968, p. 11.

93 IT 'The war of morality' 14 Feb. 1968, p. 11.

94 IT 'Danger year' 11 Jan. 1968, p. 11.

95 IT 'Neverend' 8 Mar. 1968, p. 11.

96 IT 'Alternative' 9 Mar. 1968, p. 11.

97 DE; vol. 235, col. 1858 (June 1968).

98 IT 'Duty' 16 Oct. 1968, p. 13.

99 IT 'Rebuke' 18 Oct. 1968, p. 11.

1 IT 'And the next' 18 June 1969, p. 11.

CHAPTER 9
'Have Your Cake and Eat I.T.'

1 PRO; FCO 33/768/1 – Gilchrist to W.K.K. White, 2 Oct. 1969,

2 IT 'Not an inch' 4 Oct. 1968, p. 11.

3 IT 'Baton or ballot' 7 Oct. 1968, p. 11.

4 IT 'An old city faces a new sorrow' 7 Oct. 1968, p. 1.

5 IT 'Baton or ballot' 7 Oct. 1968, p. 11.

6 IT 'Major blunder' 3 Jan. 1969, p. 9.

7 IT 'Throw-Back' 6 Jan. 1969, p. 13.

8 IT 'Nearly to midnight' 23 Apr. 1969, p. 11.

9 IT 'Minus one' 9 July 1969, p. 9.

10 IT 'The Twelfth and after' 14 July 1969, p. 11.

11 IT 'The Major's visit' 9 Aug. 1969, p. 9.

12 IT 'Time and the north' 16 Aug. 1969, p. 11.

13 Interview of Gageby by John Bowman on RTÉ radio 1974.

14 Interview with Brian Fallon, 10 Oct. 2006.

15 PRO; FCO 33/767 – Gregson to V. Hartles, 16 Sept. 1969.

16 PRO; FCO 33/768/1 – Gilchrist to White, 2 Oct. 1969.

17 CRO; IT Ltd, annual report, y/e Dec. 1969.

18 PRO; FCO 33/769 – Gilchrist to White,
    15 Oct. 1969.

19 PRO; WRR3/548/9 – White to V. Hartles,
    16 Oct. 1969.

20 PRO; WRR3/548/3 – White to Gilchrist,
    7 Nov. 1969.

21 PRO; WRR3/548/3 – White to Gilchrist,
    22 Dec. 1969.

22 See Chapter 12.

23 Interview with Brian Fallon, 10 Oct. 2006.

24 Interview with Dennis Kennedy, 4 July
    2007.

25 *Sunday Times*; 'The Major in need of a
    new strategy' 18 Nov. 2001.

26 IT 'In the Dail' 21 Oct. 1969, p. 9.

27 DE vol. 241, col.1412, Oct. 1969.

28 DE vol. 241, col.1570–1, Oct. 1969.

29 IT 'Force against NI not ruled out by
    government – Blaney' 9 Dec. 1969, p. 1.

30 IT 'Great week for cheek' 13 Dec. 1969,
    p. 12.

31 IT 'The breaking point' 6 May 1970, p. 13.

32 IT 'Review of events in politics' longest
    day' 7 May 1970, p. 6.

33 IT 'Loyalty' 7 May 1970, p. 13.

34 IT 'Come clean' 9 May 1970, p. 11

35 IT 'Unionist style' 30 Oct. 1970, p. 13.

36 IT 'Political fervour stopped just short of
    mass hysteria' 22 Feb. 1971, p. 1.

37 Interview with James Downey, 11 Apr. 2007.

38 IT 'Mr Lynch' 6 Dec. 1979, p. 13.

39 Interview with Gageby on RTÉ's 'Seven
    Days' *c.*1972.

40 IT 'In blood stept in so far' 31 Jan. 1972,
    p. 11.

41 IT 'A new chapter' 24 Mar. 1972, p. 11.

42 IT 'Attack on the *Irish Times* policy'
    7 Mar. 1972, p. 8.

43 Interview of Gageby by John Bowman on
    RTÉ radio 1974.

44 IT 'Till the pips squeak' 20 Nov. 1973,
    p. 13.

45 IT 'The real freedom' 22 Nov. 1973, p. 13.

46 IT 'Stand and run' 22 May 1974, p. 11.

47 O'Clery, C. (2006) 'The task master', pp
    103–4. See IT 28 May 1974, p. 1.

48 IT 'The Loyalist day' 24 May 1974, p. 13.

49 IT 'Wilson the wrecker?' 27 May 1974,
    p. 11.

50 Interview with Brian Fallon, 10 Oct. 2006.

51 Downey, J. (1983) *Them and us*, p. 84.

52 Gillespie, E. (ed.) (2003) *Changing the
    Times,* p. 247.

53 See McCafferty, N. (1981) *In the Eyes of
    the Law*.

54 IT 'Women seek real equality' 15 Apr.
    1971, p. 1.

55 IT 'Customs officers at Dublin rail station
    knew what hit them!' 24 May 1971, p. 13.

56 IT 'Ireland's place' 10 May 1972, p. 11

57 IT 'Two "Yes" votes' 7 Dec. 1972, p. 13.

58 IT 'New weekly journal' 14 Apr. 1973, p. 1.

59 IT 'Introducing our all-woman cabinet'
    14 Feb. 1973, p. 6.

60 IT 'The 16 women candidates' 26 Feb.
    1973, p. 12.

61 IT 'But what about us?' 7 Feb. 1973, p. 6.
    & 'The politicians reply' 27 & 28 Feb.
    1973, p. 6.

62 IT 'Disputes in Dublin newspapers
    continue' 14/15 Mar. 1973, p. 1.

63 Interview with Gerry Mulvey, 31 Jan. 2006.

64 IT 'The Irish Times Ltd and the newspaper
    disputes' 14/15 Mar. 1973, p. 1.

65 CRO; IT Ltd, annual report, y/e Dec. 1969.

66 CRO; IT Ltd, annual report, y/e Jan. 1971.

67 CRO; IT Ltd, annual report, y/e Dec. 1972.

68 The 380,000 preference shares were
    composed of 275,000 5¹/2% £1 preference
    shares and 105,000 6¹/2% £1 preference
    shares.

69 IT 'An Irishman's Diary' 18 Dec. 1975, p. 9.

70 CRO; IT Ltd, shareholders' register, Jan.
    1971.

71 CRO; IT Ltd, annual report, y/e Jan. 1972.

72 IT '£50,000 new capital for *Irish Times*'
    30 May 1972, p. 12.

73 IT '*Irish Times* rights issue approved'
    11 July 1972, p. 14.

74 CRO; IT Ltd, allotment of shares,
    Aug. 1972.

75 CRO; IT Ltd, annual report, y/e Dec.
    1972. See also IT 'Irish Times Ltd'
    15 April 1973, p. 15.

76 Letter from board to shareholders, 6 Apr.
    1973.

77 CRO; IT Ltd, shareholders' register, July
    1974.

78 IT '77% jump in profits of Irish Times
    Ltd' 1 May 1974, p. 14.

79 IT 'The *Irish Times* now a trust' 5 Apr.
    1974, p. 1.

80 IT 'New every morning' 5 Apr. 1974, p. 11.

81 Investment Bank of Ireland purchase
    document, 30 Apr. 1974.

82 Ambrose, W. (1974) 'Independent *Irish
    Times*', B&F, 10:29, 6.

83 Interview with Gerry Mulvey, 31 Jan. 2006.
84 Interview with James Downey, 11 Apr. 2007.
85 Interview with Mary Maher, 18 July 2007.
86 Interview with Paul Gillespie, 6 June 2007.
87 Correspondence with Dennis Kennedy, 4 July 2007.
88 IT '£2m *Irish Times* deal analysed' 5 Apr. 1974, p. 14.
89 Ambrose, W. (1974) 'Independent *Irish Times*'. B&F, 10:29, 6.
90 SI; 'Have your cake and eat I.T.' 7 Apr. 1974, p. 9.
91 IT '£2m *Irish Times* deal analysed' 5 Apr. 1974, p. 14.
92 Interview of Gageby by John Bowman on RTÉ radio 1974.
93 Interview with Don Reid, 28 Sept. 2007.
94 Interview with Louis O'Neill, 21 Sept. 2007.
95 CRO; IT Ltd, AoA, article 27
96 IT '£2m *Irish Times* deal analysed' 5 Apr. 1974, p. 14.
97 Whittaker, A. (2006) 'The Bank of Ireland and the *Irish Times*', p. 176.
98 CRO; IT Holdings, AoA, article 3.
99 CRO; IT Ltd, EGM special resolution, 2 July 1974.
1 Interview with Don Reid, 28 Sept. 2007.
2 CRO; IT Foundation, AoA, article 38.
3 CRO; IT Trust Ltd, memorandum of association, article 2.d.ii.a.
4 Ibid., article 2.d.ii b 1–5
5 Ibid., article 2.d.ii c 1–3
6 Kearney, R. & Moran, D. (1984) 'Public responsibility and the Press', *Crane Bag*, 8:2, 16 of 13–23.
7 CRO; IT Trust, AoA, article 43
8 Ibid., article 36
9 Ibid., article 52
10 Ibid., article 60
11 Ibid., article 45
12 CRO; IT Ltd, AoA, article 49.ii & 49.i.
13 Ibid., article 60
14 Ibid., article 51
15 Ibid., article 78
16 Ibid., article 79
17 Interview with Don Reid, 28 Sept. 2007. The ten original governors of the trust were Major McDowell, chairman of Irish Times Ltd, Thekla Beere, former secretary of the department of transport and power, William Blease, Northern Ireland officer, ICTU, John Healy, journalist, James Meehan, professor of political economy, UCD, Donal Nevin, assistant general secretary, ICTU, Peter O'Hara, group financial director, Brooks Watson Group Ltd, James Walmsley, chairman, Eason and Son, Jacob Weingreen, professor of Hebrew, TCD, and Richard Wood, chairman of John A. Wood Ltd. Interestingly, in September 1974, Donal Carroll, a director of the Bank of Ireland was appointed a trustee. For detailed biographies of the trustees see IT 'The Irish Times Trust' 19 Sept. 1986, p. 5.
18 CRO; IT Ltd, AoA, article 50.
19 Interview with Paul Gillespie, 6 June 2007.
20 IT 'Prolific author who started in *Irish Times*' 6 Nov. 2004, p. 12.
21 Interview with Louis O'Neill, 21 Sept. 2007.

CHAPTER 10
Troublesome Times

1 IT 'Gardai using North-style brutality in interrogation techniques' 14 Feb. 1977, p. 1.
2 Correspondence with Dennis Kennedy, 4 July 2007.
3 Interview with Mary Maher, 18 July 2007.
4 Interview with James Downey, 11 Apr. 2007.
5 Correspondence with Dennis Kennedy, 4 July 2007.
6 Ibid.
7 Interview with Mary Maher, 18 July 2007.
8 Interview with Renagh Holohan, 11 Apr. 2007.
9 Correspondence with Dennis Kennedy, 4 July 2007.
10 Interview with Mary Maher, 18 July 2007.
11 Interview with Gerry Mulvey, 31 Jan. 2006.
12 Interview with Brian Fallon, 10 Oct. 2006.
13 Hunter, R. (1974) 'The newspaper industry', B&F, 10:46, 10 of 10–12.
14 IT 'A new type-face for the *Irish Times* today' 3 Nov. 1975, p. 1.
15 IT 'Net sales of the *Irish Times*' 28 Feb. 1976, p. 1.
16 IT 'Net sales of the *Irish Times*' 18 Feb. 1977, p. 1.
17 IT 'Irish Times planning 10% cut in costs' 6 May 1977, p. 1.
18 IT 'The Irish Times Limited' 2 Mar. 1977, p. 1.

19 Whittaker, A. (2006) 'The Bank of Ireland and the *Irish Times*', pp 171–7.

20 IT '*Irish Times* planning 10% cut in costs' 6 May 1977, p. 1.

21 Interview with Louis O'Neill, 21 Sept. 2007.

22 Interview with Don Reid, 28 Sept. 2007.

23 IT '*Irish Times* planning 10% cut in costs' 6 May 1977, p. 1.

24 IT 'Cabinet may urge easier sentence' 11 June 1976, pp 1 & 13.

25 IT 'High court ruling on *Irish Times* case' 6 July 1976, p. 11.

26 Kerrigan, G. (1979) 'The life and *Irish Times* of Douglas Gageby', *Magill*, 3:3, 28 of 14–32.

27 IT 'High court ruling on *Irish Times* case' 6 July 1976, p. 11.

28 Interview with James Downey, 11 Apr. 2007.

29 Interview with Andrew Whittaker, 27 Apr. 2007.

30 Interview with Gerry Mulvey, 31 Jan. 2006.

31 See SI 'Keating is challenged on Bula Mine deal' 6 Feb. 1977, pp 1&8.

32 DE; vol. 297, col. 934–5, (Mar. 1977).

33 Correspondence with Richard Keatinge, 7 July 2007.

34 IT 'Gardai using North-style brutality in interrogation techniques' 14 Feb. 1977, p. 1.

35 IT 'The Law' 14 Feb. 1977, p. 9.

36 See IT 'News Focus' 15 & 16 Feb. 1977, p. 10.

37 IT 'No Garda interrogation squad exists – Cooney' 18 Feb. 1977, p. 1.

38 IT 'Questions unanswered' 18 Feb. 1977, p. 9.

39 IT 'Only one side of story, says Cooney' 19 Feb. 1977, p. 5.

40 IT 'The Saturday Column' 19 Feb. 1977, p. 10.

41 IT 'Traditional hostility alleged' 19 Feb. 1977, p. 5.

42 DE: vol. 296, col. 1770 (Feb. 1977).

43 IT 'Investigation "a job the politicians should have been doing" says Devlin' 15 Feb. 1977, p. 7.

44 Interview with James Downey, 11 Apr. 2007.

45 Interview with Gerry Mulvey, 31 Jan. 2006.

46 Interview with Renagh Holohan, 11 Apr. 2007.

47 Brady, C. (2005) *Up with the Times* p. 168.

48 IT 'Dynamic, tough and idealistic' 28 June 2004, p. 4.

49 O'Leary, O. (2006) 'Mr Gageby's republic', p. 47.

50 IT 'Fergus Pyle' 14 Apr. 1997, p. 6.

51 IT 'Wrong fingerprint circulated as assassin's' 1 Mar. 1977, p. 1.

52 IT 'Gardai said to have falsified evidence' 2 Mar. 1977, p. 1.

53 IT 'Gardai holding prints inquiry' 5 Mar. 1977, p. 1.

54 IT 'What must be done' 5 Mar. 1977, p. 9.

55 The first 'Weekend' section was published on 18 June 1977.

56 IT '*Irish Times* made profit of £306,000 last year' 7 Mar. 1978, p. 12.

57 Interview with Paul Gillespie, 6 June 2007.

58 Correspondence with Mary Maher 18 July 2007.

59 IT 'New editor of the Irish Times' 1 July 1977, p. 1.

60 Correspondence with Dennis Kennedy, 4 July 2007.

61 IT 'Fergus Pyle' 14 Apr. 1997, p. 6.

62 Interview with Renagh Holohan, 11 Apr. 2007.

63 Kerrigan, G. (1979) 'The life and *Irish Times* of Douglas Gageby', *Magill*, 3:3, 32 of 14–32.

64 IT '77,316' 26 Jan. 1980, p. 1.

65 IT '*Irish Times* made profit of £306,000 last year' 7 Mar. 1978, p. 12.

66 IT 'Joy' 1 Oct. 1979, p. 21.

67 O'Leary, O. (2006) 'Mr Gageby's republic', p. 47.

68 Tobin, M. (1984) 'Irish newspapers'. B&F, 21:2, 34 of 34–35.

69 Downey, J. (2006) 'Irish Catholics' favourite Protestant editor', p. 28.

70 House Agreement between NUJ & Irish Times Ltd 1980.

71 IT '84,408' 22 Feb. 1984, p. 1.

72 Kerrigan, G. (1984) 'Douglas Gageby and the *Irish Times*', *Magill*, 8:8, 34–9.

73 O'Dea, T. (1984) 'The Great Khan of Cortoon', *Magill*, 7:10, 32 of 24–33.

74 IT 'John "Backbencher" Healy' 7 Jan. 1991, p. 4.

75 Kilfeather, F. (1997) *Changing Times*, p. 44

76 IT 'Great start to the coursing season' 5 Feb. 1983, p. 8.

77 IT 'Mr Haughey' 8 Dec. 1979, p. 17.

78 IT 'To Work' 10 Mar. 1982, p. 11.

79 IT 'Loyalty chief test in Fianna Fáil' 20 Sept. 1982, p. 15.
80 Tansey, P. (2006) 'Mapping a new prosperity', p. 138.
81 IT 'Voters' Day' 18 Feb. 1983, p. 11.
82 Myers, K. (2006) 'By that sin fell the angels', pp 119–21.
83 Correspondence with Frank McDonald, 20 Sept. 2007.
84 IT 'Attempts to transfer Garda sergeant fails' 28 Oct. 1982, p. 8.
85 Joyce, J. & Murtagh, P. (1983) *The Boss*, pp 268–74.
86 IT 'Gardai, RUC in contact before arrest' 28 Oct. 1982, p. 6.
87 IT 'Journalists' Telephones were tapped' 18 Dec. 1982, p. 1. Both journalists later received damages from the state for this breach of their privacy.
88 IT 'Listening in' 20 Dec. 1982, p. 11.
89 IT 'Retribution' 21 Jan. 1983, p. 9.
90 IT 'In his own time' 28 Jan. 1983, p. 9.
91 IT 'Better now' 3 Feb. 1983, p. 9.
92 IT 'Parties choke on halo policies' 7 Feb. 1983, p. 11.
93 IT 'Section 4: use and abuse in Dublin' 17 Oct. 1983, p. 6.
94 IT '*Irish Times* attacked on Section 4 report' 22 Oct. 1983, p. 7.
95 IT 'The theological constitution' 3 Sept. 1983, p. 8.
96 IT 'Reinforcing unity' 14 Jan. 1983, p. 9 & 'Puzzle' 1 Feb. 1983, p. 9.
97 IT 'In the national interest' 9 Feb. 1983, p. 11.
98 IT 'The second partitioning of Ireland' 30 Aug. 1983, p. 9.
99 IT 'The theological constitution' 3 Sept. 1983, p. 8.
1 IT 'Today's Vote' 7 Sept. 1983, p. 9.
2 IT 'The North does care' 31 May 1986, p. 23.
3 IT 'Growing up beyond 1690 and 1937' 9 June 1986, p. 11.
4 IT 'With a clear conscience' 12 June 1986, p. 11.
5 IT 'A thought for others' 16 June 1986, p. 11.
6 IT 'The generous way' 26 June 1986, p. 11.
7 IT 'Sellout' 18 Nov. 1985, p. 13.
8 IT 'Taylor criticises EEC's Belfast appointment' 10 July 1985, p. 1.
9 IT 'Irish Times buys new press' 13 Mar. 1985, p. 12.

10 Interview with Louis O'Neill, 21 Sept. 2007.
11 CRO; Dowell Ltd, annual reports.
12 Gageby's company was called Fetchfer (Unlimited) and later Quarterland (Unlimited).
13 CRO; Rossdohan Ltd and Derdiu Ltd, annual returns.
14 CRO; Irish Times Holdings, memorandum of association, special resolution, 18 Feb. 1985.
15 CRO; Irish Times Holdings, annual returns 1987 & 1988.
16 Interview with Louis O'Neill, 21 Sept. 2007.
17 Brady, *Up with the Times*, p. 56.
18 Interview with Brian Fallon, 10 Oct. 2006.
19 Interview with Paul Gillespie, 6 June 2007.

CHAPTER 11
Changing Times

1 Interview with Conor Brady, 18 July 2007.
2 Brady, C. (2005) *Up with the Times*, p. 49.
3 IT 'New editor of the *Irish Times*' 16 Dec. 1986, p. 1.
4 Interview with Renagh Holohan, 11 Apr. 2007.
5 Brady, *Up with the Times*, p. 58.
6 Interview with Mary Maher, 18 July 2007.
7 Brady, *Up with the Times*, p. 58.
8 Interview with Paul Gillespie, 6 June 2007.
9 Brady, *Up with the Times*, p. 59.
10 CRO; IT Ltd, AoA, article 49 (1).
11 Ibid., article 34.
12 CRO; IT Trust Ltd, AoA, articles 2, 6, 21, 37, & 52.
13 Interview with Don Reid, 28 Sept. 2007.
14 IT 'IT reports £1.7m profit on £27m turnover' 22 Sept. 1989, p. 16.
15 IT 'IT turns in £3.6m profit on £32m Turnover' 22 Nov. 1990, p14; and IT 'IT announces marginal profit increase' 21 June 1991, p. 14.
16 Interview with Conor Brady, 18 July 2007.
17 See Martin, S. (2008) *Good Times and bad*, pp 189–209.
18 Brady, *Up with the Times*, p. 69.
19 Interview with Conor Brady, 18 July 2007.
20 Brady, *Up with the Times*, pp 90–2.
21 Ibid., p. 100.
22 *Phoenix* 'Goldhawk's criminal libel case' 23 May 2003, p. 40. See also *Phoenix* 'Stephen Hilliard: setting the record straight' 18 Oct. 1991, p. 16.

23 Brady, *Up with the Times*, p. 191.

24 SI 'A moral time for the old dowager' 12 May 1991, p. 9.

25 Keena, C. (2003) *The Ansbacher conspiracy*, pp 177–8.

26 IT 'Cayman Islands banker linked to £1.1m account' 14 Dec. 1996, p. 1.

27 Brady, *Up with the Times*, p. 188.

28 SBP 'CRH rapped by inspectors' 7 July 2002, p. 13.

29 IT 'Planners shell-shocked by scale and rapidity of rezoning decisions' 31 May 1993, p. 6.

30 IT 'Greens challenge Ahern on payments' 23 Feb. 2006, p. 23.

31 Correspondence with Frank McDonald, 20 Sept. 2007. See IT 'The rezoning scandal' 27 Sept.–28 Oct. 1982.

32 IT 'Letters to the Editor' 30 Oct. 1982, p. 17.

33 IT 'Cash in brown paper bags for councillors' 12 July 1993, p. 1.

34 IT 'Call for immunity from prosecution to facilitate rezoning inquiry' 14 July 1993, p. 7.

35 IT 'Bruton calls for inquiry into rezoning' 17 July 1993, p. 3.

36 Correspondence with Frank McDonald, 20 Sept. 2007.

37 IT 'Lawyers who prompted planning inquiry seek costs', 22 July 2005, p. 7.

38 Brady, *Up with the Times*, p. 198 & p. 188.

39 Ibid., p. 84.

40 Ibid., p. 82.

41 Ibid., p. 85.

42 IT 'The fantasy at the hearth of the consensus on the north' 7 Jan. 1993, p. 10.

43 Kennedy, D. (2005) 'Kingdom of the Bland', *Magill*, Nov. 2005, 52–3.

44 IT 'An Irishman's Diary' 14 Jan. 2005, p. 17.

45 Ibid., 15 Apr. 1998, p. 13.

46 Interview with Conor Brady, 18 July 2007.

47 Brady, *Up with the Times*, pp 86–7.

48 Interview with Conor Brady, 18 July 2007.

49 IT 'Get out and vote' 22 May 1998, p. 5.

50 Interview with Mary Maher, 18 July 2007.

51 Brady, *Up with the Times*, p. 123.

52 IT 'Hesitant candidate who restored some sense of stability' 27 Sept. 1990, p. 10.

53 Lenihan, B. (1991) *For the record*, p. 124.

54 Ibid., p. 143.

55 Ibid., p. 125.

56 O'Reilly, E. (1991) *Candidate*, p. 110.

57 IT 'Lenihan did make call to president he now denies' 24 Oct. 1990, p. 1.

58 Lenihan, *For the record*, p. 134.

59 Interview with Conor Brady, 18 July 2007.

60 Ibid. See also Dick Walsh's account in IT 'One more time just for the record' 11 May 1991, p. 10.

61 IT 'Choosing between two Irelands' 6 Nov. 1990, p. 13.

62 Lenihan, *For the record*, pp 205–6.

63 Interview with Conor Brady, 18 July 2007.

64 Lenihan, *For the record*, p. 212.

65 Interview with Conor Brady, 18 July 2007.

66 Ibid.

67 Ibid.

68 Downey, J. (1998) *Lenihan*, p. 167 & p. 174.

69 Duffy, J. (2006) 'Taping History', *Magill*, Mar., 20–23.

70 Interview with Conor Brady, 18 July 2007.

71 Ibid.

72 Correspondence with Lorna Siggins, 5 Sept. 2007.

73 Interview with Conor Brady, 18 July 2007.

74 Brady, *Up with the Times*, p. 147.

75 Correspondence with Lorna Siggins, 5 Sept. 2007.

76 Brady, *Up with the Times*, p. 147.

77 Interview with Conor Brady, 18 July 2007.

78 IT 'Dr Casey resigns as Bishop of Galway' 7 May 1992, p. 1.

79 IT 'A bishop resigns' 7 May 1992, p. 11.

80 IT 'An unacceptable silence' 9 May 1992, p. 13.

81 IT 'Dr Casey admits using diocesan funds to pay mother of his son' 12 May 1992, p. 1.

82 Correspondence with Andy Pollak, 6 Sept. 2007.

83 Interview with Conor Brady, 18 July 2007.

84 Turner, M. (2004) *Martyn Turner's greatest hits*, p. 2.

85 Interview with Conor Brady, 18 July 2007.

86 IT 'State attempts to stop girl's abortion', 12 Feb. 1992, p. 1.

87 Brady, *Up with the Times*, p. 159.

88 See IT 31 July 1993, p. 10.

89 IT 'Israeli press criticises cartoon' 17 Aug. 1993, p.6.

90 See IT 23 Nov. 1995, p.16. The minister was Mervyn Taylor, the minister for equality and law reform.

91 Correspondence with Martyn Turner, 12 Mar. 2008 & interview with Conor Brady 18 July 2007.

92 IT 'Descent into cruelty' 18 Feb. 1992, p. 13.

93 Brady, *Up with the Times*, p. 163

94 Ibid., pp 162–3.

95 Ibid., p. 225.

96 IT 'How a government sailed into a storm over clerical abuse' 23 Aug. 1997, p. 6.

97 IT 'Reynolds says Ahern withheld file on Smyth case' 10 Mar. 2007, p. 11.

98 IT 'Reynolds asked Whelehan to resign before endorsing him' 5 Dec. 1994, p. 1.

99 IT 'Paper, online editions grow together' 19 Mar. 2000, p. 21.

 1 Hubert, T. (2000) 'ireland.com – The *Irish Times*' unpublished DCU BAJ project.

 2 IT 'Logging on at the top of the world' 29 Aug. 1994, p. 17.

 3 IT 'IT website audited as having 396,000 users in month' 10 Feb. 1998, p. 9.

 4 IT 'IT website busiest, figures show' 24 Nov. 1998, p. 9.

 5 Hubert, 'ireland.com – The *Irish Times*'

 6 Interview with Conor Brady, 18 July 2007.

 7 IT '95,310' 26 Aug. 1995, p. 1.

 8 Interview with Louis O'Neill, 21 Sept. 2007.

 9 Interview with Mary Maher, 18 July 2007.

10 Interview with Paul Gillespie, 6 June 2007.

11 Interview with Conor Brady, 18 July 2007.

CHAPTER 12
Madam Editor

 1 Interview with Conor Brady, 18 July 2007.

 2 Interview with Don Reid, 28 Sept. 2007.

 3 Brady, C. (2005) *Up with the Times*, pp 182–4.

 4 Interview with Louis O'Neill, 21 Sept. 2007.

 5 Correspondence with Dennis Kennedy, 4 July 2007.

 6 Interview with Mary Maher, 18 July 2007.

 7 SBP '*Irish Times* staff object' 4 Dec. 1994, p. 9.

 8 Interview with Mary Maher, 18 July 2007.

 9 CRO; IT Trust Ltd, memorandum of association, article 2.d.ii.a.

10 Brady, *Up with the Times*, p. 184.

11 IT 'A dilemma for Labour' 23 Nov. 1994, p. 13.

12 IT 'Letters to the Editor' 29 Nov. 1994, p. 13.

13 Ibid.

14 Correspondence with Mary Maher, 18 July 2007.

15 Brady, *Up with the Times*, p. 186.

16 Interview with Louis O'Neill, 21 Sept. 2007.

17 Interview with Conor Brady, 18 July 2007.

18 Ibid.

19 Correspondence with Mary Maher, 18 July 2007.

20 Brady, *Up with the Times*, p. 221.

21 *Phoenix* 'Good Times and Bad' 30 Jan. 1998, p. 8.

22 Interview with Don Reid, 28 Sept. 2007.

23 SBP 'Profile: mutinous talk, but major stays on the bridge' 27 June 1999, p. 10.

24 IT 'IT to buy new colour printing press' 24 Jan. 2000, p. 16.

25 IT 'The IT in deal with printers' 1 Dec. 1999, p. 23.

26 O'Halloran, B. (2000) 'The *Irish Times*'. B&F, 36:49, 22 of 20–4.

27 Brady, *Up with the Times*, pp 255–7.

28 Correspondence with Mary Maher, 18 July 2007.

29 Brady, *Up with the Times*, p. 115.

30 Interview with Don Reid, 28 Sept. 2007.

31 Brady, *Up with the Times*, p. 116.

32 CRO; IT Ltd, AoA, resolution dated 22 Dec. 1994.

33 Ibid., resolution dated 23 June 1997.

34 Correspondence with Mary Maher, 18 July 2007.

35 Interview with Conor Brady, 18 July 2007.

36 Brady, *Up with the Times*, p. 118.

37 IT 'The *Irish Times* now a trust' 5 Apr. 1974, p. 1.

38 CRO; IT Ltd, AoA, resolution dated 28 Sept. 1990.

39 Interview with Conor Brady, 18 July 2007.

40 IT 'IT profit rises 51.6%' 11 June 1999, p. 2 (Business).

41 IT 'Rise in turnover helps boost IT pre-tax profits to £3.5m' 8 June 1995, p. 14; IT 'Annual pre-tax profit rises 51.1% to £5.4m at IT Trust' 14 June 1997, p. 17; IT 'Pre-tax profit up 70% at *Irish Times*' 12 June 1998, p. 51; IT 'IT profit rises 51.6%' 11 June 1999, p. 2 (Business).

42 CRO; IT Trust, memorandum of association 2.d.

43 Ibid., 2 a, b & c.

44 See O'Halloran, B. (2000) 'The *Irish Times*'. B&F, 36:49, 20–4.

45 Interview with Conor Brady, 18 July 2007.

46 Interview with Don Reid, 28 Sept. 2007.

47 Interview with Conor Brady, 18 July 2007.

48 Interview with Don Reid, 28 Sept. 2007.

49 *Phoenix* 'The Irish Times in mourning' 28 Sept. 2001, p. 9.

50 Interview with Renagh Holohan, 11 Apr. 2007.

51 SBP 'Restructuring cost Irish Times €21m' 16 Aug. 2001, p. 51.

52 SBP 'Worst of times for the Times' 11 Nov. 2001, p. 11.

53 Correspondence with Mary Maher, 18 July 2007.

54 IT 'Doomsday predictions not needed' 19 Nov. 2001, p. 8.

55 IT 'Structure of Irish Times to undergo change' 21 Dec. 2001, p. 7.

56 IT 'Keane says he will quit Ireland after world cup' 23 May 2002, pp 1, 22 & 23.

57 Phoenix 'Humphries quits over Smith' 14 Mar. 1997, p. 8.

58 Interview with Geraldine Kennedy, 15 Oct. 2007.

59 SBP 'New pay disclosures as row engulfs Irish Times' 16 Nov. 2003, p. 1.

60 SBP 'Irish Times columnist lambasts paper's self-censorship' 16 Nov. 2003, p. 13.

61 Ibid.

62 IT 'NUJ and columnist to meet Irish Times editor over dismissal' 24 Nov. 2003, p. 5.

63 IT 'Irish Times reveals details of directors' pay' 26 Nov. 2003, p. 8.

64 Interview with Ronan Fanning, 3 Apr. 2007.

65 IT 'McDowell prepared to act as link' 3 Jan. 2000, p. 8.

66 IPR 'The Archive; Letter of British Ambassador to Dublin, A.G. Gilchrist 2.10.1969' Jan. 2003.

67 SI 'Irish Times' McDowell called his editor a white nigger' 26 Jan. 2003, p. 1.

68 IT 'Major McDowell rejects UK envoy's claim' 27 Jan. 2003, p. 5.

69 SI 'Conor mounts his high horse and charges in' 2 May 2004, p. 20.

70 SI 'White nigger denial poses a real dilemma' 2 Feb. 2003, p. 8.

71 IT 'Letters to the Editor' 23 Apr. 2004, p. 19.

72 Ibid., 29 Apr. 2004, p. 17.

73 Interview with Conor Brady, 18 July 2007.

74 Interview with Andrew Whittaker, 27 Apr. 2007.

75 IT 'Haughey seen as "shrewd, ruthless"' 3 Jan. 2003, p. 6. See also O'Halpin, E. (2006) Intelligence and Anglo-Irish relations.

76 IT 'An Irishman's Diary' 8 Feb. 2005, p. 17.

77 Quoted in Village 'Crisis in the Times' 12–18 Feb. 2005, 16 of pp 14–17.

78 IT 'Letters to the Editor' 10 Feb. 2005, p. 17.

79 IT 'Media of Myersspeak' 12 Feb. 2005, p. 2 (Weekend).

80 Interview with Geraldine Kennedy, 15 Oct. 2007.

81 IT 'An Irishman's Diary' 10 Feb. 2005, p. 17.

82 IT 'Regret for the offence caused' 10 Feb. 2005, p. 17.

83 IT 'Why I chose to publish Kevin Myers' Irishman's Diary' 12 Feb. 2005, p. 13.

84 IT 'Irish Times returns to profitability in 2003' 9 July 2004, p. 2 (Business).

85 IT 'Irish Times doubles profits to €15.3m' 15 July 2005, p. 2 (Business).

86 SI 'Irish Times staff revolt at editor and directors' indefensible salaries' 7 Aug. 2005, p. 3.

87 ST 'Dispute at Irish Times getting "hot and heavy" 5 Dec. 2004, p. 4 (Business).

88 Interview with Geraldine Kennedy, 15 Oct. 2007.

89 Ibid.

90 IT 'Pre-tax profits of €14.1m for Irish Times Ltd' 27 Oct. 2006, p. 2 (Finance).

91 IT 'Irish Times Ltd reports 25% rise in operating profits to €22.7m' 13 July 2007, p. 3 (Finance).

92 IT 'Tribunal examines payments to Taoiseach' 21 Sept. 2006, p. 1.

93 IT 'Tribunal to state action over leak next week' 30 Sept. 2007, p. 8

94 IT 'An error of judgment' 28 Sept. 2006, p. 21.

95 IT 'Pressure on Ahern builds as PDs seek more details' 29 Sept. 2006, p. 1.

96 IT 'A poor reflection of ourselves' 13 Oct. 2006, p. 19.

97 IT 'Newspaper's duty was to publish story, says editor' 30 Sept. 2006, p. 8.

98 Ibid.

99 IT 'Keena refuses to identify source of leak' 30 Sept. 2006, p. 8.

1 IT 'Judges agree report in public's interest' 13 July 2007, p. 4

2 Interview with Geraldine Kennedy, 15 Oct. 2007.

3 IT 'Irish Times is told to face tribunal on source' 24 Oct. 2007, p. 8.

4 Interview with Geraldine Kennedy, 15 Oct. 2007.

5 Ibid.

6 See Browne, H. (2006) 'The Irish Times', The Dubliner, May, 39–47.

7 Interview with Geraldine Kennedy, 15 Oct. 2007.

8 Ibid.

Bibliography

PRIMARY SOURCES

Interviews /
Correspondents
Conor Brady, James Downey, Brian Fallon, Ronan Fanning, Paul Gillespie, Renagh Holohan, Richard Keatinge, Dennis Kennedy, Geraldine Kennedy, Mary Maher, Frank McDonald, Gerry Mulvey, Louis O'Neill, Cathal O'Shannon, Andy Pollak, Don Reid, Lorna Siggins, Andrew Whittaker

National Library
Arnott, J. (1886) An Alternative Policy for Ireland. Dublin
Arnott, J. (1886) Second Letter on an Alternative Policy for Ireland. Cork
The Ruhleben Irish Players: First AGM, 1916: Hon. Secretary's Report

National Archives
Dept of Justice: Office of Controller of Censorship files
Dept of Taoiseach files

Military Archives
Office of Controller of Censorship files

Dublin Diocesan
Archives
John Charles McQuaid Papers

UCD Archives
Patrick Barry Moloney Papers

DCU Library
Douglas Gageby Papers

Companies
Registration Office
Irish Times Ltd; Irish Times Holdings Ltd; Irish Times Foundation Ltd; Irish Times Trust Ltd; Dowell Ltd; Derdiu Ltd; Rossdohan Ltd; Mail Publications Ltd

Government
Publications
Oireachtas Debates available at www.oireachtas.ie

Periodicals   Business and Finance, Catholic Bulletin, Evening Mail, Foreign Affairs, Irish Independent, Irish Pictorial, Irish Political Review, Irish Press, Irish Times, Magill, Studia Hibernia, Sunday Independent, Sunday Business Post, Sunday Review, Sunday Times, Sunday Tribune, The Bell, The Dubliner, The Leader, The Phoenix, The Standard, The Times, The Word, Village.

Other Sources   Interview by John Bowman of Douglas Gageby on RTÉ Radio 1974
Interview of Douglas Gageby on RTE's *Seven Ages, c.*1972
Author's interview of Douglas Gageby, 11 Aug. 1998

SECONDARY SOURCES: BOOKS AND ARTICLES

Ambrose, W. (1974) 'Independent Irish Times', *Business and Finance*, 10:29, 6.

Andrews, C.S. (1982) *Man of no property*. Dublin, Mercier Press.

Anon. (1941) 'Meet R.M. Smyllie', *The Bell*, 3:3, 180–188.

Anon. (1952) 'Profile: Mr Robert M. Smyllie', *The Leader*, 52:11, 21–2.

Anon. (1974) 'Inside Back', *Business and Finance*, 10:42, 36.

Bowyer Bell, J. (1969) 'Ireland and the Spanish Civil War, 1936–39', *Studia Hibernia*, 9, 137–163.

Bowen, K. (1983) *Protestants in a Catholic state*. Dublin, Gill & Macmillan.

Brady, C. (2005) *Up with the Times*. Dublin, Gill & Macmillan.

Brady, C. (2005) 'Defending Fergus Pyle', *Village*, 19–25 August, 25.

Browne, H. (2006) 'The *Irish Times*', *The Dubliner*, May, 39–47.

Browne, N. (1986) *Against the tide*. Dublin, Gill & Macmillan.

Browne, S. (1937) *The press in Ireland: a survey and a guide*. Dublin, Browne and Nolan.

Browne, V. (2005) 'Crisis in the *Times*', *Village*, 12–18 February, 14–19.

Browne, V. (2006) 'Undermining the Trust', *Village*, 7–13 December, 17–20.

Bundock, C. (1957) *The National Union of Journalists: a jubilee history, 1907–1957*. Oxford, Oxford University Press.

Butler, H. (1996) *In the Land of Nod*. Dublin, Lilliput Press.

Campbell, P. (1950) *An Irishman's Diary*. London, Cassell and Co.

Campbell, P. (1960) *Come here till I tell you*. London, Hutchinson and Co.

Campbell, P. (1967) *My life and easy times*. London, Anthony Blond Ltd.

Carey, M. (2002) 'Paper cuts and bleeding hearts', *Magill*, January, 14–18.

Coogan, T.P. (2003) *Ireland in the twentieth century*. London, Hutchinson.

Cooney, J. (1999) *John Charles McQuaid: ruler of Catholic Ireland*. Dublin, O'Brien Press.

Costello, P. & Van de Kamp, P. (1987) *Flann O'Brien: an illustrated biography*. London, Bloomsbury.

Cronin, A. (1951) 'The literary pages of the daily press', *The Bell*, 17:4, 5–11.

Cronin, A. (2003) *No laughing matter: the life and times of Flann O'Brien*. Dublin, New Island Books.

Cullen, L.M. (1989) *Eason & Son: a history*. Dublin, Eason & Son Ltd.

Devoy, J. (1929) *Recollections of an Irish rebel*. New York, Chas. P. Young Company.

Downey, J. (1983) *Them & us*. Dublin, Ward River Press.

Downey, J. (1998) *Lenihan: his life and loyalties*. Dublin, New Island Books.

Downey, J. (2006) 'Irish Catholics' favourite Protestant editor' in Whittaker, A. (ed.) *Bright, brilliant days*, pp 21–30.

Duffy, J. (2006) 'Taping history', *Magill*, March, 20–3.

Dunlop, A. (1911) *Fifty years of Irish journalism*. Dublin, Hanna and Neale.

Ellmann, R. (ed.) (1966) *Letters of James Joyce: volumes 2 and 3*. New York, Viking Press.

Fallon, B. (1998) *The age of innocence: Irish culture, 1930–1960*. Dublin, Gill & Macmillan.

Findlater, A. (2001) *Findlaters – the story of a Dublin merchant family, 1774–2001*. Dublin, A&A Farmar.

Fleming, L. (1965) *Head or harp*. London, Barrie and Rockliff.

Foley, D. (2003) *Three villages*. Waterford, Ballylough Books.

Foley, M. (2004) 'Colonialism and journalism in Ireland', *Journalism Studies, 5*:3, 373–85.

Gageby, D. (1979) 'The media, 1945–70' in Lee, J.J. (ed.) *Ireland, 1945–70*. Dublin, Gill & Macmillan, pp 124–35.

Gageby, D. (1999) *The last Secretary General Sean Lester and the League of Nations*. Dublin, Town House and Country House, 1999.

Gaughan, J.A. (1980) *Thomas Johnson, 1872–1963: first leader of the Labour Party in Dáil Éireann*. Dublin, Kingdom Books.

Gaughan, J.A. (1993) *Alfred O'Rahilly. vol. 3: Controversialist; part 2: Catholic apologist*. Dublin, Kingdom Books.

Gaughan, J.A. (ed.) (1996) *Memoirs of Senator Joseph Connolly (1885–1961): a founder of modern Ireland*. Dublin, Irish Academic Press.

Gillespie, E. (ed.) (2003) *Changing the Times: Irish women journalists, 1969–1981*. Dublin, Lilliput Press.

Gray, T. (1991) *Mr Smyllie, Sir*. Dublin, Gill & Macmillan.

Healy, J. (1968) *The death of an Irish town*. Cork, Mercier Press.

Healy, J. (1991) *Healy, reporter: the early years*. Achill, House of Healy.

Hegarty, S. & O'Toole, F. (2006) *The Irish Times book of the 1916 Rising*. Dublin, Gill & Macmillan.

Hogan, T. (1943) 'Myles na Gopaleen', *The Bell, 13*:2, 129–40.

Horgan, J. (2001) *Media in Ireland: a critical history since 1922*. London, Routledge.

Horgan, J. (2006) 'Aggiornamento' in Whittaker, A. (ed.) *Bright, brilliant days*, pp 59–68.

Hubert, T. (2000) 'ireland.com – The *Irish Times*', unpublished DCU BAJ project.

Hunter, R. (1974) 'The newspaper industry: paper thin profits ahead?', *Business and Finance, 10*:46, 10–12 & 27.

Hurley, P. (1966) 'Ireland's newspapers: Douglas Gageby, editor of the Irish Times', *The Word*. June, n.p.

Inglis, B. (1962) *West Briton*. London, Faber and Faber.

Inglis, B. (1990) *Downstart: the autobiography of Brian Inglis*. London, Chatto & Windus.

Irish Times (1917) *The Sinn Féin Rebellion*. Dublin.

Irish Times (1944) *Poems from Ireland*. Dublin.

Irish Times (1950) *The liberal ethic*. Dublin.

Joyce, J. & Murtagh, P. (1983) *The boss*. Dublin, Poolbeg.

Kenna, C. (2003) *The Ansbacher conspiracy*. Dublin, Gill and Macmillan.

Kennedy, D. (2005) 'Kingdom of the bland', *Magill*, Nov, 52–3.

Kenneally, I. (2008) *The paper wall: newspapers and propaganda in Ireland, 1919–1921*, Cork, Collins Press.

Kenny, I. (1987) 'Douglas Gageby' in *In good company: conversations with Irish leaders*. Dublin, Gill and Macmillan, pp 172–94.

Kenny, I. (1994) 'Conor Brady: the *Irish Times*' in *Talking to ourselves: conversations with editors of the Irish news media*. Galway, Kenny's Publishing, pp 263–84.

Kearney, R. & Moran, D. (1984) 'Public responsibility and the Press: Richard Kearney and Dermot Moran talk to Douglas Gageby', *Crane Bag*, 8:2, 13–23.

Kerrigan, G. (1979) 'The life and Irish Times of Douglas Gageby', *Magill*, 3:3, 14–32.

Kerrigan, G. (1984) 'Douglas Gageby and the *Irish Times*', *Magill*, 8:8, 34–9.

Kilfeather, F. (1997) *Changing Times: a life in journalism*. Dublin, Blackwater Press.

Krause, D. (ed.) (1980) *The letters of Sean O'Casey, 1942–1954 (Vol. 2)*. New York, Macmillan.

Krause, D. (ed.) (1992) *The letters of Sean O'Casey, 1959–64 (Vol. 4)*. Washington, Catholic University of America Press.

Lenihan, B. (1991) *For the record*. Dublin, Blackwater Press.

Martin, S. (2008) *Good times and bad*. Cork, Mercier Press.

McCafferty, N. (1981) *In the eyes of the law*. Dublin, Ward River Press.

McCourt, F. (1996) *Angela's ashes*. London, HarperCollins.

McDowell, R.B. (1997) *Crisis and decline: the fate of the Southern Unionists*. Dublin, Lilliput Press.

McGarry, F. (1999) *Irish politics and the Spanish Civil War*. Cork, University Press.

Mercereau, J. (2003) 'Irishness according to one of Ireland's leading newspapers: the *Irish Times*, 1949–2001' in Gonzales, R. (ed) *The representation of Ireland/s: images from outside and from within*. Barcelona, PPU, pp 61–72.

Mercier, V. (1945) 'The *Times* (Irish)', *The Bell*, 9:4, 290–7.

Mikhail, E.H. (ed.) (1977) *W.B. Yeats, interviews and recollections, (vol. 2)*. London, Macmillan.

Moloney, P. (1952) 'A survey of the development of Dublin daily newspapers, 1850–1914'. MA Thesis, UCD.

Myers, K. (2000) *From the Irish Times column 'An Irishman's Diary'*. Dublin, Four Courts Press.

Myers, K. (2006) 'By that sin fell the angels' in Whittaker, A. (ed.) *Bright, brilliant days*, pp 119–26.

Nesbitt, R. (1993) *At Arnotts of Dublin, 1843–1993*. Dublin, A&A Farmar.

O'Brien, M. (2001) *De Valera, Fianna Fáil and the Irish press: the truth in the news?* Dublin, Irish Academic Press.

O'Cleary, C. (2006) 'The task master' in Whittaker, A. (ed.) *Bright, brilliant days*, pp 99–106.

Ó Conaire, B. (1986) *Myles na Gaeilge; lámhleabhar ar shaothar gaeilge Bhriain Ó Nualláin*. Dublin, An Clochomhar Tta.

O'Connor, G. (1988) *Sean O'Casey: a life*. London, Hodder & Stoughton.

O'Donovan, D. (1998) *Little old man cut short*. Bray, Kestrel Books.

O'Dea, T. (1984) 'The Great Khan of Cortoon', *Magill*, 7:10, 24–33.

O'Drisceoil, D. (1996) *Censorship in Ireland, 1939–1945: neutrality, politics and society*. Cork, Cork University Press.

O'Halloran, B. (2000) 'The *Irish Times*: where charity stays at home'. *Business and Finance*, 36:49, 20–4.

O'Halpin, E. (2006) 'Intelligence and Anglo-Irish relations, 1922–73' in O'Halpin, E., Armstrong, R. & Ohlmeyer, J. (eds) *Intelligence, statecraft and international power*. Dublin, Irish Academic Press, pp 135–50.

O'hEithir, B. (1986) *The begrudger's guide to Irish politics*. Dublin, Poolbeg.

O'Hegarty, P.S. (1998) *The victory of Sinn Féin*. Dublin, UCD Press.

O'Keefe, T. (ed) (1973) *Myles: portraits of Brian O'Nolan*. London, Martin Brian and O'Keefe.

O'Leary, O. (2006) 'Mr Gageby's Republic' in Whittaker, A. (ed.) *Bright, brilliant days*, pp 45–8.

O'Nolan, K. (ed.) (1989) *The best of Myles: a selection from 'Cruiskeen Lawn' Flann O'Brien (Myles na Gopaleen)*. London, Grafton.

O'Reilly, E. (1991) *Candidate; the truth behind the presidential campaign*. Dublin, Attic Press.

O'Toole, F. (1999) *The* Irish Times *book of the century*. Dublin, Gill & Macmillan.

Oram, H. (1983) *The newspaper book: a history of newspapers in Ireland, 1649–1983*. Dublin, MO Books.

Oram, H. (1993) *Paper tigers: Stories of Irish newspapers by the people who make them*. Belfast, Appletree Press.

Orr, C. (1989) *Splash! drama and comedy in a newspaperman's career*. Devon, Merlin Books.

Quinn, A. (2001) *Patrick Kavanagh: a biography*. Dublin, Gill and Macmillan.

Richardson, C. (2007) 'Transforming Anglo-Ireland: R.M. Smyllie and the Irish Times'. *New Hibernia Review*, 11:4, 17–36.

Schulz, T. (1999) *Das Deutschlandbild der* Irish Times, *1933–45*. Frankfurt-am-Main. Peter Lang.

Sheehy Skeffington, A. (1991) *Skeff: The Life of Owen Sheehy Skeffington, 1919–1970*. Dublin, Lilliput Press.

Sheridan, N. (1973) 'Brian, Flann and Myles' in O'Keefe, T. (ed.) *Myles: portraits of Brian O'Nolan*, pp 32–53.

Smyllie, R.M. (1938) *Carpathian contrasts*. Dublin, Irish Times.

Smyllie, R.M. (1938) *By the banks of the Dordogne*. Dublin, Irish Times.

Smyllie, R.M. (1946) 'Unneutral Neutral Eire', *Foreign Affairs*, 24, 317–26.

Tansey, P. (2006) 'Mapping a new prosperity' in Whittaker, A. (ed.) *Bright, brilliant days*, pp 135–8.

Tobin, F. (1984) *The best of decades: Ireland in the 1960s*. Dublin, Gill & Macmillan.

Tobin, M. (1984) 'Irish newspapers', *Business and Finance*, 21:2, 34–5.

Turner, M. (2004) *Martyn Turner's greatest hits*. Dublin, Gill & Macmillan.

Viney, M. (2006) 'Y' in Whittaker, A. (ed.) *Bright, brilliant days*, pp 155–8.

Whelan, G. & Swift, C. (2002) *Spiked: church-state intrigue and the rose tattoo*. Dublin, New Island.

White, J. (1973) 'Myles, Flann and Brian' in O'Keefe, T. (ed.) *Myles: portraits of Brian O'Nolan*, pp 62–76.

White, J. (1975) *Minority report: the Protestant community in the Republic of Ireland*. Dublin, Gill & Macmillan.

Whittaker, A. (2006) 'The Bank of Ireland and the *Irish Times*' in Whittaker, A. (ed.) *Bright, brilliant days*, pp 171–7.

Whittaker, A. (ed.) (2006) *Bright, brilliant days: Douglas Gageby and the* Irish Times. Dublin, A&A Farmar.

Whyte, J.H. (1980) *Church and state in modern Ireland, 1923–1979*. Dublin, Gill & Macmillan.

Woodman, K. (1985) *Media control in Ireland, 1923–1983*. Southern Illinois University Press.

Yeates, P. (2000) *Lockout: Dublin 1913*. Dublin, Gill & Macmillan.

Index